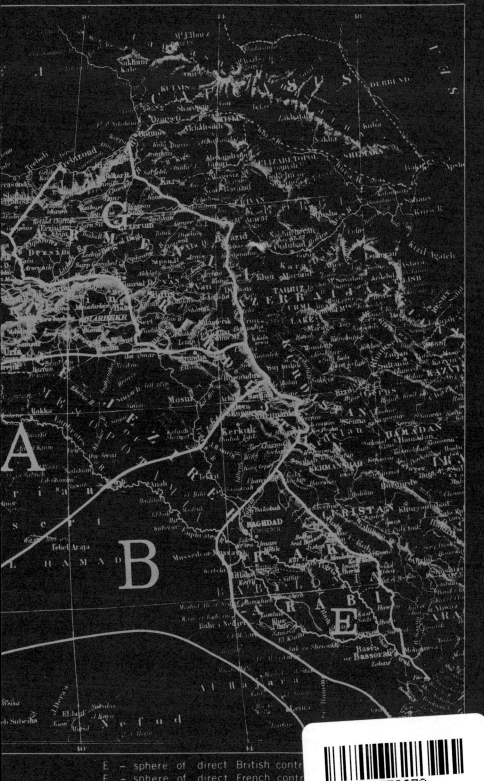

Foundations of British Policy in the Arab World

FOUNDATIONS OF BRITISH POLICY IN THE ARAB WORLD: The Cairo Conference of 1921

Aaron S. Klieman

THE JOHNS HOPKINS PRESS

Baltimore and London

END PAPERS   Map illustrating the Sykes-Picot Agreement of 1916 included in a secret memorandum by the Foreign Office, "Synopsis of our Obligations to our Allies and Others," G. T. Paper 3917 of February, 1918, CAB 24/45, War Cabinet. Reproduced by permission of the Public Record Office, London. The key has been altered for purposes of clarification.

MEMBERS OF THE CAIRO CONFERENCE OF 1921   Photo by Radio Times Hulton Picture Library, courtesy of BBC Publications, London.

DE BUNSEN COMMITTEE MAPS   Originally printed in CAB 27/1 as part of the de Bunsen committee report. Reproduced by permission of the Public Record Office, London. The key to the maps has been altered for purposes of clarification.

The Johns Hopkins Press, Baltimore, Maryland 21218
The Johns Hopkins Press Ltd., London

Library of Congress Catalog Card Number 73-103613

ISBN-0-8018-1125-2

To my parents,
for their faith and encouragement

Preface

The decade of war and peace between 1914 and 1923 witnessed the dissolution of the Ottoman Empire, and with it the foundation of Great Britain's policy in the Near and Middle East. Against this background of change—in England, in the Arab world, and internationally—those responsible for such policy sought its reconstitution in fidelity to traditional interests and in accord with existing political conditions. A policy of drift, of reaction rather than initiative, nevertheless persisted until 1921, when a conference of leading British authorities convened at Cairo and Jerusalem from 12 to 30 March under the direction of the secretary of state for the colonies, Mr. Winston Churchill. The Cairo Conference, as it was known officially, represented a major attempt to satisfy the imperative need for policy revision.

As they assembled, the participants had before them three immediate objectives: first, to consolidate gains and effect economies through more efficient administration at the local level in the various parts of the Arab world; second, to reconcile the different perspectives held by the British officials and governmental agencies involved in Middle Eastern affairs by means of a centralized control exercised effectively from London;

and third, by means of the above, to arrive at a comprehensive framework, incorporating previous commitments and existing realities, for future relations with the Arabs.

In 1921 the conference was regarded by many people as the logical culmination to a long period of growing British involvement in, and control of, the strategic area between the Mediterranean Sea and the Persian Gulf. Finally, after years of competition with France, post-Bismarck Germany, and czarist Russia, England stood virtually unrivaled upon the ruins of the Ottoman Empire. Others saw the Cairo Conference as perhaps the inauguration of a new era of British preeminence, but certainly one which would present grave responsibilities as well as opportunities. Still other individuals, however, took a dim view of the conference, opposing it as a futile attempt to contain the rising force of nationalism whereby the Arab people demanded the right to be active subjects, rather than passive objects acted upon and spoken for by the European powers, in determining their political future.

Until now, the Cairo Conference and the events preceding and resulting from it have not received scholarly attention. The only official account to be made public was presented in an address by Mr. Churchill before the House of Commons in June, 1921, shortly after his return from the Middle East. One contemporary historian, attempting to explain this "curious fact," has written: "The reason (apart from the distressing British passion for secrecy) is not, so far as can be seen, that shameful conspiracies were laid in Cairo, but rather that amid the fearful preoccupations of the postwar years the importance of this meeting was not noticed."[1] Today, the earlier preoccupations having been disposed of, the relevant documents are available for analysis, and it has become possible to remedy the deficiency.

The purpose of this study, therefore, is to consider the Cairo Conference as an episode important to the complete history of British relations with the Middle East by relating the events that led to its convocation and its more immediate repercussions. The many traditions, pressures, and considerations involved can perhaps be best described by approaching the conference as a prism through which these were filtered, emerging to form the new foundation for British policy in the interwar period.

1. Christopher Sykes, *Crossroads to Israel* (Cleveland: World Publishing Co., 1965), p. 56.

Consideration is given as well to the impact of the conference on the political evolution of those countries most directly affected: Iraq, Palestine, Syria, Transjordan—comprising the Fertile Crescent—and Arabia. Thus elements of European diplomacy and a chapter in the modern history of the Arab world are combined with a political study of the complexities inherent in any country's decision-making process.

In pursuing this task I have been fortunate in receiving counsel and support from Professor Majid Khadduri of the School of Advanced International Studies. Drafts of the manuscript have benefitted from his suggestions. Professor Harry Howard also offered useful comments. Extended research overseas was made possible through the assistance of The Johns Hopkins University and The National Foundation for Jewish Culture.

I had access to original documents at the Public Record Office in London, in addition to several collections of personal papers belonging to public officials involved in some capacity with the Cairo Conference. Consequently, I wish to acknowledge the assistance rendered by personnel of these various institutions in England and in Israel: the British Museum and its newspaper archives at Colindale, the India Office, the House of Lords Library, Miss Elizabeth Monroe of St. Antony's College, Oxford, Professor A. J. P. Taylor and The Beaverbrook Library, the Central Zionist Archives, the Israel State Archives, and, lastly, the Weizmann Archives. Citations of Crown-copyright records in the Public Record Office appear by permission of the Controller of Her Majesty's Stationery Office.

I am endebted most recently to Mr. John Gallman and Miss Penny James of The Johns Hopkins Press for guiding the manuscript through publication. My wife, by sharing the frustrations no less than the rewards of student life, research, writing, and editing, has helped bring this work to fruition.

A. S. K.

Table of Contents

Contents

Notes on Arabic Transliteration and Usage

Because the following study deals with a period in Great Britain's diplomatic relations with the Middle East notable for its inconsistency, it is not surprising to find this reflected even in the matter of Arabic transliteration. At no time did officials of the various governmental departments conform to one pattern of spelling or usage when referring to personalities and locations within the Arab world. Thus the first king of Iraq—or Mesopotamia—was written of as Faisal, Feisul, or Feisal; his father, the shareef (or sherif) of Mecca was known as Hussein, Husain, or Hussain. In like fashion, the area east of the Jordan River was rendered on occasion Trans-Jordania, Trans-Jordan, or Transjordania.

Rather than seek at this late date to impose uniformity on the individuals and institutions responsible for British policy, the author prefers to retain the original spelling when quoting directly from documentary sources. However, he has adopted one form—for example, Faysal, Husayn, sharif, Amir Abdullah, Transjordan, the Hijaz—in striving for consistency in his own writing.

The following abbreviations will be used in the footnotes:

CAB   Cabinet Meetings
C.P.   Cabinet Paper
C.Z.A.   Central Zionist Archives
C.O.   Colonial Office
Cmd.   Command (Parliamentary) Paper
E.C.   Eastern Committee
F.O.   Foreign Office
G.O.C.   General Officer Commanding
I.O.   India Office
I.S.A.   Israel State Archives
O.E.T.A. (S)   Occupied Enemy Territory Administration (South)
W.O.   War Office
W.A.   Weizmann Archives

The key to the filing system used by the Foreign Office is as follows. The figures preceded by a letter are the numbers of individual papers. These are followed successively by file number and index number, the last indicating the country and archives division. For example, footnote 9 on page 48 reads:

E8118/38/44 [no. 742], F.O. 406/44.

Once decoded, this refers to individual paper 8118, which is part of file 38 pertaining to Turkey (44) under Eastern affairs (E). Egypt (16), Persia (34), Palestine (88), Syria (89), Arabia (91), and Mesopotamia (93) were other subdivisions under Eastern affairs. Paper 8118 happened to be a cable, no. 742, which is available to the researcher in volume 406/44 of Foreign Office documents.

Transliteration and Usage

CHAPTER 1 # Wartime Commitments, 1914–18

The problem now is not how to keep the Turkish Empire permanently in being ... but how to minimize the shock of its fall, and what to substitute for it.—Viscount Bryce

By electing to align itself with the Central Powers shortly after the outbreak of war in 1914, the Ottoman Empire not only affected British policy but initiated as well a new chapter in the history of the Near and Middle East.

In the decades before 1914, British statesmen had sought an underlying consistency in policy toward the enduring, complex Eastern Question. Great Britain encouraged widespread economic and administrative reforms within the Ottoman Empire, extending diplomatic or military support when necessary. Yet she also partook of the spoils— Cyprus and Egypt, for example—when expedient, or if only to prevent their coming under the control of rival powers. Thus she endorsed the principle of the survival of an Ottoman Empire while at the same time helping to incorporate into the continental balance of power the fact of that empire's forced withdrawal from European and Mediterranean territories.

The Great War of 1914 afforded Britain an opportunity at last to resolve this inconsistency. Thereafter the problem for London became one of measuring its response to the outright partition of the constricted

1

empire in Asia and the transition from an Ottoman imperial structure to a narrower Turkish nationalism. Also inherent in this larger problem was the need to determine the political future of those Arab regions which lay within the former Turkish Empire.

When the final session of the Paris Peace Conference ended on 21 January 1920, the future status of Turkey still remained unresolved. Discussion had taken place among the victorious Allied and Associated Powers, but these had produced acrimony rather than accord and served only to emphasize the complex nature of the subject. Although the mandate system had been embodied in Article 22 of the Covenant of the League of Nations, no comprehensive agreement could be arrived at which would govern such specific aspects as the detailed provisions for a definitive peace treaty with Turkey, designation of the actual mandatories, and a delineation of boundaries for the mandated territories. The conference, content after providing the framework for an era of international peace and cooperation through its principal achievements, the Treaty of Versailles and the League covenant, consigned the entire question of the Near and Middle East[1] to further consultations between the interested parties, particularly England and France. As a result, this latter phase of the Eastern Question was allowed to persist beyond fifty-one months of hostilities and secret diplomacy and the succeeding twelve months of peacemaking as an unsettling factor in postwar world politics and in the reconstitution of the Near and Middle East, as well as in British foreign policy.

From the single perspective of Great Britain, the domestic and external status of those lands comprising the Ottoman Empire had been of importance since at least the beginning of the nineteenth century. Anglo-Turkish concert had been possible at that point because of a mutual in-

---

1. One outcome of the 1919–21 rethinking of British policy was the distinction made between the terms "Near East" and "Middle East." The former was used thereafter with some degree of consistency in reference to Turkey proper and to matters relating to Asia Minor, while "Middle East" came to be reserved for the Arab world. See Roderic H. Davison, "Where Is the Middle East?" *Foreign Affairs*, July, 1960, p. 668. For the purpose of this study, the narrower term "Fertile Crescent" will be taken to include the geographical area presently comprised of Iraq, Israel, Jordan, Lebanon, and Syria, as described in P. M. Holt, *Egypt and the Fertile Crescent, 1516–1922* (London: Longmans, Green & Co., 1966), pp. 1–9.

British Policy in the Arab World

terest in frustrating the efforts at direct political penetration made by Napoleonic France; it was strengthened as the century progressed under the pressure of Russian expansionism.[2]

With the consolidation of control in India, successive British governments came to hold the strategic value of the Ottoman Empire's Arab regions in ever greater regard. Generals and statesmen alike acknowledged the necessity for retaining unimpeded access to the two routes linking England with her Indian empire and the Orient: the northern overland route across Syria and Mesopotamia to the Persian Gulf; and, after the opening of the Suez Canal in 1869, the southern waterway connecting the Mediterranean Sea with the Indian Ocean.[3] D. G. Hogarth, later a prominent member of the Arab Bureau in Cairo, in 1902 summed up both the attraction and the danger offered by the region:

... it is a Debatable Land, distracted internally by a ceaseless war of influence, and only too anxious to lean in one part or another on external aid. Therefore, it is always prone to involve in its own unrest those responsible for the peace of the world, and ultimately to endanger the balance of power in Europe.

Nor it is only as a Debatable Land that the Nearer East has a disquieting influence on the outer world, but also as an Intermediate Land, that is to say, a thoroughfare—the region through which must lie, and by which can be endangered, the communication between the West and the West-in-East.[4]

Great Britain, although conscious of the excessive centralization of authority at Constantinople and of the corruption and decay weakening

2. The so-called eastern question and Britain's relationship to it are most thoroughly discussed in three basic books on the subject: Sir John A. R. Marriott, *The Eastern Question: An Historical Study in European Diplomacy* (London: Oxford University Press, 1940); H. W. V. Temperley, *England and the Near East* (London: Frank Cass & Co., 1964); and M. S. Anderson, *The Eastern Question, 1774–1923* (New York: St. Martin's Press, 1966).
3. Strategic considerations governing Britain's Middle Eastern policy in the nineteenth and twentieth centuries are emphasized in Halford L. Hoskins, *British Routes to India* (London: Longmans, Green & Co., 1928), and in the Royal Institute of International Affairs, *The Political and Strategic Interests of the United Kingdom* (London: Oxford University Press, 1939), pp. 100–186. In 1839 British troops occupied Aden, and British influence spread thereafter along the Persian Gulf and into the interior of Arabia.
4. D. G. Hogarth, *The Nearer East* (London: William Heinemann, 1902), pp. 280–81.

the Sublime Porte in its foreign relations, nevertheless saw little choice but to support the existence of the empire and to encourage reform.[5] Upon the assumption of power by the Young Turks in 1908, Foreign Secretary Edward Grey wrote to Sir G. A. Lowther, British ambassador at Constantinople, that "the rejoicing at the upset of the old and the prospect of a new régime is genuine; our course is clear: we must welcome and encourage this prospect as long as it continues."[6] Even as the threat of war drew near and hope for Turkish reform became dimmer, Grey continued to assert the traditional rationale: "A grave question of policy is involved and the only policy to which we can become a party is one directed to avoid collapse and partition of Asiatic Turkey. The effect of the opposite course upon our own Mussulmans in India would be disastrous to say nothing of the complications that would be produced between European Powers."[7]

Given this legacy of support for the territorial integrity of the Ottoman Empire—despite such departures as the annexation of Cyprus in 1878 and the occupation of Egypt in 1882—the conversion of Turkish policy from professed neutrality to belligerency in late 1914 forced a complete revision of British military and political thinking. After considerable delay, and only in response to intense diplomatic pressure from France and Russia,[8] the British government sought to formulate its ultimate war aims and territorial ambitions in the Middle East. An interdepartmental committee was specifically constituted under the chairmanship of Sir Maurice de Bunsen to consider British desiderata in Turkey-in-Asia. The committee reviewed in detail the existing interests of Great Britain in the region and then submitted a secret report to the War Council on 30 June 1915.

Addressing itself to the basic question of whether the acquisition of

5. Efforts made to revive the Ottoman Empire through social, administrative, and military reform are detailed in Frank E. Bailey, *British Policy and the Turkish Reform Movement* (Cambridge, Mass.: Harvard University Press, 1942), and in Roderic H. Davison, *Reform in the Ottoman Empire, 1856–1876* (Princeton: Princeton University Press, 1963).
6. Grey to Lowther, 11 August 1908, in *British Documents on the Origins of the War*, vol. 5: *The Near East, 1903–9*, ed. G. P. Gooch and Harold Temperley (London: His Majesty's Stationery Office, 1928), p. 266.
7. Grey to Lowther, telegram (no. 498), 4 July 1913, in *ibid.*, vol. 10 (1936), pt. 1, "The Near and Middle East on the Eve of the War," p. 481.
8. See the author's article "Britain's War Aims in the Middle East in 1915," *Journal of Contemporary History* 3, no. 3 (July, 1968) : 237–51.

British Policy in the Arab World

new territory was advisable or not, the committee argued the necessity of maintaining

a just relation between the prospective advantages to the British Empire by a readjustment of conditions in Asiatic Turkey, and the inevitable increase of Imperial responsibility. Our Empire is wide enough already, and our task is to consolidate the possessions we already have, to make firm and lasting the position we already hold. . . . It is then to straighten ragged edges that we have to take advantage of the present opportunity, and to assert our claim to a sphere in settling the destiny of Asiatic Turkey.[9]

In conformity with this general claim (albeit a reluctant one) to benefits from Turkey's eventual defeat, nine specific desiderata in the Arab region were distinguished. The committee called for a final recognition and consolidation of Britain's position in the Persian Gulf which would entail security for the development of such undertakings as oil production, river navigation, and construction of irrigation work; exploiting Mesopotamia as a granary and an area for Indian colonization; and retaining Britain's strategic position in the eastern Mediterranean and Persian Gulf, plus security for British communications, by means of a "minimum increase of naval expenditure and responsibility." Three of the desiderata pertained to the Arab peoples. They called for the fulfillment of pledges under consideration or already given to the several *shaykhs* of the Arabian peninsula and, "generally, maintenance of the assurances given to the Sharif of Mecca and the Arabs"; insurance that Arabia and the Muslim holy places would remain "under independent Moslem rule"; and, lastly, a settlement of the question of Palestine and the holy places of Christendom. These, then, were the elements singled out as the constants for any future policy at a time when the exigencies of war, the effects of uncoordinated decision-making, and the excesses of secret diplomatic bargaining had not yet complicated Great Britain's position in the former Turkish territories.

The de Bunsen committee concluded its report by advocating that a policy of decentralization be imposed upon Constantinople which, "while securing the vital interests of Great Britain, will give to Turkey in Asia some prospect of a permanent existence" and would at the same time

9. Cabinet, Ad Hoc Committees (secret), "Report, Proceedings and Appendices of a Committee Appointed by the Prime Minister. 1915. British Desiderata in Turkey-in-Asia," CAB 27/1, p. 4.

free the five great provinces of Anatolia, Armenia, Syria, Palestine, and Jazirah-Iraq from "the vampire-hold of the metropolis, . . . [thus giving] them a chance to foster and develop their own resources."[10] Such a scheme, it was thought, would satisfy Britain's allies in their insistence upon an alteration of the *status quo ante bellum* and an end to Ottoman independence, while avoiding such direct responsibilities as would result from the other, more extreme alternative of partition.

This proposal, however, never received the endorsement of the British government. As the War intensified, nothing less than the dissolution of the Turkish Empire could justify the many sacrifices demanded of the public. In addition, the leaders of the country had become so resentful of the Turks that Lord Curzon, who was undersecretary of state for foreign affairs at the time, reflected their sentiment when he said later that "the presence of the Turks has been a source of unmitigated evil to everybody concerned."[11] This feeling was reinforced by the fear that Britain would deny herself the spoils of victory while her present allies—but potential rivals—acquired new territory. As Prime Minister Asquith rationalized, if "for one reason or another, because we didn't want more territory, or because we didn't feel equal to the responsibility, we were to leave the other nations to scramble for Turkey without taking anything ourselves, we should not be doing our duty."[12]

Although the moderate proposals of the de Bunsen committee were rejected, its basic assumptions and considerations were those which the Foreign Office, India Office, and War Office shared in their future dealings with the Arabs, the French, and the Zionists. The latitude possessed by each department in selecting the means deemed appropriate for achieving these aims stemmed in part from the conspicuous absence during the war years of any comparable evaluation of Britain's Middle Eastern interests, or of a comprehensive plan of government-sanctioned action for their implementation. This fact in turn explains many of the

10. *Ibid.*, pp. 28, 24. "Al-Jazirah" and "al-'Iraq" were used generally by the de Bunsen committee in reference to the northern and southern halves of present-day Iraq.
11. Lord Curzon before the Eastern Committee in December, 1918, quoted in David Lloyd George, *The Truth About the Peace Treaties*, vol. 2 (London: Victor Gollancz, 1938), p. 1014; see also Harold Nicolson, *Peacemaking, 1919* (London: Methuen & Co., 1964), p. 35.
12. Asquith on 19 March 1915, in CAB 42/2 ("Papers of the War Council, Dardanelles Committee and the War Committee").

difficulties subsequently encountered by Great Britain in the first years of peace.

Stalemate along the western front, having become more pronounced during the latter part of 1915, guided British energies toward a dual strategy: militarily, to attack the eastern flank of the Central Powers, and, politically, to arrest the decline in morale within the Entente while securing support from previously uncommitted parties. The military offensive had already resulted in the ill-fated assault upon the Gallipoli peninsula and would yet inspire campaigns against the Turks through Mesopotamia and along the eastern coast of the Mediterranean.[13] The diplomatic phase induced simultaneous contact with the Arabs, the Allies, and spokesmen for the Zionist movement.[14]

The emergence of the Arabs as a distinctive entity, and their recognition as such by the British government, was one of the major effects of Anglo-Turkish hostility. Whereas previously the Arabs, as nominal subjects of the Sultan-Caliph, could be approached independently only at the risk of offending the sensitivities of the Sublime Porte, a state of war permitted Britain to exploit grievances between Arab and Turk and to deal directly with Arab spokesmen.[15] As early as November, 1914, a message had been sent to Sharif Husayn of Mecca, ruler of the Hijaz, at the instruction of Lord Kitchener, the secretary of state for war. It advised that,

if the Amir and Arabs in general assist Great Britain in this conflict that has been forced upon us by Turkey, Great Britain will promise not to inter-

---

13. The official account of military operations in the East is provided by Sir George Macmunn and Cyril Falls, *Military Operations: Egypt and Palestine*, 2 vols. (London, 1928–30), and by F. J. Moberly, *The Campaign in Mesopotamia, 1914–1918*, 2 vols. (London, 1923–24).
14. In January, 1915, the Cabinet had before it a secret memorandum submitted by Herbert Samuel, then president of the Local Government Board, on "The Future of Palestine." It referred to "a stirring among the twelve million Jews scattered throughout the countries of the World" and urged the annexation of Palestine by Britain (CAB 37/123). In March Samuel wrote a revised memorandum stressing the political advantages for Britain in a claim to Palestine (CAB 37/126, no. 1).
15. Zeine N. Zeine, *Arab-Turkish Relations and the Emergence of Arab Nationalism* (Beirut: Khayats, 1958). See also Bernard Lewis, *The Emergence of Modern Turkey* (London: Oxford University Press, 1961); Philip P. Graves, trans., *Memoirs of King Abdullah of Transjordan* (London: Jonathan Cape, 1950), esp. pp. 84–92, 97–98; and Arnold J. Toynbee and Kenneth P. Kirkwood, *Turkey* (New York: Charles Scribner's Sons, 1927), p. 53.

vene in any manner whatsoever, whether in things religious or otherwise.
. . . Till now we have defended and befriended Islam in the person of the
Turks: henceforward it shall be in that of the noble Arab. . . . It would be
well if your Highness could convey to your followers and devotees, who are
found throughout the world in every country, the good tidings of the freedom
of the Arabs and the rising of the sun over Arabia.[16]

This message and an earlier visit by the sharif's son, Abdullah, to the
British Residency in Cairo soon led to a direct correspondence between
the British high commissioner for Egypt and the ruler of the Hijaz
concerning prospects for an alliance.[17]

In his opening letter of 14 July 1915 Sharif Husayn sought to gain
the endorsement of Great Britain for his definition of Arab aspirations.
He began by stating that "the whole of the Arab nation without exception have decided in these last years to live, and to accomplish their
freedom, and grasp the reins of their administration both in theory
and practice."[18] He then asked approval of several "fundamental propo-
sitions," the most important being that England should acknowledge
"the independence of the Arab countries, bounded on the north by
Mersina and Adana up to the 37° of latitude . . . ; on the east by the
borders of Persia up to the Gulf of Basra; on the south by the Indian
Ocean, with the exception of the position of Aden to remain as it is; on

16. CAB 27/1, p. 144 (note on Arabia made by the India Office on 26 April 1915).
    It should be noted that from the outset the British contributed to their own diffi-
    culties by encouraging the sharif in his personal ambitions, even intimating to
    him that "it may be that an Arab of true race will assume the Khalifate at Mecca
    or Medina." They also tended to overestimate the scope of his prestige and au-
    thority and the extent of Arab homogeneity. The title "sharif" indicates descent
    from the prophet Muhammad and is a mark of distinction within the Islamic
    community.
17. For Abdullah's role as an intermediary, see Graves, *Memoirs of King Abdullah*,
    pp. 112–14. There are a number of books dealing in whole or in part with the
    Husayn-McMahon correspondence, the foremost being: George Antonius, *The
    Arab Awakening* (Philadelphia: Lippincott, 1939), which provides the text of
    the letters as well as a detailed exposition of the Arab interpretation; Zeine N.
    Zeine, *The Struggle for Arab Independence* (Beirut, 1960), pp. 1–12; and Harry
    N. Howard, *The Partition of Turkey* (Norman: University of Oklahoma Press,
    1931). The official British translation was first published (with modifications)
    in 1939 as a parliamentary command paper: "Correspondence between Sir Henry
    McMahon, His Majesty's High Commissioner at Cairo, and the Sherif Hussein
    of Mecca, July, 1915–March, 1916" (Cmd. 5957); hereinafter cited as Cmd.
    5957.
18. Cmd. 5957, p. 3.

British Policy in the Arab World

the west by the Red Sea, the Mediterranean Sea up to Mersina, England to approve of the proclamation of an Arab Khalifate of Islam."[19] In return the sharif promised to acknowledge the preferential position of England in all economic enterprises in the Arab countries. Replying on 30 August, Sir Henry McMahon expressed satisfaction that "Arab interests are English interests and English Arab," and that "our desire [is] for an independent Arabia." Regarding the question of limits and boundaries, he advised that "it would appear to be premature to consume our time in discussing such details in the heat of war."[20]

This first exchange of letters set the tone for future correspondence by revealing divergent emphases. In communicating with the king of the Hijaz, McMahon had but one immediate objective: to have the Arabs commit themselves against their political suzerain and co-religionists. He thus sought to avoid lengthy, detailed negotiations over exact boundaries and spoke initially only of an independent Arabia. The sharif, on the other hand, was specific both with regard to the nature of military and financial support expected from Britain and to the territorial dimensions of future Arab rule. His vagueness, however, appeared in a matter of less immediate concern; he did not specify what form this future independence might take: whether one vast kingdom or several units, each with a separate form of government yet leagued together in some type of confederation. Thus, for example, on 9 September Husayn wrote, "I am myself with all my might carrying out in my country . . . all things which tend to benefit the rest of the Kingdom," to which McMahon replied on 24 October: Great Britain would give advice and assist to establish "what may appear to be the most suitable forms of government in these various territories."[21]

Husayn continued to press for a discussion of frontiers, and McMahon,

19. Cmd. 5957, p. 3. It has been suggested that Sharif Husayn was influenced in his claim by a protocol drawn up early in 1915 by secret societies of Arab nationalists at Damascus; see Antonius, *The Arab Awakening*, pp. 157–58.
20. Cmd. 5957, p. 3. All maps drawn by the de Bunsen committee, whether for schemes of partition, zones of interest, Ottoman independence, or decentralization, provided for an independent Arabia but confined it to an area whose northern frontier began just south of Aqaba and extended across the desert to a point south of Basra on the Persian Gulf; it was therefore not expected to include any area of the Fertile Crescent. These maps are located in CAB 27/1; see also Appendix A of the present volume.
21. Cmd. 5957, p. 6.

having realized that the sharif regarded this question as one of vital and urgent importance and would delay entering the war, sought instructions from London. He was then authorized to make the following statement in his letter of 24 October:

> The two districts of Mersina and Alexandretta and portions of Syria lying to the west of the districts of Damascus, Homs, Hama and Aleppo cannot be said to be purely Arab, and should be excluded from the limits demanded.
> With the above modification, and without prejudice to our existing treaties with Arab chiefs, we accept those limits. As for those regions lying within those frontiers wherein Great Britain is free to act without detriment to the interests of her ally, France, I am empowered in the name of the Government of Great Britain to give the following assurances and make the following reply to your letter:—
> (1) Subject to the above modifications, Great Britain is prepared to recognize and support the independence of the Arabs in all the regions within the limits demanded by the Sherif of Mecca. . . .[22]

Relieved at this acceptance of his principal demand for independence, Husayn wrote back on 5 November, retracting his insistence upon the inclusion of the *vilayets* of Mersina and Adana in the Arab kingdom. At the same time, however, he did stress that the *vilayets* of Aleppo and Beirut and their sea coasts were purely Arab and that the *vilayets* in Mesopotamia were historically bound to the Arabs. But he was willing to leave the latter under British administration for a short time in return for a "suitable sum paid as compensation to the Arab Kingdom for the period of occupation." With this he claimed to have made the utmost in concessions for the sake of agreement.

Having consented only reluctantly to the sharif's territorial claims, the British government subsequently introduced modifications. By the time McMahon sent his letter of 14 December to Mecca, three reservations were apparent: first, further consideration would have to be given to Aleppo and Beirut, "as the interests of our ally, France, are involved in them both"; second, since Britain could not repudiate agreements already in existence, those which were then in effect with Arab chiefs would still apply "to all territories included in the Arab Kingdom"; and, finally, Britain insisted that her established position and interests in Mesopotamia would necessitate special administrative arrangements.

22. *Ibid.*

Twenty thousand British pounds sterling, an "earnest of intentions," accompanied the letter in hopes of softening the sharif's reaction.

Any apparent deadlock was averted by the next exchange of letters in January, 1916. On 1 January, out of a wish to avoid "what may possibly injure the alliance of Great Britain and France," Husayn agreed to cease pursuing his original claim. Yet he took the occasion to record his own enduring reservations: ". . . we find it our duty that the eminent minister should be sure that, at the first opportunity after this war is finished we shall ask you (what we avert our eyes from to-day) for what we now leave to France in Beirut and its coasts. . . . it is impossible to allow any derogation that gives France, or any other Power, a span of land in those regions."[23] McMahon's reply was forthcoming on 25 January. Setting aside Husayn's warning of future friction, it judged his decision to be "entirely in the interests of the Arab peoples" and ended with a strong statement of Anglo-French solidarity from which Husayn was invited to benefit "to the mutual welfare and happiness of us all."

The Arab revolt against the Ottoman Empire commenced on 10 June 1916. In the course of the war it facilitated British military campaigns in the area and contributed to the Turks' retreat from the Arab provinces. Even more important, it created for Great Britain a sense of obligation to the Arabs in general and to the sharifians in particular, while permitting the extension of sharifian influence from the Arabian peninsula to the Fertile Crescent, a movement symbolized by the entry of the Hijazi army into Damascus on 1 October 1918.

A month before the start of the Arab revolt, the foreign ministers of France, Great Britain, and Russia entered into a secret agreement governing their own partition of the Ottoman Empire. Russian demands in March, 1915, for Constantinople and control of the straits had prompted her allies to consider their own claims. When unofficial discussions during the autumn of 1915 reached a satisfactory stage, Sir Mark Sykes and M. Georges Picot were selected by their governments to draft the actual provisions for a formal agreement.[24] On 9 May 1916 M. Paul

---

23. *Ibid.*, p. 13.
24. An evaluation of the role played by Sir Mark Sykes, who had been a member of the de Bunsen committee, is offered in Elie Kedourie, *England and the Middle East* (London: Bowes & Bowes, 1956). Three useful accounts of the negotiations are provided in Jean Pichon, *Le Partage du Proche-Orient* (Paris, 1938); H. W. V. Temperley, *A History of the Peace Conference of Paris*, vol. 6 (London:

Cambon, French ambassador to London, conveyed to Sir Edward Grey the acceptance by his government of *"les limites telles qu'elles ont été fixées sur les cartes signées . . . , ainsi que les conditions diverses formuleés au cours de ces discussions."*[25]

In his reply the following day, Grey enumerated twelve conditions as a basis for the understanding, the first being the most important.

That France and Great Britain are prepared to recognise and protect an independent Arab State or a Confederation of Arab States in the areas (A) and (B) marked on the annexed map, under the suzerainty of an Arab chief. That in area (A) France, and in area (B) Great Britain, shall have priority of right of enterprise and local loans. That in area (A) France, and in area (B) Great Britain, shall alone supply advisers or foreign functionaries at the request of the Arab State or Confederation of Arab States.[26]

The remaining points provided for the establishment of administrative systems within the respective spheres; an international administration for that area known to the Arabs as southern Syria and to Europeans as the Holy Land or Palestine;[27] control of the key ports of Acre, Haifa, and Alexandretta, the latter two being open to French and British trade respectively; and other measures concerning tariffs, arms control, and railway facilities. This accord, altered only to satisfy minor Russian claims and to comply with a French request that the word "protect" in the first clause be changed to "uphold,"[28] remained secret until published by the Bolsheviks in November, 1917 (to the discomfiture of

Henry Frowde, Hodder & Stoughton, 1924), pp. 1–22; and Jukka Nevakivi, *Britain, France and the Arab Middle East, 1914–1920* (London: The Athlone Press, 1969). France, given the opportunity in 1915, immediately asserted a claim to Syria together with the region of the Gulf of Alexandretta and Cilicia up to the Taurus range.

25. E. L. Woodward and Rohan Butler, eds., *Documents on British Foreign Policy, 1919–1939*, 1st ser., vol. 4 (London: Her Majesty's Stationery Office, 1952), p. 244; hereinafter cited as *Documents*, 4.

26. *Ibid.*, pp. 245ff. For the map, see the end papers of the present volume.

27. In a handbook prepared by the Naval Intelligence Division of the Admiralty at the end of the war, "Syria" was defined "in its broadest acceptation" as "the country that lies between the eastern shore of the Mediterranean and the deserts of Arabia. In a narrower sense the name denotes that part of Syria which is not included in Palestine" (*Handbook of Syria [Including Palestine]* [London: His Majesty's Stationery Office, 1920], p. 9).

28. Cambon to Grey, 25 August 1916, *Documents*, 4:249. "Il me semble que les mots 'soutenir' et 'uphold' rendraient plus exactement notre pensée."

the British, the French, and the Arabs alike), and formed the basis for Anglo-French discussions on the Middle East at the Paris Peace Conference.

The Sykes-Picot agreement—a striking example of traditional diplomacy within a Middle Eastern context—amounted to a calculated division in advance of territorial spoils of war. And, for analytical purposes, its specific terminology, provisions, and implications were no less significant. First, it assumed that a spirit of close cooperation and consultation would continue to govern relations between the two powers in peacetime, in disregard of the long record of Franco-British rivalry in the area. Second, both parties appear to have held a limited definition of Arab sovereignty; they considered themselves "the protectors of the Arab State" and believed that any administrative systems which might be established could be only "as they desire and as they may think fit to arrange" with the Arab state. Yet they agreed to negotiate with the Arabs over the boundaries of the Arab state and were prepared to accept the king of the Hijaz as an equal to be consulted together with the other allies in matters pertaining to that area reserved for international control. Third, the signatories were vague in their conception of the form which Arab rule would take; the clause "Arab State or a Confederation of Arab States" appears five times in the document. Finally, Grey made acceptance of the agreement by His Majesty's Government conditional, provided that "the co-operation of the Arabs is secured, and that the Arabs fulfil the conditions and obtain the towns of Homs, Hama, Damascus, and Aleppo."[29] It was apparent that Great Britain, in accepting the role of intermediary between the Arabs and the French, judged her undertakings up to that point to be complementary, and that in any event the specific interests of all three parties could be adjusted reasonably and honorably once Turkey had been defeated.

In this spirit, and out of lingering anxiety as to the course of the war, the British government proceeded to take upon itself a further obligation in November, 1917, this time to the Jewish people. Leaders of the Zionist movement—Dr. Chaim Weizmann and Nahum Sokolow in particular—and their supporters in England had become increasingly active in seeking official support for their cause since Herbert Samuel first tabled his memoranda on Palestine before the Cabinet in the early

29. *Ibid.*, p. 245.

months of 1915. In audiences with individual members of the government they sought British endorsement of their claim to Palestine as the historical and spiritual homeland of the Jewish people. In return the Zionists volunteered to assert their influence in rallying Jewish communities throughout the world to the Allied cause.

By the late summer and early fall of 1917 the British government was moving toward an acceptance of the Zionist proposal. After several sessions devoted to discussion of the wisdom and wording of a declaration, the Cabinet authorized Foreign Secretary Arthur Balfour to issue the following statement, in the form of a letter to Lord Rothschild, on 2 November: "His Majesty's Government view with favour the establishment in Palestine of a national home for the Jewish people, and will use their best endeavours to facilitate the achievement of this object, it being clearly understood that nothing shall be done which may prejudice the civil and religious rights of existing non-Jewish communities in Palestine, or the rights and political status enjoyed by Jews in any other country."[30]

By issuing the Balfour Declaration the British government had committed itself even further to the emerging struggle for the Middle East, a struggle between Britain and France for regional pre-eminence, between the Arabs and France for Syria, and between the Arabs and Zionists for Palestine. The statement of sympathy with Zionist aspirations appears to share certain features with its precursors. A deeply felt need for additional support may have made the government prone to exaggerate the ability of the Jewish people to substantially influence the war's outcome.[31] Similarly, the likelihood of immediate returns made

30. The letter was first published by the *Jewish Chronicle* in London (9 November 1917, p. 10) and is reproduced on the frontispiece of Leonard Stein, *The Balfour Declaration* (London: Valentine-Mitchell, 1961), which is the most authoritative and scholarly presentation of its evolution, the role of Zionist diplomacy, and factors contributing to the British decision. In contrast to its open circulation in Europe, the declaration was kept a secret from the Arab communities. A copy was supplied by the general headquarters in Cairo to the chief administrator of O.E.T.A.(S) on 9 October 1919, but with instructions to treat it as "extremely confidential, and on no account for any kind of publication" (I.S.A., file 2108). A public reading of the declaration apparently did not take place in Palestine until April, 1920.

31. In the case of both France and Russia the need was rather to sustain them in their existing war effort. Thus the given rationale for British acceptance of Petrograd's 1915 demands was "to avoid anything in the nature of a breach with

British Policy in the Arab World

the endorsement of such abstract principles as "Arab independence" and "a national home for the Jewish people" politically expedient. Lastly, British statesmen assumed a willingness on the part of their allies to grant concessions: Arab nationalists would passively accept another limitation of their claim to sovereignty over the entire Arab region while the French approved a revision of the Sykes-Picot agreement which would allow a special role for Britain in Palestine.

Liberation of the principal cities became the occasion for public statements by British military commanders as the Allied forces swept through the Fertile Crescent in 1918. The address by Lieutenant General Sir Stanley Maude to the people of Baghdad on 19 March 1917 is representative.

O people of Baghdad remember that for 26 generations you have suffered under strange tyrants who have ever endeavoured to set one Arab house against an other in order that they might profit by your dissensions. This policy is abhorrent to Great Britain and her allies, for there can be neither peace nor prosperity where there is enmity and misgovernment. Therefore I am commanded to invite you, through your nobles and elders and representatives, to participate in the management of your civil affairs in collaboration with the political representatives of Great Britain who accompany the British Army, so that you may be united with your kinsmen in North, East, South, and West in realising the aspirations of your race.[32]

Such declarations could not but serve to excite the expectations of the local populace.

From the point of view of the Arabs, however, the major British undertaking still remained the personal one involving the king of the Hijaz.

Russia, or any action which would incline Russia to make a separate peace" (Sir Edward Grey, 3 March 1915, CAB 42/2). This sensitivity to Russian attitudes contributed to the signing of an Anglo-French-Russian agreement which immediately preceded the more limited Sykes-Picot agreement. Grey recalled afterward that this same sentiment prevailed in negotiating the Sykes-Picot agreement: "Having regard to the tremendous task upon which Britain and France were jointly engaged, the British Government were anxious to avoid any suspicion which might interfere with the cordiality of our cooperation" (Lloyd George, *The Truth About the Peace Treaties*, 2:1022). Winston Churchill later characterized the entire series of secret agreements as "simply compulsive gestures of self-preservation" (*The World Crisis, 1911–1918*, 3 vols. [New York: Charles Scribner's Sons, 1931], pt. 1, p. 130).
32. Political Department memoranda, B. 253, I.O.

In order to counter any adverse effects from the Bolsheviks' publication of the secret Sykes-Picot agreement, but also to allay Arab suspicions arising from British military-political occupation of the liberated areas, D. G. Hogarth was instructed on 4 January 1918 to inform the sharif that the "Entente Powers are determined that the Arab race shall be given full opportunity of once again forming a nation in the world."[33] This meeting with the sharif allowed the British emissary to inform the sharif as well that, "since the Jewish opinion of the world favours a return of Jews to Palestine," the British government "are determined that in so far as is compatible with the freedom of the existing population, both economic and political, no obstacle shall be put in the way of this ideal." Husayn's reaction, as recorded by Hogarth, was not without an element of incongruity, for while "the King seemed quite prepared for [the] formula and agreed enthusiastically, I have no doubt that in his own mind he abates none of his original demands on behalf of the Arabs, or in the fullness of time, of himself."[34]

With each succeeding Allied statement disclosing new reservations and distinctions, the seeds were planted for future estrangement from the sharifians. On 16 June 1918, in response to a memorial submitted by seven Arab leaders resident in Cairo concerning the liberated areas, the British government distinguished among four categories: areas in Arabia which had been free and independent before the war; areas emancipated from Turkish control by the action of the Arabs during the war; areas formerly under Ottoman dominion but occupied by the Allied forces; and those areas still under Turkish control. In the first two categories the British reaffirmed their intention to "recognise the complete and sovereign independence of the Arabs," while expressing their desire that in the third sector "the future government of these regions . . . be based upon the principle of the consent of the governed. . . ."[35]

Anglo-French intentions were even more explicit in the last document

33. "Statements made on behalf of His Majesty's Government during the year 1918 in regard to the Future Status of certain parts of the Ottoman Empire" (Cmd. 5964), 1939, miscellaneous no. 4, p. 3; hereinafter cited as Cmd. 5964.

34. *Ibid.*, pp. 4–5. On 2 November 1916 Husayn proclaimed himself "King of the Arab Countries"; but the Entente Powers refused to accept his title. Instead, on 10 December France, Great Britain, and Russia formally recognized the independence of the Hijaz and Husayn as "King of the Hijaz" (U.S., Department of State, Division of Near Eastern Affairs, *Mandate for Palestine* [Washington, D.C.: Government Printing Office, 1927]).

35. Cmd. 5964, pp. 5–6.

British Policy in the Arab World

of consequence to emerge from the war period. A declaration was issued jointly by the two countries in November, 1918, and was given wide publicity. After repeating the desire of France and Great Britain to foster the emancipation of the peoples in the Middle East and the establishment of freely chosen national governments and administrations, it stated:

Far from wishing to impose on the populations of these regions any particular institutions, they are only concerned to ensure by their support and adequate assistance the regular working of Governments and administrations freely chosen by the populations themselves. To secure impartial and equal justice for all, to facilitate the economic development of the country . . . , to favour the diffusion of education, to put an end to dissensions . . . , such is the policy which the two Allied Governments uphold in the liberated territories.[36]

Heightened self-interest, anxiety as to Arab fears and suspicions, facts created by the military campaigns, and the impact of President Wilson's espousal of self-determination[37] had combined to produce a document which encouraged Arab hopes while in effect compromising that endorsement of Arab independence first extended by Great Britain in 1915. These factors also reversed the earlier British equation of Sharif Husayn's wishes with those of the region as a whole. The assumption that Husayn would become sovereign of a monolithic Arab nation was abandoned in favor of separate relationships with the several narrower political, administrative, and geographical units.

With the signing of the Armistice of Mudros by the Entente Powers and Turkey on 30 October 1918, fighting ceased in the Middle East. In the period 1915–18, events had been determined largely by military strategy on the battlefield. In 1919 the emphasis was upon diplomatic maneuvering within the council chambers at Versailles. Only two months separated these two phases as the nations and their leaders, weary from the protracted war effort, turned without respite to the challenges of peace.

36. *Parliamentary Debates* (Commons), 5th ser., 145:36.
37. Zeine (*The Struggle for Arab Independence,* p. 47) cites Lloyd George in stressing concern for Arab feelings as the motivation behind the Anglo-French declaration, while Arnold T. Wilson, writing at the time from Mesopotamia, condemned it as the unfortunate product of Wilsonian idealism (Sir Arnold T. Wilson, *Mesopotamia, 1917–1920: A Clash of Loyalties* [London: Oxford University Press, 1931], 2:102–3).

CHAPTER 2 The Difficulties of Peace, 1919

The war was one thing—a perfectly tremendous strain,
but one was carried along by the bigness of the thing.
Everybody was working above his or her usual capacity.
Now comes the inevitable "slump". We are all tired to
death. We have lost the old stimulus. . . . The problems of
peace are nearly as big really as the problems of war.
But the nervous exhaustion from which we are all suffering
prevents our rising to the new call.—Colonial Secretary
Lord Milner, 8 August 1919

In preparing for and engaging in discussions about the Arab world at
the Paris Peace Conference, the British delegation, headed by Prime
Minister David Lloyd George and Foreign Secretary Arthur James Balfour, had to deal with certain existing facts. At the climax of military
operations, troops of the British Empire were positioned throughout the
Fertile Crescent, from Sinai to the Persian Gulf. They exercised sole
control of Palestine and Mesopotamia and shared control of Lebanon
with France and of Syria with the Hijazi army, which was under the
command of Amir Faysal, second youngest son of King Husayn of
the Hijaz. Over-all command of the region was held by General Allenby,
whose headquarters were in Cairo. Because the Arab region had originally been part of the Ottoman Empire, it was legally regarded as occupied enemy territory pending a treaty whereby the Turkish government
would be compelled to relinquish its title. In the interim, military administrations were instituted.[1]

1. Syria and Palestine were divided into three administrative areas, Occupied Enemy Territories South, North, and East. Before 1914 the Fertile Crescent had

19

In terms of both men and matériel, the overwhelming expenditure in this theater of war had been British—a factor which weighed heavily on the thinking of British leaders, generals, and the public. Too great an investment had been made by Great Britain, it was felt, for her simply to withdraw. Rather, the opposite was argued: a continued presence would be necessary in order to protect British interests, often equated with tranquility in the region.[2] Instead of diminishing, these interests were expanding as the occupation became institutionalized, and new economic, social, and educational projects, first hinted at in the 1918 Anglo-French declaration, were begun. In Mesopotamia, for example, an influx of civil officials bent upon consolidating the victory stimulated a large increase in the bureaucracy. An Irrigation Department was established to cope with the menace of floods, to economize in the use of water, and to drain marshes. An Agricultural Department directed the cultivation of irrigated lands and sought to grow cotton. A railway was constructed from Basra to Baghdad which, when opened to commerce in 1919, became an integral part of the Constantinople-Basra system. There was every indication that "the British were in Mesopotamia to stay"[3] as efforts to secure existing interests led to the creation of new ones and strengthened the inclination to remain.

Earlier promises constituted a further restraint upon British diplomatic flexibility. At the war's end the government found itself a party to three major undertakings: an official correspondence with the Arab

---

been governed as eight units: Mesopotamia was divided into the *vilayets* of Mosul, Baghdad, and Basra and the *mutasarrifiyah*, or governorship, of Dair al-Zur; Syria into the *vilayets* of Aleppo, Damascus, and Beirut and the governorships of Jerusalem and Mount Lebanon.

2. The chief political officer in Palestine assured the Foreign Office on 22 September 1919, "as long as British troops remain, it is my opinion we need anticipate no trouble" (Colonel Richard Meinertzhagen, *Middle East Diary* [London: The Cresset Press, 1959], p. 49). Writing in 1918, the civil commissioner in Baghdad, Sir Percy Cox, maintained that "we should still hope to annex the Basrah Vilayet and exercise a veiled protectorate over the Baghdad Vilayet" (Political Department memoranda, B. 284 ["The Future of Mesopotamia"], 22 April 1918, I.O.). This was in keeping with the prevalent military argument: "With Palestine, Arabia and Persia, Mesopotamia forms an important link in a chain of contiguous areas under British influence, extending from Egypt to India" ("Memorandum by the General Staff on Mesopotamia," 12 November 1919, app. 1, p. 2, C.P. 120 in CAB 24/93).

3. Edward M. Earle, *Turkey, the Great Powers, and the Baghdad Railway* (New York: Macmillan Co., 1924), p. 297.

chief regarded as leader of the Arab peoples, a secret treaty with the plenipotentiary of a sovereign nation, and a public declaration to the Zionist leaders viewed as unofficial spokesmen for the Jewish people. Whatever their individual distinctions, these commitments were considered to be binding, not only by Husayn, France, and the Zionists, but, more importantly, by the British themselves. It soon became apparent, however, that inconsistencies did exist among these undertakings, as Balfour admitted in August, 1919.

These documents are not consistent with each other; they represent no clear-cut policy; the policy which they confusedly adumbrate is not really the policy of the Allied and Associated Powers; and yet so far as I can see, none of them have wholly lost their validity or can be treated in all respects as of merely historic interest. Each can be quoted by Frenchmen, Englishmen, Americans, and Arabs when it happens to suit their purpose. Doubtless each will be so quoted before we come to a final arrangement about the Middle East.[4]

Even if their incompatibility was debatable, it was clear by 1919 that events had conspired to make the promises obsolete. The interests of the Arabs, the British, the French, and the Zionists were seen to be no longer (if they ever had been) harmonious. Thereafter the emphasis and the dilemma of British policy lay in attempting to reconcile these divergent interests and demands. Foreign Secretary Balfour himself concluded:

Since the literal fulfilment of all our declarations is impossible, partly because they are incompatible with each other and partly because they are incompatible with facts, we ought, I presume, to do the next best thing. And

4. *Documents*, 4:343; see also Albert H. Hourani, *Great Britain and the Arab World* (London: John Murray, 1945), p. 19, for a valid interpretation of the agreements as "an attempt . . . to please everybody up to a certain point." Writing two months later, Lloyd George took exception with Balfour's interpretation, maintaining instead that the "obligations do not conflict with one another, but are complementary" (*Documents*, 4:487).

Conspicuously missing from Balfour's list of obligations was the declaration on Palestine bearing his own name. Quite possibly he continued to regard it as consistent. He certainly did not dismiss it lightly, for in the memorandum dated 11 August 1919 he expressed the opinion that the "four Great Powers are committed to Zionism. And Zionism, be it right or wrong, good or bad, is rooted in age-long traditions, in present needs, in future hopes, of far profounder import than the desires and prejudices of the 700,000 Arabs who now inhabit that ancient land" (*ibid.*, p. 345).

the next best thing may, perhaps, be attained if we can frame a scheme which shall, as far as possible, further not merely the material interests, but the hopes and habits of the native population; which shall take into account the legitimate aspirations of other peoples and races, in particular, of the French, the British, and the Jews; and which shall embody, as completely as may be, the essential spirit of the various international pronouncements, whose literal provisions it seems impossible in all cases to fulfil.[5]

Nor was the task of reconciliation made easier by developments within the Near and Middle East. With the demise of Turkish rule, Arab nationalist leaders returned from exile to compete for the support of the masses, and a number of political groups emerged from hiding. Comprising the Arab nationalist movement, these particularistic societies differed over fundamental issues: Was the emphasis to be pan-Islamic or pan-Arab? Could unity be achieved with a European presence, and if so, peacefully or through militancy? Did the sharifian dynasty, headed by Husayn, represent the appropriate instrument for achieving nationalism and independence? Which was most desirable, local or broad nationalism? Despite such doctrinal differences, however, concern over the fate of the *watan al-'arabi*, or Arab homeland, had by 1919 led most of the groups toward a common awareness of what the nationalist thinker al-Afghani had warned: "By God's Life! Madness and infidelity are leagued together, and folly and greed are allied to destroy religion, to abrogate the Holy Law, and to hand over the Home of Islam to foreigners without striking a blow or offering the least resistance."[6]

Few British statesmen as yet appreciated the potential of this undercurrent of nationalist sentiment. Sir Arthur Hirtzel of the India Office expressed a minority opinion when he ventured, "Is it not then better to

---

5. *Documents*, 4:346.
6. Quoted in E. G. Browne, *The Persian Revolution of 1905–1909* (Cambridge: The University Press, 1910), p. 26. According to T. E. Lawrence, the term "Arab Movement" encompassed all the vague discontent against Turkey which existed in the Arab provinces before 1916 (Kedourie, *England and the Middle East*, p. 103). See also Albert H. Hourani, *Arabic Thought in the Liberal Age, 1798–1939* (London: Oxford University Press, 1962), particularly chap. 11; *Documents*, 4:360–65, for a description of four specific societies operating in Jerusalem; and Majid Khadduri, " 'Azīz 'Alī Miṣrī and the Arab Nationalist Movement," *St. Antony's Papers*, no. 17 (Middle Eastern Affairs no. 4) (London: Oxford University Press, 1965), pp. 140–63.

do voluntarily what one will, sooner rather than later, be compelled to do? . . . We must swim with the new tide which is set towards the education, and not the government, of what used to be subject peoples."[7] But resistance to such pleas was part of a general European insensitivity— traced as far back in Middle Eastern history as the Urabi revolt in Egypt in 1882—to the force of nationalism. Consequently, the British negotiated the future of the Middle East in Paris with insufficient attention to local conditions.

If for the time being Great Britain could afford to ignore such a force, Sharif Husayn could not, for Arab nationalist sentiment directly affected his status and prestige. To some Muslims Husayn's opposition to the Caliph during the war was inexcusable. Many natives of the Fertile Crescent considered themselves intellectually and culturally superior to the Hijazis of the Arabian desert. The mufti of Jerusalem allegedly said in 1919: "I have been asked if the Hedjaz Kingdom will satisfy our national aspirations. Not at all. That is for the Bedouins across the Jordan. We are different peoples. Our native country is Palestine."[8]

Similar antipathy toward the sharif and his family was reported from Baghdad several weeks earlier by Colonel A. T. Wilson. Instructed by London to make inquiries into local sentiment at the possible candidacy of Amir Abdullah for ruler of a united Mesopotamia, Wilson replied that hostility toward any member of the sharif's family was growing because "Hedjaz politicians and persons have no connection with or hold upon Mesopotamia and even [the] idea that King Husein should be prayed for in Mosques has found little favour there."[9] Still others, more extreme and anti-European, viewed Husayn as subservient to British wishes.

Husayn's personal authority over the Arab provinces was further diminished by the appearance of a rival in the more immediate arena of Arabia. The bitter contention between the Hashimi family, led by King Husayn, and Ibn Sa'ud had resumed after the armistice, and on 19 May 1919 Sa'udi forces defeated the Hijazi troops commanded by Amir Ab-

7. Hirtzel to A. T. Wilson, private letter of 17 September 1919, Arnold T. Wilson Papers, British Museum.
8. General Headquarters of Egyptian Expeditionary Force to the Foreign Office, 3 March 1919, copy of an article of 10 February "written by a certain Miss Weinstein of Jerusalem to the Associated Papers of New York" (F.O. 608/98).
9. Curzon to Balfour (cipher telegram), 26 January 1919, F.O. 608/96.

dullah at Turaba. Husayn was spared further defeat only through Britain's diplomatic intervention with Ibn Sa'ud. Not only had it been true in wartime that "automatically, the Sharif's control of affairs waned as the fighting receded farther and farther from his seat of power,"[10] but his domestic position in peacetime was being undermined as well. Angered at Abdullah's military failure, Husayn also criticized the statesmanship of Faysal in strong terms during the tense period over Syria at the end of the year.[11]

Having become estranged from his own sons, Husayn compounded his difficulties by allowing relations with the British to worsen. In November, 1919, General Allenby paid an official visit to the king at Jidda. Husayn insisted upon full British compliance with their promises and opposed French designs on Syria, leaving the impression with Abdullah that these discussions "resulted only in increased misunderstanding" on the subject of Syria, Palestine, and Iraq.[12] As Husayn's stature diminished, so did British hopes—for the time being—of solving their Arab problem through the agency of the sharifians.

The rise of two revolutionary forces beyond the immediate perimeter of the Arab provinces and the danger of their coalescing into an anti-British drive also had an important effect on British attitudes toward the Middle East. On 19 May 1919 a Turkish officer, Mustafa Kemal, landed at Samsun on the Black Sea coast of Anatolia and, in defiance of his superiors in Constantinople, proceeded to organize a movement for Turkish nationalism and against an imposed peace settlement. When added to the lingering animosity toward the Turks, the fact that this resistance jeopardized Allied arrangements for the partitioning of Turkey sufficed to set British policy against the Kemalists. For not only did

10. Elizabeth Monroe, *Britain's Moment in the Middle East, 1914–1956* (Baltimore, Md.: The Johns Hopkins Press, 1963), p. 47. Abdullah portrays his father as "bad tempered, forgetful and suspicious" and as having lost "his quick grasp and sound judgment" (Graves, p. 183).

11. Dispatch no. 571 of 22 November 1919 transmitted a literal translation of a letter from Husayn to Faysal, who was then in Paris: "Therefore, the result is, Sir, that if I encounter an incident (notwithstanding the patience and tolerance promised), and if anything interferes with my decisions as you have already done more than once, I will withdraw that same moment. . . . Moreover, if the Syrians decide to fight for their liberty and independence, I will not hesitate in going over to them to co-operate with them . . . so that they may know that I did not betray them. God will not guide traitors" (*Documents*, 4:550).

12. Graves, *Memoirs of King Abdullah*, p. 190.

these nationalists intend to oppose the Sublime Porte in their fight to retain an independent Turkey in Anatolia, but they sought solidarity with their fellow Muslims to the south, as was first articulated in the Turkish National Pact at Angora.[13]

Emanating from Russia, communism was the second force bent on reversing the status quo. Unlike the Kemalists, the Bolsheviks had sought quite early to feed on Middle Eastern discontent. Within a month of their seizure of power the Council of People's Commissars issued an "Appeal to the Muslims of Russia and the East" seeking their support for the revolution. Addressing itself to "Moslems of the East! Persians, Turks, Arabs and Hindus," the appeal condemned the "rapacious European plunderers," expressed Bolshevik opposition to the seizure of foreign territory, and ended by asking for Muslim support "in the work of regenerating the world."[14] Anti-Bolshevik resistance in the Caucasus collapsed and the Red Army advanced along a wide front in the wake of a general British troop withdrawal. Alarm grew in London and Paris at the prospect of a Turco-Bolshevik drive aimed at menacing India through the Middle East. One result was the greater emphasis placed upon the strategic importance of this region, Mesopotamia in particular, by those responsible for military planning.[15] The specific threat posed by the Turks and the Bolsheviks, in addition to the general unrest in

13. The first article of the pact referred to a link between the Arab Middle East and the Turkish Near East: ". . . the whole of these parts . . . imbued with sentiments of respect for each other and of sacrifice . . . form a whole which does not admit of division for any reason in truth or in ordinance" (text in Temperley, *History of the Peace Conference of Paris*, 6:605–6).
14. Jane Degras, ed., *Soviet Documents on Foreign Policy*, vol. 1: *1917–1924* (London: Oxford University Press, 1951), pp. 15–17.
15. On 12 January 1920 the Eastern Committee of the British government was of the opinion that "in view of our inability to find the force entailed in the holding of line (a) [Constantinople-Batum-Baku-Kraznovodsk-Merv] or (b) [Constantinople-Baku-Enzeli-Tehran-Meshed], of the difficulties of reinforcing troops in areas south and east of Caspian, and of military argument that such a force would be more profitably employed in aggressive action elsewhere, it was inevitable that we should fall back on alternative (c) [Northern Palestine-Mosul]" (Lord Hardinge at the Foreign Office to Earl of Derby, Paris, for Curzon's attention [telegraph], 13 January 1920, in 169528/ME58, F.O. 406/43). The record of friction and cooperation between the two revolutionary groups and against the Allies is presented in Arnold J. Toynbee, *Survey of International Affairs, 1920–1923* (London: Oxford University Press, 1927), pp. 316–76 ("Russia, Transcaucasia, and Turkey"), and in Firuz Kazemzadeh, *The Struggle for Transcaucasia (1917–1921)* (New York: Philosophical Library, 1951).

Asia at this time, contributed to a British regional view in which the Fertile Crescent would form the base for dealing with a crisis in any of the adjoining areas of tension.

Despite the above challenges—incompatible promises, national exhaustion, the logic of imperialism, a tendency to react with condescension toward nationalism, Turkish and Bolshevik rejection of the status quo, general turbulence, and the failure of Husayn to fulfill British expectations—France and Great Britain might have dealt effectively with the Fertile Crescent in the early postwar years had they been able to concert policy. Instead, under the pressures of peace in Europe and Asia, the wartime coalition began to break apart. Divergence became increasingly apparent in their respective approaches to Europe, the Rhine, the future of Germany, and Turkey, but it was especially evident in matters concerning the Middle East. The last of the Ottoman Empire to be divided was the Fertile Crescent north of Arabia, and the contenders for control of the area were Britain and France. In 1919 events revealed that the Anglo-French relationship had been an *alliance de convenance*, one without a firm, lasting foundation. Mutual distrust and recrimination exposed the Entente Cordiale of 1904 as a façade which had suppressed deep historical differences instead of resolving them.

On the one hand, France was determined to retain at least one sphere of influence in the region, both as compensation for her heavy sacrifice in the European fighting and in keeping with her traditional interests in the Levant. Premier Clemenceau therefore insisted upon France's right to Syria, a claim based on the Sykes-Picot agreement. The French were also concerned that Britain, a former rival in the Middle East, might achieve unchallenged pre-eminence in this area of economic potential and strategic importance.[16] Consequently, they began to think in terms of an Anglo-Syrian conspiracy whereby the Syrians would be encouraged to resist the French occupation of Beirut and claim to primacy in

16. Professor Toynbee has placed this phase of the rivalry in its proper historical perspective: "One cannot understand—or make allowances for—the postwar relations of the French and British Governments over the 'Eastern Question' unless one realizes this tradition of rivalry and its accumulated inheritance of suspicion and resentment. . . . The French are perhaps more affected by it than the English, because on the whole they have had the worst of the struggle in the Levant as well as in India, and failure cuts deeper memories than success" (*The Western Question in Greece and Turkey* [London: Constable & Co., 1923], pp. 45–46).

Syria.[17] Moreover, their suspicions were not entirely unfounded; the unauthorized activity of certain British agents, who allegedly were unaware of the official British position, was damaging the credibility of claims in London to a "policy of *désintéressment*" in Syria.[18] Finally, the French refused to be governed in their Arab policy by the promises of His Majesty's Government to Sharif Husayn, as Clemenceau duly informed Lloyd George on 9 November.[19]

On the other hand, French uneasiness at the state of the alliance was reciprocated by the British. The apparent unwillingness of the French to compromise with Arab demands was viewed as a threat to the influence and prestige of Britain with the Arabs; the need to consult Paris, to consider French interests, and to restrain the Syrians on behalf of France pointed up the liabilities inherent in the alliance. When asked for an appraisal of Arab potential to resist France, General Allenby reported deep misgivings. If the French were given a mandate in Syria, he submitted, there would be serious trouble and probably a war involving Great Britain; "the consequences would be incalculable."[20]

The extent of the Anglo-French divergence was reflected in an exchange of letters between Clemenceau and Lloyd George in October, 1919. On the 14th the French Premier wrote, *inter alia*, to the Earl of Derby, British ambassador in Paris: "Je comprends fort bien l'embarras où se trouvent les négociateurs anglais, qui sous le coup des nécessités politiques, ont été amenés à prendre au Hedjaz, au Nedjd [Ibn Sa'ud] et avec la France des engagements sinon opposés, du moins difficiles à ajuster."[21] On the 18th a reply was forthcoming from the British

17. The fact that a British officer, Colonel T. E. Lawrence, accompanied Amir Faysal in his appearance before the peace conference contributed to mounting French suspicions. On 21 August a member of the Foreign Office expressed criticism of Lawrence's role: "We and the War Office feel strongly that he is to a large extent responsible for our troubles with the French over Syria . . ." (*Documents*, 4:354).

18. Upon learning of such activity, Balfour termed it "most unfortunate" and "of a nature to lend some colour to these repeated French complaints" (Balfour to Curzon from Paris, 28 July 1919, no. 1208 [telegram], *ibid.*, p. 323; see also French charges on pp. 321, 327–28).

19. Clemenceau to Lloyd George, 9 November 1919, *ibid.*, p. 521.

20. Quoted in Ray Stannard Baker, *Woodrow Wilson and World Settlement*, vol. 3 (London: William Heinemann, 1923), p. 15.

21. *Documents*, 4:469.

Prime Minister in which he expressed surprise at the "complete change from the friendly tone you adopted in our discussions on this subject in Paris" and said that it would be hard for him to conceive "of a more offensive imputation made by one Ally to another, after five years in comradeship in arms."[22] He went on to charge the French government with being under a "complete misapprehension" as to British policy, of communicating messages of a "somewhat insulting form," and of advancing unfounded accusations. Lloyd George ended by pleading that Anglo-French relations not become estranged, yet warned that his government would be compelled to publicly refute French accusations if they continued, though "certainly nothing would be more calculated to encourage the enemies of that Anglo-French Alliance which was the principal cause of the Allied victory in the war. But they will not shrink from this duty if it is thrust upon them."[23]

In the absence of mutual good faith, little could be done to conciliate differences in outlook toward the Arabs, the engagements of 1916, or the most appropriate formula for removing at least the Middle Eastern obstacle to Anglo-French amity. Thus the breach, first reopened in the final stages of the war and widened in the clash of ideas and personalities in 1919, persisted thereafter as an important irritant in the triangular relationship among the French, the Arabs, and the British.

Controversy within Great Britain over ends and means further limited the capacity of her statesmen to deal effectively with Arab affairs. English society as a whole was weary from the unprecedented war effort—an effort which was to affect British imperial relations profoundly. D. G. Hogarth was one of the few people who at the time grasped its full implications. "The empire has reached its maximum and begun the descent. There is no more expansion in us . . . and that being so we shall make but a poor Best of the Arab Countries; Had the capture of Baghdad ended the War we could have done much; but the rest of 1917 and all of 1918 and 1919 have lowered our vitality permanently. We started in 1914 young and vigorous and we have come out in 1919 to find we are old and must readjust all our ideas."[24] Even to the less perceptive it was clear that people were exhausted, anxious to return to normalcy as

22. *Ibid.*, pp. 479ff.
23. *Ibid.*, p. 489.
24. Hogarth to Miss Gertrude Bell, Oriental secretary to the acting civil commissioner, Mesopotamia, 11 April 1920, Wilson Papers.

soon as possible, and therefore impatient with foreign adventures or expensive overseas commitments.

Public impatience asserted itself in a demand for military demobilization. When questioned about the disposition of a large number of British forces abroad, Sir Henry Wilson, chief of the Imperial General Staff, advised: "get out of the places that don't belong to you and hold on to those that do."[25] In January, 1919, Winston Churchill assumed the office of secretary of state for war and in the next twelve months succeeded in demobilizing more than four million soldiers.

Nevertheless, continuing public pressure dictated the need for a diplomatic initiative in the Near and Middle East: either to quickly achieve a peace settlement with Turkey or to withdraw the occupation troops from Constantinople and Syria. Churchill strongly advocated decision and action in his letter of 12 August to the foreign secretary in Paris:

I know how great your difficulties are, but I trust you will realise that the length of time which we can hold a sufficient force at your disposal to overawe Turkey is limited. . . . All the men we are raising in this country are needed either to hold down Ireland, to maintain order here, or to relieve our demobilisable garrisons in Egypt or India. The delays in demobilisation caused by the delay in reaching Peace with Germany and Turkey have already added more than 60 millions to the Army Estimates, for which no Parliamentary sanction has been obtained, and I must really ask for assistance in this matter, which is from day to day assuming greater prominence in the House of Commons and throughout the country.[26]

The fact that the logic of public discontent and financial limitations had impressed itself upon the government was reflected in a decision on Syria communicated by Curzon to Amir Faysal on 9 October. Britain would begin a troop withdrawal from Syria on 1 November because:

the peoples of the British Empire have lost over 950,000 lives, and they have incurred a debt of £9,000,000,000 in securing the freedom of the nations of Europe and of the peoples who formerly languished under the Turkish yoke. . . . It has sustained the onerous and expensive burden of maintaining law

25. Quoted in Field Marshal Viscount A. P. W. Wavell, *Allenby in Egypt* (London: George G. Harrap & Co., 1943), p. 52.
26. Churchill to Balfour, 12 August 1919, Arthur James Balfour Papers, British Museum; see also Stephen R. Graubard, "Military Demobilization in Great Britain," *Journal of Modern History* 19, no. 4 (December, 1947) : 309.

and order in countries just liberated from alien rule in the hopes that the Peace Conference would come to a rapid and peaceful solution of the difficult problems connected with the future of the Middle East. But it is unfair to the British taxpayer to ask him to bear any longer the burden of occupying provinces for which the Empire does not propose to accept permanent responsibility.[27]

While the debate over demobilization, economy, and disengagement from the increasingly complex Middle East situation affected British policy significantly, the lack of coordination hampered the policy-making establishment itself. Historically, the extension of British influence into the Fertile Crescent during the nineteenth century had occurred from two directions, the Mediterranean Sea and along the Persian Gulf. Because the first thrust involved Britain in continuous diplomatic relations with the Ottoman Empire, and frequently in competition with other European powers, responsibility for British policy in the Levant had rested with the Foreign Office. Similarly, because economic penetration of Mesopotamia and Persia had been stimulated by considerations particular to Britain's Indian empire, jurisdiction in that sphere had been entrusted traditionally to the India Office.

By the turn of the century this division of authority had been made more permanent through the growth of separate bureaucratic and administrative structures, each with its priorities and particular regional perspective. Not only did the war reinforce this distinction, but it also injected the War Office into Middle Eastern affairs, as evidenced by Lord Kitchener's diplomatic initiative toward Sharif Husayn late in 1914 and Churchill's concern in 1919–20.

As a consequence the several departments possessed different sensitivities. The Foreign Office sought to meet the susceptibilities of Britain's allies (France, Greece, Italy, and the United States), to punish the Turks, and to devise a comprehensive foreign policy of which the Arab provinces were but one element. Conversely, in its capacity as spokesman for the government of India, the India Office was more concerned with the sensitivities of millions of Indian Muslims. The Arab Bureau in Cairo came to support the sharifians as the instrument most suitable

27. Curzon to Faysal, 9 October 1919, *Documents*, 4:447. Lloyd George claimed that, with regard to Syria, domestic pressures "left no other course open to the British Government" (*The Truth About the Peace Treaties*, 2:1093, "Extract from Aide-Memoire of September 13th, 1919").

to British interests and Arab aspirations, whereas officials in the India Office urged support for the Sa'udis as the rising power in Arabia. Differing over whether to court the Arabs specifically or to appease the Islamic world as a whole by dealing leniently with the Turks, whether to retain British influence by direct control or by indirect means, and whether to endorse the primacy of Husayn or that of Ibn Sa'ud, the so-called Mediterranean and Indian schools of thought continued along separate paths even after the 1919 armistice.[28] Any efforts at coordination, such as the Interdepartmental Conference on Middle Eastern Affairs,[29] proved too slow and cumbersome.

This failure to provide the necessary guidance from London was resented and criticized by British personnel stationed in the Middle East, and one of the more outspoken men was Colonel A. T. Wilson. "It was generally useless to refer questions to London, for the administrative machinery at home was so complicated that telegrams seldom elicited a reply in less than a month, and the answers were often insufficiently definite and specific to be useful as a guide to action."[30] His view from Mesopotamia was reaffirmed in Palestine, objection being taken, for example, to the faulty lines of communication between London and that region: ". . . we had but the slightest and vaguest information about the Sykes-Picot negotiations . . . and there was far too little realization of Indian operations in Iraq and of Indian encouragement of Ibn Sa'ud. So far as we were concerned it seemed to be nobody's business to harmonize the various views and policies of the Foreign Office, the India Office, the Admiralty, the War Office, the Government of India and the Residency in Egypt."[31] Although Balfour had brushed aside repeated criticism of the lack of effective, integrated machinery by promising

28. For a fuller treatment of the Foreign Office–India Office rivalry, see Monroe, *Britain's Moment in the Middle East*, pp. 35–38, 54; John Marlowe, *The Persian Gulf in the Twentieth Century* (London: The Cresset Press, 1962), pp. 42–50; Hubert Young, *The Independent Arab* (London: John Murray, 1933), pp. 271–72.
29. The Eastern Committee of the War Cabinet held thirty-eight meetings from 28 March to 21 November 1918 and was then replaced by the Interdepartmental Conference with Curzon as chairman. A great many of the latter's forty-one meetings between 7 January 1919 and 16 June 1920 were taken up with the unsettling events in Persia and the Caucasus. The full records of both committees are in P. 940/19, I.O.
30. Wilson, *Mesopotamia, 1917–1920*, 2:140.
31. Sir Ronald Storrs, *Orientations* (London: Nicolson & Watson, 1937), p. 179.

The Difficulties of Peace, 1919　　　　　　　　　31

that the question of control would be dealt with after the war,[32] existing arrangements persisted through 1919. Consequently, instead of presenting a well-defined formula for dealing with the Middle East, which might have succeeded in breaking the deadlock that developed at Versailles, the government found itself subjected to a number of conflicting opinions, interests, and pressures from within its own ranks. Nor was this fundamental weakness alleviated with the replacement of Balfour by George Nathaniel Curzon as secretary of state for foreign affairs on 27 October 1919.

32. Balfour to Edwin Montagu, 27 July 1918, and secret memorandum E.C. 24A, 13 August 1918, both in CAB 21/186.

CHAPTER 3

Failure at the Paris Peace
Conference

*Appetites, passions, hopes, revenge, starvation, and
anarchy ruled the hour; and from this simultaneous
welter all eyes were turned to Paris.*—Winston Churchill,
The World Crisis

Great Britain shared in the mood of optimism and expectation surrounding the formal opening of the Paris Peace Conference on 18 January 1919. The Fourteen Points enunciated by President Woodrow
Wilson had excited the world's imagination as a framework for restruc-
turing international relations; the assembly of leaders offered an unprecedented opportunity to translate these principles into reality.[1] The
agenda items, as complex as they were diverse, included disarmament,
reparations, Germany's boundaries, peace treaties, a League of Nations,
and the dissolution of four empires—of which the Arab regions comprised but one portion.

Those Arabs of the Fertile Crescent and Arabia who were politically
alert looked to the conference as an international forum prepared to
acknowledge their contribution to the war and qualified to approve their
aim of independence. But as the months passed, and as what President

1. Analysis of the peace conference is facilitated by access to the participants'
many diaries, memoirs, and descriptions as well as by studies of specific aspects.
Temperley's *History of the Peace Conference of Paris* remains the standard work
on the subject.

Wilson termed "the whole disgusting scramble" for territory became apparent in the Arab provinces, disillusionment set in and moderation yielded to militancy. This regression in relations between the Arab world and the European powers and, on a secondary level, between France and Great Britain, is illustrated by the chronology of events originating in Damascus as well as in London and Paris. Two events of significance occurred shortly before the conference opened, the first providing one of the few instances of accord during 1919, the second establishing the tone for dialogue between Premiers Lloyd George and Clemenceau regarding the Arab question.

On 3 January an agreement was signed between Dr. Weizmann, on behalf of the Zionist Organisation, and Amir Faysal, acting as representative of the kingdom of the Hijaz. Its nine articles looked to "the most cordial goodwill and understanding" in relations between "the Arab State and Palestine." Effect was to be given to the British declaration of November, 1917, in return for which the Zionist Organisation would use "its best efforts to assist the Arab State in providing the means for developing the national resources and economic possibilities thereof."[2] The Weizmann-Faysal agreement, while but a footnote to the later record of enmity between Arab and Jewish nationalisms, was regarded by the British in 1919 as an auspicious beginning to an era of cooperation in Palestine.[3]

Faysal's willingness to enter into such an agreement stemmed largely from the nature of his mission and the reception accorded him in Europe. Having only begun to establish an Arab government in Damascus

2. The text is in Moshe Pearlmann, "Chapters of Arab-Jewish Diplomacy, 1918–1922," *Jewish Social Studies* 6, no. 2 (April, 1944) : 135–36. The original English version, with Faysal's handwritten proviso in Arabic, is in the possession of St. Antony's College, Oxford. Although Faysal later claimed to be unable to recall the agreement, his letter to Sir Herbert Samuel, dated 10 December 1919 and found in the Samuel Papers at the Israel State Archives, contains the following: "J'ai la ferme conviction que la confiance réciproque établie entre nous et le parfaite accord de notre point de vue qui a permis une parfaits compréhension entre le Dr. Weizmann et moi. . . ."
3. The fact that the British encouraged such contacts is reflected in the remark by Gilbert Clayton that Weizmann's earlier visit to Faysal in June, 1918, "was instigated by me and not by Weizmann himself" (G. S. Clayton to Symes, 13 June 1918, Reginald Wingate Papers). The British helped foster the impression among the Arabs that "the friendship of world Jewry to the Arab cause is equivalent to support in all States where Jews have a political influence" (Cmd. 5964, p. 3).

on 1 October 1918, he was called away two months later by his father, Sharif Husayn, and ordered to proceed to the Paris Peace Conference as head of the Arab delegation and there to act in concert with the British.[4] While his father viewed boundaries and the form of an Arab government as subjects for negotiation, Faysal, being directly involved in the struggle for Syria, sensed that the more fundamental issue of Arab independence was as yet unresolved. This conviction was reinforced in the course of his brief visits to France (26 November–9 December) and to England (10 December–7 January), where it became apparent that the Arabs, contrary to their expectations, were to be regarded as supplicants rather than as equal members of the victorious coalition and that the Sykes-Picot agreement remained very much an obstacle to Arab self-government.

In London Faysal was advised to accept French control in Syria, while at the same time his visit was used to encourage contact with the Zionists. Conscious of French opposition to Arab claims and uncertain of British intentions, Faysal was led to regard the Zionists as a potential ally in the coming struggle of wills. In signing the agreement with Dr. Weizmann, Faysal personally appended a proviso to the effect that this agreement would be deemed void and of no account or validity if the Arabs failed to obtain the independence which they sought through the good offices of Great Britain. Arab-Zionist relations were to be affected thereafter by the Great Powers' treatment of the Arabs, a fact all too often overlooked by analysts of the Palestine problem.

Anxiety on Faysal's part was fully justified by the outcome of several meetings between Clemenceau and Lloyd George in London from 2 to 4 December. While Faysal was being given a cool reception in France, the British prime minister pressed for an alteration of the Sykes-Picot agreement, asking that Mosul and Palestine be transferred from the French to the British sphere. His request, based on an expanded conception of Britain's strategic needs in the Fertile Crescent and stemming from what Hogarth termed "the passion of possession" following conquest, was accepted by Clemenceau. But the price for this concession was a reaffirmation by the British government of France's claim to

4. Faysal's title and instructions to act on the basis of an exclusive relationship with Great Britain are contained in Ḥafīẓ Wahbah, *Jazīrat al-'Arab fi'l Qarn al-'Ishrīn* (Cairo, 1935), p. 307.

Cilicia and Syria. Their agreement was to govern all future discussions at Versailles about Syria, and it further complicated Britain's position as mediator of Arab and French claims.

On 1 January 1919 the Hijazi delegation submitted a memorandum to the peace conference. The aim of the Arab nationalist movements was stated to be the eventual unification of all the Arabs into one nation. King Husayn asserted his claim to a privileged place among Arabs, although the diversity of the various provinces necessitated their being considered individually. The Great Powers were asked to think of the Arabs as potentially one people and not to take "steps inconsistent with the prospect of an eventual union of these areas under one sovereign government." In concluding its request that independence be conceded and local competence be established, this initial postwar statement of Arab aspirations expressed the hope that the conference would not attach "undue importance to superficial differences of condition" nor consider the Arabs "only from the low ground of existing European material interests and supposed spheres," offering in return "little but gratitude." Citing President Wilson's principles as a defense, a supplementary note of January 29 on the "Territorial Claims of the Government of the Hedjaz" restated the Arab hope that the powers would attach "more importance to the bodies and souls of the Arabic-speaking peoples than to their own material interests."[5]

Although this hope was to be articulated shortly thereafter in Article 22 of the Covenant of the League of Nations, the discrepancy between Arab and European thinking was more readily evidenced in such discussions of the Syrian question as took place on 20 March at a meeting of the Council of Four. Faysal's presentation of the Arab case in his brief appearance before the larger policy-making body on 6 February had stimulated intense consideration of the problem, and the chief delegates now seemed prepared to offer concrete proposals. Instead, the meeting constituted a reversal, for the British and French representatives engaged in an argument deriving from their persistent differences over the secret treaties, apportioning responsibility for them, and the degree to which they were still binding upon their respective governments. At this point President Wilson intervened, proposing that an in-

5. The two memoranda are reproduced in David Hunter Miller, *My Diary at the Conference of Paris, 1918–1919*, 22 vols. (New York: Appeal Printing Co., 1924), 4:297–300.

terallied commission be sent to ascertain the actual wishes of the people in the Fertile Crescent, to which neither Clemenceau nor Lloyd George raised any serious objections.[6]

Amir Faysal expressed his approval also, for the commission would "enable the Arabs to make their voices heard above the cries of success raised by the victors in this War."[7] On 21 April he took leave of the conference and of the intricacies of formal diplomacy in order to prepare for the commission's arrival. Returning to the Arab world, on 5 May he addressed a conference of Syrian notables at Damascus, pledging himself to the independence program and beseeching his audience to "depend and trust in our Allies who helped us, and who wish us good success and have no ambitions but to help us to progress."[8] Whether because of renewed optimism or out of desperation to keep the activists under his personal direction, the notables declared their support for his policy. Faysal then proceeded to instruct the Syrian people in how to answer inquiries from the commission. "The people have been told to ask for complete independence for Syria, and, at the same time, to express a hope that it will be granted to other Arab countries. By this compromise Faysal has reconciled the 'Ittihad-es-Suri', which thinks only of Syria, with the pan-Arab empire enthusiasts represented in the 'Istikhal [sic]-el-Arabi.' "[9] Only through moderation and with the sup-

6. Lawrence Evans, *United States Policy and the Partition of Turkey, 1914–1924* (Baltimore, Md.: The Johns Hopkins Press, 1965), pp. 135ff., provides an account of the meeting on 20 March as well as a description of the American role in Turkish and Arab problems; see also Baker, *Woodrow Wilson and World Settlement*, pp. 6–15, and Zeine, *The Struggle for Arab Independence*, pp. 76–79.
7. Faysal to President Wilson, 24 March 1920, cited in Evans, *United States Policy and the Partition of Turkey*, p. 141.
8. Faysal's address and its enthusiastic reception, which illustrated the degree of support he still possessed in the early part of 1919, are reported in *Documents*, 4:267–72. Such support enabled him to inform the British that he would tell the commission: "Advice and assistance to the Syrian State to be given by Great Britain, should they refuse, by America; if America refuses, by Great Britain, America, and France; in no case by France alone(?)" (*ibid.*, p. 265).
9. Report from Damascus by British liaison officer Lieutenant Colonel Kinahan Cornwallis on the "Political Situation in Arabia," 16 May 1919, *ibid.*, p. 264. On 2 July the first General Syrian Congress issued its "statement of desires," asking that "there should be no separation of the southern part of Syria, known as Palestine, nor of the littoral western zone, which includes Lebanon, from the Syrian country" and seeking assurances against "partition under whatever circumstances." Notable for its moderate tone (demonstrated by repeated use of the words "request" and "ask"), the statement explicitly stated: "We do not

port of the Great Powers could Faysal hope to reconcile his personal dilemma of direct involvement in Syrian affairs with loyalty to his father and the dream of a larger Arab independence and unity, a dilemma summarized in the distinction between the terms "Arabia" and "Syria."

In retrospect it would appear that these protestations of support for Faysal and his diplomatic approach, coupled with the preceding, momentary Allied consensus in support of a commission, were the turning point for both the Arabian and European phases of the Middle East problem in 1919. Basic divergencies expressed at the Big Four meeting of 20 March subsequently reasserted themselves and contributed to a steady decline in Anglo-French understanding. This in turn deprived Faysal of his chance for a peaceful solution through accommodation and contributed to the erosion of his authority until, by 1920, he had become captive of those extremists who were determined to resist any extension of French authority east of the Damascus-Homs-Hama-Aleppo line.

Several days before his departure from Paris on 21 April, Amir Faysal had met with Clemenceau in an apparent effort to arrive at a compromise. The French premier asked that, as a minimum, Faysal consent to the replacement of British troops with French units in Syria, but assured him that France had no desire to conquer the country. He added, however, that the French people would not be pleased if no trace of France's presence in Syria were to remain. If France were not to be represented in Syria by her flag and troops, the people would consider it a disgrace, like the flight of a soldier from the battlefield.[10]

Faysal was noncommittal in his reply, preferring to let the proposed interallied commission hear the wish of the Syrians for independence. By the end of May, however, the very formation of the commission had become a source of controversy between Clemenceau and Lloyd George; in the end both retracted their earlier assent, imposed mutually unacceptable preconditions, and finally disassociated themselves from the

---

acknowledge any right claimed by the French Government in any part whatever of our Syrian country and refuse that she should assist us or have a hand in our country under any circumstances and in any place" (J. C. Hurewitz, *Diplomacy in the Near and Middle East*, vol. 2 [Princeton: D. Van Nostrand, 1956], pp. 63–64).

10. Account provided by a confidant of Faysal, Sāṭiʿ al-Ḥuṣrī, *Day of Maysalun*, trans. Sidney Glazer (Washington, D.C.: The Middle East Institute, 1966), p. 59.

project.[11] Nevertheless, since the American members appointed to the commission had already departed for the Middle East, they were instructed to carry out the inquiry, which lasted from June until August. And, while their final report confirmed the Syrians' rejection of a French mandate, it was neither acted upon by the peace conference nor even supported in its conclusions by the American government, which refused to accept responsibility for mandated territories in the Near and Middle East.[12]

As the year progressed, those factors through which Faysal had hoped to assure Syrian independence were removed one at a time: the support of world opinion for the principle of self-determination; multilateral negotiation and the influence of disinterested third parties; the endeavor to use the techniques of European diplomacy; reliance upon Great Britain to implement her Arab undertaking and to intervene with the French on the Arabs' behalf; direct bilateral discussions with the French leader; and, finally, the report of an impartial commission.

Faysal and the Arab moderates were to suffer one more rebuff when it became clear by the autumn of 1919 that Britain was proceeding with plans to withdraw her troops from Syria and Cilicia. Confirmation was provided by the agreement reached between Lloyd George and Clemenceau on 15 September, after a British initiative two days earlier. The British *aide-mémoire* gave 1 November as the date for the evacuation to commence and enumerated, *inter alia*, the following guidelines:

3. In deciding to whom to hand over responsibility for garrisoning the various districts in the evacuated area, regard will be had to the engagements and declarations of the British and French Governments, not only as between themselves, but as between them and the Arabs.
4. In pursuance of this policy the garrisons in Syria west of the Sykes-Picot line and the garrisons in Cilicia will be replaced by a French force, and the garrisons at Damascus, Homs, Hama, and Aleppo will be replaced by an Arab force. . . .
6. The territories occupied by British troops will then be Palestine, defined in accordance with its ancient boundaries of Dan to Beersheba, and Meso-

---

11. Zeine, *The Struggle for Arab Independence*, pp. 88–94.
12. An exhaustive study of the American mission to Syria and Palestine is provided by Harry N. Howard, *The King-Crane Commission* (Beirut: Khayats, 1963); see also Evans, *The United States and the Partition of Turkey*, pp. 138–59.

potamia including Mosul, the occupation thus being in harmony with the arrangements concluded in December 1918. . . .

7. The British Government are prepared at any time to discuss the boundaries between Palestine and Syria and between Mesopotamia and Syria.[13]

This decision was made despite a personal letter from Faysal to Lloyd George delivered on 9 September by General Allenby. Addressed to "Your August Excellency," the message began with a warning that "affairs have reached a most dangerous climax" and were threatening Faysal's own position. ". . . I find myself torn asunder by different National Parties, which have now united through alarm at this delay and through the assurance of an evil augury. They are all agreed to perish utterly, rather than witness the division and mutilation of this Country, and put no further assurance in promises. . . ."[14] Recalling that "Mecca was upheld against Constantinople and the Turks in order to maintain the 'national principle,' " Faysal advised that the dignity of his own person and family as well as the prestige of Great Britain would suffer from any division of Syria, for it was "the brain of the Arab Provinces." Urging that only a guarantee of Syrian unity could prevent his demise and a state of anarchy, the amir informed Lloyd George that he was leaving immediately for Europe with the hope of arriving "before any decision is taken in London or disaster overtakes us both here and there." Yet Faysal reached London three days after the conclusion of the Anglo-French agreement over British troop withdrawals.

Faysal nevertheless participated in a series of three meetings with the British prime minister on 19 and 23 September and 13 October.[15] He sought cancellation of the troop withdrawals, or at least their postponement. But in a letter of 10 October Lloyd George made it clear that His Majesty's Government saw no recourse but to implement its decision. In view of compelling domestic considerations and the announcement six months earlier that Britain would not accept a mandate for Syria under any circumstances, the government regarded as impossible the occupation of Syria or Cilicia until such time as the peace conference could settle its eastern question.[16] With this decision and its presenta-

13. Text in *Documents*, 4:700–701.
14. *Ibid.*, p. 386.
15. Minutes of all three meetings, together with supplementary correspondence, are presented in *ibid.*, pp. 395–404, 413–19, and 458–63.
16. *Ibid.*, p. 451. At their second meeting Lloyd George placed responsibility for

tion to Faysal as a *fait accompli*, the government had served notice of its desire to abstain from the Syrian problem and to thereby extricate itself from the costly, awkward, and unappreciated position of intermediary between the two contenders.

The amir, under criticism from his father and from his Syrian followers, saw but one alternative: to deal directly with the French. Abandoned by the British, Faysal traveled to Paris, arriving on 20 October. Much had happened in the short interval since he had assured Clemenceau on 20 April of his being "a warm friend of France and of your administration." Still, the desperate situation warranted the effort, and Faysal lingered in Paris for more than two months.

In his absence the tension within Syria mounted. On 1 November British troops began to withdraw from forward positions, and by early December their evacuation from Syria had been completed. French and Arab troops now faced each other across the new zones of occupation. Incidents of military clashes increased in both frequency and intensity. The administration in Damascus proved unable to control the populace in the amir's absence; nor did the reduction of Great Britain's monthly subsidy from £150,000 to £75,000 contribute to its stability. General Henri Gouraud's arrival in Beirut on 21 November as French high commissioner for Syria and Cilicia provided one more sign of France's determination to secure her position in Syria, even at the risk of displeasing her British allies and despite resistance by the local inhabitants.

This new resolve on the part of France manifested itself during Faysal's uneasy stay in Paris. An exchange of letters and a series of meetings proved to no avail in the face of French adamance.[17] All options thus exhausted, Faysal turned away from Europe and diplomacy for the last time, departing for Beirut on 7 January with the knowledge that the

---

the delay in resolving the Turkish problem squarely upon the United States, "who have not yet made up their minds to the acceptance of mandates." In his letter of 10 October and at the final meeting he cited the illness of President Wilson, "without whose participation no final decisions can be arrived at." See also Lloyd George, *The Truth About the Peace Treaties*, 2:1093.

17. Upon arriving in Beirut, Faysal told Colonel Waters-Taylor that he had come to an agreement with France but wished to gain the consent of his people to the clauses before signing it. He regarded the agreement as distasteful, but said that he had been "handed over, tied by feet and hands, to the French." A carbon copy of this Temporary Agreement is found in C.S. 229, I.S.A.

Arab cause—and, by implication, that of the sharifians—would be won or lost by a direct confrontation in Syria during 1920.

What had begun as a year of hope ended in great disillusionment for all those concerned with the fate of the Fertile Crescent. The events of 1919, corresponding approximately to the period in which the Paris Peace Conference was in session, produced significant changes in the approaches, attitudes, and ultimate objectives of each of the participants. Within the first few months the focus of attention shifted from Versailles and multilateral diplomacy to Downing Street, the Quai d'Orsay, and secret, bilateral negotiations.

The British government had initially sought to free itself from incompatible undertakings through a conciliatory approach. As late as 18 October, in a letter to Clemenceau, Lloyd George had continued to insist that "the British Government are so impressed with the importance of bringing about an understanding between the Arabs and the French."[18] When Clemenceau and Faysal demonstrated conclusively their insistence upon the full rights provided by the Sykes-Picot and Husayn-McMahon documents respectively, British policy was transformed into one of disengagement. Henceforth, His Majesty's Government would devote its energies to securing Britain's Middle Eastern interests in Arabia, Mesopotamia, and Palestine while divorcing itself as much as possible from France's policy toward Syria.

The French position moved from a willingness to control Syria with Arab assistance to control despite the Arabs. The Arabs, who began by seeking the aid of the European powers, faced the new year alienated from France and disappointed with Great Britain. Thus the year 1919 left the Arab goal of independence and unity more remote than it may have seemed in 1914, the Anglo-French alliance seriously weakened, and the principle of self-determination virtually inapplicable to the Fertile Crescent.

On 22 January 1917 President Wilson had cautioned:

No peace can last, or ought to last, which does not recognize and accept the principle that Governments derive all their just powers from the consent

---

18. *Documents*, 4:486. It has been suggested that conciliation was the guiding principle for Lloyd George in all his dealings in foreign affairs; see C. L. Mowat, *Britain Between the Wars, 1918–1940* (London: Methuen & Co., 1955), p. 53.

British Policy in the Arab World

of the governed, and that no right anywhere exists to hand peoples about from sovereignty to sovereignty as if they were property.[19]

Failure to heed this advice was the salient feature of Middle Eastern politics in 1919. As a result the year constituted only a brief, uneasy interlude between the fighting of 1915–18 and the outbreak of renewed violence in 1920.

19. "The Essentials of Permanent Peace" (address delivered to the Senate of the United States), in *President Wilson's Foreign Policy: Messages, Addresses, Papers,* ed. James Brown Scott (New York: Oxford University Press, 1918).

CHAPTER 4 The Year of Violence, 1920

Indifference to the significance of the Near East in the scheme of world affairs has been carried so far that it is not appreciated that almost irreparable harm is being done to British interests.—The Near East, 2 January 1920

Stalemate characterized the Middle East at the beginning of 1920. The suspicion and intransigence of the Arabs, the British, and the French— and the inability of any two parties to compose their differences in a common front against the third—worked to preclude a diplomatic solution. The initiative, therefore, was transferred for the first time since the war from the chancelleries of Europe to the centers of ferment and activism in the Fertile Crescent: Baghdad, Damascus, Jerusalem, Amman.

Disillusioned by the Great Powers and by Wilsonian principles, and impatient after the unfruitful efforts of Faysal, the Arabs became increasingly concerned about the pervasive Anglo-French presence in the liberated areas. This atmosphere of resentment and unrest, in the rural areas as well as in the cities, contributed to a series of events which was to make the year memorable for its chronology of violence. By the end of 1920 the foundations of British policy would be upset, and with them prospects for a peaceful era of British dominance. Similarly, in the annals of Arab history 1920 would be referred to as *'Amm al-Nakba*, the Year of Catastrophe,[1] a phrase derived from the unfortunate series of events shortly to transpire in Syria.

1. Antonius, *The Arab Awakening*, p. 312.

Yet 1920 began peacefully enough. On 12 February Lloyd George and Clemenceau participated in the first Conference of London, which initiated an irregular sequence of *ad hoc* international conferences held after the conclusion of the Paris Peace Conference on 21 January.[2] The conference, reflective of the gradual manner in which Middle Eastern affairs still were approached, was devoted to the terms of peace with the Ottoman Empire. The premiers agreed to leave the Sultan in Constantinople but were unable to progress beyond that point, and the conference adjourned on 23 February.

Shortly thereafter, on 8 March, the second General Syrian Congress sat in Damascus and passed a resolution proclaiming both the independence and integrity of Greater Syria as a sovereign state and constitutional monarchy under Amir Faysal. A group of twenty-nine Iraqis passed a similar resolution on Mesopotamia and chose Amir Abdullah as their first monarch.[3] When news of these decisions reached Europe the effect was instant, shattering complacency and evoking strong verbal reactions from London and Paris.

M. Cambon, French ambassador in London, was summoned to the Foreign Office on 13 March to hear a thorough evaluation by Lord Curzon of recent French actions in Syria and of how they had contributed to the unilateral decisions made by the Syrian congress. Curzon accused General Gouraud of creating a sense of irritation in the Syrian people. He openly accused the French of "forcing themselves into areas where [they] . . . were not welcomed by the inhabitants," and felt it necessary to place on record that "the responsibility was not ours, but belonged in the main, if not exclusively, to the French."[4]

The situation seemed to ease slightly on 18 March when General Allenby reported the intended policy of Gouraud, his equal in the Levant,

2. A. L. Kennedy, in his *Old Diplomacy and New* (London: John Murray, 1922), p. 342, lists seventeen conferences in the period February, 1920–March, 1922. These are described in greater depth in Toynbee's *Survey of International Affairs, 1920–1923*, pp. 1–55.
3. At the same time, an "orderly and solemn demonstration" took place in Palestine and the military governor of Palestine was presented with a petition demanding an independent Syria with natural boundaries, no separation of Palestine from Syria, and an end to Zionism and Jewish immigration. See Meinertzhagen to War Office, 12 March 1920, no. 25, W.O. 106/195.
4. E. L. Woodward and Rohan Butler, eds., *Documents on British Foreign Policy, 1919–1939*, 1st ser., vol. 13 (London: Her Majesty's Stationery Office, 1963), p. 228; hereinafter cited as *Documents*, 13.

to avoid any manifestations of hostility against Faysal unless the latter attempted to give practical effect to the declaration of the Damascus congress.[5] Allenby urged that Faysal's sovereignty over an Arab nation or confederation be acknowledged, but that France be responsible for the administration of Syria, Britain for that of Palestine and Mesopotamia. "If Powers persist in their attitude of declaring null and void the action of Feisal and Syrian Congress, I feel certain that war must ensue. If hostilities arise, the Arabs will regard both French and English as their enemies and we shall be dragged by the French into a war which is against our own interests and for which we are ill-prepared."[6]

Such reasoning, however, was viewed in London as tantamount to capitulation to Arab pressure and was rejected. Officials in India, Egypt, and Mesopotamia had already been advised by the War Office that His Majesty's Government would not recognize the right of any self-constituted body at Damascus to regulate such important matters.[7] Allenby was further instructed by Lord Curzon on 1 April to notify both Faysal and Abdullah that the Mesopotamians in Damascus had no authority and that Mesopotamia's future could be decided only by the peace conference after it ascertained the wishes of the inhabitants.[8]

Allied anger at the actions of the Syrian congress remained unabated. The Supreme Council reconvened at San Remo on 19 April and proceeded to repudiate the proclamations issued at Damascus. On the 25th the mandates for Mesopotamia and Palestine were issued to Great Britain while the Syrian mandate was given to France, thus producing a direct test of wills between the European Allies and the Syrian nationalists.

The decisions taken at San Remo were made public on 5 May and their promulgation fostered further contempt by the Arabs for the West. In a letter three days later, General Haddad, head of the Hijazi delegation in Paris in Faysal's absence, submitted a formal protest to the secretary general of the League of Nations over the assignment of the mandates, pointing out that the wishes of the inhabitants had not been taken into account and noting "a certain contradiction" between the

5. Allenby to War Office, 18 March 1920, no. 265, W.O. 106/195.
6. Allenby to Curzon, 18 March 1920, no. 271 (telegram), *Documents*, 13:231.
7. Secret paraphrase from War Office to India, Egypt, and Mesopotamia, 13 March 1920, W.O. 106/195.
8. Curzon to Allenby, 1 April 1920, no. 292 (telegram), *Documents*, 13:239.

principles implied by this decision and "the promise of liberty and self-determination so solemnly proclaimed." He warned that "the moderate elements in the young nation, who have endeavoured, and are still endeavouring, to guide it towards a policy of sincere collaboration with the Allies, are now discouraged and rendered powerless by this decision."[9]

The Arab moderates' admitted loss of control over the situation, when added to the existing tension and uncertainty, produced a spiral of demonstrations and armed clashes which led to major crises in Syria and Mesopotamia and to disorder in Palestine on both sides of the Jordan River. Although the three newly mandated territories shared certain features in common, they differed in the nature and extent of their uprisings and must therefore be examined individually.

The right to control over Syria, and the geographic extent of that control, had been a source of contention between France and the sharifians since Syria's liberation from the Turks in October, 1918. By the spring of 1920 neither side showed much flexibility, and an outbreak of violence appeared to be inevitable. To the sharifians, Syria, as the center of Arab nationalism and the seat of an Arab government, was theirs by right of conquest and the expectations fostered by the Husayn-McMahon correspondence. They regarded its independence as non-negotiable and believed that the choice of a mandatary and the selection of advisers should at least be subject to approval by the Damascus government.

At the same time Syria had become no less central to the hopes and pride of France. Speaking in the Chamber of Deputies on 28 July 1920, M. Victor Bérard conveyed the attitude of many Frenchmen toward Syria. "In 1916, we had Syria, Cilicia, Mesopotamia, a part of Kurdistan, and our international share of Palestine. Now, when we reopened the accords in 1920, we saw that M. Clemenceau had abandoned *en route* Mesopotamia and Kurdistan, by giving Mosul to the English, and that he had also abandoned Palestine by transforming it from an international land into an English land."[10] All that remained to France were

9. E7414, F.O. 371/5036. In June Allenby suggested to Curzon that the San Remo decisions had come as a shock to Husayn and "probably brought home to him, for the first time, the fact that no words of his could alter the decree as regards Syria and Mesopotamia and that his hopes of expansion beyond the Hedjaz had ended in failure" (E8118/38/44 [no. 742], F.O. 406/44).
10. *Journal officiel de la République française*, Débats du Sénat, 28 July 1920, cited in Harry H. Cumming, *Franco-British Rivalry in the Post-War Near East* (London: Oxford University Press, 1938), p. 66.

Syria and Cilicia, with control over the latter already being forcefully disputed by the Kemalists. Earlier, in 1919, M. Maurice Barrès, a well-known author, deputy, and member of the French Academy, had written in *Echo de Paris* on the eve of one of Faysal's visits:

The Feisal comedy has gone far enough. No nation other than France possesses in so high a degree the particular kind of friendship and genius which is required to deal with the Arabs. . . . The British theory of installing in Syria an Arab Government of the Hedjaz is untenable. The Emir Feisal has no right to be in Damascus, Homs, Hama or Allepo [*sic*]. France knows how to give these towns a Syrian Government. What is Feisal to us or to the Syrians? A man of straw set up by England, without a title, without influence. . . . If England wishes to give a kingdom to this Emir, let her set him up in Bagdad.[11]

This self-righteousness and a hardened attitude toward the person of the amir became translated into official policy when Clemenceau wrote to Lloyd George that "the essential difficulty lies not in the excessive ambitions of France, but in the absolute designs of the Emir, who does not seem yet really to understand the necessity for the Arabs to accept a French mandate. . . ."[12]

As each side, confident in the validity of its cause, reaffirmed its resolve not to yield, and as a struggle of force rather than of words became imminent, the French demonstrated the absolute priority they placed on Syria by concluding an armistice with the Kemalists on 30 May. By this action they further indicated a willingness to act unilaterally, without British approval, in the Near and Middle East.[13] More

11. Earl of Derby (Paris) to Curzon, 20 October 1919, *Documents*, no. 1018, 4:491. A striking British parallel to the first part of M. Barrès' statement was provided by a "Memorandum on Changes in the General International Situation Since the Date of the Main British Commitments Regarding the Middle East" (undated), prepared in the Political Intelligence Department of the Foreign Office: "Our record . . . gives us a claim to a voice in the future of these regions which puts into the shade our previous claims as well as those of our Allies. This claim rests upon a relation with the native population which grows closer every day . . ." (E8063, F.O. 371/5036).
12. *Documents*, 4:522.
13. According to Mustafa Kemal the French sought to communicate with his nationalists "after the beginning of May." See *A Speech Delivered by Ghazi Mustapha Kemal, October, 1927* (Leipzig: K. F. Koehler, 1929), p. 390. At the end of June R. G. Vansittart, in Paris for discussions on boundaries, reported M. Berthelot's remark that the French considered that "the time for joint action in regard to Feisal was over and that further communication to him should be

immediately, the armistice freed them from a two-front clash with both Arab and Turk, and thereby allowed for the full application of French diplomacy and military power in securing the Syrian mandate.

Given the disparity in their capabilities, the Syrians were forced to pursue a more limited strategy, aimed at exploiting the differences between Britain and France, in the hope that at the decisive moment Britain would still choose to support the Arab cause. In an urgent cable to Lord Curzon on 19 June, Faysal stressed the grave consequences likely to result from the Franco-Turkish armistice, calling it "the commencement of a series of defeats in [the] Near East" which would shortly menace the peace of Mesopotamia, Mosul, and other places and lead to the overwhelming influence, both actual and moral, of the Turks in the regions to the south.[14] Appeals to British self-interest were mixed with emotionalism: writing to Allenby on 3 July, Husayn begged Britain to give him Mesopotamia, Syria, and Palestine, "in every way because Arabs deserve Britain's sympathy and pity."[15] In the end, however, these appeals failed to alter the earlier British decision not to interfere directly in the contest for Syria.

Deprived of Britain's support, the sharifian government was powerless to resist French pressure. A list of French demands calling for Syria's acknowledgment of the mandate and consent in the French occupation of Homs, Hama, and Aleppo was communicated to Faysal by General Gouraud in an atmosphere of confusion and agitation. Faysal finally acceded to the ultimatum but not in time to prevent the French army from marching on Damascus and forcing the Syrian government to evacuate the city on 24 July. A brief confrontation ensued at Maysalun, during which the remnants of the Syrian army were routed. Fay-

---

from them alone," especially since Britain was being left alone in Mesopotamia and Palestine (Earl of Derby to Curzon, 29 June 1920 [unnumbered telegram], *Documents*, 13:297–98). This was separately confirmed by Sir Herbert Samuel, who quoted Berthelot as saying that France had "no special desire to come to an understanding with Feisal" (Samuel to Curzon, 24 June 1920, private papers, St. Antony's College).

14. *Documents*, 13:289. Calling Britain's attention to the implications likely to result from a Turkish revival did not deter Faysal from secretly establishing contact with Kemalist agents for his own purposes, as admitted by al-Husrī (*Day of Maysalun*, esp. p. 86).

15. Allenby to Curzon, 3 July 1920, no. 650 (telegram), *Documents*, 13:306.

sal and his entourage fled to Daraa and eventually to exile in Europe, thus terminating the brief Syrian experiment in self-government.[16] In succeeding months the French consolidated their hold, meeting with virtually no overt resistance from the local population. A new cabinet was formed of Syrian notables willing to collaborate with the French. On 1 September General Gouraud announced that in the future Syria would be administered as four distinct units: Great Lebanon, Damascus, Aleppo, and Alawiya. By December the French were in complete control. When challenged to state what part of Syria he intended to retain and for how long, Prime Minister Leygues replied: "The whole of it, and for ever." Then, called upon by the Financial Committee of the Chamber of Deputies to furnish additional information, he declared: "Our position in Syria is excellent. We consider our presence there more than necessary; it is indispensable. We possess schools in Syria and, above all, our influence goes back for centuries. We could not, without losing our rank as a great Mediterranean, African and Moslem Power, renounce our action there, which will cost us less and less as time goes on."[17] The committee, impressed by the government's firmness, approved the credits requested for Syria for the period January–February, 1921, which amounted to 106 million francs. Clearly, France was giving full notice of her intention to remain in complete control of Syria.

In terms of British policy, the demise of the Damascus government ended the first phase of what might be called the sharifian policy—an attempt to promote British interests in the Fertile Crescent and Arabia through support for Husayn and his sons.

In the last desperate days before Maysalun, General Haddad had returned to this theme. He had sought to place before the Foreign Office the advantages of British-sharifian cooperation, the latter being "the only family which can find support from every party throughout the Arab provinces" and which, with British assistance, could soon "put an end to every outside intrigue." Instead of being a source of trouble, the

16. Accounts have always varied over the exact course of events preceding Maysalun. The French interpretation is provided in General Catroux, *Deux missions en Moyen-Orient, 1919–1922* (Paris: Librairie Plon, 1958), while al-Ḥuṣrī (*Day of Maysalun*) portrays the view of those close to Faysal at the time in accusing the French of intentionally precipitating the crisis.
17. Lord Hardinge of Penhurst (Paris) to Curzon, 21 December 1920, E16025/2/44 (no. 3786), F.O. 406/44.

Arab provinces would then be a "means for establishing peace throughout the Middle East."[18] Five factors, however, precluded British enthusiasm at this time: (a) a basic tenet of Curzon's policy that Anglo-French unity in European matters was more important than the sharifians and Syria; (b) the San Remo decision to leave Syrian affairs to France, and the reciprocal arrangement for the British mandates; (c) the military fact that the sharifian forces were woefully unequal to the French army of the Levant; (d) France's and Faysal's rejection, in effect, of the British effort at mediation in 1919; and (e) a preoccupation with unfavorable developments in Palestine and Mesopotamia.

Nevertheless, despite British silence during Faysal's hour of need, there was an enduring sense of responsibility toward him. This was made explicit in two important communiqués, one to the government of France and the other to Faysal personally. On 28 July, at the second Conference of Boulogne, Lord Curzon informed M. Berthelot that ". . . although Syria had been placed under the mandate of France with our consent . . . yet Feisal was brought into certain relations with us. . . . We therefore could not view his possible disappearance from the scene without some concern, and we felt that no step in this direction, if it were contemplated, should be taken without consultation with us."[19] Even more crucial for an understanding of future events was the urgent telegram of 5 August from Curzon to the high commissioner in Palestine, where Faysal was awaiting embarkation for Europe. "You should inform Feisal that His Majesty's Government appreciate his desire to create no complications between England and France. They are fully aware that he has made every effort to sustain a difficult position with due regard to the interests of the Allied Powers, and they trust that they may in the future have an opportunity of showing to him that his loyal attitude to the British Government has not been forgotten."[20]

French steadfastness and Arab dissatisfaction continued to dominate Syrian politics throughout the interwar period, giving rise to a futile yet

18. Confidential note by General Haddad, Syrian diplomatic agent in London, to the Foreign Office, received 14 July 1920, E8205/2/44, F.O. 406/44, pp. 240–43.
19. Curzon to Sir G. Grahame (Paris), 28 July 1920, no. 2615 in E. L. Woodward and Rohan Butler, eds., *Documents on British Foreign Policy, 1919–1939*, 1st ser., vol. 8 (London: Her Majesty's Stationery Office, 1958), p. 321; hereinafter cited as *Documents*, 8.
20. Curzon to Sir H. Samuel (Jerusalem), 5 August 1920, no. 69 (urgent telegram), *ibid.*, p. 330.

symbolic insurrection at the end of 1925. For Britain the events of July, 1920, essentially removed Syria from the sphere of direct British concern in the Fertile Crescent. However, an opportunity to compensate Faysal soon presented itself, due to developments in Mesopotamia.

In contrast to Syria, Mesopotamia had enjoyed a period of comparative tranquility in 1919 and the first part of 1920. Under the British occupation public works had been started and security ensured.[21] Because confidence in the system of direct administration was seemingly widespread (obedience from the natives being generally assumed), Great Britain had willingly accepted the mandate for Mesopotamia. The country seemed far removed from that resentment of European influence being manifested in adjacent Syria, and violence was not expected. Consequently, when disorder did break out it proved all the more embarrassing to the British government and forced a reappraisal of Britain's entire Middle Eastern policy.

The individual responsible for Mesopotamia at the time was Acting Civil Commissioner Colonel Arnold T. Wilson. Criticizing the Anglo-French declaration of 8 November 1918 for its undesirable effect of prematurely arousing native expectations, Wilson offered his personal opinion: "If the future status of this country is to be dealt with successfully, it must, I am convinced, be treated independently of Arab problems elsewhere. . . . I submit, therefore, that our best course is to declare Mesopotamia to be a British Protectorate, under which all races and classes will be given forthwith the maximum possible degree of liberty and self-rule that is compatible with that good and safe Government to which all nations aspire but so few now enjoy."[22] Wilson steadfastly reiterated the importance of a direct British presence and sought its implementation in the following two years. Thus, as late as June, 1920, he cabled Edwin Montagu, the secretary of state for India: "Having set our hand to task of regenerating Mesopotamia we must be prepared to furnish alike men and money and to maintain continuity of control for years to come. We must be prepared, regardless of League of Nations, to go very slowly with constitutional or democratic institutions, the application of which to Eastern Countries has often been attempted of late

21. At the end of 1920 a "Review of the Civil Administration of Mesopotamia," prepared by Gertrude Bell and containing detailed information on Britain's contribution to the stability and growth of the country, was published as Cmd. 1061.
22. Wilson, *Mesopotamia, 1917–1920*, 2:104–5.

years with such little degree of success."[23] Wilson's approach, in keeping with the tradition of British colonial tutelage, was one of gradualism; however, three influences—friction within the administration he headed; the impact of nationalism, which he tended to underestimate; and Great Britain's official commitment to the mandate principle—were already at work in 1919 to refute his premises.

The records indicate that considerable discord existed among the civilians attached to Wilson's staff. Gertrude Bell, the famous orientalist and Wilson's political secretary, frequently confided her sharp differences of temperament and perspective with Wilson in letters to her family.[24] These feelings were reciprocated by Wilson, who viewed her as a legacy from his predecessor and an outspoken proponent of introducing an amir as ruler of the country. He accused her of failing to take into account sufficiently "the jealousies and sectional quarrels which in a country like this would in a few years time wreck any logical scheme of constitution that could be devised."[25]

Civil-military relations were also strained, for Wilson, charged with directing the civil administration of Mesopotamia, felt hampered by his exclusion from military affairs. Nor did he hold a high opinion of his military equivalent, General Aylmer Haldane.[26] Wilson disagreed with the War Office aim of reducing the garrison stationed in Mesopotamia. He countered by criticizing military extravagance in a number of areas. In his cable of 9 June to the India Office, he flatly warned that Britain could not possibly give effect to the mandate without the risk of disaster, "unless we are prepared to maintain for the next two years at least as many troops in the country as we may have, and in a state considerably

23. Wilson to Montagu, 9 June 1920, no. 6948 (cipher telegram, clear the line), Wilson Papers.
24. See Elizabeth Burgoyne, *Gertrude Bell: From Her Personal Letters, 1914–1926* (London: Ernest Benn Limited, 1961), pp. 140ff. Another personality clash existed between Wilson and H. St. John Philby, at the time a junior member of the administration, for Philby later referred to Wilson, along with T. E. Lawrence, as his "principal antagonists"; see Philby, *Arabian Days* (London: Robert Hale, 1948), p. xvi.
25. Wilson to Dobbs, Foreign and Political Department, Delhi, 26 January 1920, Wilson Papers.
26. Wilson described Haldane as "too old and too tired for the job. He came out tired, thinking it was a peace job and has found out his mistake" (Wilson to General Macmunn [India], 10 September 1920, Wilson Papers). See also Wilson, *Mesopotamia, 1917–1920*, 2:277.

more efficient than they are now. . . . To restore shaken confidence of public if we stay, or to enable us to evacuate if we go, more troops are needed."[27]

Wilson's position was certainly an excellent one from which to appreciate the intimate relationship between the Syrian crisis and mounting discontent inside Mesopotamia. As civil administrator he would have noted that, in the confusion following Maysalun, a number of refugees formerly of the Hijazi army had crossed into Mesopotamia and sought to arouse emotions against the Europeans. But whether he was particularly attuned to the tension lurking beneath the surface of Mesopotamian society and outside the country's borders or was merely seeking ways to deter the War Office, he alone sounded the alarm of impending crisis. In a letter dated 31 March to Sir Arthur Hirtzel, the undersecretary of state for India, he warned of anticipated trouble on the Euphrates during the summer. But his warnings were dismissed both in London and in Baghdad. Secretary of State Montagu submitted several of his telegrams before the Cabinet on 15 June with the comment: "It will be seen that Sir A. Wilson takes a very serious view of the military situation, the dangers of which I am inclined to think he overstates."[28]

Upon taking up his assignment in Baghdad, General Haldane was briefed by Wilson about trouble expected "before many weeks" in the lower Euphrates area. He chose to ignore the warning, preferring the less pessimistic appraisal of his own intelligence staff and fearing the reaction his appeal for reinforcements would occasion in London. His main support was a letter sent by Miss Bell, "who knew the Arabs more intimately than any other member of the civil staff," a day or two after Wilson's warning of 3 June, in which she confidently reported that "the bottom seems to have dropped out of the agitation, and most of the leaders seem only too anxious to let bygones be bygones."[29]

Although the exact starting point of the Mesopotamian uprising has never been determined, by mid-summer it was obvious to all concerned that the foundation for Britain's presence was in danger. By 14 June

27. Wilson to Montagu (secret, clear the line), 9 June 1920, P. 4593, I.O. (C.P. 1475 of 15 June 1920).
28. C.P. 1475, 15 June 1920.
29. General Sir Aylmer Haldane, *A Soldier's Saga* (London: William Blackwood & Sons, 1948), pp. 374–75.

Miss Bell had reversed her position, noting that the nationalists had created a reign of terror and that practically no business had been done for the previous fortnight.[30] By September she was of the opinion that Britain was "in the middle of a full-blown Jihad," challenged by "the fiercest prejudice of a people in a primeval state of civilisation."[31] Yet it was not until 2 August that the crisis was formally recognized as such by General Headquarters, which announced: "In consequence of aggression of certain tribes on the Euphrates it is notified that a state of war exists through-out Mesopotamia."[32]

With the sharp increase of incidents and the spread of violence, the British garrisons in Mesopotamia were hard-pressed. As the full extent of the disorders became apparent, a call for reinforcements was answered promptly. On 26 August the secretary of state for war informed Lloyd George that because "every effort must be made to procure vigorous action and decisive results," twenty additional battalions were being sent in relief from England, Persia, and India, raising the joint battalion strength of Mesopotamia and Persia from forty-nine to sixty-eight.[33]

The danger reached its peak in early August. Reporting on the unfavorable situation, Wilson told of troop columns withdrawing under attack, of railway lines being damaged, and of anticipated internal troubles in Baghdad. He expected the disturbances to spread as well among the tribes, where the movement appeared to him to be "largely anarchic and bolshevistic in that it is a revolt against all authority, including very

30. In his analysis Haldane stressed that an incident on 30 June, "trivial in itself," had lit "the fire of insurrection." It occurred at Rumaithah, where a local *shaykh* had been arrested by "the injudicious action" of a district political officer. The *shaykh* was rescued by his tribesmen, who were joined by others, and the British troops had been extricated with difficulty. Thereafter, the outbreaks of resistance seemed to spread rather spontaneously (*ibid.*, pp. 376–77). In general see Haldane, *The Insurrection in Mesopotamia, 1920* (London: William Blackwood & Sons, 1922), for full details of the military expeditions. Philby, by contrast, points to the May attack by Jamil al-Midfa'i on the garrison at Tel Afar as the signal for revolt (Philby, *Arabian Days*, p. 185).
31. Lady Bell, ed., *The Letters of Gertrude Bell*, vol. 2 (London: Ernest Benn, 1927), pp. 497–98.
32. Wilson to Montagu, telegram of 9 August 1920, E10172, F.O. 371/5229.
33. Churchill to Lloyd George, 26 August 1920, F/9/2/41, Lloyd George Papers, Beaverbrook Library. Churchill gave the directives only after the Cabinet had decided "that we are to plough through in that dismal country."

often that of the Shaikhs."[34] But British lines held. Reinforcements began to arrive and Baghdad remained under control. The situation improved slowly and by late October London was advised: "If rebellion has not entirely subsided it no longer gives cause for serious anxiety and it only remains to clear up debris in certain localities."[35] Such assurances were welcomed with relief at the Foreign Office, although it was not until February, seven months after the beginning of the troubles, that General Haldane was able to inform the War Office that the operations had ceased, having "taught the tribesmen what it meant to cross swords with the British Empire."[36]

Renewed self-confidence of this type was not readily shared by those engaged in assessing the great damage done to the prestige and policy of Great Britain. Like Miss Bell, many were painfully aware of "the waste it all means and the inevitable bitterness it must engender, the difficulty in putting anything straight after this terrible upheaval."[37] Of equal concern was the fact that the uprisings had seriously weakened the British claim to the Mesopotamian mandate, which was based on the consent of the governed. Order had been restored, "but the future was dubious in the extreme."[38]

Important for an understanding of Britain's Middle Eastern policy are the diverse explanations of the causes of the Mesopotamian uprising provided for policy-makers in London. Arnold Wilson submitted a comprehensive list of thirteen contributing factors, but stressed above all the alleged intervention of Syrian and Turkish nationalists aided by American oil interests.[39] Rising in Parliament to defend expenditures for troops in Mesopotamia, Colonial Secretary Milner backed Wilson's emphasis on external forces by arguing: "It is not Mesopotamia . . .

34. Wilson to India Office, 30 July 1920, no. 9218 (telegram), Wilson Papers.
35. Sir Percy Cox to India Office, 26 October 1920, no. 12987, W.O. 106/201; see also G.O.C. Mesopotamia to War Office, 17 October 1920, E13014, F.O. 371/5231.
36. Haldane, *A Soldier's Saga*, p. 383; see also p. 379.
37. Lady Bell, *Letters of Gertrude Bell*, 8 August 1920, 2:494.
38. Churchill, *The World Crisis, 1918–1928: The Aftermath* (New York: Charles Scribner's Sons, 1929), p. 491 ("A Memorandum upon the Pacification of the Middle East").
39. Wilson, *Mesopotamia, 1917–1920*, 2:310–12 (Wilson to Montagu, telegram of 12 August 1920). Wilson voiced his suspicion of the Standard Oil Company in a secret telegram to Montagu, 17 June 1920 (no. 7321, I.O.), contained in the Wilson Papers.

which is responsible for the necessity of keeping up these large forces. It is the condition of warfare or something next to warfare which is existing all around. . . ."[40] In the opinion of the prime minister, General Gouraud's violent action against the Faysal regime in Syria had been the catalyst. "The feeling created by the disregard of solemn treaties with the Arabs spread throughout the Arab world and left the impression that the only straight word spoken by the Western nations was the one that was bellowed from the cannon's mouth. It made the Arabs hostile in Mesopotamia and Palestine. . . ."[41]

The compulsion to see a universal conspiracy at work was fostered by Major N. N. E. Bray, the Special Intelligence officer attached to the Political Department of the India Office, in his several analyses. On 14 September his very secret "Preliminary Report on Causes of Unrest" was distributed to the Cabinet, together with a chart demonstrating "the far wider conspiracy" and implicating Amir Faysal as well. Bray contended that "both the Nationalist and Pan-Islamist movements derive their inspiration from Berlin—through Switzerland and Moscow. The situation is further complicated with Italian, French and Bolshevist intrigues."[42] He admitted, however, that while there was evidence of interference from outside Syria and Mesopotamia, it was still necessary to track down, "by a process of careful and methodical elimination," the "comparatively small central organization" from which the various secret societies received their inspiration. This, of course, was never done.

A more balanced interpretation might be that British statesmen of the period shared with later Arab historians the tendency to impart to events a sense of order which in truth had not existed at the time. Influenced by the reports of Wilson and Bray, members of the government initially accepted the thesis of closely coordinated intervention from outside Mesopotamia, while Arab historians have referred to events of the summer of 1920 as an "Iraqi revolution" and "an insurgence against the denial of independence and the arbitrary imposition of the manda-

40. *Parliamentary Debates* (Lords), 5th ser., 40 (1920) : 892. Mesopotamia was discussed on 25 June; see *ibid.*, cols. 848–94.
41. Lloyd George, *The Truth About the Peace Treaties*, 2:1113.
42. E12339, F.O. 371/5230. Sir John Tilley minuted the Foreign Office file: "Bray has written a nice little essay but he does not begin to prove that the origin of the troubles was elsewhere than in Mesopotamia." Bray persisted and submitted a second report on 18 October 1920 (E12966, F.O. 371/5231).

tory system."[43] In retrospect the uprising appears to have been more decentralized than concerted, spontaneous rather than premeditated, and ignited by diverse motives on the individual or tribal level. Within a short span of time these actions assumed a dynamic of their own, building upon each successive act of defiance and the ineffective British response in the early stage.

Whether it was in fact a true revolution or a series of uprisings, the Mesopotamian crisis was given a meaningful perspective by several members of the Foreign Office, the most persuasive being Colonel Kinahan Cornwallis. He criticized Major Bray's first report for its over-emphasis of external factors and reasoned that the government should work to remove the sources of dissatisfaction within Mesopotamia proper. In the sense that the British government adopted the latter point of view, it can be said that the uprising was indeed revolutionary, because of its impact on the British policy-making apparatus.

One less desirable result of the disturbances was a renewal, or rather an increase, of rivalry within the government, particularly between the Foreign Office and the India Office. At the height of the crisis the secretary of state for India implied that both the War Office and the Foreign Office were dealing inadequately with the military and diplomatic aspects of Mesopotamia, interfering excessively in that country's government, and failing to gain the support of the pro-British nationalists. Indicative of the interdepartmental rivalry was Lord Curzon's notation to Major Hubert Young: "Mr. Montagu has seized the occasion to make a series of absurd charges against the F.O. Please put together the facts tomorrow and let me have a few counter charges against the India Office."[44] The continued division of authority made all the more difficult any effective determination of policy, let alone its implementation.

Even before the crisis, steps had been underway to alter the administration of Mesopotamia, with the aim of allowing the country a greater degree of self-government. On 6 April 1919 Colonel Wilson had suggested that Sir Percy Cox, who had been transferred to Persia, be invited to return eventually as the first high commissioner of Mesopota-

43. See, for example, Jalāl Yahyā, al-Thawra al-'Arabīyya (Cairo, 1959), p. 248, and Antonius, The Arab Awakening, p. 313.
44. C.P. 1680, 23 July 1920, E9020, F.O. 371/5228.

mia.[45] At the time, Cox was personally involved in negotiating the important Anglo-Persian treaty; in any case, he insisted upon having undivided authority before he would consent to return to Mesopotamia. Lord Curzon wrote to Cox the following November describing the unsatisfactory situation in Baghdad due to the predominance on the staff of young officers lacking in experience and to "a system of British Government advised by Arabs rather than [one] of Arab Government [advised] by British."[46] He conveyed the feeling in London that Cox's return to Mesopotamia as high commissioner was the first condition for recovering confidence. But by the end of 1919 Curzon still was unable to satisfy Cox's demand for full power.

Following the San Remo conference early in 1920, the Cabinet decided to proceed with plans for transforming the status of Mesopotamia and Palestine from military to civilian rule, despite the absence of a peace treaty with Turkey. Pursuant to this, on 7 June the Cabinet instructed that Wilson be informed of the decision of His Majesty's Government to entrust Sir Percy Cox with the task of framing an organic law for approval by the League of Nations. Cox was also authorized to call into being a predominantly Arab Council of State under an Arab president and an Assembly representative of the people as a whole.[47] Wilson's reaction was negative. On 6 July he wrote, "All my personal instincts make me doubt whether H.M.G. can possibly pull off such a scheme as they propose," and at the end of the month he predicted that "an Arab State though not on the lines desired by H.M.G. may yet come to pass, but it will be by revolution and not by evolution."[48]

Although the decision was reached in June, due to a controversy between the War Office and the India Office over its wording and to the summer crisis, the formal announcement was not made public until 17 September in Baghdad. The final version read: "In capacity as High Commissioner, Cox will be chief British representative in Mesopotamia

45. Wilson to India Office, Political Department memoranda, B. 317, I.O. Cox had apparently been approached earlier, in February, but pronounced himself "not really keen" (Cox to Bell, 9 February 1919, and Wilson to Hirtzel, 8 March 1920, both in Wilson Papers).
46. Curzon to Cox (Teheran), 14 November 1919 (unnumbered telegram), *Documents*, 4:531.
47. Montagu to Wilson, 7 June 1920, P. 4216(3), C.P. 1475.
48. Wilson to Hirtzel (telegram), 6 July 1920, and Wilson to Cox, via Montagu, 29 July 1920, both in the Wilson Papers.

and will be responsible for civil administration of country until he shall be able to give effect to the fixed policy of His Majesty's Government of setting up Arab State in Mesopotamia. This will be his primary task to be accomplished as soon as conditions permit."[49]

Three days later, Wilson delivered his valedictory and sought to exonerate himself and his administration by indicting the government in London for its indecision: "Our orders were clear; we were not to build. We could not know what the Peace Conference would decide, but we could, and did foresee that delay meant trouble."[50] He then proceeded to London where he defended his policy before the Cabinet and his personal reputation before the English press.

Sir Percy Cox assumed responsibility for Mesopotamia on 4 October. One of his first official acts was the issuing of a proclamation to the tribes and communities expressing his intention to assist in creating a national government, but warning that this could occur only if all active opposition ceased. By 11 November he was able to announce, as "an immediate expedient," the formation of a Council of State as the provisional government, with 'Abd al-Rahman al-Gaylani, the Naqib of Baghdad, as president of the council.[51]

Several of Cox's dispatches during this period suggest, however, that any differences between himself and Wilson were more procedural than substantive. In a report completed for Cabinet consideration after his appointment, Cox showed himself sensitive to Mesopotamia's importance for Britain and of the need to retain ultimate control in some form. He also confided that "it would smooth our path from the point of administration if the creation of an Emir could be postponed for some years, and if the British representative could fill his place in the meanwhile."[52]

49. Montagu to Baghdad, 17 September 1920, P. 6861, F.O. 371/5230.
50. Wilson, *Mesopotamia, 1917–1920*, 2:319; see also Burgoyne, *Gertrude Bell*, pp. 166–67.
51. Text of Cox's proclamation of 11 October is in Colonial Office, *Report on 'Iraq Administration, October, 1920–March, 1922* (London, n.d.), p. 123. The report also contains a list of the members of the provisional government and the work it accomplished (*ibid.*, pp. 4–10).
52. "Appreciation of Mesopotamia-Persia Situation," report by Sir Percy Cox, 24 July 1920, submitted to the Cabinet by Lord Curzon on 30 July (E13975, F.O. 371/5231). Evidence of Cox's strong control over affairs is found in his telegram of 26 October to the India Office (E13471, F.O. 371/5231), and in Haldane, *A Soldier's Saga*, p. 381.

As the year 1920 ended, Mesopotamia entered into a new period of calm under the façade of an Arab government. Yet there was no mistaking its being subject to the ultimate authority of Great Britain in the person of High Commissioner Sir Percy Cox.

The upheavals in Syria and Mesopotamia made manifest two problems plaguing British policy in the Fertile Crescent: the unavoidable association with France, and the need to create a feasible third alternative to what Colonel Wilson posited as the choice of either governing or evacuating. Events in Palestine during 1920 indicated a third dilemma: how to reconcile the emerging conflict of interests between two nationalist forces—one Arab, the other Jewish—each of which claimed sole rights to Palestine.

Since obtaining the Balfour Declaration the Zionists, much like Faysal, had worked at strengthening their case in two areas. In Europe they relied on diplomatic means when dealing with the victorious powers, Britain and France in particular. In Palestine their emphasis was on practical achievements, such as immigration, land settlement and reclamation, capital investment—in general, on participation in the daily social and economic life of the country. While the former gave the Zionists important contacts with leaders like Balfour, Clemenceau, Faysal, and Lloyd George, the latter tactic tended to irritate vocal, important segments of the Palestinian Arab community; it also alienated members of the British government, who were resentful of any element likely to disturb the country's equilibrium.

At the beginning of 1920 the wave of protests which had agitated Syria for more than a year spread to Palestine. Peaceful demonstrations were held against the European intention to separate Palestine from Greater Syria and against Zionist activities. On 8 December 1919 the military governor of Jerusalem received a letter from two leading Arab societies, *Nadi al-'Arabi* and *Muntada al-'Arabi,* advising that "Southern Syria forms a part of the United Syria beginning from Taures to Rafa, the separation of which we do not tolerate under any circumstances, and we are as well prepared to sacrifice ourselves towards its defense with all our power."[53] The following February he received a similar note which warned against "helping the Jews to possess our land." Demon-

53. The letter is preserved in Pol. 2095 in the Israel State Archives, as is the note of February, 1920.

strations organized by the Muslim-Christian League in Jerusalem and in other Palestinian centers passed quietly on 27 February.[54]

An actual outbreak of violence did not occur until 4 April, which was, symbolically, the day of the Christian Easter, Jewish Passover, and Muslim festival of Nebi Musa. When the fighting ended in Jerusalem, 5 Jews and 4 Arabs lay dead; 211 Jews and 21 Arabs had been wounded.[55] British leaders suddenly realized the difficulty of their position in Palestine, for this outbreak inaugurated a period of bloodshed in the history of the Holy Land which was to continue intermittently during the next half-century. But Palestine's strategic importance dictated British acceptance of the mandate.[56]

While at San Remo, Lloyd George, Balfour, and Curzon determined to introduce civilian government to Palestine, although the legality of such an action was questionable because Ottoman Turkey had not as yet formally relinquished its claim to sovereignty over the area. The three leaders considered the selection of a high commissioner and chose Herbert Samuel, although because he was a Jew and a Zionist the appointment was made with a certain amount of hesitancy. Upon being offered the position on 24 April, Samuel sought the advice of Zionist leaders present at San Remo; when they urged him to accept, he wrote a letter to that effect to the prime minister the next day, explaining that he was motivated by a sense of duty. "The fulfilment of the Zionist programme must, from the nature of the case, be gradual, and very considerate for the interests of the Arabs and Christians. Jewry in Palestine would be more likely to practice patience, without losing enthusiasm, if the pace were set by an Administrator who was known to be in full sympathy with the ultimate aim."[57]

Meanwhile, however, Curzon became hesitant and on 12 May asked Samuel to reconsider his acceptance at least for a year. But, writing on

54. Meinertzhagen (Cairo) to Curzon, no. 15 (telegram), *Documents*, 13:219–20.
55. Details of the riot are found in Cmd. 5479 of 1937; see Paul Hanna, *British Policy in Palestine* (Washington, D.C.: American Council on Public Affairs, 1942), pp. 43–44.
56. See, for example, Curzon's remarks on Palestine as quoted in Lloyd George, *The Truth About the Peace Treaties*, 2:1146–47.
57. The episode at San Remo is described in J. B. Hobman, ed., *David Eder: Memoirs of a Modern Pioneer* (London: Victor Gollancz, 1945), pp. 158–59. Samuel's personal account is in file A/65 of the Herbert Samuel Papers, Library of the House of Lords.

the 14th, Samuel again accepted the post, citing encouragement from Palestinian Jewish leaders and from two influential officials in Egypt, Wyndham Deedes and Sir Gilbert Clayton.[58] Lloyd George also remained in favor of the appointment, which was officially confirmed by Lord Curzon on the 19th, with one reservation. "The Army have approved the assumption by you of the title of Commander-in-Chief of the troops in Palestine with the proviso that the possession of this title will not give you any right of interference in details of operations or movement of troops. . . ."[59]

A further indication of the difficulties awaiting the new high commissioner was the mixed reception given his appointment. One Zionist in Palestine called it "the biggest and most satisfactory news of my public life," while the Jewish writer Israel Zangwill viewed it as "a mere cover for the practical repudiation of the Balfour Declaration." To a British Jew in the Palestine administration it seemed a "great stroke of Providence," and the governor of Jerusalem called it the start of "The Great Adventure."[60] Conversely, in Damascus, a letter signed by Arif al-Arif on behalf of the Arab Palestinian Society termed the decision "the first step to realize the Zionists' desires" and warned that it would cause trouble and riots.[61]

To the relief of the British government, Sir Herbert Samuel's arrival in Palestine on 30 June passed without incident.[62] In his inaugural speech in Jerusalem on 7 July he spoke optimistically, stressing the need for cooperation and progress in the areas of civil service, an advisory council, banks, and public works.[63] Seeking to capitalize on the early

58. Curzon had received a cable from General Allenby warning that the appointment of a Jew was very likely to unleash attacks on Jews in Palestine. But Samuel was able to report more favorable reactions from other British officials. See Samuel's minutes of a meeting with Curzon on 12 May 1920, Samuel Papers.
59. Letter of appointment from Curzon, dated 19 June 1920, *ibid*.
60. Eder to Samuel, 1 May 1920, private papers, St. Antony's College; Zangwill, letter to the editor of *The Spectator*, 3 July 1920, quoted in ESCO Foundation for Palestine, Inc., *Palestine: A Study of Jewish, Arab, and British Policies*, vol. 1 (New Haven, Conn.: Yale University Press, 1947), p. 259; interview with Norman Bentwich, 15 December 1967; Storrs to Samuel, 7 June 1920, Samuel Papers.
61. Letter from Palestinian Arab Society to chief administrator O.E.T.A.(S), 25 June 1920, C.S. 65, I.S.A.
62. On the occasion of his appointment as high commissioner, Herbert Samuel was made a Knight Grand Cross of the Order of the British Empire.
63. The text of his speech is found in E8599/85/44, F.O. 406/44. Prior to his

British Policy in the Arab World

calm, he quickly began to translate British intentions into tangible measures, the most important being the formation of an advisory council composed of Arab, Jewish, and British representatives. At the initial meeting of the council on 6 October, the high commissioner described it as "a first step in the development of self-governing institutions."[64]

Maysalun and the decline of Damascus as the center for Arab activism contributed indirectly to the air of calm which enabled Samuel to introduce needed changes. By October he was able to report definite progress: restrictions on travel were reduced; pilgrims and tourists were being encouraged to visit Palestine; and Jewish immigrants were being employed immediately upon arrival. All these measures, he felt, illustrated that "the process of the establishment of the Jewish national home will benefit and not injure the non-Jewish population."[65] At the end of October, after four months as high commissioner, Samuel wrote a personal letter to the prime minister which reflected his unaltered confidence. "So far, the measures that have been taken appear to be popular. I find not the slightest difficulty in getting all the different sections to work together. . . . The tranquility of the country is remarkable."[66] It was also superficial, since both the Arabs and Zionists had lists of grievances which could not be satisfied merely by economic reforms.

The influx of Jewish immigrants and capital threatened the privileged position of the land-owning class in Palestine while luring away the *fellah* and laborer with offers of higher salaries and better working conditions. To the political élite, Britain's policy of balancing the aspirations of both communities was a means of delaying the establishment of fully representative bodies based on majority rule. In general, the sudden burst of energy by the Jewish pioneers—regarded as usurpers in an Arab land—contrasted sharply with the structured, tradition-oriented, and more static patterns of behavior within the Arab community and constituted a cultural irritant.

---

appointment Samuel had toured Palestine at the invitation of General Allenby in December, 1919. In his final report on 31 March, Samuel addressed himself primarily to the country's great economic potential, calling the political difficulties "by no means insuperable" if all the inhabitants benefited from economic progress.

64. Enclosure 2 in no. 83, 10 October 1920, E13008/85/44, F.O. 406/44.
65. *Ibid.*
66. Samuel to Lloyd George, 28 October 1920, F/44/8/3, Lloyd George Papers.

Growing Arab dissatisfaction became verbalized when on 18 December the third Palestinian Congress concluded its meetings in Haifa and presented the high commissioner with a memorandum. It appealed to Great Britain to form a native government responsible to a legislative assembly whose members would be representative of, and elected by, "the Arabic-speaking population living in Palestine up to the beginning of the war." Aware of the public debate then taking place in England over foreign expenditures, the congress urged prompt action since "the hesitation of according it amounts to the continuance of the unnecessary and unavoidable discontent of the Arab people, and the burdening of the British people with too heavy expenses for the sake of internal and external peace, as this congress, speaking in the name of the people, is unsatisfied with the present Administration. . . ."[67] The administration's response came in a letter from Civil Secretary Wyndham Deedes to the president of the congress, Musa Kazim al-Husayni. Instead of addressing himself to the issues raised in the memorandum, Deedes wrote that in the eyes of the government the congress was "by no means representative of the population," its delegates having been chosen arbitrarily by small groups, and that more information would be needed before the resolutions could be considered officially.[68]

Dialogue between the Arabs and Zionists became strained too, partially because the latter sought for, and failed to find, any Palestinian Arab leader who was a competent spokesman for the entire Arab community. Writing to Herbert Samuel from Palestine in 1919, Dr. Weizmann complained: "I see the real difficulty in the fact that there is no responsible head of the Arab Nation with whom one can deal here. They are broken up in factions, each lead [sic] by one or two agitators who give vent to their feelings in abusing us, grossly threatening us and insulting us sometimes very vulgarly, but all that is not deep enough. It is a movement which develops simply par richochet from Egypt and Damascus. I had numerous proofs that the Fellah is friendly to us."[69] Unable to formalize these perceived signs of friendliness, the Zionists compounded the problem by going beyond Palestine to cultivate Arab

67. Samuel to Curzon (no. 244), 1 January 1921, enclosure in E501/35/88, F.O. 406/45, pp. 145–46.
68. Ibid.
69. Weizmann to Samuel, 22 November 1919, W.A.

British Policy in the Arab World

ties, particularly with Amir Faysal.[70] Any hopes of controlling the Palestinian Arabs through the agency of Faysal, however, were crushed by the events of July and August, 1919, in Syria.

For their part, by late 1920 the Zionists were also dissatisfied with the form and substance of the mandate and uneasy as to Britain's intentions. Her hesitation in permitting foreign investment and in granting concessions was thought to be impeding Palestine's economic growth, and hence its capacity for large-scale Jewish immigration. Certain clauses of the draft mandate for Palestine appeared to be inimical to Zionist interests. And Anglo-French negotiations on frontier lines between Syria and Palestine, which culminated in an agreement on 23 December 1920, seemed to neglect the importance of the headwaters of the Jordan River for Palestine's economic future.[71] Even earlier, Weizmann had written to Justice Brandeis: "I was most loyal to the idea that Great Britain was the best Government to which the mandate should be entrusted. I now fear that they are playing with us as a cat plays with a mouse."[72]

Consequently, by December, 1920, the assumption by many English-

70. A Zionist emissary was summoned by Faysal to Damascus "in June, or July, 1919" and set down unofficially a plan for an Arab-Jewish settlement "somewhat like a basic constitution." The plan is described in Haim Kalvarisky, *Tochniot U'niumim* (Jerusalem, 1939). On 12 August 1919 Colonel Waters-Taylor wrote: "In my opinion Weizmann places undue reliance on Feisal" (confidential letter to G.H.Q., Weizmann Archives). But on 25 March 1920 Weizmann called Faysal "a broken reed." "I can see other forces coming up which will break F., break all he is concerned with, break the European influence. New problems, new methods and new tactics are awaiting us in the nearest future" (W.A.).

71. Letters from Weizmann and his colleagues to Curzon, Balfour, and other British leaders in the fall of 1920 complained of alterations in the draft mandate. In writing to Churchill on 22 November, Weizmann singled out the elimination of the clause in the preamble recognizing the historic connection of the Jewish people with Palestine, substitution of "self-governing institutions" for "self-governing commonwealth" in Article 4, and, under Article 13, the withdrawal of the provisions guaranteeing the Jewish Agency a favorable opportunity for undertaking the execution of public works and the development of natural resources. These and similar pleas for draft reconsideration are in Z4/10: 287 of the Zionist office in London which is now part of the Central Zionist Archives. The boundary question was virtually the only one on which the Palestinian Arabs and Zionists could agree (14139, C.O. 733/1). "Franco-British Convention of December 23, 1920," was printed as Cmd. 1195.

72. Weizmann to Brandeis, 1 May 1919, W.A.

men that their three objectives in Palestine—establishing a Jewish national home, protecting Arab rights, and fostering self-government for the over-all community—might be accomplished without excessive difficulty was itself challenged. In submitting his summary report for 1920, the high commissioner acknowledged that "the present favourable appearances may be deceptive"; for inside Palestine there were elements "which would be ready to respond to propaganda from abroad."[73] Still, taking comfort in the fact that the political situation was satisfactory, with "no signs that the complete tranquility which now prevails throughout is soon likely to be disturbed," Sir Herbert Samuel believed that his personal enthusiasm, philosophy of government, and policy had been vindicated. Tranquility would be preserved, "given an Administration which shows concrete results in measures that directly benefit the people, and which treats all sections with sympathy and complete impartiality."[74] Yet no amount of good will could erase the precedent already established for the use of violence between the two communities and, more important, the mutual antagonism which it had brought to the surface in Palestine.

Although order was restored to Syria, Mesopotamia, and Palestine by the end of 1920, a fresh source of concern—and a fourth dilemma—for Great Britain appeared on the eastern side of the Jordan River. Regarded with imprecision for centuries, this large area had been virtually *terra nullius* under the Turks and was left undefined in the partition of the Ottoman Empire. Some measure of jurisdiction had been brought to the area by the Damascus government, but with its overthrow the whole situation in Transjordan once again became fluid and dangerous. As Sir Herbert Samuel described it: "The line from west to east between the French and the British mandatory areas . . . cut right across the territory that had been put by Allenby under the Emir's administration. When the French drove him out of the northern part—Eastern Syria— the southern part was left in the air. This was the country east of the Jordan and stretching far to the south. The area of my Commission included it, and it fell to me to make some provision for its government."[75]

73. Samuel to Curzon, 8 January 1921, E1062/401/88 (no. 11), F.O. 406/45.
74. *Ibid.*
75. Viscount Samuel, *Memoirs* (London: The Cresset Press, 1941), p. 159. For the background of the problem, see Norman and Helen Bentwich, *Mandate Memories, 1918-1948* (London: The Hogarth Press, 1965), pp. 51–52; P. J. Vatikiotis,

British Policy in the Arab World

Instability in Transjordan affected the security of both Syria and Palestine as well as the territorial claims of the Zionists. After their dispersal by General Gouraud, supporters of the Faysal regime fled the country, some going to Europe, some to Mesopotamia, and others to the more remote region of Transjordan. The town of Amman and its environs thus became a potential center for attacks against the French. Anxious for revenge, many of the political refugees began to raise forces and to organize raiding parties with the purpose of marching against, or at a minimum harassing, Syria.

For the British, unrest in the area adjacent to Palestine and raids across the Jordan River presented an intolerable situation. General Congreve, reporting on 4 May that Palestine was still far from quiet, attributed this in part to constant raids by tribes east of the Jordan. He indicated that serious attacks had been made on Beisan and Semakh and warned: "This attack was repulsed but there is likelihood of further raids being made, as aeroplane reconnaissances and intelligence reports show large encampment on the north-east and eastern frontiers of Palestine."[76]

Of even greater concern was the prospect that France would use the raids as a pretext for expanding southward. Hubert Young, writing after Faysal's downfall, sought to raise within the Foreign Office what he regarded as an important point. "What is the 'Syria' for which the French received a mandate at San Remo? Does it include Trans-Jordan, or does it only come down to the British sphere of influence as defined in the Sykes-Picot Agreement of 1916? . . . We must be prepared with a policy in case the French not only occupy Damascus but advance down the Hejaz railway towards Deraa, Amman, and Maan."[77] But to establish effective control over the area Britain would have to dispatch and station troops there—a prospect not readily acceptable to the British in 1920.

Politics and the Military in Jordan (London: Frank Cass & Co., 1967), pp. 37–38; *Peace Handbook no. 60, Syria and Palestine* (1920), pp. 42–43; and George Adam Smith, *The Historical Geography of the Holy Land* (London: Hodder & Stoughton, 1894), esp. pp. 527–79.

76. "Appreciation of the Situation: Egypt and Palestine," by General Walter Congreve, commander of Egyptian expeditionary force, app. C of C.P. 1467, CAB 24/126.

77. Young's note for Lord Hardinge, 27 July 1920, in E8974 of F.O. 371/5124.

The sudden prominence of Transjordan in British military and political considerations was paralleled by the Zionists, for they had included that region in their geographical definition of Palestine even prior to the Balfour Declaration.[78] In their statement presented before the peace conference on 3 February 1919, the Zionists defined the eastern extremity of Palestine as "a line close to and West of the Hedjaz Railway terminating in the Gulf of Akaba."[79] On the following day, in a letter to Sir Henry Wilson, Weizmann wrote: "It is absolutely essential for the economic development of Palestine that this line be drawn so as to include the territories east of the Jordan which are capable of receiving and maintaining large Jewish mass settlements."[80]

The Zionist effort was rewarded by endorsements from leading British statesmen. Lord Milner advised Nahum Sokolow "to insist upon as large a portion of Trans-Jordania as possible," while Lord Balfour urged that the eastern frontier be drawn "as to give the widest scope to agricultural development on the left bank of the Jordan, consistent with leaving the Hedjaz railway completely in Arab possession."[81] Lord Curzon, although not regarded by the Zionists as particularly sympathetic to their cause, also recognized the need to consider Zionist claims in any decision on the future of the Transjordanian lands.[82]

These were some of the considerations when in the middle of 1920 the British government began its debate over directions to be given Sir Herbert Samuel for coping with Transjordanian unrest. The first discussion took place at the end of July as policy-makers in London and Jerusalem began to foresee the implications of Faysal's defeat. On 27

78. A frequent theme of *Palestine*, published by the British Palestine Committee early in 1917, was the "vital necessity of having the country east of Jordan included in Palestinian territory"; see issues of 15 February (pp. 25–30) and 21 July (pp. 201–4). In a book, *Eretz Israel*, published at this time, the authors, David Ben-Gurion and Isaac Ben-Zvi, argued that the eastern boundary of Palestine rightfully included the two sanjaks of Hauran and Kerak and a part of the sanjak of Damascus.
79. No. 1627, F.O. 608/99. The first article in the draft of the Faysal-Weizmann agreement recognized the need to fix the boundary of "Palestine East of the River Jordan" (W.A.).
80. Weizmann to Sir Henry Wilson, 4 February 1919, W.A.
81. Sokolow's interview with Milner at the Colonial Office, 4 November 1919, C.Z.A. Balfour's opinion was expressed in his memorandum to Lloyd George, "Disposal of Turkish Territories," 26 June 1919, *Documents*, 4:302.
82. Quoted in Lloyd George, *The Truth About the Peace Treaties*, 2:1146–47.

July the British embassy in Paris received a very urgent cable from the Foreign Office asking what the French claimed was the southern boundary east of the Jordan for the area given them under the Syrian mandate; the reply was that south of the Sykes-Picot line "we can lay down the frontier as we wish."[83] Sir Herbert Samuel reported two days later that British occupation had been invited by the sharifian governor of Hauran and several other *shaykhs* in the Kunaytra area. As for the opinion of his staff, "We are unanimous in view that this is the right time to occupy the country from Beisan to Deraa and with the troops at our disposal without any fighting."[84] Since existing conditions required an immediate decision, he therefore strongly recommended "not losing present most favourable opportunity to secure proper boundaries of future Palestine."

Added urgency was lent on 6 August by reports of unilateral French action in occupying Kunaytra, appointing new governors to Hauran and Salt, and summoning to Damascus all the *shaykhs* from as far south as Kerak.[85] That same day the Foreign Office suggested to Samuel that he immediately let it be known that in the area south of the Sykes-Picot line "we will not admit French authority and that our policy is for this area to be independent but in closest relation with Palestine."[86] Curzon also informed the British ambassador in Paris of reports from the area which indicated a violation of the Sykes-Picot agreement regarding zone B and instructed him to convey the position of His Majesty's Government that "we cannot recognise any French rights in that area."[87]

By early August, however, the councils in London against armed occupation prevailed, their reluctance to use troops strengthened by French denials of any intention to move south of the original Sykes-Picot line. General Wilson, in principle long opposed to further military commit-

83. Foreign Office to Lord Derby for Vansittart, no. 833 (cipher telegram), W.O. 106/198; Lord Derby's reply, 28 July 1920, no. 876, *ibid.*
84. Hicom to Prodrome (secret communiqué), 29 July 1920, C.S. 106I, I.S.A. The military commander in Palestine confirmed Samuel's confidence in maintaining Transjordan "without reinforcements"; see Egypforce to Troopers (secret, clear the line), 3 August 1920, *ibid.*
85. Samuel to Prodrome (secret intelligence report from Tiberias), 6 August 1920, *ibid.*
86. Foreign Office to Samuel, 6 August 1920, no. 70 (urgent cipher telegram), 6048 in file P. 6002, I.O.
87. Curzon to Paris (repeated to Hicom), priority paraphrase telegram, 7 August 1920, C.S. 106I, I.S.A.

ments, wired General Congreve on 7 August: "we are in no position to take what appears to me to be an unnecessary risk and under the circumstances the proposal to occupy Trans-Jordania can only meet with my opposition. . . ."[88] That same day Churchill notified Congreve of his opposition to the proposal and of his intention to so inform the Foreign Office.

Because of this strong opposition from the War Office, on 11 August Lord Curzon informed Samuel of the government's refusal to approve the military occupation of Transjordan. At the same time, he noted the government's awareness of the danger of continued anarchy and relayed its belief that "the best means of securing a genuine and lasting desire for any extension of British administration towards the East is to give the people of Trans-Jordania an opportunity of realising gradually the benefits which this administration will give them."[89] Accordingly, Samuel was instructed to send six suitable political officers to Transjordan—but without military escort—to encourage local self-government, to give advice, and to foster trade with Palestine. He proceeded to implement this policy of gradualism and on 20 August traveled to Salt where he addressed the Arab notables assembled there. He assured them that Britain did not propose to bring the area under the system of administration which existed in Palestine. "The general instructions of the British Government to the officers in those districts would be above all to help the people to govern themselves, while maintaining those principles of honesty and justice which are the marks of British Administration in all parts of the world and which are the foundations of all good government."[90] The promise was for "a separate administration"; but this only evaded the question of Transjordan's ultimate political status.

Although the *shaykhs* were satisfied with this arrangement, which offered the hope of stability and security, both Amir Faysal, then in Haifa, and the Zionists questioned the meeting and its implications for the future. Notified on 17 August of Samuel's intended visit, Faysal

88. War Office to Congreve (message from C.I.G.S.), W.O. 106/198.
89. Foreign Office to Samuel, no. 80, *ibid.*
90. The official text is located in the Central Zionist Archives. For a description of what Samuel referred to as "an entirely irregular proceeding, my going outside my own jurisdiction," see John Bowle, *Viscount Samuel* (London: Victor Gollancz, 1957), p. 207, and *Documents*, 13:342–43.

British Policy in the Arab World

wrote in reply: "I see no objection to the presence of British Officers in all the country during my absence; but I do not understand exactly what Your Excellency means by saying 'To appoint a small number of officers to assist the people of Trans-Jordania to organise their own Government'. Does that mean the organization of a new government permanently separated from Syria politically and in administration, or is it only a temporary arrangement until the present situation is clear?"[91] The Zionists likewise expressed concern at Samuel's speech, assuming uneasily that he "could not have meant that [the] entire region east of the Jordan is to be excluded from Palestine and from the operation of our mandate."[92] In reporting the speech, the editors of *Palestine* asked:

But what are to be the boundaries of Transjordania? What are to be its relations with Palestine? What is to be its political status? . . . Does that mean . . . that Transjordania is to be a separate *state* distinct from Palestine, or to be a separate *province* of Palestine furnished with an administrative system peculiarly adapted to its own conditions? . . . From the point of view of Palestine this matter is vital. Cisjordania and Transjordania are geographically, economically, historically, and strategically inseparable: they are two halves of one single entity—Palestine.[93]

Additional questions were raised as a new phase of Britain's involvement with Transjordan began shortly thereafter, the result of increasing agitation. Various tribes challenged the authority of the local councils and thus revealed the inadequacy of such a loose system of rule. By the end of August, British representatives reported on the unsatisfactory state of affairs, stressing the need to guarantee security and to prevent the region from becoming a center for Arab nationalist activities and political propaganda.[94]

91. Samuel to Curzon, 17 August 1920, 6830, I.O.
92. Benjamin V. Cohen, Zionist Office (London), to Weizmann, 26 August 1920, W.A.
93. *Palestine* 8, no. 4 (25 September 1920) : 26.
94. Samuel acknowledged the inadequacy of the Foreign Office's plan to rule indirectly. "An Interim Report on the Civil Administration of Palestine during the period 1st July, 1920–30th June 1921" (Cmd. 1499), p. 21. Captain C. D. Brunton and Major I. N. Camp, both sent to Transjordan as advisers, reported that troops were needed to guarantee public security and to gain the confidence of the local tribes; see St. Antony's Papers and Israel State Archives. Another

Sharifian involvement was identified as the primary cause of unrest when on 21 September the War Office received an urgent telegram from Samuel advising that King Husayn had issued an appeal to the *shaykhs* of Kerak, Adwan, and the Balka which read in part: "This is the time to show your ardour and zeal in connection with your religion and country. Be united and assist your co-religionists to a deliverance of our country from the infidels. One of my sons is proceeding to you with funds and provisions."[95] A note from the French government on 29 September warned that Husayn's sons, Ali and Abdullah, were preparing an attack against Daraa and called attention to *"l'intérêt commun que nous aurions à éviter des intervention de ce genre dans les territoires à mandat."*[96] Curzon gave assurances that while there was as yet but a minimal danger to French interests, the British government was watching developments, and "no opportunity will be lost of taking whatever steps circumstances may render practicable."[97] But this satisfied neither the French nor Samuel; both preferred that British troops be sent to maintain order.[98]

Upon receipt of Samuel's request for a thousand troops, the Foreign Office once again sought the advice of the military, suggesting that the Army Council consider "as a precautionary measure" the possibility "of improving communications, and possibly of preparing landing-grounds for air-craft across the Jordan."[99] On 31 October British headquarters in Alexandria wired reports from Jidda that Amir Abdullah had left Madina for Ma'an, the northernmost town in the Hijaz, preparatory to entering Transjordan.[100] Samuel asked the Foreign Office for an indication of the steps to be taken should Abdullah cross into

---

of the six officers, Sir Alec Kirkbride, in an interview with the present author on 13 December 1967, termed as "nonsense" the early attempt at pacifying the region. For an additional description of the anarchic situation, see Alec Kirkbride, *A Crackle of Thorns* (London: John Murray, 1956).

95. Samuel to War Office (urgent), no. 268, W.O. 106/198.

96. W.O. 106/200.

97. Foreign Office reply, 7 October 1920, *ibid.*

98. Samuel to Curzon, 12 October 1920, no. 92 (report of conversation with M. de Caix), F.O. 406/44, p. 352; Samuel to Lord Stamfordham, 17 October 1920, Samuel Papers; Samuel to Lloyd George, 28 October 1920, Lloyd George Papers.

99. Foreign Office to War Office, 25 October 1920, in E12874/85/44 of F.O. 406/44, p. 349.

100. E13480/9/44, F.O. 371/5065.

the unsettled region. He was assured that the amir was unlikely to move north and, even so, would "not stir up active trouble."[101]

It became apparent that the government had been seriously misled on this point when reports were received of a message sent by Abdullah to all the districts in Transjordan announcing that as "Vice-king of Syria" he was asking members of the Syrian congress and all officers and troops of the Syrian army to come to Ma'an. On 5 December Abdullah issued a further call for support, urging the need to oppose French colonization of Syria and to restore Faysal to his rightful throne.

As rumors spread and tension mounted once again, a temporary respite was gained by the Foreign Office. Upon being informed of Abdullah's activities, Faysal, then in London for important discussions with the British government, promised to communicate with his father in order to restrain Abdullah. In conjunction with Faysal's initiative, British representatives at both Jidda and Jerusalem let it be known that His Majesty's Government "will not countenance any action being taken by the Hejaz authorities of a nature to conflict with French interests in Syria."[102]

Despite these efforts, Samuel and the British representatives in the area refused to share in the optimism; in fact, they became even more concerned. On 12 December, Samuel, in reply to assurances that Faysal had successfully intervened with Abdullah, warned of the possibility that Abdullah might still proclaim a sharifian government over Transjordan "contrary to the wishes of the great majority of the inhabitants." "If such an event took place the consequences which I have repeatedly pointed out ... must ensue. Inter-tribal disorder and recurrence of raids into Palestine together with insecurity of Palestine's chief source of food supply would threaten serious re-action here. . . . I should be remiss if I did not call attention to the seriousness of situation which may be now developing."[103] Samuel provided for such a contingency by instructing the officers in Transjordan to: (1) withdraw if their mission

101. Foreign Office to Samuel, 19 November 1920, no. 256, W.O. 106/202.
102. Curzon to Hardinge (Paris), 8 December 1920, no. 3949, *Documents*, 13:412. Abdullah nevertheless reserved the right to "act as circumstances dictated." As late as March, 1921, Husayn assured the British of his efforts to restrain Abdullah. See Batten to Curzon (secret), 11 March 1921, in E3859/455/91 (no. 21) of F.O. 406/46.
103. Samuel to Curzon, 12 December 1920, no. 425 (telegram), *Documents*, 13:413.

of promoting local self-government and public order became impossible; (2) avoid local or anti-French entanglements; and (3) prevent themselves from falling into the hands of any hostile party.[104] Meanwhile Transjordan's future remained undecided, pending a sharifian move, while the status quo proved ineffective as well as unsatisfactory to all parties concerned. Samuel captured the feeling of uneasiness as the year ended: "The position in Trans-Jordania is satisfactory for the moment. Feisal's intervention came at the nick of time, and relieved what might have become a troublesome situation. We can now wait for the next crisis."[105]

On balance the position of Great Britain had been strengthened in the Fertile Crescent during the latter half of 1920 by the appointment of Sir Percy Cox and Sir Herbert Samuel as high commissioners. Cox had calmed the people of Mesopotamia by providing a sense of progress while safeguarding British interests through forceful, if indirect, control. Samuel, while less accustomed to the exercise of power, appeared to be favorably affecting Palestinian affairs through his sense of obligation and emphasis on benefits for the entire country. Through their presence the British government and public enjoyed a temporary respite in which to debate discredited policies, draw conclusions from the disorders that had characterized 1920, and transform such conclusions into the foundations for a new, more realistic policy in the Fertile Crescent. Events in Syria, Mesopotamia, Palestine, and Transjordan had posed a serious challenge. A suitable response—the Cairo conference—was forthcoming.

104. Hicom to the Foreign Office, 16 November 1920, no. 376, I.S.A.
105. Samuel to Curzon, 19 December 1920, Samuel Papers.

CHAPTER 5 **London: Prelude to Cairo**

As I sit in the Foreign Office and look out on the scene
I am reminded of one of those lava-lakes . . . where you
observe a great liquid expanse, an uneasy movement
troubling the surface, a seething and bubbling going on.
From time to time a violent explosion occurs; here the
banks slip down into the mud and are engulfed, while there
you see new landmarks emerge. That is a picture of what
is going on all over the world at the present moment.
—Foreign Secretary Lord Curzon, 1921

In its larger perspective, the unrest in the Fertile Crescent was but one in a series of crises which taxed British diplomacy in 1920. Changes in many parts of the empire partially explain the inability of the Foreign Office to respond promptly and effectively to the Middle Eastern challenge. Excluding specifically European problems, such as reconstruction, Germany's future, the Irish question, Anglo-French relations, the League of Nations, and international security, the British government was subjected to discouraging reports throughout the year from Persia, Egypt, Arabia, and Turkey, countries on the perimeter of the Fertile Crescent; these reports prompted Gertrude Bell's exasperated description of Asia from the Mediterranean to the Indian frontier as a "devil's cauldron."[1]

Empire strategists, appreciating Persia's importance as a barrier to Russian expansion and beginning to sense the potential value of oil, had sought to protect British interests through an Anglo-Persian treaty drafted in 1919 by Sir Percy Cox. Because of its unfavorable recep-

1. Burgoyne, *Gertrude Bell*, p. 181 (4 November 1920).

77

tion and the restless climate of nationalist agitation within Persia, however, the treaty was as yet unratified, to the growing anxiety of the British government, especially in the face of Bolshevik advances through the Caucasus. If implemented, the treaty would have become the cornerstone for a great imperial design stretching from the Nile to the Indus and from the Taurus Mountains to the Indian Ocean.[2] By the end of 1920 the issue was still unresolved, and Curzon and the military seriously considered evacuating Persia, a move which would make control of Mesopotamia all the more important.[3] If Persia was secured, existing schedules for a reduction of expenditures and forces could be effected; the loss of Persia would necessitate retrenchment in Mesopotamia.

Egypt, at the southern extremity of the Arab world, had been tense since the outbreak of violence there in March, 1919. Nationalist demands, presented by Sa'd Zaghlul and the *Wafd*, centered on the termination of the protectorate status, particularly since Britain had shown herself willing to recognize the independence of more backward areas, such as the Hijaz and, for a while, Syria.

A special commission was appointed under the chairmanship of Lord Milner to investigate the situation and to submit recommendations to the Cabinet. The Milner commission visited Egypt from 7 December 1919 until the first week of March, 1920, and then returned to London for secret negotiations with Zaghlul. Finally, on 9 December 1920 the full report was submitted. Acknowledging for the first time the bankruptcy of any return to the prewar system, or reforms of a merely departmental character, it called for a more radical change "to meet the new conditions." The commission, regarding the moment as favorable, advised that Egypt be restored in practice to what it had been in theory during the occupation: "a Government of Egypt by Egyptians," with British interests assured by a treaty.[4] On the one hand, the Milner report reflected a new realism on the part of some British leaders toward the

2. Harold Nicolson, *Curzon: The Last Phase, 1919–1925* (New York: Harcourt, Brace & Co., 1939), pp. 121–22; the text of the treaty appears in *Parliamentary Papers*, Cmd. 300 (1919).
3. C.P. 1320 ("Mesopotamia Expenditure"), memo by secretary of state for war, 1 May 1920, CAB 24/106; Hardinge to Curzon, 20 May 1920, *Documents*, 13:488.
4. See Major General Sir Charles W. Gwynn, *Imperial Policing* (London: Macmillan and Co., 1936), chap. 4; see also Mahmud Zayid, *Egypt's Struggle for Independence* (Beirut: Khayats, 1965). Cmd. 1131 (1921) contains the "Report of of the Special Mission to Egypt."

appeal and strength of nationalism. But at the same time, even a diminution of authority in Egypt would duplicate the Persian-Mesopotamian
relationship, since the utility of Palestine then would be enhanced as a
base for British troops in close proximity to the Suez Canal.

As long as the war lasted, Britain's position in the Arabian peninsula
remained relatively uncomplicated because of a policy of subsidizing
the several paramount chiefs. But with the war's termination, old
suppressed rivalries—sharifians against Sa'udis, the imam of Yemen
against the idrisi of Asir—broke out anew.[5] Moreover, King Husayn,
valued for his prestige in the Muslim world as protector of the holy
cities, was becoming more difficult to control. Unable to crush the Sa'udi
menace, by 1920 the sharif also had a number of grievances against
Great Britain: wartime promises had not been fulfilled, he and his delegation had been regarded as less than allies at the Paris Peace Conference, the European powers had refused to confirm his self-appointment
as king of Arabia, and, most galling, Britain had kept silent while
France crushed Faysal's regime but had supported Zionist development
in Palestine. If left unappeased, Husayn might fully support an uprising
against Syria, or incursions into Palestine through the long corridor of
Transjordan, or, even worse, effect a reconciliation with the Turks.

Two comparatively minor uprisings in fringe areas during 1919–20
were also to influence British military strategy toward the Fertile Crescent. On 13 April 1919 an anti-British campaign had been launched in
Afghanistan by Amanullah, but was quickly suppressed. So, too, a revolt inspired by the "mad Mullah" in the Somaliland protectorate was
ended with equal swiftness in only twenty-three days.[6] In both instances
success resulted from the use of airplanes and thus strengthened the
doctrine of controlling and pacifying large areas from the air rather
than with infantry units on the ground.

Far more difficult to cope with was the unsatisfactory situation in

5. The complications inherent in Britain's playing a mediatory role in Arabia are
revealed in the abortive mission of Lieutenant Colonel H. F. Jacob to Yemen
to establish Imam Yahya as autonomous ruler in preference to the idrisi. Seized
by tribesmen, he was forced to agree that Britain would also sustain the intermediate tribes from both the imam and the idrisi (E246/166/44, F.O. 406/43).
6. "Papers regarding Hostilities with Afghanistan, 1919" (Cmd. 324), 1919; "Report of the Intelligence Section, King's African Rifles" (secret), 12106, C.O.
732/4.

Asia Minor, "the anarchic zone," engendered by the Kemalist resistance. Implications of continued Turkish defiance of the San Remo decisions and the subsequent Treaty of Sèvres were numerous. Legality for the mandates was still lacking. As Lord Curzon informed the Italian government, "The one hope of His Majesty's Government is that their position in these territories may be definitely legalised without delay, so that administration and finance can at last be placed on a proper footing and order maintained in the name of duly constituted authority. They are accordingly most anxious to secure the definite issue of the mandates."[7] Yet Italy joined with France in advocating accommodation with Kemal against the more forceful stand taken by Greece and Great Britain, thus further straining the postwar Allied coalition. Indian Muslims were alienated by British hostility to the Sultan-Caliph. The Arabs of the Fertile Crescent had before them an example of effective resistance to European power.[8] British energies were being sapped. And revolt in Anatolia offered an opening for the spread of Bolshevist influence.

The latter prospect truly alarmed many British officials, for the Bolshevik threat to established British positions in the Near and Middle East showed signs of succeeding through propaganda as well as the force of arms. The new rulers in Russia were alert to the fertile field offered by Arab discontent, as evidenced in the invitation (published in *Izvestia* on 3 July 1920) issued by the Third International to the peoples of the East to send delegates to a conference in Baku. Citing specific situations in Armenia, Mesopotamia, Syria, and Arabia, it urged "the workers and peasants of the Near East" to organize and to arm themselves. ". . . You will defeat the English, French, and American capitalists, you will liberate yourselves from your oppressors, you will secure freedom, you will be able to organize a free, peaceful republic of toilers, you will use the riches of your land in your own interests. . . ."[9] Although there were only three Arabs among the 1,891 delegates in

7. Curzon to Marquis Imperiali, 28 December 1920, F.O. 406/46.
8. In response to the Allied occupation of Constantinople, Kemal issued a proclamation on 16 March which ended: "We shall have won the applause of mankind and shall pave the road to liberation which the Islamic world is yearning for, if we deliver the seat of the Caliphate from foreign influence . . ." (Kemal, *A Speech*, pp. 362–63). The proclamation was brought to the attention of the Muslim communities by various means of propaganda and by word of mouth.
9. Quoted in Ivar Spector, *The Soviet Union and the Muslim World, 1917–1958* (Seattle: University of Washington Press, 1959), pp. 48–52.

attendance, the Baku congress approved in principle the issuing of an "Appeal (Manifesto) to the Peoples of the East": "Many times you have heard from your governments the summons to a holy war, you marched under the green banner of the Prophet; but all these holy wars were deceitful and false. . . . Now we summon you to the first genuine holy war under the red banner of the Communist International. . . . Arise, Arabs and Afghans. . . . May the holy war of the Peoples of the East and the toilers of the whole world burn with unquenchable fire against imperialist England!"[10]

Soviet efforts went beyond inflammatory declarations, as evidenced by the deteriorating situation in the Caucasus. At the end of September, with the Turkish seizure of Kars and Ardahan and the Bolshevik invasion of Armenia, there existed for the first time a direct connection between the two revolutionary regimes. Throughout the year urgent reports reached London emphasizing the dire implications of a Soviet-Kemalist alliance. Reporting from Tiflis on 6 January, a British agent warned that upon reaching the Caspian Sea the Soviets would be able "to form a coalition of Mohammedan States for the overthrow of British rule in India, Mesopotamia and Egypt."[11]

Such reports were taken most seriously by the India Office, which was particularly sensitive to repercussions in India. This departmental view was summed up in a memorandum dated 3 January 1921: "Great Britain, forming . . . the main barrier to the emancipation of the world and to the institution of a universal Soviet regime, must be destroyed; this may be done by detaching India from the Empire. As India cannot be taken by a direct assault, it is necessary, as a preliminary step, to create Soviets right up to the Indian borders. . . . It is part of their policy to use Islam in so far as it may be utilised in an anti-British sense. . . ."[12] The author pointed out signs of strain within "the tenuous alliance" resulting from mutual suspicion and competitive territorial ambitions and therefore urged that these be exploited by British recognition of the Kemalists as, in essence, the lesser of the two evils.

Influential voices had been heard on behalf of such a response to the Turko-Bolshevik threat in recent months. Count Sforza, the Italian foreign minister, had openly suggested this step to Curzon during the Allied

10. *Ibid.*, p. 296.
11. Memorandum on Central Asia by Mr. E. W. Birse, *Documents*, 13:431.
12. Shuckburgh (I.O.) to Young (F.O.), F.O. 371/6342.

Conference at Spa on 10 July; likewise, M. Leygues expressed France's desire to reach an agreement with Kemal.[13] Within the Cabinet, Montagu had long been the leading proponent of a softer line toward the Kemalists, his ardor at one point resulting in a sharp rebuke from Lloyd George.[14] For strategic reasons the War Office also lent support to this course of action. But the sharpest critic of the government's policy, which was in effect forcing both the Turks and Arabs into the arms of the Bolsheviks, was Winston Churchill. Writing to the prime minister on 24 March, he expressed himself in unequivocal terms: "Compared to Germany, Russia is minor; compared to Russia, Turkey is petty. . . . With military resources which the Cabinet have cut to the most weak and slender proportions, we are leading the Allies in an attempt to enforce a peace on Turkey which would require great and powerful armies and long costly operations and occupations."[15]

Of central importance for Churchill, whose interest in, and influence upon, Britain's Middle Eastern policy grew during 1920, were his commitment to demobilization and his implacable hostility toward bolshevism. In 1919 he had written to Balfour, "The ruin of Lenin and Trotsky and the system they embody is indispensable to the peace and revival of the world."[16] He was to repeat this theme incessantly in public speeches and confidential memoranda, thus prompting Lloyd George to describe him as having "Bolshevism on the brain."[17] Yet Churchill

13. Curzon to Buchanan (Rome), 10 July 1920, in E8098/1435/44 (no. 643) of F.O. 406/44; Hardinge (Paris) to Curzon, 12 December 1920, *Documents*, 13: 202. French agents had sought to contact the Kemalists after the beginning of May (Kemal, *A Speech*, p. 390).
14. See Montagu memorandum of 24 December 1919, in E318 of F.O. 371/6349. Lloyd George wrote Montagu on 25 April 1920: ". . . it is clear that neither you nor any Mohammedan can expect to impose your views on the British Government or the Peace Conference against their better judgment or have any ground for believing that your advice has not been respected because it has been overruled" (F/40/3/5, Lloyd George Papers).
15. Churchill to Lloyd George, F/9/2/20, *ibid*. In a speech at Dundee on 14 February he called for "a peace with Turkey soon," one which "does not unite against us the feelings of the whole Mohammedan world"; see Winston S. Churchill, *The Position Abroad and at Home* (London: Harrison & Sons, 1920).
16. Churchill to Balfour, 23 August 1919, Arthur James Balfour Papers, British Museum.
17. Quoted in W. N. Medlicott, *Contemporary England, 1914–1964* (London: Longmans, Green & Co., 1967), p. 149. For insight into Churchill's thinking, see his *Reason and Reality*, a speech delivered at Sunderland on 3 January 1920 (Lon-

persisted in calling for a definite change in policy aimed at averting the union of Mustapha Kemal with the communists.

Despite their more sympathetic stand toward the Turkish nationalists, which admittedly was based on expediency, the Allied governments and British Cabinet members failed to persuade the prime minister and his secretary of state for foreign affairs, both of whom insisted upon support for the Greeks and toughness toward the Turks.[18] Their resolve found expression in the treaty of peace with Turkey signed at Sèvres on 10 August 1920.[19] The treaty, with its harsh terms placing limitations on Turkish sovereignty, was humiliating and only strengthened the resolve of Kemal and his supporters to contest its implementation and, indeed, its validity. Yet Lord Curzon placed great emphasis on the Treaty of Sèvres, calling its nonratification "a purely technical point" and viewing its revision "with the utmost reluctance."[20] Thus the anti-Kemalist policy endured into 1921 and was one aspect of the debate which took place in England during 1920, both in the press and within official circles, over the policy of His Majesty's Government in Asia and particularly in the Arab world.

At all levels of English society the cry in 1920 was for economy and an end to domestic problems. In January the government admitted a deficit of £473 million, and there was talk of an income tax. In the single year since Churchill had entered the War Office, four million men had returned to civilian life, yet the public clamored for more troop reductions. In Parliament it was stated that the weekly cost of troops in occupied Ottoman territories alone amounted to £750,000. In an edi-

don: Harrison & Sons, 1920); his speech before United Wards' Club of the city of London, *The Times*, 5 November 1920, p. 9; *The World Crisis, 1911–1918*, pt. 1, pp. 70–103, 232–61; and his memoranda "Russian Policy," 12 November 1919, Paper 128, CAB 24/93, and "Greece and Middle Eastern Policy," 10 December 1920, CAB 23/23.

18. Dispatches from Admiral de Robeck in Constantinople influenced thinking at this time. He deprecated Kemalist strength and insisted that the Turk "only understands force" (10 November 1920, no. 1190 [telegram], *Documents*, 13: 174–75). He was replaced shortly thereafter by Sir Horace Rumbold, who in January, 1921, suggested to the Foreign Office that it cease regarding Kemal "any longer as a brigand chief" since his Angora government was able to exercise "all functions of Government with average efficiency as efficiency goes in Turkey" (20 January 1921, in E1006/1/44, of F.O. 406/45).

19. See the text in "Treaty of Peace with Turkey," Cmd. 964 (1920).

20. Conference of Ministers, 18 February 1921, minutes, CAB 23/24, p. 179.

torial on 8 March *The Times* warned, "there can be no real economy in Whitehall until Parliament finds a way of controlling financial operations of the Executive." On 16 June the League to Enforce Public Economy held its first meeting, at which the position in Mesopotamia and Palestine was singled out for criticism on military and financial grounds. Whereas the government had adopted as its motto, "Let us keep steady," *The Times* preferred "Let us keep solvent." Statistics during the year indicated falling exports, diminishing production, "creeping paralysis" in industry, increasing joblessness, and inflation, together with heavier taxation.

The Mesopotamian uprising in the middle of the year was therefore most inopportune for the Lloyd George government, since it shattered the illusion of Arab satisfaction with Great Britain and demanded immediate additional expenditures to pacify the country. The uprising also provided the antiwaste movement and critics of the government with concrete evidence of failure. The daily press seized upon the Mesopotamian example in editorial comment. Opposing "adventures in the Middle East," *The Times* wrote: ". . . if the Government . . . think that their policy in Mesopotamia during the past year has redounded to the glory of the Empire they are alone in their belief. . . . Every sane critic of Government expenditure must deplore the waste which still marks War Office outlay at a time when the nation is financially embarrassed."[21] It called, instead, for "the constant pressure of . . . public opinion" to "chasten Government extravagance and the tendency towards the 'Indianization' of Mesopotamia, replacing these with an Arab State and reduced direct responsibilities."[22] Prominent figures, such as Colonel T. E. Lawrence and the Agha Khan, were invited to offer their opinions. Lawrence chose to single out "the willfully wrong policy of the civil administration in Bagdad" as the main reason for Britain's loss of men, money, and supplies.[23] The Agha Khan, described

21. *The Times*, 6 November 1920, p. 11.
22. *Ibid.*, 26 June 1920, p. 17.
23. *Ibid.*, 22 August 1920, p. 7. Lawrence, at the time a Fellow at All Souls College, Oxford, freely volunteered his opinions, as in a special correspondent's interview with him which appeared on page 1 of the *Daily News* on 25 August. His criticism of the administration in Mesopotamia—in editorials, interviews, and letters to the editor—returned him to national prominence and brought him to Churchill's attention as an expert on the Arabs. It also caused Gertrude Bell to hold him guilty of "the unpardonable sin of wilfully darkening counsel" (Burgoyne, *Gertrude Bell*, pp. 164–65).

as "one of the foremost of the Mohamedan princes of India," castigated the government for warmongering, exploiting Indian troops, and penetrating into "areas outside [its] legitimate Asiatic sphere."[24]

Public pressure and newspaper criticism were carried over into parliamentary debates, where the attack was led by former Prime Minister Herbert Asquith. Addressing himself to Mesopotamia on 23 June, Asquith declared: "Whatever may be its possibilities of resurrection, reconstruction, or revitalization, it is certainly not a duty which it is incumbent upon us to take upon our already overburdened shoulders."[25] Some members, ignoring the Middle Eastern context, extended their attack to a general critique of wastefulness and mistaken priorities. Others, however, addressed themselves to the specific weaknesses of Middle Eastern policy which had led to heavy expenditures: shortsightedness in not having reconciled Arab and Frenchman; nineteenth-century imperialist methods no longer applicable; or "the tragic absurdity" of British troops being killed by Arabs who were assumed to be friendly to England and for whose security and economic growth such large expenditures were being incurred.[26]

The debates reached their peak in December when Churchill had the unpleasant duty, as he put it, of defending a proposal that a supplementary sum, not exceeding £39,750,000, be granted to the government to meet expenditures not provided for in the original army estimate for the year regarding the garrisons in Mesopotamia and elsewhere.[27] Although the government emerged successfully from the heated debates, these sessions, and the coverage given them, illustrated the extent of dissatisfaction and provided the final stimulus for change, in policymaking if not immediately in actual policy. Such a move, however, had long been under discussion, albeit sporadically, within the Cabinet itself.

Even in the midst of the war a modest effort had been made to bring greater efficiency to the conduct of Near and Middle Eastern affairs. On 5 July 1918 Edwin Montagu, secretary of state for India, submitted a paper on "The War in the East" to the Eastern Committee of the War Cabinet, in which he advocated a change, since the East, he felt, was being neglected. He proposed that a new department be established as a condominium of the Foreign Office and India Office. In September

24. *The Times*, 5 November 1920, pp. 13–14, and 6 November 1920, p. 11.
25. *Parliamentary Debates* (Commons), 5th ser., 23 June 1920, col. 2236.
26. Mr. Lambert, 26 July 1920, in E8991 of F.O. 371/5228.
27. *Parliamentary Debates* (Commons), 5th ser., 136 (15 December 1920) : 527–638.

General Smuts stated before the same body that unity of direction was urgently required in the eastern theater so that the German menace might be met more effectively.[28] However, the committee accepted as a temporary solution the appointment of Lord Robert Cecil, another advocate of centralization, as the person responsible for all Middle Eastern questions within the Foreign Office. Replying to Montagu's initiative, Foreign Secretary Balfour made an important distinction between the two elements high policy and machinery, advising that the latter—regardless of whether control of policy would be left to the Foreign Office or given to a new office to be created at 10 Downing Street—was a problem "which may be left alone till after the war."[29] Yet, despite such promises, the reliance upon old procedures—the system in which no minister was "formally and definitely accountable for what was going forward, nor for its expense"[30]—continued even after the armistice.

Nor did the replacement of Balfour by Curzon improve matters. In the opinion of some of his colleagues Curzon was personally unsuited to the task of remedying the bureaucratic confusion or of proceeding on definite and consistent lines. Churchill, for example, upset over the damage done to his demobilization plan and measures of economy by Foreign Office mistakes in the Arab world, described Curzon as presiding over the scene "with much complacency."[31] A more indirect criticism of Curzon was delivered in the House of Commons on 19 July 1920 by Mr. Ormsby-Gore, a former assistant secretary of the Middle Eastern Committee under Curzon and a leader in the campaign for reorganization. Speaking of the French ultimatum to Faysal, he warned that it would prove harmful to Great Britain since "we are all Feringhis—Franks—in the eyes of the Arabs. We stand for Europe, and we stand together." "What is wanted is a spirit in the Foreign Office that is energetic, that is interested in these Middle Eastern questions, with foresight, with knowledge, ready to listen to people who have been in

28. Both memoranda are printed in CAB 21/186; see secret E.C. 24A of 13 August and secret E.C. 31st minutes of 17 September.
29. Balfour to Montagu, 27 July 1918, secret E.C. 24A, CAB 21/186.
30. Winston S. Churchill, "Mesopotamia and the New Government," *Empire Review* 38, no. 270 (July, 1923) : 695.
31. *Ibid.* On a later occasion Churchill wrote that one of Curzon's characteristic weaknesses was that "he thought too much about stating his case, and too little about getting things done"; see Winston S. Churchill, *Great Contemporaries* (London: Thornton Butterworth, 1937), p. 281.

British Policy in the Arab World

the country recently and not merely thirty years ago, and who will determine that the *entente* between Britain and France shall continue, and that between Britain and the Arabs shall continue, and that will determine to bring them together and put an end to these months and months of procrastination."[32]

After the long, costly period of delay, the unsettling events of 1920 in all parts of the Arab world led His Majesty's Government to conclude that the system of dividing control among the Foreign, India, and War offices had to be ended and that responsibility for the region should be transferred to a single department under the control of one secretary of state. The renewed campaign was conducted simultaneously on three levels: within the Cabinet, by the Foreign Office, and in Parliament.

The presentation of a memorandum on the "Mesopotamian Expenditure" by the secretary of state for war on 1 May formally opened the Cabinet debate on reorganization. Warning that "unless and until the decisions in principle are given, no effective progress can be made towards a curtailment of our responsibilities and our expenditure," he argued for:

(1) The transfer of Mesopotamia, and, if possible, of the Mandated Territories, to the Colonial Office.
(2) The fixing of a Grant-in-Aid for each by agreement between the Treasury and Colonial Office.
(3) The transference of the military responsibility for maintaining order in Mesopotamia to the Air Ministry as soon as possible.
(4) The immediate contraction of the area of occupation in Mesopotamia, with concentration of troops only along the railroads.

In his opinion, control over Mesopotamia should be turned over to "a Department of State which has a real knowledge and experience of the administration and development of these wild countries, which is accustomed to improvisations and makeshifts, which is accustomed to measure the territory it occupies by the amount of force at its disposal, and to measure the amount of the force at its disposal by the exiguous funds entrusted to it."[33] Churchill praised the Colonial Office for

32. *Parliamentary Debates* (Commons), 5th ser., 132 (19 July 1920) : 153.
33. C.P. 1320, CAB 24/106. T. E. Lawrence claimed to have planted in Lloyd George's mind the idea of divesting Curzon of responsibility for the Middle East; see Liddle Hart, *T. E. Lawrence* (London: Jonathan Cape, 1934), p. 408.

its "extraordinarily cheap and extremely successful" control of East Africa, which he attributed to "a patient policy of waiting for opportunities, of knowing how and when to take appropriate action, and, above all, a frugal policy [which] has kept us out of any trouble or expense. . . ." At the same time, he rejected any possible claim by the Foreign Office, because it "is the great Department of State the whole of whose experience and special aptitudes is devoted to the conduct of the relations of this country with foreign States, and to mix up with this the administration of provinces is to impair the discharge of both functions."

As individual Cabinet members expressed their opinions, Churchill found himself supported once again by Montagu and opposed by Lord Milner. On behalf of the India Office Montagu recommended in his memorandum of 2 June that all the Middle Eastern areas be placed under a single controlling agency in London, preferably a special Middle East Office, to be created *ad hoc*.[34] Failing that, the Colonial Office should be renamed and reorganized; but "the Foreign Office should be definitely ruled out." Lord Milner, on the other hand, rejected Churchill's first premise that prompt, drastic curtailment of expenditures was the paramount necessity of the moment and cautioned against any change, fiscal or administrative, prompted by "the rage for immediate saving."[35] Although the Mesopotamian crisis then assumed priority in Cabinet sessions, the questions raised by Churchill continued to be the subject of discussion through the summer and autumn.

Inside the Foreign Office, Hubert Young had presented for departmental consideration a "Note on the Future Control of the Middle East," dated 17 May.[36] He described the deficiencies of the existing arrangement: Egypt, Yemen and Asir, Persia, Syria, and the Hijaz were the responsibility of the Foreign Office, Palestine and Mesopotamia were controlled by the War Office under military administrations, and the Persian Gulf coast, Nejd and Hail, Aden, and the Hadhramaut fell under the jurisdiction of the India Office, with a number of intermediary agencies and areas of dual control as further complicating factors.

34. "Mesopotamia and Middle East: Question of Future Control," C.P. 1402, CAB 24/107.
35. Secret memorandum by the secretary of state for the colonies, 24 May 1920, C.P. 1337, CAB 24/106.
36. E4870/4870/44, F.O. 406/43.

Calling this arrangement makeshift, he saw three alternatives—divided control, control by a new department, or control by an Eastern department of the Foreign Office—and proposed that the Foreign Office support the third alternative as the least objectionable. His argument was incorporated by Lord Curzon when, in a battle of memoranda, he defended the Foreign Office's record.[37] Curzon began by criticizing the India Office, then derided Churchill's preference for the Colonial Office by claiming that it stemmed from Churchill's being "very imperfectly acquainted with the views or interests of the States of the Middle East"; he concluded by advising the creation of a Middle Eastern department headed by a parliamentary undersecretary who would be "responsible to and taking his orders from the Secretary of State for Foreign Affairs." The several positions thus were drawn sharply.

A third initiative was undertaken during this period by several members of Parliament. A letter was sent to the Cabinet secretary on 26 May by Lord Winterton. Bearing the signatures of twenty prominent public and parliamentary figures, the letter called for the creation of a new department to handle the Middle East, for the present arrangement, if allowed to continue, would "result in conflicts of policy, misunderstandings, delays and unavoidable expense."[38]

As the need for a decision became evident, the Cabinet resumed debate on the subject at its meeting on 13 December, Churchill again having urged a definite change in policy. After a presentation by Colonel A. T. Wilson, recently returned from his post in Mesopotamia, the Cabinet could not agree except to require further consideration before reaching a decision on the government's future policy in Mesopotamia. Finally, on 31 December the full Cabinet met to consider a number of documents relating to the situation in Persia, Mesopotamia, and the Middle East generally. By the end of the session, after a sharp division of opinion, the Cabinet agreed:

(1) that responsibility for the whole of the administration of the mandatory territories of Mesopotamia and Palestine should be concentrated in a single Department, which should bear on its financial Votes the whole of the expenses both Civil and Military;

---

37. "Future Administration of the Middle East," 8 June 1920, C.P. 1434, CAB 21/186.
38. Secret letter, C.P. 1372, *ibid.*

(2) that, as a counsel of perfection, the best plan would be the establishment of a new Ministry for the purpose, but that at the present time this proposal would not be acceptable to Parliament;

(3) (by a majority) that the New Department should be set up as a branch of the Colonial Office, which should be given some new title, such as the "Department for Colonies and Mandated Territories";

(4) that the Secretary of State for the Colonies, in consultation with the heads of the other Departments concerned, should appoint an Interdepartmental Committee to work out details, including the date of the transfer;

(5) that, in the meantime, the responsibility should remain as at present. . . .[39]

Governmental inertia and the forces resisting change had been overcome just enough to offer the prospect of a break in the impasse that characterized the conduct of Middle Eastern affairs.

With responsibility now entrusted to the Colonial Office, the way was opened for one further, even more unexpected development. On 9 January the Cabinet was informed by the prime minister of Lord Milner's resignation. Winston Churchill would succeed him as colonial secretary and therefore be entrusted with the new task of reordering British policy toward the Arab world.

Churchill's appointment was made possible by Milner, who on 27 November advised Lloyd George of his intention to resign before the end of the year.[40] Exhausted by his involvement in Egyptian affairs, Milner refused to be deterred, especially when on 31 December the Cabinet added to his responsibilities by directing him to work out the details of the proposed transfer; he responded to this in a note to the prime minister on 3 January 1921. "I will not discuss the merits of the scheme, with which I do not agree. It is a Government decision and has to be carried out—by members of the Government. But not by me, who am on the very eve of retirement, and only hanging on from day to day. . . ."[41] He closed by asking to be relieved from official duties as soon as practicable. It is not clear when the position was first offered to Churchill, but it would appear to have been prior to 3 January, for by

39. Cab. 82 (20), 31 December 1920, CAB 23/23.
40. Milner to Lloyd George, 27 November 1920, Alfred Milner Papers, Bodleian Library, Oxford University.
41. Milner to Lloyd George, 3 January 1921, F/39/2/37, Lloyd George Papers; see also Hankey to Lloyd George, 5 January 1921, CAB 21/186.

the 4th he was already writing his acceptance to the prime minister. "I have carefully considered the task which you wish me to undertake; and in view of all the circumstances I feel it is my duty to comply with your wish. . . . While I feel some misgivings about the political consequences to myself of taking on my shoulders the burden and the odium of the Mesopotamian entanglement, I am deeply sensible of the greatness of the sphere you are confiding to my charge, of the honour which you have done me in choosing me for such critical employment. . . ."[42]

Originally attracted to the Middle East because of his direct personal responsibility for the safety and proper usage of British troops, Churchill in the course of 1920 came to feel that matters had reached "a point where my responsibility to prevent a great disaster has become a real one."[43] Whether by coincidence or design, out of genuine concern or political ambition—or perhaps a combination of these—he was now to be entrusted with a mandate for change in the relations between Great Britain and the Arab world.

In compliance with the Cabinet decision of 31 December a special Interdepartmental Committee was constituted on 11 January 1921 with Sir James Masterton Smith as Chairman and with representatives from the Treasury and the Colonial, Foreign, India, and War offices. On 31 January it presented the new colonial secretary with its final report.[44]

The first section of the Masterton Smith report provided a definition of the territorial sphere of the new department, which in principle was to encompass Mesopotamia, Aden, and Palestine, the latter term covering Transjordan as well. But this narrow sphere presented the committee with a problem at the outset: the three territories were not coterminous,

---

42. Churchill to Lloyd George, 4 January 1921, F/9/2/51, Lloyd George Papers. At least one party to the events, Lord Curzon, thought it was "a put up job between L.G. and Churchill" (Curzon to Samuel, quoted in Bowle, *Viscount Samuel*, pp. 210–12). Curzon also accused Churchill of wishing to be "a sort of Asiatic Foreign Minister" (Leonard Mosley, *Curzon: The End of an Epoch* [London: Longmans, Green & Co., 1960], p. 216). Lord Riddell relates an interesting anecdote wherein Lloyd George had first considered Churchill for the position on Christmas Day, 1918; see G. A. Riddell, *Lord Riddell's Intimate Diary of the Peace Conference and After, 1918–1923* (London: Victor Gollancz, 1933), p. 8.
43. Churchill to Prime Minister, 5 August 1920, in F/9/2/37, Lloyd George Papers.
44. F.O. 371/6343, pp. 16–26. Curzon, resenting the Cabinet action as an affront to himself and to the Foreign Office, insisted that the Committee meet at once, for "the sooner we are absolved from all responsibility the better" (Curzon to Hankey [confidential], 2 January 1921, Cab. 82 [20], CAB 21/186).

their land boundaries had not yet been demarcated, and the large intervening area was sparsely inhabited by nomadic tribes. On the assumption that the Cabinet had intended the Middle Eastern problem to be
treated as an organic whole, the committee recommended that the sphere
of the new department be bounded on the west by the Mediterranean,
on the southwest by the frontier of Egypt and the Red Sea, on the south
and southeast by the Indian Ocean, on the northeast by the northeastern
boundary of Mesopotamia and the Arabian littoral of the Persian Gulf.
In essence, this entailed the department's assumption of responsibility
for all of Arabia, too, but left the Foreign Office as the channel of communication between the governments of Great Britain and the Hijaz.

The scope of the Middle East Department was extended to administration and policy in Mesopotamia, Palestine, and Aden; "policy in other
Arab areas within the British sphere of influence"; delimitation of
boundaries between British spheres and territories of independent Arab
rulers; and all expenditures, whether civil or military. The report suggested a pattern of relations among the Colonial Office, War Office, and
Air Ministry and proposed financial arrangements and a plan for creating one body of Arab political officers liable for service in any part
of the territorial sphere outside Palestine.[45] It concluded by recommending that the new department be manned at the outset by officers loaned
from parent services, with the transfer of responsibilities to become
effective on 1 March.

The Cabinet met once again on 14 February to consider the recommendations of the Masterton Smith committee. At this meeting Churchill pressed strongly for the right to initiate and regulate policy in Arabia.
He had expressed himself on the subject a month earlier when familiar-
izing himself with the Middle East.

The Arab problem is all one, and any attempt to divide it will only reintro-
duce the same paralysis and confusion of action which has done so much
harm during the last two years. . . . Feisal or Abdullah, whether in Mesopotamia or Mecca; King Hussein at Mecca; Bin Saud at Nejd; Bin Rashid at
Hail; the Sheikh of Kuweit; and King Samuel at Jerusalem are all inextrica-
bly interwoven, and no conceivable policy can have any chance which does

---

45. The committee cited as reasons for this distinction the arrangements, already
far advanced, for a Palestinian civil service and "the special international importance of the country" (F.O. 371/6343, p. 22).

not pull all the strings affecting them. To exclude Arabian relations would be to disembowel the Middle Eastern Department.[46]

But Lord Curzon resisted this extension of control, emphasizing the incongruity of transferring the king of the Hijaz, who was an independent sovereign, to the Colonial Office. Moreover, he feared a situation in which the government might be committed by the Colonial Office to a definite policy without the knowledge and consent of the Foreign Office on issues involving international politics of the first magnitude. In an effort to reach a compromise the Cabinet generally approved the recommendations contained in the report, required that the Colonial and Foreign secretaries consult together to reach a working agreement on Arabian policy, and authorized the colonial secretary to visit Egypt in the early part of March for the purpose of "consulting with the British authorities in Palestine and Arabia as proposed."[47]

Churchill took up his new assignment with customary energy and enthusiasm. By early February preliminary arrangements had been made for consultation with several experts on the Middle East. He was particularly anxious to meet Sir Percy Cox, for he considered the Mesopotamian situation to be extremely urgent. Describing himself as having "a great deal to learn, but at least I have a completely virgin mind on the subject,"[48] Churchill surrounded himself with a highly competent staff. Sir James Masterton Smith became permanent undersecretary; John Shuckburgh of the India Office was made assistant undersecretary; Roland Vernon of the Treasury and Hubert Young of the Foreign Office became assistant secretaries. Eric Forbes Adam and Reader Bullard were the principal officers, while Colonel Richard Meinertzhagen served as military adviser. Lastly, using "arguments which I could not resist," Churchill prevailed upon Colonel T. E. Lawrence to act as political adviser to the Middle East Department. Every possible point of view was thus represented and Churchill was assured of expert advice.

Churchill's original intention was to meet Sir Percy Cox in Mesopotamia to discuss the new ruler, the size, character, and organization

46. Churchill to the Prime Minister from Nice, 12 January 1921 (private and personal), F/9/2/54, Lloyd George Papers.
47. E2603/533/65, F.O. 371/6342; also in Cab. 7 (21), 14 February 1921, CAB 23/24.
48. Young, *The Independent Arab*, p. 324.

of the future garrison, a timetable for reducing the existing garrison, the amount of the grant-in-aid required, and the extent of the territory to be held and administered.[49] However, the meeting soon became enlarged, for Sir Herbert Samuel and the resident in Aden were invited to participate. Similarly, in his reply of 14 February Cox asked to discuss additional questions connected with Mesopotamia; for this purpose he requested permission to bring a larger delegation, including the Arab ministers of finance and defense, "both quite unexceptionable socially," to show the national government it was being taken into Britain's confidence. An alternative site thus became necessary, and Cairo was chosen, although not before both Curzon and Allenby had been assured that Churchill would not take the opportunity to involve himself in Egyptian affairs.[50]

Preparations for the meeting continued throughout February. On the 18th Churchill asked that an effort be made to persuade the Council of the League of Nations to defer consideration of the "A" mandates for Mesopotamia, Palestine, and Syria; he wanted time to consider the terms of the mandates at his forthcoming meeting. The Cabinet agreed to this request.[51] That same day Churchill instructed Shuckburgh to consider the agenda carefully and provided him with extensive notes of his own as a guide.[52]

Churchill also had occasion to express what he felt to be his task and

49. Churchill to Cox (telegram), 7 February 1921, in E2322/533/65 of F.O. 371/6342.
50. Ostensibly, Cairo had been selected for its suitability as a "half-way house" (Churchill to Samuel, 12 February 1921, Samuel Papers). But a Reuters dispatch, claiming that Churchill would "confer with heads of Egyptian Government," aroused Allenby's concern. The Foreign Office urged Jerusalem or even Ismailia or Port Said as alternatives because, as one member put it, any British minister was likely to "find himself in Cairo the object of demonstrations from these excitable monkeys which would be embarrassing both to himself and to the Administration" (R. C. Lindsay, E2225/533/65, F.O. 371/6342). Allenby was calmed by Curzon, who wrote on 21 February that Churchill's visit "is not connected with the Milner Report nor with the future of Egypt, for which he is not responsible, and you are authorised to let this be known" *(ibid.)*. This episode illustrates not only the suspicion with which Churchill was regarded but the uneasiness which British officials felt over the tense situation in the Middle East.
51. Cab. 8 (21), p. 91, CAB 23/24; see also the French ambassador's *"très urgent"* note of the 16th asking Britain to urge immediate council approval but which met with a request for further delay (E2188, F.O. 371/6378).
52. 17262, "Conference at Cairo," C.O. 722/4.

what he hoped to accomplish at Cairo. These thoughts offer an insight into his motivation and a standard by which to evaluate the subsequent conference. One of the earliest expressions appeared in a message to Cox, who, having misunderstood Churchill's intention to supervise a policy of withdrawal from Mesopotamia, offered his resignation on 13 January. The colonial secretary hastened to assure Cox that "I intend to try my utmost to preserve our control. . . . No province in the British Empire has ever been acquired by marching in and maintaining a large regular army at the cost of the British Exchequer, but always by skilful and careful improvisations adapted to its special needs."[53] In his farewell speech at the War Office on 15 February Churchill voiced his hope that "I may not only lighten your burdens but the burdens of the taxpayer by reducing these commitments and by bringing these regions into a less extravagant condition. . . ."[54] Shortly before his departure for the conference Churchill wrote to Sir George Ritchie to inform his constituents in Dundee of the reasons and purpose for his expected absence from the country. Refuting newspaper accusations that his object was to build up a costly and vainglorious Middle Eastern empire at the expense of the taxpayer, he expressed the desire to devise and carry through a better and much cheaper scheme as the only alternative to total withdrawal from Mesopotamia.

We marched into Mesopotamia during the war and rooted up the Turkish Government . . . We accepted before all the world a mandate for the country and undertook to introduce much better methods of government in the place of those we had overthrown. If, following upon this, we now ignominiously scuttle for the coast, leaving sheer anarchy behind us and ancient historic cities to be plundered by the wild Bedouin of the desert, an event will have occurred not at all in accordance with what has usually been the reputation of Great Britain.[55]

To uphold the honor and vital interests of Great Britain, to realize economies, and to reduce commitments—these constituted the major ends of British policy in the Fertile Crescent as conceived by the indi-

53. Churchill to Cox (priority A, personal and secret), 16 January 1921, P. 3795, I.O.
54. *The Times*, 15 February 1921, p. 12.
55. 25 February 1921, in 10749 of C.O. 732/3; see also the criticism of Churchill and the new department in *The Times*, 23 February 1921, p. 11.

vidual to whom its conduct was entrusted on the eve of the Cairo Conference.

What Churchill could not yet elaborate on in public was the one missing element, the specific means by which to achieve the above goals, an agency which might satisfy his desire to pull together all the strings in the Middle East and justify his opinion that "the Arab problem is all one." Yet this, too, had emerged during the latter part of 1920. Termed for convenience "the sharifian solution," it denoted a revival of the thesis (thought to have been discarded after Faysal's failure at Damascus) that King Husayn and his family were worthy of British support in Arabia and the Fertile Crescent.

The genesis of the sharifian solution can be traced back to 1918. In October of that year T. E. Lawrence appeared before the Eastern Committee and suggested that Abdullah be installed as ruler in Baghdad and Lower Mesopotamia, with his brothers Zayd and Faysal similarly provided for in Upper Mesopotamia and Syria respectively.[56]

Such an arrangement apparently had been given consideration even earlier, for on 22 April Percy Cox stated that he could not see "the least justification or necessity for introducing one of the family of the Sherif of Mecca" to fill the role of "nominal headpiece" in the desired British administration in Mesopotamia. He went further by objecting to Husayn's being recognized as king of Arabia and sovereign of a group of confederate states. Similarly, Gilbert Clayton, in describing the attitudes of the Palestinian Arab, confided that the sharifian movement left him absolutely cold. Despite these disparaging reports, the Eastern Committee gave much attention early in 1919 to the possible candidature of Abdullah for titular amir of a united Mesopotamia.[57]

The combined negative effect of the Syrian congress's unilateral declaration of Faysal and Abdullah as monarchs of Syria and Mesopo-

---

56. Thirty-seventh meeting of Eastern Committee, 29 October 1918, Milner Papers. See Lawrence's initial impressions of Faysal and Abdullah in his *Seven Pillars of Wisdom* (New York: Doubleday, Doran & Co., 1935), pp. 44 and 68, and his praise for "the oldest, most holy, and most powerful family of the Arabs" in David Garnett, ed., *The Letters of T. E. Lawrence* (New York: Doubleday, Doran & Co., 1939), p. 267.

57. Curzon to Balfour, 26 January 1919, no. 73 (cipher telegram), F.O. 608/96. Foreign Office files 1376 and 1747 contain unfavorable appraisals of Abdullah by two members of the Arab Bureau in Cairo, D. G. Hogarth and Kinahan Cornwallis.

tamia, Faysal's inability to avert the Syrian tragedy, and a decline in Husayn's power in the Arabian heartland appeared at the time to have removed the sharifian family as a potent factor in the Middle East. But during the summer of 1920 support for the sharifians re-emerged among many British authorities. Allenby reported that in a visit with him in Egypt Abdullah had spoken with moderation and restraint and was content to leave his fate in the hands of Great Britain; and that during the Syrian crisis he had strongly advised recognition of Faysal as sovereign over an Arab nation.[58] The letters of Gertrude Bell at this time portray her increasing interest in either Faysal or Abdullah for the throne in Mesopotamia.[59] Herbert Samuel, after a tour of Palestine in the spring of 1920, came to advocate a loose confederation of the Arab-speaking states, with its government seat in Damascus and with Faysal recognized not only as sovereign in his own state but also as the honorary head of the confederation.[60] On 25 June, in a debate in the House of Lords, the idea of placing a sharifian in Mesopotamia was put forth by Lord Lamington and Lord Sydenham.[61] Sensing the time and climate of opinion to be appropriate, General Haddad, in a note to the Foreign Office received on 14 July, outlined his plan for re-establishing peace throughout the Middle East by working in conjunction with the sharifians.[62]

Ironically, given his consistent opposition earlier, Arnold T. Wilson set the stage for further serious consideration of the idea. In his dispatch of 31 July he replied to the news of Faysal's departure from Syria by inquiring whether the government might consider the possibility of offering him the amirate of Mesopotamia. "We have always regarded Feisal as booked for Syria. Nothing that I have heard during the last few months has led me to modify my views of unsuitability of Abdullah and . . . [it is] fairly clear that no local candidate will be successful in obtaining sufficient local support to enable him to make good. Feisal alone of all Arabian potentates has any idea of practical difficulties of running a civilised government on Arab lines."[63] He offered as addi-

58. Allenby to Curzon, 16 May and 18 March 1920, *Documents*, 13:260, 231.
59. See, for example, her letters of 14 June, 16 August, 3 and 24 October, and 25 December 1920 in Burgoyne, *Gertrude Bell*.
60. Samuel to Curzon (personal), 2 April 1920, Samuel Papers.
61. *Parliamentary Debates* (Lords), 5th ser., 25 June 1920.
62. E8205/2/44, F.O. 406/44, pp. 240–43.
63. Wilson to India Office, no. 9249 (telegram), in E9252 of F.O. 371/5038.

tional reasons the likelihood that Faysal would realize the need for foreign assistance as well as the danger of relying on an Arab army. What could not fail to impress officials in London after their abandonment of Faysal in Syria was Wilson's argument that renewed support for Faysal would re-establish British prestige in Arab eyes and wipe out the accusation of bad faith otherwise made against Great Britain.

As the idea circulated, it acquired two new proponents who thereafter were to share significantly in its implementation. Hubert Young, in a "Foreign Office Memorandum on Arabian Policy" drafted on 23 October, strongly recommended that "whatever may be decided about our relations with the other rulers of Arabia, it is essential, if we are to preserve our prestige in the Moslem world, that steps should be taken without delay to restore confidence in the mind of the guardian of the Holy Places of Islam [i.e., Sharif Husayn]."[64] Kinahan Cornwallis also supported the sharifian plan. Reacting to a report that Husayn's attitude toward Britain had become one of "studied obstruction," he commented: "King Hussein as a personality is nothing; as a symbol of the Arab Revolt he stands for a good deal in Moslem minds and his disappearance by our agency would not only be a confession of the failure of our whole Arab policy but would be eagerly seized upon by our ill wishers as a proof of our cynicism. I am afraid we must make the best of a bad job."[65] Despite this negative motivation regarding Husayn, Cornwallis was enthusiastic about Faysal and was to act as unofficial intermediary for the government when it decided to approach Faysal concerning the throne of Mesopotamia in January, 1921, an occasion provided by Faysal's presence in London despite French objections and Foreign Office hesitation.

Having sailed from Haifa a forlorn and abandoned figure, Faysal proceeded to Milan, where he contemplated an uncertain future and the prospect of exile, his only contact being General Haddad Pasha in London.[66] The opportunity to enter England came about, in the first

64. Confidential, E13523/9/44, F.O. 371/5065. On 6 October Young wrote: "The acceptance by the French of the suzerainty of Feisal in Syria is not an essential condition to the fulfilment of our pledge to the Arabs . . . nor is Feisal irretrievably estranged from us" (*Documents*, 13:378).
65. 30 September 1920, in E12529/9/44 of F.O. 371/5065.
66. It is not known why Faysal chose not to return to the Hijaz; the most plausible explanation lies in his estrangement from his father. The fact that he was de-

instance, at the request of his father, who, seeking to preserve a semblance of his former prestige, asked His Majesty's Government to receive Faysal as his personal emissary; in essence this meant the resumption by Faysal of his original role as head of the Hijazi delegation. The request coincided with a plan, conceived in the India Office, to summon Husayn and Ibn Sa'ud, or their plenipotentiaries, to London for a conference on Arabia.

The Foreign Office, however, viewed Husayn's request as awkward. Given the early stage of their consideration of Faysal for monarch of Mesopotamia, it was deemed desirable to avoid any action or language likely to be regarded as a commitment to him. A visit by Faysal, including an audience with King George V, was certain to bring unwanted publicity, and equally undesirable was the enmity of France which surely would develop from such a visit so soon after the Syrian episode.

An indication of the implacable hostility of France toward Faysal was given at Hythe on 8 August when Lloyd George and Curzon casually mentioned the possibility that Faysal would be chosen by the Mesopotamians, and that in such a case Britain would be bound seriously to consider such a request.[67] Millerand and Berthelot explained how Mesopotamia would then become a focus of intrigue against Syria and how the effect in France would be disastrous. On 17 August the French chargé d'affaires volunteered that the enthronement of Faysal would be regarded as *"un acte peu amical vis à vis de la France."*[68] On 9 October a note arrived from the French government raising objections even to Faysal's coming to London, which led Curzon to suggest that the visit be postponed.

Nevertheless, on 16 November Curzon informed M. Cambon that "we could find no excuse for further postponement" and that Faysal would be received early in December on a "complimentary mission." He studiously avoided making the assurance that Mesopotamia would not be discussed. He simply noted with "absolute candour" the prospect that Faysal would wish to discuss certain aspects of the Arabian question

---

pressed is evident in his plea to Haddad on 29 September in which he reported twelve telegrams from his father, each telling him to proceed at once, and closed: "I want you to do your utmost to get me out of this place" (Haddad to Cornwallis, 6 October 1920, in E12391/9/44, *ibid.*).

67. *Documents*, 8:716–22.
68. M. de Fleuriau, 17 August 1920, in 5876, I.O.

and the future of the "large block of territory between or adjoining . . . Syria and Mesopotamia," adding that the position of France in Syria, past or present, would not be brought up.[69]

Accordingly, Faysal had an audience with the king on 4 December, gave assurances that Abdullah would cause no trouble in Transjordan, and participated in three discussions at the Foreign Office, on 2 December and on the 13th and 20th of January.[70] It was immediately apparent that agreement was lacking as to the purpose of these meetings. The British government viewed the presence of Faysal as an opportunity to "bring restraining influences to bear on King Hussein and the Emir's brothers," the first object being to induce the Hijaz to ratify the Treaty of Versailles and to sign and ratify the Treaty of Sèvres.[71] Instead, Faysal sought to reopen the question of the promises contained in the original Husayn-McMahon correspondence dealing with the sharifians.

At the first meeting (with Sir John Tilley) there was a reaffirmation of loyalty and friendship and a request by Faysal for a statement of British intentions. In his encounter with Curzon at the meeting on 13 January, Faysal dwelt entirely on the precarious situation in Arabia proper: the menacing activities of Ibn Sa'ud and the threat of invasion, which Curzon deemed exaggerated. Faysal also complained bitterly of the withdrawal of the wartime subsidy to Husayn while Ibn Sa'ud was receiving a handsome payment. Curzon advised him that a plan of balanced subsidies to all the Arabian chieftains was under consideration and could be used as a deterrent, through the threatened stoppage of payments, against acts of belligerency. Again, no mention was made of either Mesopotamia or Transjordan.

At the third meeting, chaired by R. C. Lindsay, Faysal accepted the principle and manner of equal subsidies but expressed differences of interpretation with regard to the 1915–16 correspondence. He made specific reference to the Arab right to Palestine and the Syrian towns of

69. Curzon to Earl of Derby (Paris), no. 3724, W2113/1946/17, F.O. 406/44; this was reaffirmed on 23 December (Curzon to M. de Fleuriau, E16027/9/44, W.O. 106/204).

70. Minutes of the meetings are found respectively in E16103/9/44, F.O. 406/44; E757/4/91, F.O. 406/45; and E986/4/91, *ibid*.

71. Tilley to Army Council, 14 December 1920, 8846 of P. 6002, I.O.; see also "Foreign Office Memorandum on Possible Negotiations with the Hedjaz," prepared by Young on the eve of Faysal's visit, 29 November 1920 (confidential, 11615), E14959/9/44, C.O. 732/3.

Damascus, Homs, Hama, and Aleppo, and to Arab apprehensions, which were preventing ratification of the Treaty of Versailles, as to the meaning of the word "mandate" and about the mandate principle. The meeting ended with Lindsay advising that the right of the king of the Hijaz to have a voice in the future of all the Arab peoples could not be acknowledged until the Arabs themselves expressed a wish for him to represent them.

Although Curzon described the meetings as "quite infructuous," having been "devoted to a now belated and rather controversial analysis of the meaning of old pledges and the extent to which they have or have not been observed,"[72] they did succeed in illustrating Faysal's personal desire to cooperate with Great Britain, his powers of conciliation, and the plausibility of using the sharifians once again for British purposes, in the original spirit, if not in the letter, of the Husayn-McMahon correspondence.

The logical beginning was Mesopotamia, but overtures to Faysal were delayed until advice could be received from Sir Percy Cox. Finally, on 2 January, Cox wired that consultation with local notables was extremely undesirable and that there were no really suitable native candidates; the initiative in the matter of Faysal would have to come from London.[73]

With Cox's go-ahead in hand, on 7 January Curzon provided Cornwallis with confidential instructions on how to approach Faysal. He was to offer advice on a personal basis, suggesting that Faysal terminate the London discussions by coming to a reasonable settlement without delay, return to Mecca, and persuade Husayn for his own benefit to ratify the Treaty of Versailles. At the same time Husayn should propose a son as a candidate for Mesopotamia, preferably Faysal, who would then inform the Mesopotamians of his willingness; if they accepted him, Faysal would have his "chance of uniting a large portion of the Arab race under a single Arab Government."[74]

At the private meeting between Faysal and Cornwallis on 8 January,

72. Curzon's minutes on negotiations with Faysal, undated, 8675, C.O. 732/3.
73. Cox to India Office, telegram 148S (clear the line), 2 January 1921, in E277 of F.O. 371/6349.
74. E583, *ibid.* No evidence of an earlier meeting on 17 December could be found in the Foreign Office records, although it was alluded to by P. W. Ireland in *Iraq: A Study in Political Development* (London: Jonathan Cape, 1937), p. 309.

Faysal's response was to be deeply grateful but to reject the proposal. "My father, who really wants Abdulla to go to Mesopotamia would never approve, and he and all the people would believe that I am working for myself and not for my nation, in agreement with the British. I will never put myself forward as a candidate. My honour is my dearest possession and I will never allow myself to be accused of self-interest. I have already caused enough strife in Islam."[75] Faysal expressed full support for the claim of Abdullah to the Mesopotamian throne; however, he did say that he would accept the task if the Mesopotamians said they wanted him and if Great Britain rejected Abdullah. Thus Cornwallis concluded that two paths were open to the British: either they could arrange for Abdullah to go to Mesopotamia, or Cox could "quietly and unostentatiously . . . engineer the election of Feisal." Cornwallis personally preferred the latter, since Faysal was "by far the better man and would serve us loyally and well." But Churchill was as yet unconvinced. "A little more time and consideration are needed before definitely launching Feisal. I must feel my way and feel sure of my way."[76] Nevertheless, by the time of Churchill's departure for Cairo, the Middle East Department had committed itself to a sharifian for Mesopotamia, and preferably Faysal.[77]

By March, 1921, after years of vacillation and drift, hope was offered for a fresh approach to the Arab world because of an unusual conjunction of favorable aspects: (1) men deemed competent were stationed at various points in the Middle East; (2) the area itself presented an opportunity, perhaps the last, for Great Britain to regain her former prestige; (3) the aims of British policy had been debated and refined; (4) a single department, reflecting the important distinction at last made between the Near East and the Arab Middle East, was coordinating and

75. E583, F.O. 371/6349.
76. Churchill to Lloyd George, 8 January 1921, in F/9/2/53, Lloyd George Papers.
77. The first item on the agenda drawn up by the Middle East Department (primarily by Young and Lawrence) prior to the conference regarded the selection of an Arab ruler in Mesopotamia as an essential preliminary and stated that "Feisal should be the ruler" (9837, C.O. 732/3). Lawrence mentions talks between Churchill and Faysal, although no evidence of this could be found by the author in either the Colonial Office or Foreign Office files; see Robert Graves and Liddell Hart, *T. E. Lawrence to His Biographers* (London: Cassell, 1963), p. 144. However, the detailed memorandum by the Middle East Department does confirm Lawrence's claim that the important decisions had been made in London.

British Policy in the Arab World

implementing policy from London; (5) a person of admitted energy, enterprise, and imagination had been empowered to safeguard Britain's empire in the East; and (6) a conference of all the leading experts was about to take place to blend these assets into a coherent policy adapted to change and appropriate for governing relations in the decades ahead.

Thus, despite the opinion of *The Times* that "no more disturbing proceeding than the suggested gathering at Cairo" was imaginable,[78] the secretary of state for the colonies, accompanied by a select group of experts, departed for Marseilles on 3 March en route to Cairo.

78. *The Times*, "Mesopotamia and Mr. Churchill," 23 February 1921, p. 11.

THE CAIRO CONFEREES Front row: *Winston Churchill, center, with Sir Herbert Samuel on his right, Sir Percy Cox on his left. Second row: Sir Arnold T. Wilson, first from left; Gertrude Bell, second from left; Ja'far Pasha, center; T. E. Lawrence, fourth from right; Hubert Young, first from right.*

CHAPTER 6 **The Cairo Conference,
March, 1921**

*It made straight all the tangle, finding solutions fulfilling
(I think) our promises in letter and spirit (where humanly
possible) without sacrificing any interest of the peoples
concerned. So we are quit of the war-time Eastern
adventure, with clean hands, but three years too late to
earn the gratitude which peoples, if not states, can pay.*
—T. E. Lawrence, *Seven Pillars of Wisdom*

The Cairo Conference opened formally on 12 March 1921. In attendance were forty experts on one or more facets of British policy in the Middle East—the high commissioners and general officers commanding in Palestine and Mesopotamia, the general officer commanding in Persia, the resident for the Persian Gulf, the governor of Somaliland, the resident at Aden, and their respective civilian and military staffs.

At the first session Winston Churchill explained his object in calling the conference and outlined the program to be followed. The participants then split up into two groups to conduct the business of the conference: a Political Committee, presided over by the secretary of state for the colonies, and a Military and Financial Committee, presided over by Sir Walter Congreve. The two committees would meet together when political and military proposals were coordinated or considered side by side. Between forty and fifty sessions were held at the Semiramis Hotel during the next twelve days in what was described as "utmost secrecy."[1]

The discussants on Mesopotamia were to confine themselves to three

1. *The Times*, dispatch from Cairo, 26 March 1921, p. 8.

105

political and interrelated considerations. First was the question of the immediate reduction of British military commitments, for "no local interest can be allowed to stand in the way. . . ."[2] However, this resolve could not be considered independently of the political future of Mesopotamia, which necessitated the prior formation of a local government "of real prestige and authority," which in turn posed the question of the relative positions of His Majesty's Government and the future Mesopotamian government under the mandate. As prior agreement had been reached between Sir Percy Cox and General Haldane on military reductions, the second item was given the closest attention under the following points:

(a) Whether there was to be an Arab ruler or not.
(b) If yes, whether he should be a member of the family of the sharif of Mecca.
(c) If so, whether there was any member of that family who was clearly preferable to all others, both from the British point of view and from that of the people of Mesopotamia.
(d) Whether the Arab ruler should be selected by the British government or by the Arab Council of State in Baghdad.
(e) Whether it was desirable or necessary that the National Assembly should meet before the ruler assumes office.
(f) Whether the ruler should offer himself as a candidate or be invited by Mesopotamia to accept the office.
(g) At what stage the offer or invitation should be made.
(h) On what date the ruler should proceed to Baghdad to take up his position.

At the first meeting of the Political Committee Sir Percy Cox was invited by Churchill to describe the steps he had found it necessary to take when he arrived in Mesopotamia. Late in 1920 it had been essential to set up at once some form of provisional government under the respected Naqib of Baghdad; yet it was deemed impossible that Mesopotamian affairs should be conducted by this government indefinitely. Cox felt that another long delay in replacing the provisional Council of State with a more competent authority could not be tolerated.

2. "Report on Middle East Conference Held in Cairo and Jerusalem" (secret), F.O. 371/6343, p. 36. Unless otherwise indicated, succeeding quotations in this chapter will be from these official minutes contained in F.O. 371/6343.

British Policy in the Arab World

As alternative candidates for ruler, Cox mentioned the Naqib, Sayyid Talib, who was minister of the interior in the Council of State, the *shaykh* of Muhammara, Ibn Saʻud, the Agha Khan, and a Turkish prince, Burhan al-Din. But he dismissed each of these on grounds of politics or character, and only one alternative remained: a member of the sharifian family. This solution would, he thought, be welcomed by the majority of Mesopotamians, provided it was not too obvious that the sharifian was being nominated by the British government. Cox proposed that since machinery was already in full swing for the election of the promised National Assembly, the Assembly could be convened to vote for a ruler within six weeks of his return.

Churchill, however, challenged this approach on procedural and political grounds, his main point being that if Britain was to spend money on Mesopotamia she could not be expected to acquiesce in the selection of whatever ruler the Assembly might choose. Consequently, the candidate's name had to be put before the British government at some stage for its approval; and this could not really be done after a legislative assembly had voted for him. Before proceeding to discuss the exact method of selection, Churchill, as chairman, asked Cox to explain the reasons why, among the sons of Husayn, Faysal was preferable to Abdullah from the Mesopotamian point of view. Cox replied that Faysal's previous military experience during the war and his experiences with the Allies made him better qualified as a ruler than any of his brothers. Although this explanation charitably avoided reference to the *débâcle* at Maysalun or French antipathy toward Faysal, it was supported by Colonel Lawrence, who depicted Abdullah as lazy and by no means dominating, while Mesopotamia needed a ruler who would be an active and inspiring personality.

The chairman broadened the discussion by offering a strong argument in support of the sharifian policy in general, since it enabled the British to bring pressure to bear in one Arab sphere in order to attain their ends in another. If Faysal knew that his father's subsidy, the protection of the Holy Places from Saʻudi-Wahhabi attack, and Abdullah's position in Transjordan were all dependent upon his own good behavior, he would be much easier to deal with. The same argument applied, *mutatis mutandis*, to King Husayn and Amir Abdullah. Lawrence and Miss Bell joined Churchill in rejecting the French warning that by adopting a sharifian policy Churchill would risk being destroyed by a monster of his own creation.[3]

By the end of the first day of the conference it was apparent that agreement existed as to the wisdom and utility of a sharifian solution to the Mesopotamia question in the person of Faysal.[4] The necessity for British approval and for speed were also acknowledged. Only the process of selection presented real difficulties.

The second meeting of the Political Committee (on the 13th) therefore was devoted to various aspects of a timetable drawn up by Cox on the procedure to be adopted in the event of Faysal's appointment. It was generally agreed that Faysal should arrive in Mesopotamia by the end of May, on the assumption that his presence in Mesopotamia would have such an inspiring effect on the population that there would be little if any opposition to his candidacy. As Lawrence emphasized, "it was most undesirable that the Sherif should in any way carry on an election campaign in person."[5]

Churchill then sent a personal, secret cable to the prime minister which began: "Prospects Mesopotamia promising." He expressed the likelihood of a unanimous conclusion that Faysal offered "hope of best and cheapest solution" and suggested that the formula be: "In response to enquiries from adherents of Emir Feisal the British Government have stated that they will place no obstacles in the way of his candidature as Ruler of Iraq, and that if he is chosen he will have their support." He continued:

On the receipt of your assent to this formula I shall tell Lawrence he can communicate formula to Feisal. On this, Feisal will at once proceed to Mecca, passing through Egypt on the way. We do not want any announcement, even in guarded terms, of formula if it can be possibly avoided until . . . the middle of April. Method of choice will require careful study in order to avoid confused or meaningless expression of Mesopotamian opinion.

---

3. While vacationing in Nice after accepting his new position, Churchill had met with M. Millerand and leading officials of the French Foreign Ministry in Paris on 11 January. He confided to Lloyd George his impression that the French were "very ready to be conciliatory and accommodating to us at the present time" (Churchill to the Prime Minister, 12 January 1921, in F/9/2/54, Lloyd George Papers).
4. Agreement was facilitated by the fact that the London and Baghdad delegations had arrived in Cairo fully intent upon promoting the candidacy of Faysal.
5. F.O. 371/6343, p. 42.

Time is short as Sir P. Cox must return, and all my plans depend on clear settlement with him before we separate.[6]

Churchill ended by asking the prime minister to telegraph favorable answers on this and related points within three or four days so that a definite and detailed program of action could be drawn up.

A reply was forthcoming from London on the 16th.[7] Since the government had hinted on several occasions that it would not veto Faysal's candidacy if there was a strong demand for him and if peace might thereby be restored in Iraq, it would be hard to reconcile this attitude with the procedure proposed by Churchill. The prime minister, also citing concern for French reaction, therefore insisted that the real initiative in any demand for Faysal should come from Mesopotamia. Lloyd George reminded Churchill of Faysal's insistence that he would not become a candidate until the claims of Abdullah had been disposed of.

Two days earlier the Political Committee had met for the third time to discuss the question of the foreign relations of Iraq under the mandate, but again had failed to reach any conclusion. Instead, the discussion returned to the subject of Faysal. General agreement was reached on the revised timetable submitted by Cox, Lawrence, and Miss Bell. According to the schedule, when Faysal arrived in Mecca he would telegraph influential figures in Mesopotamia saying that, because he had been repeatedly urged by his friends to come to Mesopotamia, and because the British government had assured him that if the people wanted him it was not disposed to stand in his way, he had discussed the matter with his father and brothers and had decided to offer his services to Iraq. On 23 April, having seen the primary effect of this message, it would be announced that he or a representative would come to Mesopotamia during the month of Ramadan. The enthusiasm engendered by the announcement and arrival of Faysal, it was hoped, would be so great as to remove the need to ask the Assembly to discuss the question of a ruler; they would simply convene to confirm his nomination. Thus, by 8 June Faysal would be in a position to dissolve the provisional govern-

6. Churchill to the Prime Minister, received at the Colonial Office on 14 March 1921, F.O. 371/6342, p. 1. Largely due to the influence of Sir Percy Cox, "Iraq" was used with increasing frequency as a desired alternative for "Mesopotamia," and the two terms will be used synonymously hereafter.
7. *Ibid.*, p. 2.

ment and to call upon the Naqib, or someone else, to form a cabinet. The two Mesopotamians accompanying Cox to Cairo, Sassoon Effendi and Ja'far al-'Askari, ministers of finance and defense, respectively, in the existing Council of State, were then called in and asked for their views. Both agreed that of the three men whom they considered as the most prominent candidates—namely, the Naqib, Sayyid Talib, and Sharif Faysal—the last-named would be most welcomed by the country at large.

A fourth and final meeting of the Political Committee was held on 15 March to discuss the future of Kurdistan. Sir Percy Cox, reflecting the opinion of the Mesopotamians and supported by the loyal Miss Bell, maintained that those divisions in which the Kurds were predominant—Kirkuk, Sulaimaniya, and districts north of Mosul—formed an integral part of Iraq.

He was immediately challenged by Major Young, who countered with a proposal to set up a Kurdish state without delay, one which would be under the direct control of the high commissioner and not a part of, or responsible to, the Iraqi government. Young was supported by Major Noel, the foremost British authority on the Kurds, who thought the Kurds would prefer home rule and might be a useful buffer state against both Turkish pressure from without and Iraqi anti-British movements from within.

Churchill was inclined to agree with the latter suggestion and, with remarkable prescience, conceived a situation in which a future ruler, "with the power of an Arab army behind him, . . . would ignore Kurdish sentiment and oppress the Kurdish minority."[8] The committee finally adopted Major Young's recommendation to keep Kurdistan separate from Iraq but it mollified Cox by stipulating that this arrangement be maintained until such time as a representative body of Kurdish opinion might opt for inclusion in Iraq.

Important decisions affecting British financial and military responsibilities in Mesopotamia were taken during concurrent sessions of the combined Political and Military committees. On 13 March Churchill set the tone for these meetings when he pointed out that it was essential that the reductions of troops be accelerated by all possible means, and that very considerable economies be effected without delay. On the as-

8. F.O. 371/6343, pp. 60–61.

sumption that the program to install Faysal could be carried out satis-factorily, it was decided that the garrison in Mesopotamia would be reduced from thirty-three to twenty-three infantry battalions as fast as shipping could be made available. Proportionate reductions in staff, auxiliary services of all kinds, followers, and animals would follow. Resultant savings were estimated at £3,750,000 and would reduce the anticipated expenditure for Mesopotamia and Palestine in 1921–22 from £31,000,000 to £27,250,000. A second stage of reduction might then begin in October to bring the forces in Mesopotamia down to ap-proximately the number in a permanent garrison, about 15,000 men.

In pursuing the prospects for a second stage of reduction, the joint committee was under pressure from Churchill, who termed as "quite insufficient" the saving of nearly four million pounds from the immedi-ate reductions already arranged. Success depended to an even greater extent upon two rather uncertain factors: first, the development of a local Kurdish force and Arab levies of 5,000 Mesopotamians, promised by Ja'far Pasha, to relieve British garrisons on the border; and second, the adaptation and development of air power.

The utility of airplanes for reducing expenditures was advocated by Air Marshal Sir H. M. Trenchard. He had submitted memoranda to the Cabinet several times during 1920 propounding greater emphasis on the air force. Finding Churchill increasingly receptive, he chose the Cairo Conference as an opportune occasion for presenting a "Scheme for the Control of Mesopotamia by the Royal Air Force."[9] Essentially, his scheme called for the concerted use of an Arab army, the Royal Air Force, and armored cars, the latter forces operating from not more than three main bases. Auxiliary aerodromes would be maintained, guarded by detachments of the Arab army, at various points throughout the country. Wireless communication, armored cars, an efficient intelligence system, and the positioning of main bases along the railroad would all help to ensure the principal value of the air in maintaining internal order: its ability to answer requests for assistance "with an air of celer-ity which no other arm is capable of." Trenchard estimated that twelve squadrons of the Royal Air Force would be adequate to fulfill this role.

On 16 March, impressed by the savings inherent in such a scheme,

9. *Ibid.*, pp. 74–78. For an example of his earlier efforts, see "Air Staff Memoran-dum on the World Situation, May 1920," C.P. 1467 in CAB 24/107.

and giving consideration to "the vital necessity of preparing and train-ing an Air Force adequate to our needs in war, the importance of testing the potentialities of the Air Force, the need for giving its superior offi-cers and staffs the experience in independent command and responsibil-ity,"[10] the joint committee accepted in principle Trenchard's proposal. The air scheme, with its attendant desert routes, was to become a central feature of British strategic thinking thereafter.

Two other items pertaining to Mesopotamia had been entered on the formal agenda: refugees and various financial questions. About 14,000 Armenians and 800 Russian refugees were in camps near Basra, while nearly 20,000 Assyrians were located near Mosul. Sir Percy Cox warned that it would be difficult to provide for the support of these refugees after 1 April; it was neither desirable nor thought possible that they might be absorbed into Mesopotamia. The conference therefore recom-mended that the Armenians be transferred to some port on the Black Sea; that the Russians be shipped to Egypt to join others of their com-patriots until such time as political conditions allowed for their return to Russia; and that no alternative existed but to give the Assyrians some arms for their protection and turn them out to make their way back to their own country if possible. But such measures, despite their severity, hardly touched the surface of the far more pervasive problem of minor-ity groups dispersed throughout the Arab world. These would contrib-ute to the area's heterogeneity, and therefore to its complexity, while frustrating any simplified version of Arab nationalism.

In the matter of financial relations with the Mesopotamian govern-ment, it was agreed that the British government would be responsible for any net difference between all expenditures and receipts up to 31 March 1921. Imperial assets were to be disposed of as soon as it was convenient. They were to be offered to the Mesopotamian government at a fair valuation, but if that failed, they would be offered to private persons or companies. This quest for revenue, however, did not prevent Churchill from rejecting a bid by Sir Arnold Wilson to purchase the Mesopotamian railways on behalf of an English firm. Churchill consid-ered such a transaction inadvisable, for, if the conference policy proved successful, more advantageous offers could be expected in the future. Thus one more reason was added for achieving political stability in Iraq: it would attract British private enterprise and thus relieve the

10. F.O. 371/6343, p. 73.

government of the liability of finding fresh capital for the railways and other sectors of the economy. The Mesopotamian budget, it was decided, should meet all civil charges in the future, and in addition provide a contribution to imperial military charges in the form of an Arab army.

Despite careful attention to such military and financial matters, Churchill was cognizant of the importance of Faysal's enthronement for the success of his policy of economy with honor. His primary concern, therefore, was to gain Cabinet sanction for the formula briefly suggested in his telegram of the 14th, especially since decisions were being made at Cairo on this assumption. Not having yet received the prime minister's reply of 16 March, the colonial secretary dispatched a telegram that day in which he presented definite proposals for action on which the authorities "have reached complete agreement on all points, both political and military."[11] He appended the proposed procedure regarding Faysal, policy in Iraq and Kurdistan, military forces, and the three stages of reducing the garrisons, with resultant savings, all of which were contingent upon the course of events, successful political administration, and "immediate energetic action."

Upon receiving Lloyd George's telegram of 16 March, which expressed concern that publication of the suggested formula would antagonize the already sensitive French, Churchill realized that misunderstanding had arisen between Cairo and Downing Street. This prompted him to send a further cable on the 18th assuring that the formula had not been intended for publication but as "a definite indication of the limits within which our policy could be framed."[12] He concurred in the need to secure "a spontaneous movement" for Faysal but warned that "unless we have a mind of our own on the subject it is by no means certain that this will occur." He described the variety of claimants, none of whom was judged suitable, as complicating the situation and jeopardizing the sharifian system, which was deemed the "only workable policy."

In justifying the selection of Faysal over Abdullah, Churchill pointed

11. Churchill to the Prime Minister, received at the Colonial Office on 16 March 1921, F.O. 371/6342, pp. 3–5. Despite this claim of unanimity, the minutes of the conference reveal an occasional sharp divergence, such as that between Cox and Young on the Kurds, as well as personality clashes. For an alleged heated exchange between Lawrence and Gertrude Bell, see Sir Reader Bullard, *The Camels Must Go* (London: Faber & Faber, 1961), p. 121.
12. Churchill to the Prime Minister, 18 March 1921, F.O. 371/6342, pp. 5–6.

not only to the comparative weakness of the latter but to an important political consideration. Choosing Abdullah for Mesopotamia would only ensure the failure of British policy in two directions at once by putting the weak brother on the throne of Iraq while leaving the active brother loose and discontented to work off his grudges against the French by disturbing Transjordan. Apparently the willingness of an unrequited Abdullah to foment trouble against the British in Transjordan and Palestine still was not fully appreciated in Cairo, except perhaps by Samuel. Churchill also offered insight into later attitudes toward the election of Faysal when he defended the need for the amir to come to Mesopotamia personally. Only his evocation of mass enthusiasm would make an election unnecessary; anything less than this course might lead to "an incoherent verdict by a small majority in favour of an unsuitable candidate at elections scarcely worthy of [the] name in so scattered and primitive a community."

Because all the proposals for Mesopotamia were contingent upon the choice of Faysal, the colonial secretary feared that the reservations expressed by Lloyd George would endanger the work thus far accomplished at Cairo. Consequently, he ended the telegram with a strong statement.

I have given my closest attention to this whole matter, and am supported by the advice of best and most responsible authorities on the subject. Considering that you were in favour of Feisal before I took this office, and that I even had to exert myself to delay a Cabinet decision in his favour till I had considered the question more fully, I could not help being disconcerted by the first part of your telegram of the 16th. I do hope you will give me personally the support to which I am entitled in a task which I certainly have not sought.

Having argued that French dislike of Faysal could not stand in the way of British interests, Churchill also dismissed the notion that Faysal would not contest Abdullah's claim: "we think we are very much better informed of his real views and wishes." For the sake of Great Britain Faysal had to be installed in Baghdad.

With the arrival of Sir Herbert Samuel on 16 March, the Cairo Conference turned its attention to that portion of the agenda which dealt with Palestine. In opening the first meeting of the Palestine Political and Military Committee the following day, Churchill stated that the policy of His Majesty's Government in Palestine would be discussed under two topics, the first being the local development of Palestine, with particular reference to the Zionist question. How had the four intervening years affected the British-Zionist relationship as originally conceived in the Balfour Declaration? Could Palestinian Arab opposition to the latter and the demand for self-determination still be reconciled with a Jewish national home? The second topic was a general and external view of developments in Palestine as affected by both present and future British policies in Mesopotamia and Arabia. In other words, how might the sharifian solution, its unlikely application to Palestine, and the need to reduce the imperial garrison all be related to the critical situation in Transjordan?

In a memorandum prepared earlier in London, the Middle East Department set forth those factors which had contributed to the dilemma over Transjordan. Under the terms of the draft mandate Great Britain would be responsible for establishing a national home for the Jews in Palestine. She was also bound by the assurances given to Sharif Husayn in 1915 to recognize and support Arab independence in those portions of the Turkish *vilayet* of Damascus in which she was free to act without detriment to French interests. The western boundary of that *vilayet* had been the Jordan River. Palestine and Transjordan were not, therefore, on quite the same footing. Transjordan, the intervening territory between Palestine and Mesopotamia, had essentially comprised area B as defined in the Sykes-Picot agreement, but the Anglo-French separation in 1920 virtually precluded the formation of an Arab state under their joint auspices.

As originally drafted, the mandates for Palestine and Mesopotamia had assumed the two territories to be coterminous. At the same time, the areas were economically interdependent, and it was felt that their development ought to be considered as a single problem. Yet His Majesty's Government had been entrusted with the mandate for "Palestine." If the British wanted to assert a claim to Transjordan and to avoid raising with the other powers the legal status of that area, they could do so only by proceeding on the assumption that Transjordan formed part of the area covered by the Palestine mandate. After all, neither the Balfour Declaration nor the draft mandate contained a definition of actual boundaries. In default of this assumption, according to the Treaty of Sèvres the area would be left to the disposal of the principal Allied Powers. Then again, if Transjordan were subsumed under the Palestine mandate, some means would have to be found of giving effect to the terms of the mandate there which were consistent with the "recognition and support of the independence of the Arabs." But criticism, especially from the Zionists, could be expected if all the terms of the Palestine mandate were not applied literally to the whole territory for which responsibility was accepted. Urgency was added to complexity by the news received at Cairo that Abdullah had advanced from Ma'an into Transjordan and had entered Amman.[13]

Sir Herbert Samuel agreed with the departmental view that Transjordan should be included under the British mandate. He advocated that the territory be administered on different lines from Palestine, partly owing to the question of Zionism, but that it definitely should not be regarded as an independent Arab state. He felt, however, that the main concern of the moment was to deal with Abdullah—who continued to regard Faysal as king of a Syria embracing Transjordan—if possible by combining "our Sherifian with our mandatory policy."

Churchill expressed the hope that the decision which had been arrived at in previous meetings of the conference with regard to Mesopotamia might also prove to be a solution for Transjordan. "It had seemed best to support the Sherifian cause; in fact no other alternative presented itself."[14] To support a sharifian in Iraq and not in Transjordan, Churchill reasoned, would be to court trouble. Efforts were being made in Iraq and Arabia to obtain the good will of the sharifian family and, most important for the future, to place them as a whole under an obligation to Great Britain; admittedly, Abdullah's moral influence was therefore of great importance. As the colonial secretary viewed the situation, objections to the enduring argument for garrisoning Transjordan were compelling: the force might be either more than Britain could afford financially or, alternatively, so small as to be unsafe. In Churchill's own words, "we must make more bricks with less straw." The only alternative left was to make satisfactory arrangements with Abdullah aimed at curbing his activities, in the first instance against the French, and possibly against Zionist settlements.

13. See *The Times*, 18 March 1921, p. 9. For an account of Abdullah's exploits and reception, see Khayr al-Dīn al-Ziriklī, *'Āmān fī 'Ammān* (Cairo, 1925), esp. pp. 27–34.
14. F.O. 371/6343, p. 98.

British Policy in the Arab World

Although Churchill's opinion was received favorably, most of the conferees voiced strong reservations as to the desirability of appointing Abdullah as ruler. Samuel was the first to register an objection and was followed by Lawrence, who thought a governor should be appointed. Lawrence feared that the French might make overtures to Abdullah regarding the vacant throne in Damascus and that these would lead to the absorption of Transjordan into the French orbit. Major Young was also in favor of an alternative to Abdullah, if it was possible to find one.

The absence of a more suitable candidate proved decisive in the debate; the fact was that Abdullah now sat in Amman. When asked for his opinion, Deedes opposed the appointment of Abdullah, but felt that the only course was to accept his appointment as a *fait accompli*. Major Somerset similarly pointed to the strength inherent in Abdullah's position; in his opinion it would be impossible to get rid of Abdullah in the event of his not being appointed, or of his refusing to agree to the conditions of the appointment. By the close of the meeting three possible alternatives had been discerned: (1) appointment of Abdullah, for which it would be necessary to obtain his good will; (2) appointment of a local governor endorsed by Abdullah, who would himself withdraw from the territory; (3) dispatch of a military expedition to eject Abdullah. The third alternative was regarded as out of the question, despite General Radcliffe's opinion that the reduction of British forces in the Black Sea, Mesopotamia, and Constantinople now made it possible actually to occupy Transjordan by force. Colonel Lawrence typified the shift of sentiment which had taken place in the course of the day. Having originally discounted the amir, he now thought the appointment of a loyal and amenable, but inactive, sharif to be unobjectionable; it was his belief that neither Britain nor Amir Abdullah was strong enough at present to hold Transjordan without assistance from the other.

The Palestine Military Committee was therefore appointed to consider and submit a report on the first two alternatives mentioned above. It met that same day, proceeding on the assumption that either Abdullah or his nominee, both of whom were friendly to Great Britain, would be appointed governor of Transjordan with the general consent of the inhabitants. It was at this meeting, devoted to military matters, that Captain Peake first submitted a scheme for the composition, strength, and cost of the local forces which was eventually to lead to the creation of the Arab Legion. While it was agreed that the Palestine garrison would consist of 7,000 men (having been reduced in the last six months from 25,000), Air Vice Marshal Salmond provided a plan for the future governance of Transjordan which was similar to that proposed for Iraq. Accordingly, the R.A.F. squadron in Palestine, reinforced when necessary from Egypt, would fly over Transjordan once a month; attention would be given to possible types of air force action, and landing grounds, wireless stations, and petrol storage centers would be established at Irbid, Amman, and Kerak.

Another subject for discussion between Churchill, Samuel, and their military advisers was the proposed Palestine defense force. The high commissioner indicated his intention to form a defense force of two battalions—one each from the Jewish and Arab communities—during the forthcoming fiscal year. In supporting the plan, he cited the feeling of the Jews that it was only equitable for them to defend their own national home, especially since the state of British public opinion regarded the shedding of British blood and the spending of British money in defense of the Zionists as unjust and unnecessary. By appealing to the patriotism of young Jews, he hoped to obtain sufficient recruits, and at a low rate of pay. Then, in order to avoid arousing grievances among the Arabs, he proposed to make them the same offer. Although he doubted that the Arabs would be satisfied by these conditions, at least there would then be no justification for complaints against the Jewish force. Even if this ambitious scheme succeeded, Samuel candidly admitted that Palestine would, for "political reasons," require British troops in the country for as long as could be foreseen.

His proposal met with immediate criticism from the conference's military members, who preferred an efficient and adequate gendarmerie to local forces, which they viewed as a thinly veiled attempt to create a Jewish national army. The latter force could not be employed in Palestine except within restricted Jewish areas; nor was its use in operations outside Palestine advisable, because of the religious feeling that would be provoked throughout the Arab world. Still, Samuel persisted, and he eventually received the support of Churchill, who thought that, bearing in mind the international character of the Zionist movement and the desire expressed by the Jews to help in their own defense, it would be better to opt for troops rather than a gendarmerie.

These discussions of a Palestine defense force illustrate at a glance the obstacles that would be encountered repeatedly by the British and

the Zionists in the decades ahead. Great Britain would instruct her officials to treat both communities impartially, delicately balancing the interests of both Arab and Jew. Yet, in the last analysis, she would have
to fill the thankless role of arbiter, with no prospect of a terminal point.
The Zionists, despite their efforts on behalf of the land, would find themselves opposed by the Palestinian Arabs and regarded as intruders by
the larger Arab world.

On the basis of the joint sessions of the Political and Military committees, Churchill was in a position to send a telegram to the prime
minister on 18 March 1921.[15] He began by advising that, given the large
troop reductions already effected in Palestine, he could not recommend
any further measures at the moment. Then, surprisingly, he continued:
"We consider it necessary immediately to occupy militarily TransJordania." He offered the following reasons for reversing his previous and
long-standing opposition: (1) to secure a settled government there
which would prevent Palestine's being disturbed by raids; (2) to stop
the present intrigues against the French, which incidentally provided the
only means Britain had of "gilding the Feisal pill"; (3) to facilitate
the reopening of the Hijaz Railway and the re-establishment of the pilgrimage to Mecca.

Churchill admitted that military occupation was only one of the re-
quirements for effecting this revised policy toward Transjordan; reaching a satisfactory arrangement with Abdullah was another. "As we cannot contemplate hostilities with Abdullah in any circumstances, there is
no alternative to this policy. We must therefore proceed in co-operation
and accord with him." As his main justification for abandoning resistance to the idea of armed occupation, Churchill offered the following:
"Abdullah with best will in the world will not be able to restrain his
people from disturbing the French and even making war upon them unless he is fortified and restrained at once by presence of a British force,
which must be strong enough to provide for its own safety." He also
termed the development of this projected policy a definite part of the
more general policy of friendship and cooperation with the sharifians,
which also harmonized with the adopted plan for Mesopotamia. By his
own admission Churchill had been swayed by the arguments presented
by Sir Herbert Samuel, General Congreve, and Colonel Lawrence. Yet

15. Churchill to the Prime Minister, F.O. 371/6342, pp. 6–7.

he personally accepted full responsibility, informing Lloyd George: "I have no doubt whatever that occupation of Trans-Jordania on basis of an arrangement with Abdullah is right policy for us to adopt, and that it will afford best prospect of discharge of our responsibilities with future reductions of expense."

Once the comprehensive nature of the sharifian policy—which would regulate British involvement in Mesopotamia, Palestine, Transjordan, Arabia, and, indirectly, Syria—was fully impressed upon Churchill, he became its leading proponent. If "my policy" of an arrangement with the sharifians were fully accepted and successfully carried, he wrote the prime minister, then Palestine and Mesopotamia together ought not to require more than £8,000,000 in 1922–23, as against the present £30,000,000.

So great was Churchill's enthusiasm, so meticulous his planning both before and at Cairo, that he even volunteered the proposed text of a message intended to reassure the French: "So far from our acquiescence in a Feisal candidature for Mesopotamia, if desired locally, being an embarrassment to you, it is, in fact, through our concomitant arrangements with Abdullah in Trans-Jordania the surest means of securing you from disturbance and annoyance from Arabs in south." The colonial secretary then concluded his long telegram of the 18th by notifying Lloyd George of his intention to meet Amir Abdullah on the 28th in Jerusalem and requesting authority to approach him, then, in order to "settle with him on line above set forth."

While awaiting a reply to his several cables, Churchill and his aides continued to dispose of agenda items. Regarding Aden and Somaliland, the conference decided on several measures for reducing expenditures, including the use of airplanes on both sides of the strategic Gulf of Aden.

In order to ensure a further reduction of the Aden garrison it was judged necessary to establish satisfactory relations with the ruler of Yemen. The imam was proving an irritant by his claims to Aden and all of the Tihama and by his conflict with the idrisi of Asir. With Ibn Saʿud supporting the latter, King Husayn felt inclined to endorse the claims of the imam. Should they materialize, these alliances would destroy the fragile equilibrium on the Arabian peninsula, upon which British preponderance depended.

On 18 March the Cairo Conference accepted the recommendation of

Sir Geoffrey Archer, governor of Somaliland, for the complete amalgamation of the Aden and Somaliland administrations as part of the ambitious effort to bring economy and greater efficiency to the Middle Eastern and African possessions or "sacred trusts" of Great Britain. This measure helped to solidify British control in the Red Sea and to enhance the strategic value of Aden during the next half-century.

The conference next turned its attention to a number of subjects listed under the agenda's general category. The colonial secretary approved the recommendations of a committee which had discussed the question of the civil services for the countries dealt with by the Middle East Department. Then, on 21 March, at the fifth meeting of the Political Committee, the subject of subsidies was raised as a possible instrument for balancing the rival forces in Arabia mentioned previously.

Churchill set the tone for the discussion by stating that in all matters he was anxious to effect economies, though he fully realized it might pay in certain cases to grant subsidies, provided a corresponding relief was effected in expenditures on the maintenance of garrisons. The conference proceeded to frame a comprehensive policy for subsidies to the independent rulers of Arabia. The subsidy to Ibn Sa'ud was increased from £5,000 a month to £100,000 per annum. In strange contrast to the general spirit of confidence in the sharifians which prevailed at Cairo, a subcommittee referred to Ibn Sa'ud as "the greatest factor in Arabian politics"[16] and as a moderating influence on his Wahhabi subjects, who were restrained mainly by his skillful use of the British subsidy. Great Britain's interests required that he refrain from armed action against Kuwayt, the Hijaz, and Mesopotamia. With particular reference to the latter, the committee concluded: "To increase his subsidy during the uncomfortable period appears prudent."[17]

As for King Husayn, it was decided that enough subsidy be paid to enable him "to put his house in order" and, on grounds of principle, that he be paid the same rate as Ibn Sa'ud and on identical terms—that is, monthly payments in arrears conditional upon fulfillment of certain obligations. In the case of Husayn the obligations were: ratifying the Treaty of Versailles and signing and ratifying the Treaty of Sèvres, which implied acceptance of both the mandatory principle and the dis-

16. F.O. 371/6343, p. 189.
17. *Ibid.*, p. 190.

posal of the Arab countries; respecting the British treaties already in existence with Ibn Sa'ud and the idrisi, and refraining from all aggression against them; improving the condition of the pilgrimage to Mecca; recognizing the rights and interests of British subjects in the Hijaz; accepting a British consul and agent at Jidda and, if necessary, a British Muslim agent in Mecca; preventing the holy places from becoming a focus for anti-British or Pan-Islamic intrigue; and dissuading branches of the sharifian movement from taking anti-French action, particularly in Syria.

It was anticipated that the institutions of representative government in Mesopotamia and Transjordan, together with the renewal and increase of his subsidy, would satisfy King Husayn and persuade him to accept British advice as he had in the past. The Cairo Conference completed its scheme for neutralizing the several warring camps of the Arabian peninsula through subsidies to each by providing comparable largesse to the idrisi, Imam Yahya, and to Fahad Bey of the Anizah tribe, which occupied land vital to the projected air route across Mesopotamia.

The colonial secretary repeatedly emphasized the necessity for carrying out a farsighted policy of imperial aerial development in the future. He foresaw the day when the route connecting Egypt with Mesopotamia and India would be one of the main air routes of the British Empire, shortening the distance to Australia and New Zealand by eight or ten days. At his direction a committee examined the possibilities of opening up a motor route across the desert from Palestine to Iraq and recommended that it should run through Ma'an, Jauf, and Baghdad. Anticipating the significance of oil in the area, attention was also given to the cost and feasibility of a railway and pipeline traversing the Fertile Crescent, linking the Persian Gulf fields to the Mediterranean port of Haifa.

Given the presence of the high commissioners for Mesopotamia and Palestine, the opportunity was taken to discuss the draft mandates and the Anglo-French accord reached the previous December. As to the latter—which provided for a joint delimitation of boundaries between Palestine and Mesopotamia and the French territory of Syria—it was decided to begin with the Palestine-Syria line, leaving Mesopotamia for later action. No opposition to the wording of the draft mandates was expressed by either Cox or Samuel, although the validity of proposed arrangements for Kurdistan and Transjordan was questioned.

Accordingly, Churchill cabled the Colonial Office on 21 March, asking whether the Cairo proposals would necessitate any special provisions being made in the two mandates. "If it is absolutely necessary from a legal point of view that slight inconsistencies in our treatment of these areas should be authorised . . . it would be better to specify areas affected without referring in detail to proposed difference in treatment."[18] Upon receipt of this cable informal consultation took place between the Colonial Office legal adviser and the assistant legal adviser to the Foreign Office. Their suggestion, relayed to Cairo on the 25th by Shuckburgh, was that, "however undesirable it may be for His Majesty's Government themselves to propose alterations of the mandates at this stage,"[19] a clause be inserted in each of the mandates. Article 16 of the Mesopotamian mandate would read thereafter: "Nothing in this mandate shall prevent the mandatory from establishing such an autonomous system of administration for the predominantly Kurdish areas in the northern portion of Mesopotamia as he may consider suitable." Similarly, a new Article 25 was proposed for insertion in the Palestine mandate. It read:

In the territories lying between the Jordan and the eastern boundary of Palestine as ultimately determined, the mandatory shall be entitled to postpone or withhold application of such provisions of this mandate as he may consider inapplicable to the existing local conditions, and to make such provision for the administration of the territories as he may consider suitable to those conditions, provided no action shall be taken which is inconsistent with the provisions of articles 15, 16 and 18.[20]

Those assembled having deliberated on the mandates and having endorsed a proposal to constitute the Hijaz Railway as a single *waqf*, or

18. *Ibid.*, p. 208.
19. *Ibid.* Minutes of the informal consultations are in file 13896 of C.O. 732/5.
20. The first draft of Article 25 was originally worded "to postpone the application of such provisions," but was altered at Shuckburgh's initiative since " 'postpone' means, or may be taken to mean, that we are going to apply them eventually. I suggest 'withhold.' " In an urgent letter to the Foreign Office on 24 March, the Colonial Office explained that Article 25 had been framed in such a way as to enable Britain "to set up an Arab administration and to withhold indefinitely the application of those clauses of the mandate which relate to the establishment of the National Home for the Jews" (13896, C.O. 732/5). At the same time the economic interests of the League members, the religious freedom of the inhabitants, and the liberty of missionary enterprises in Transjordan were expressly safeguarded by Articles 15, 16, and 18.

Muslim trust, to be managed jointly by agents of France, Great Britain, and the Hijaz, the Cairo phase of this unprecedented Middle Eastern conference came to an end. Further meetings would be held in Jerusalem to discuss questions affecting Palestine and Transjordan. Thus far the conference had run smoothly and, with perhaps the one exception of Transjordan, according to the recommendations embodied in the memorandum drawn up beforehand by the Middle East Department.

Much of the work accomplished by Churchill and his colleagues in Cairo, however, was jeopardized by Lloyd George's continued silence. Having been alerted to a Cabinet meeting scheduled for the following day, Churchill cabled the prime minister (requesting Cabinet circulation) on 21 March, pleading for a vote of confidence and reasonable latitude in the handling of Faysal's Mesopotamian candidacy. Admitting that there would be local opposition to Faysal, "owing to vigorous pressing of personal claims by rivals on the spot," and noting that "much intrigue is rife" in the absence of Sir Percy Cox, he nevertheless stated unequivocally his position and that of the Cairo conferees: ". . . we have no doubt whatever that the best guarantee for stability of government and quick reduction of expense and responsibility would be adoption of Feisal by a substantial preponderance of public opinion. In all the Arab world there is no other competing principle capable of maintaining an Arab State on modern lines than the Shereefian."[21] What had begun as an exercise in pragmatism had been expanded at Cairo into a principle to be applied wherever possible, beginning with Mesopotamia and then spreading to Arabia and Transjordan. Endorsed by the professionals at Cairo and championed by no less a political figure than Churchill, the sharifian idea was to prevail in London and become a pillar of the British imperial structure.

Finally, on 22 March Lloyd George sent a very urgent and secret cable to Churchill which began, "Cabinet devoted exhaustive consideration to your proposals this morning. They were much impressed by collective force of your recommendations. . . ."[22] It went on to assure Churchill of Cabinet approval for his timetable on Mesopotamia, noting Cox's return to Baghdad after as little delay as possible, Faysal's de-

---

21. Churchill to the Prime Minister, cable received 21 March 1921, F.O. 371/6342.
22. Prime Minister to Churchill, 22 March 1921, *ibid.*, p. 9; see also CO14449 in C.O. 730/9.

parture for Mecca for consultations with his father, "who appears from our latest reports to be in a more than usually unamiable frame of mind," and the precaution that no announcement or communication would be made to the French until Faysal had offered himself to the people of Mesopotamia. Approval was also given to the Cairo proposals regarding Kurdistan and the steps leading to troop reductions, while the question of proposed subsidies to the Arab chiefs, not appearing to demand an immediate decision, was left for closer scrutiny by the India, Foreign, and Colonial offices and the Exchequer in London.

Lloyd George then informed Churchill of the considerable misgivings entertained by the Cabinet in discussions of the proposals for Transjordan. Three arguments were presented. First, it was thought that the almost simultaneous installation of the two brothers in regions contiguous to the French sphere of influence would be regarded with great suspicion by the French as a deliberate plot to menace their position in Syria. Second, Churchill was reminded of his former opinion, still maintained in London, that occupation would involve a military commitment, the extension and duration of which it was impossible to forecast. Third, it was not clear that Abdullah would quietly accept his position in "a territory too small for a Kingdom." Abdullah's presence and the general desire to fulfill earlier promises to Husayn were seen as favoring "an Arab rather than a Palestinian solution"; but the price to be paid, as calculated from London, seemed to be high and the results doubtful. Wishing to acquaint Churchill with these misgivings, the Cabinet advised him: "you should not exclude other plans from your mind," for instance, treating Transjordan as "an Arab province or adjunct of Palestine" while preserving the Arab character of the area and administration.

Churchill's reply to the Cabinet telegram, making particular reference to Transjordan, was delayed twenty-four hours while he, contrary to assurances given Lord Curzon and the press, involved himself personally in Egyptian affairs. Aware of the anti-British sentiment prevailing in the streets of Cairo and Alexandria,[23] and buoyed by his success

---

23. Descriptions of the climate in Egypt at the time of the Cairo Conference are offered in Jack Frishman, *My Darling Clementine: The Story of Lady Churchill* (London: W. H. Allen, 1963), pp. 67–74, and by Major Somerset in a letter of 12 March to his father, Somerset Papers, St. Antony's College.

at the conference, Churchill accepted an invitation to meet with the Sultan. On the morning of 22 March, accompanied by High Commissioner Allenby, Churchill presented himself at Abdin Palace and listened while the Sultan of Egypt criticized his own prime minister, Adli Pasha, denounced the extremists, and voiced the hope that no agreement would be reached. Churchill could not resist venturing a personal belief that the premature publication of the Milner report had gravely prejudiced British interests, but that "we shall not surrender" to the demands of Zaghlul and the agitators.[24] In commenting before the Cabinet on 21 April, Lord Curzon criticized this intervention by Churchill and used the opportunity to denigrate Churchill's ability to deal with the Arabs. ". . . the Sultan displayed in this interview many of those characteristics which a closer familiarity with the regions which the Colonial Secretary has now taken under his sway will teach him are inseparable from the conversations of Oriental potentates, and, indeed, that His Highness consistently and successfully 'pulled the leg' of my colleague."[25]

After this brief digression Churchill returned to the sphere of his responsibility—the Fertile Crescent—and drafted a reply to the prime minister's telegram of the 22d. If disappointed, he offered no such indication; rather, his tone was conciliatory. He expressed gratitude for the approval given his general policy and provided a message for Faysal from Lawrence which read: "Things have gone exactly as hoped. Please start for Mecca at once by quickest possible route leaving Haddad temporarily as Hedjaz representative in London. I will meet you on the way and explain details. Say only that you are going [to see?] your father, and on no account put any [thing?] in press."[26] With Faysal's cooperation steps would be undertaken to implement the Mesopotamian decisions of the Cairo Conference; with the attitude of Abdullah as yet undetermined, Transjordan was proving far more difficult.

The remarks made by Churchill in this cable on the intended ruler

---

24. "Memorandum on the Situation in Egypt" (secret), 22 March 1921, C.P. 2832, CAB 24/122.
25. C.P. 2871, *ibid.* To this Churchill retorted in a letter to the prime minister on 13 June: "I am not at all prepared to sit still and mute and watch the people of this country being slowly committed to the loss of this great and splendid monument of British administration, skill and energy" (F/9/3/56, Lloyd George Papers).
26. Churchill to the Prime Minister, received at the Colonial Office on 23 March 1921, F.O. 371/6342, p. 11.

and status of Transjordan are important in light of later developments. Claiming not to have made himself quite clear in previous dispatches, he stated: "We do not expect or particularly desire, indeed, Abdullah himself to undertake Governorship. He will, as Cabinet rightly apprehend, almost certainly think it too small. . . . But that his influence should be upon our side . . . is the vital point. . . . The actual solution which we have always had in mind and for which I shall work is that which you described as follows: 'while preserving Arab character of area and administration to treat it as Arab province or adjunct of Palestine.' "[27] If such were Churchill's intentions, they were to be altered by his next conversation with an "Oriental potentate," Amir Abdullah ibn Husayn, in Jerusalem.

Shortly after his arival at Government House, the official residence of the high commissioner in Jerusalem, Churchill received a deputation of the Executive Committee of the Haifa Congress on 28 March. The president of the congress, Musa Kazim Pasha, presented him with a lengthy memorandum setting forth the position of the Palestinian Arabs. It began by questioning the impartiality of Sir Herbert Samuel, who, it was charged, persisted in ignoring the Arab congress while, on the other hand, "he recognised Zionist Congresses, congratulated them, encouraged them and wished them good luck."[28] Nevertheless, Churchill was assured of the friendship of the Arab for the Englishman, if only Great Britain would rectify her policy. The Arabs, confident of the justice of their cause, were convinced that "this unnatural partitioning of their lands must one day disappear." Yet, if Britain did not take up the cause of the Arabs, other powers, perhaps Russia or even Germany, would eventually do so.

The memorandum next turned to the Zionists, describing them as incapable of being true to anyone and having only one aim in life, from which they could not be diverted. Taking issue with the Jewish quest for a national home while underlining the threat inherent in Jewish immigration and the selection of Jews for high positions in the administration, the delegation proceeded to dissect the Balfour Declaration from a legal, historical, moral, and economic perspective, at one point term-

27. *Ibid.*, p. 10.
28. F.O. 371/6343, pp. 142–50; see also Appendix B. The memorandum, sent to the League of Nations in April, is document C.3.M.3 in *Records of the Permanent Mandates Commission,* 1921.

ing it "an act of modern Bolshevism, pure and simple." The memorandum went on in this strident tone until it concluded with a request for five immediate actions by the British government: (1) abolition of the very principle of a national home for the Jews; (2) creation of a national government; (3) cessation of Jewish immigration; (4) a halt as well to new legislation until a national government came into being; and (5) an end to the separation of Palestine from her sister states.

Churchill delivered himself of a forceful and direct reply. He reaffirmed Sir Herbert Samuel's role as the responsible representative of the Crown in Palestine. Describing what he had just heard as a "partisan statement," he refused to repudiate the Balfour Declaration or to veto Jewish immigration; "it is not in my power to do so, nor, if it were in my power, would it be my wish."[29] Taking issue with the interpretation offered by the delegates as to who had liberated Palestine from Turkish rule, he declared Britain's presence there to be based on trust and right. Similarly, he considered that a national center would be good for the world, the Jews, the British Empire, and, ultimately, for the Arabs dwelling in Palestine. Churchill concluded by seeking to assuage the Arabs' fears, calling them unfounded; he predicted that a Zionist success would be accompanied by a general diffusion of wealth and that the Arabs would yet come to see the validity of his policy of promoting good will among all sections of the Palestine community.

The Arab deputation was followed by one representing the Jewish community which also presented Churchill with a memorandum.[30] In sharp contrast to the approach taken by members of the Arab congress in their first encounter with the new colonial secretary, the Jewish National Council of Palestine began by expressing its gratitude toward the British government for the Balfour Declaration, acceptance of the mandate, and the appointment of Sir Herbert Samuel. They struck a cordant note by voicing the hope that a Jewish renaissance would have an invigorating influence on the Arabs and promised to assist the mandatory in its "historic task."

In reply, Churchill professed himself to be "perfectly convinced that

29. F.O. 371/6343, pp. 150–53; see also Appendix C of this volume.
30. Ibid., pp. 153–55; see also Appendix D of this volume.

the cause of Zionism is one which carries with it much that is good for the whole world."[31] Still, he warned of Arab alarm and suspicion which it would be the task of the Zionists to dispel. In describing his own duty to try to reassure and encourage both groups, he called for "enthusiasm and energy, restraint and forbearance," on the part of the Zionists. Wary of the opponents awaiting him in England, he candidly told the deputation on 28 March: "You must provide me with the means, and the Jewish community all over the world must provide me with the means of answering all adverse criticism. I wish to be able to say that a great event is taking place here, a great event in the world's destiny."[32]

That same day, his energy and enthusiasm unabated, Churchill met Amir Abdullah, who had been escorted across the Jordan River by Lawrence, in the first of their three conversations on Transjordan and the proposed sharifian policy of Great Britain. At this and subsequent meetings Churchill was accompanied by Sir Herbert Samuel, Deedes, Colonel Lawrence, and Major Young, while Auni Abdul Hadi acted as secretary and translator to the amir.

Churchill began by indirectly criticizing the old British policy in the Middle East for its want of coordination; he then assured his Arab listener of Britain's wish to "revert to the original policy of supporting Arab nationality on constructive lines, using the Sherifian family as a medium,"[33] although not in Syria or "Palestine west of the Jordan," nor in Arabia, where sharifian suzerainty was unacceptable. The possi-

---

31. *Ibid.*, pp. 155–56; see also Appendix E. Churchill had given an earlier indication of his attitude toward the Zionist effort in an article which appeared in the *Illustrated Sunday Herald* on 8 February 1920 under the title "Zionism versus Bolshevism: A Struggle for the Soul of the Jewish People," p. 5. It was his thesis that Zionism should be fostered as an effective counterweight to the appeal of Marxism among the Jews.

32. F.O. 371/6343, p. 155. M. Medzini's *Eser Shanim shel Mediniut AretzYisraelite* (Tel Aviv, 1928), p. 173, contains the Hebrew text. The following day Churchill repeated his avowal that "my heart is full of sympathy for Zionism," this time at a public gathering at the proposed site of the Hebrew University on Mount Scopus (F.O. 371/6343, pp. 156–57) ; see Appendix F.

33. F.O. 371/6343, p. 107. Although Churchill in his memorandum on Transjordan (submitted on 2 April 1921 as C.P. 2315; see CAB 24/122) refers to four interviews with Abdullah, the official minutes of the Cairo and Jerusalem conferences contain the records of only three; see F.O. 371/6343, pp. 107–14, and Graves, *Memoirs of King Abdullah*, pp. 202–5.

bility of Faysal's being invited to Mesopotamia was disclosed in the hope that it would dissuade Abdullah from taking any direct, unilateral action against the French during the ensuing critical period. The amir's response to these remarks was positive. As to Mesopotamia he said he had no personal feeling, claiming that his having been proclaimed king of Mesopotamia in 1920 was Faysal's doing and against his own warning that it would embarrass His Majesty's Government.

Abdullah repeatedly emphasized this desire to cooperate with Great Britain and to make the policy as outlined for Mesopotamia a success. Churchill thus felt that such a warm climate justified an exploratory discussion of Transjordan. He described it as a part of the mandate responsibility accepted by Great Britain, which recognized Transjordan's Arab character but which thought it was too small to stand alone and therefore proposed that it be constituted as an Arab province under an Arab governor responsible to the high commissioner for Palestine. When asked for his view, the amir urged an Arab ruler over Palestine and Transjordan who would have the same relationship to the high commissioner as Faysal would in Iraq.

Having taken up the Palestinian cause momentarily, and meeting resistance from both Churchill and Samuel, Abdullah allowed the conversation to return to the narrower question of Transjordan. He asked for a more detailed explanation of what the duties and responsibilities of the Arab governor would be. These were outlined for him by Churchill, who volunteered that a British force would be put at the governor's disposal in order to help him establish and maintain peaceful conditions. He was also advised that Transjordan would not be included in the administrative system of Palestine, "and therefore the Zionist clauses of the mandate would not apply." Abdullah pronounced himself impressed by the policy outlined and prepared to consider the matter in the light of these new proposals, especially since the colonial secretary depicted the pacification of Transjordan as vital to France's eventual acceptance of the sharifian solution.

At the second meeting between Abdullah and Churchill, speaking for himself personally, Abdullah guaranteed to keep Transjordan quiet, submitting that his recent presence in the territory had been merely to defend it from French attacks. But he made the guarantee temporary, pending his father's decision on the British proposals being carried to him by Faysal. Replying to a question by Churchill, he said he would rather not have British troops in Transjordan during the month which would elapse before King Husayn could make a decision.

While the colonial secretary appreciated Abdullah's frankness, he believed that something more definite and lasting should be arranged. At their third meeting, therefore, he made a private proposal to the amir, suggesting that the amir himself remain in Transjordan for a period of six months to prepare the way for the appointment, with his consent, of an Arab governor under the high commissioner at the end of that time. Such support in money and troops as was necessary would be given Abdullah; in addition, a British political officer would act as his chief adviser, assisting in the restoration of order and setting the revenues of the territory on a proper basis. In return for this support Abdullah was asked to guarantee that there would be no anti-French or anti-Zionist agitation, to cooperate in establishing secure conditions under the British mandate, and to assist in opening up the transdesert route to Mesopotamia.

The amir replied that after full consideration he had decided to accept the proposal, asking only that he be regarded as a British officer and trusted accordingly.[34] He was grateful to Churchill for having realized the difficulties of his position and promised to do everything he could to ensure the success of the proposed arrangement. He cautioned, however, that it would be difficult to restrain the tribes from their traditional, periodic raids against Syria, but agreed to Lawrence's suggestion that the attention of the raiders be drawn to their more immediate neighbors within Transjordan. Nor was this the last time that Abdullah used rival factions within Transjordan to balance his personal position as ruler.

Both sides were pleased at this informal arrangement, which did not necessitate the use of British troops, and the amir took his leave, while an exuberant Churchill informed the Cabinet: "Abdulla has now returned to Amman to begin work for us." Both on financial and military

---

34. Churchill's invitation apparently did not come as a surprise to Abdullah, for he claimed that Lawrence had informed him of the prospect on their way to Jerusalem. (Suleiman Mousa, *T. E. Lawrence: An Arab View* [London: Oxford University Press, 1966], p. 240). Both Lawrence and Churchill intimated to the amir that his controlling the territory effectively could lead to a personal reconciliation with the French and "might even lead to his being instated by them as Emir of Syria in Damascus" (*ibid.*, p. 8).

grounds, Churchill had felt justified in independently modifying the two major decisions at Cairo regarding Transjordan: the positioning of British troops in strength at Amman, and the preference for an Arab governor recommended by Abdullah rather than Abdullah himself. In addition, and at his own discretion, he had promised the amir a grant of £180,000. As he explained to the Cabinet: "It is no use pretending that this plan will be as satisfactory as the sending of the force originally specified, but it will cost very little and we run no risk of an entanglement. . . . If the matter had not been treated in this general way, no local agreement would have been possible, and a very disturbed situation would quickly have arisen."[35] Thus the deep reluctance of the former war secretary to commit British soldiers and the willingness of Abdullah to convert his presence in Amman into personal gain[36] combined to extend the general sharifian policy, almost as an afterthought, to Transjordan.

Because the arrangement with Abdullah depended so heavily upon its acceptance by France, Churchill took pains to consult with the two leading French authorities in Syria. While in Jerusalem he met with M. de Caix in what he described as "a long and not unsatisfactory interview." The French deputy high commissioner began by pressing strongly for a British garrison south of Syria, but after listening to Churchill's explanation he accepted the arrangement without objection of any kind.

Still not content, on 31 March, while en route to Alexandria, Churchill sent a personal letter to General Gouraud expressing disappointment at their not having been able to meet during his visit to Palestine. He briefly explained the sharifian orientation of British policy and the arrangement with Abdullah "of an informal and temporary character," noting that the principal difficulty for the amir would be the Syrian exiles in the northern part of Transjordan. Accordingly, he suggested a French political amnesty which would be synchronized with one already intended for Mesopotamia so as to give the Arab world the impression that the two European powers were working hand in hand. He concluded by assuring Gouraud that the Colonial Office would do everything in its power to further and facilitate French interests and the se-

35. C.P. 2815, CAB 24/122.
36. Sir Alec Kirkbride, in an interview with the author, described Churchill's action as "an academic exercise" and a case of "justifying after the event."

British Policy in the Arab World

curity of French territory and hoped for similar aid from the French.[37]

On 30 March Churchill left Jerusalem and returned to England via Alexandria, having for nineteen days engaged in examining and discussing the Middle Eastern problem, in all its manifestations, with the officials concerned. He could reflect upon his successful experiment with satisfaction. Questions which normally might have involved protracted correspondence between departments in London and continual references to the respective authorities on the spot were settled in a few hours' friendly discussion. In addition, Churchill could claim, as the official report chose to do subsequently, that "not only did the Conference work out the measures necessary to ensure an immediate and substantial reduction in Imperial expenditure, but opportunity was taken to frame a common policy for the future."[38] British officials in the Arab world had been included in the decision-making process; basic decisions had been made regarding particularly the Fertile Crescent; personal contact had been established with both the Palestinian Arabs and the Zionists; the threat posed by Abdullah no longer seemed relevant; and French cooperation had been solicited once again.

Churchill, however, could not afford to be content with these accomplishments in Cairo. Returning to the Colonial Office in London on 11 April, he immediately began to prepare for a defense of his policy before the Cabinet, Parliament, and the press. While the daily press, straining to break the secrecy surrounding the Cairo deliberations, engaged in conjecture and reported numerous accounts and rumors,[39] the colonial secretary wished first to gain Cabinet approval before reporting publicly on his mission. To those of his colleagues who took issue with his arbitrary handling of Abdullah, Churchill offered assurance that his proposals really involved a diminution rather than an increase of responsibility.[40] He was able to convince skeptics and opponents, such as

---

37. F.O. 371/6343, p. 114. The fact that Churchill's effort at coordinating policy with the Syrian authorities failed is indicated in a letter from Curzon to Lord Hardinge (Paris) on 15 September in which Curzon noted that neither a reply to nor an acknowledgment of Churchill's letter of 31 March had been received; see E10247/7250/89 (no. 2448), F.O. 406/47.

38. F.O. 371/6343, p. 12.

39. See, for example, *The Times* of 26 March (p. 8), 5 April (p. 10), 6 April (p. 9), and 12 April (p. 9) 1921, and the *Daily Mail* of 23 March (p. 6) and 9 May (p. 6) 1921.

40. Conference of Ministers, 11 April 1921, CAB 23/25, vol. 7.

Lord Privy Seal Austen Chamberlain and Curzon, that the subsidies were not on an extravagant scale and thus gained their grudging consent.

At a morning session of the Cabinet on 31 May, Churchill complained that before his departure for Cairo the chancellor of the Exchequer had agreed on a sum of £39,000,000 for the Middle East but that during his absence the sum had been reduced by more than nine million pounds, thus making it impossible for him to make a financial statement which would be satisfactory to the House of Commons. The Cabinet agreed to make the necessary adjustment. Later that day Churchill presented the Cabinet with a more comprehensive exposition of the proposed policy in light of developments within the Arab world since the conference. Reviewing once again his action in Transjordan, Churchill claimed that summoning Abdullah to Jerusalem had frustrated by only forty-eight hours the probability of his taking serious action against the French.[41] Because of this need to convince his colleagues and to clarify minor differences with his successor at the War Office, Churchill's speech to the House of Commons, originally scheduled for early April, was postponed until 14 June.

A sense of the importance which he gave to the preparation of this speech is imparted in a minute from the colonial secretary to Shuckburgh on the morning of the 14th.

There are a few questions to be settled. (1) Let me have a note in about three lines as to Feisal's religious character. Is he a Sunni with Shaih [sic] sympathies, or a Shaih with Sunni sympathies, or how does he square it? What is Hussein? Which is the aristocratic high church and which is the low church? What are the religious people at Kerbela? I always get mixed up between these two. (2) You do not seem to have checked the Palestine figures at all. I only put them in out of my head. Vernon must check them all—troops, money, population. Every figure must be checked and ticked.[42]

Then, despite his own lack of expertise about the underlying aspects of the Arab world, its social, cultural, historical, and religious background, Churchill concluded: "You must remember that my audience, both those who will hear and those who will read, are almost entirely ignorant of

---

41. Cabinet meetings 44 (21) and 45 (21) of 31 May 1921, CAB 23/25, vol. 7.
42. 14 June 1921, 29674, C.O. 732/5. Despite Churchill's ignorance of the religious qualification, considerable concern did exist over a sharifian Sunni for the throne of Iraq (with its large Shiite population) ; see The Times, 5 April 1921, p. 9.

the whole story and take hardly any interest in any part of it except how much money is to be taken out of their pockets." His meticulous preparation, together with this correct assessment of his audience, resulted in a presentation which Austen Chamberlain called "a great success," one that "changed the whole atmosphere of the House on the Middle East question."[43]

The Commons had before it a motion that a supplementary sum be granted to defray salaries and expenses in connection with Middle Eastern services, and Churchill rose to defend it before a full gallery.[44] He began by emphasizing his belief with regard to the pledges given and responsibilities accepted in the Middle East, that "it is our duty to persevere" and by doing so to find "an honourable and inextravagant and ultimately prosperous issue from our affairs." Indeed, it was such confidence which had led him to accept the position of secretary of state for the colonies and to organize the Cairo Conference. He reported that it had been decided in London that Britain would pursue a policy of achieving enormous reductions in military strength and expenditures while at the same time carrying out the undertakings accepted during the years immediately before and after the armistice; in Cairo procedural and substantive conclusions had been reached easily and unanimously. As a direct consequence of the conference, "we have a single clear policy upon which all the authorities, military and civil, are at the present time agreed."

Churchill then proceeded to enumerate the measures being taken to carry out successfully this "policy of reduction and appeasement" in Iraq, Palestine, Transjordan, Syria, and Arabia. The Cairo decisions, if fully implemented and if "our anticipations are not overthrown by events," would result in a reduced expenditure for the year 1922–23 of from nine to ten million pounds, thus constituting a considerable relief to the British taxpayer.

Having alerted his listeners to possible savings, Churchill spoke at length about Iraq—the largest single item of expenditure—and of the quest for a qualified ruler. He cautioned his audience: "We have no intention of forcing upon the people of Iraq a ruler who is not of their own choice. At the same time, as the Mandatory Power . . . we cannot

43. Note to the Prime Minister, 14 June 1921, F/7/4/10, Lloyd George Papers.
44. *Parliamentary Debates* (Commons), 5th ser., 143 (14 June 1921) : 267–90.

remain indifferent or unconcerned in a matter so vital to us. . . . The situation is not free from delicacy or uncertainty, and I must pick my words very carefully." Still, he could report that Faysal, already on his way to Iraq, had been assured of the countenance and support of Great Britain, since he offered the best prospects for a happy and prosperous outcome.

Mention of Faysal enabled Churchill, warming to his subject, to expand upon the relationship between Great Britain, the Arabs, and the sharifians. Great Britain, should she so desire, could perpetuate the policy of keeping the Arabs divided, "of discouraging their national aspirations, of setting up administrations of local notables in each particular province or city, and exerting an influence through the jealousies of one tribe against another." Or, as was the decision, she could give satisfaction to Arab nationality; and, for this purpose, "the very best structure around which to build, in fact, the only structure of this kind which is available, is the house and family and following of the Sherif of Mecca." Working in concert with King Husayn and his sons would enable Great Britain to further disengage from "the problems, burdens, and responsibilities of these embarrassing regions." On this central point events were to prove Churchill wrong, however, for subsequent decades witnessed rather a deepening engagement by Great Britain in all parts of the Arab region based on the commitments made in 1921.

Emphasis was next given to several features of the new policy toward Palestine: the Zionist movement was described as the "only cause" of unrest in Palestine; the Arabs were assured that their position would be protected, while the Jewish pioneers were praised for their dedication and achievements; the British role was to persuade the former to concede, the latter to forbear, and, despite the apparent difficulties, "with patience, coolness, and a little good fortune we may find a way out of them"; the status of Transjordan was reaffirmed to be "one of the most valuable parts of Palestine." In mentioning the subsidies Churchill added a dimension which had not been stressed at Cairo: "We shall pay only in so far as good behaviour is assured, and if injury is done by one of these parties to the other a deduction will be made from the subsidy of the aggressor and handed over, in the form of compensation, to the victim." Bringing his speech to a climax, he appealed once more for a return to Anglo-French cooperation in both the Near and Middle East. Likewise, he warned that all these efforts would be frustrated unless combined with a peaceful, lasting settlement with Turkey. Churchill, champion of the British Empire, ended on a note of determination: "We must have the means of defending our vital interests, and we must show that we possess those means, and that in the last resort we are not incapable of using them. Otherwise there is absolutely no limit to the extent of humiliation and maltreatment which will be inflicted."

Although the supplementary allocation was approved a month later, the immediate reaction to Churchill's speech was somewhat mixed. Earl Winterton praised it as "closely reasoned and well-knit" and thought the Cairo Conference would be "of the greatest possible present and future benefit to the whole British Empire."[45] A writer for *The Times* described the speech as built upon optimism, but with first-rate intellectual material; an accompanying editorial, however, was more cautious: "His speech leaves an impression that he is building upon foundations dangerously unstable and that he is incurring contingent liabilities which, should they eventuate, this country might not be able to sustain."[46] Editorializing, the *Daily Mail* feared that the policy as a whole simply could not be afforded, while the *Morning Post* confined its criticism to Palestine, where "the Jewish Government" had to be supported by British bayonets and British machine guns.[47] The Jewish press also was divided in its comment. The *Palestine* welcomed the speech as "a corroboration of our Zionist hopes," despite one or two less satisfactory passages; the *Jewish Chronicle*, on the other hand, viewed it with deep disappointment, terming it an attempt to whittle down the Balfour Declaration and "no other than a piteous piece of political dissimulation."[48] Perhaps the strongest criticism came from Mr. Asquith, leader of the Opposition. Rising to debate the Colonial Office vote on 14 July, he attacked Churchill's plans as a "staircase of fragile, precarious, crumbling hypotheses."[49]

Nevertheless, given the accumulated grievances over past and present details of Great Britain's policy, or lack of policy, toward the Arab world, the speech by Churchill was regarded as a triumph for his fresh initiative. He had succeeded in gaining Cabinet endorsement, in placat-

45. *Ibid.*, cols. 290 and 298.
46. *The Times*, 15 June 1921, pp. 10 and 11.
47. *Daily Mail*, 15 June 1921, p. 6; *Morning Post*, 15 June 1921, p. 10.
48. *Palestine*, 9, no. 14 (18 June 1921) : 106; *Jewish Chronicle*, 17 June 1921, p. 7.
49. *Parliamentary Debates* (Commons), 5th ser., 144 (14 July 1921) :1526 and 1528.

ing Parliament, and in marshaling public support for his effort in the Middle East—this at a time when Great Britain was straining under the threat of labor strikes and the Irish rebellion and with the London Conference on Turkey having ended in disappointment. Yet, whatever the reaction at home, the Cairo Conference could succeed or fail only to the extent that its decisions were properly implemented in Iraq, Palestine, and Transjordan.

CHAPTER 7 **Iraq**

> *...The progress of this country is dependent on the
> assistance of a nation which can aid us with men and
> money. And as the British nation is the nearest to us and
> the most zealous in our interests we must seek help and
> cooperation from her alone in order that we may reach our
> goal as speedily as possible.*—King Faysal in his accession
> speech, August, 1921

Selection of the first monarch of Iraq dominated that country's politics throughout most of 1921. It was of central importance for Sir Percy Cox and the Colonial Office, as well as for the leading urban and tribal figures within Mesopotamian society. The coronation of King Faysal on 23 August, in conformity with the general decision taken at Cairo, thus represented a turning point in the modern history of Iraq, bringing a degree of stability which contrasts sharply with the strife, uncertainty, and partial breakdown in administration that characterized the period 1914–20 and the deep social and political instability that has continued in Iraq since World War II. However, the enthronement was also the culmination of a process, engaging the full effort of the British authorities, which itself bears closer examination.

Rumors of British support for Faysal had been rife in Baghdad since the latter part of 1920. As early as 11 August the French paper *Matin* reported that Faysal was being offered Mesopotamia as compensation for the loss of Syria.[1] These rumors stimulated intense debate, with

1. Vol. 5876 of 1920, I.O.

support for Faysal, or Abdullah, countered by the advocacy of other potential candidates. Sharifian propaganda and suspicion of British intentions increased in February with the return to Mesopotamia of a party of ex-sharifian officers and their families from Syria; one of them, Nuri al-Sa'id, was particularly "anxious to boom Faisal" and took an increasingly active role in the campaign.[2] The delegation accompanying Sir Percy Cox, comprised of known sharifian supporters—Miss Bell, Garbett, and especially Ja'far Pasha al-'Askari—also was regarded as ominous. Nevertheless, the colonial administration was able to report that as of 1 March "the political situation remains quiet, and the work of the National Government is proceeding smoothly. Any consensus of opinion as to the appointment of an Amir seems to be as far off as ever."[3]

Then, in Cox's absence, the anti-sharifian forces began to emerge, led by the elderly Naqib of Baghdad and the ambitious minister of the interior, Sayyid Talib. Edgar Bonham Carter, left in command in Baghdad by Cox, sent an urgent cable on 23 March to his superior in Cairo.

Since your departure the situation has changed considerably. There is no doubt that in anticipation of the arrival of the Sherifian officers and expected propaganda on behalf of Faisal, Talib came to an agreement with the Naqib; . . . they put forward the claims of an Iraqi ruler for Iraq. There are indications that this claim receives a considerable measure of support, and there is I think no question but that Faisal's candidature will be strongly resisted. . . .[4]

The news occasioned serious concern among those assembled at Cairo that local opposition in Mesopotamia would frustrate the most important element of the sharifian policy. Consequently, Cox was asked to hasten his return and to direct the delicate project.

2. The officers, expelled from Syria by the French, languished in Egypt while their case became a subject of interdepartmental discussion in mid-1920. Although a good deal of political importance was attached to them, it was not until 24 September that Montagu cabled Mesopotamia: "It has been decided to take action at once for repatriation. . . . Incidence of cost can be determined later." See W.O. 106/200 and vol. 5268, I.O. Shortly after his arrival, General Nuri, brother-in-law of Defense Minister Ja'far Pasha al-'Askari, was given the position of chief of the General Staff; see Intelligence Report no. 8, 1 March 1921, in 17770, C.O. 730/1.
3. *Ibid.*
4. Hicom (Baghdad) to Cox (clear the line), telegram T/99 (no. 63), C.O. 730/14.

Arriving at Basra in the first week of April, Cox was confronted by a list of six individuals who might stand in the way of Faysal, and therefore of British interests. Several of those named posed no real threat. Place of origin, religious sectarianism, or political affinities disqualified them from the outset, whether in the eyes of the Mesopotamians or the British.[5] One such person was Sharif Ali Haydar, an Hijazi rival of Husayn, wartime collaborator with the Turks and political exile in quest of a throne. Early in 1920 he had contacted the British and the French regarding Mesopotamia and Syria respectively; the British had informed him that the matter was not as yet under consideration but that, in any case, "when the moment arrives for the installation of a native ruler . . . to be rendered possible, they have no intention . . . of making any effort to compel the acceptance of a special candidate."[6] He persisted, however, through indirect means until finally, in March, 1921, Shuckburgh advised Churchill that Haydar be discounted. "So far as is known here Ali Haidar is practically unknown in Mesopotamia and quite without a following there. He has no claims whatsoever to be made ruler of the country. He did nothing for us during the war and is entitled to no consideration at our hands."[7]

Another such unwelcome candidate was the *shaykh* of Muhammara. Arriving at Basra on 7 April, Cox met with the *shaykh*, who expressed confidence in his ability to obtain support from a majority of the people, a confidence based on invitations from the Shi'ite leaders at Najaf and Karbala. Speaking as an old friend, the high commissioner advised him to abandon the idea. Yet, in reporting to Churchill, Cox indicated a dilemma: there was no logical *prima facie* reason why Britain should object to the *shaykh*'s candidacy—he was, after all, an Arab and a staunch supporter of Great Britain; yet the mere fact of his campaigning might create "a troublesome diversion."[8] The reply from Churchill, while permitting Cox to dissuade the *shaykh*, reveals the differences of

5. See 'Anīs Ṣāyigh, *al-Hāshimīyūn wa al-Thawra al-Arabīyya al-Kubrā* (Beirut. 1966), p. 204; Ireland, *Iraq*, pp. 304–9.
6. George Stitt, *A Prince of Arabia: The Emir Shereef Ali Haider* (London: George Allen & Unwin, 1948), pp. 223 and 225; see the *Near East*, 9 September 1920, for a long letter by Sirdar Ikbal Ali Shah, an Afghan, in support of Haydar.
7. The Stitt family were active campaigners on Haydar's behalf and aroused the ire of the British government; see C.O. 730/13 for their activities which occasioned Shuckburgh's reply.
8. Paraphrase telegram, received 12 April 1921, in 17766 of C.O. 730/1.

approach between the two men. "Here [in England], unless he splits his vote, an additional candidate is sometimes a help to the strongest candidate. It is presumed you have satisfied yourself about this. I had rather pictured three or four candidates of whom one was pre-eminent. But the decision rests with you."[9] Cox persisted and informed Churchill on 3 June that the *shaykh* of Muhammara had ceased to compete.

A somewhat different approach was adopted toward another rumored candidate, Ibn Sa'ud. What concerned the British was not so much his actual candidacy—Wahhabi extremism alienated him from the Shi'ites—as his hostility toward the sharifians and his ability to intervene in Mesopotamia. When Cox learned of the Cabinet decision to table the Cairo proposals on subsidies in Arabia, he protested to Churchill. "As regards proposal made in the case of Bin Saud it is most urgent that decision should be come to before I reach Baghdad. I beg to observe that increase of his subsidy is an essential factor in the general scheme of Policy presented by conference."[10] On 4 May a letter was sent to Ibn Sa'ud through his agent in Baghdad, Ahmad Ibn Thanayan, informing him of some of the measures decided upon at Cairo. Cox assured Ibn Sa'ud that the subsidy would be continued and offered him a special cash gift of £20,000 "in case at the present juncture you might be troubled with any temporary inconvenience."[11] In addition, he stated that Britain was prepared to acknowledge his title of Sultan of Najd and its dependencies—if he wished to assume it. But in return Ibn Sa'ud was asked to refrain from any aggressive action against the Hijaz, Kuwayt, or Iraq; to cooperate in facilitating the pilgrimage to the holy cities of Arabia; to accept British guidance in his foreign policy; and "should such a contingency arise as the accession of a son of the Sherif to the rulership of Iraq you should be prepared to enter into a treaty of neighbourly peace with him."

This tactic succeeded, to the relief of both Churchill and Cox. In a letter to Cox, written prior to his receipt of the above letter, Ibn Sa'ud referred to rumors of Faysal's coming to Iraq and explained how impossible it would be for him to accept such a development.[12] By contrast, on 22 August Cox reported a most satisfactory reply from Ibn

9. Churchill to Cox, 14 April 1921, *ibid*.
10. Cox to Churchill, received 29 March 1921, in 15549 of *ibid*.
11. 29463, C.O. 730/2.
12. Cox to Churchill, no. 214, 22 June 1921, in 32183 of *ibid*.

Sa'ud to his letter of 4 May. He had accepted the Faysal decision while acknowledging Britain's warm attitude toward his own assumption of a royal title; he also accepted "with thanks and dignity" the financial assistance offered him.[13]

Yet another source of concern arose from the persistent sentiment on behalf of a Turkish prince—Burhan al-Din, a son of Sultan Abdul Hamid, being the one most frequently mentioned. This sentiment can be partially explained in terms of the recrudescence of pro-Turkish support, the decline in British prestige in the wake of 1920, and Kemalist activity within Mesopotamia. Fear of Turkish resurgence had in fact become so strong by January, 1921, that it was used as an argument in justifying the need for a sharifian candidate. As Gertrude Bell wrote: "I believe that if we could put up a son of the Sharif at once he might yet sweep the board; if we hesitate, the tide of public opinion may turn overwhelmingly to the Turks."[14] Sir Percy Cox reported that among the politicians of Baghdad the candidates stood in the following order: a Turkish prince first, followed by a son of the sharif, the Naqib, and Sayyid Talib; in his opinion the choice rested between the first two.[15]

Further disconcerting news arrived telling of Turkish activity along the northern border of Iraq and of propaganda among the Indian troops. This activity was alleged to be under the direction of *Shaykh* Ahmad al-Sanusi, either the deputy of Burhan al-Din or himself a candidate. While neither the threat of Turkish attack nor of a Turkish candidate actually materialized, they did contribute to a great deal of uneasiness during the summer months of 1921.

As the Turkish challenge to Faysal receded, it was replaced by the far more serious one posed by the Naqib and Sayyid Talib. The Naqib of Baghdad had long been a valuable associate of the British administration in Mesopotamia. His candidacy might have received full support from Great Britain but for two major handicaps: his advanced age; and the poor character of his sons, which would endanger a monarchy founded upon the principle of filial succession.

13. Paraphrase telegram from Cox, no. 414, 22 August 1921, in 42702 of C.O. 730/4. To this Churchill replied: "I congratulate you on successful result of your diplomacy. General purport of letter is most gratifying."
14. Lady Bell, *The Letters of Gertrude Bell*, 2:585 (22 January 1921).
15. Note on "Mesopotamia: Question of a Turkish Ruler," submitted to the Colonial Office on 15 February 1921 by the Political Department of the India Office (8843, C.O. 730/13).

When his political views were solicited in 1919, the Naqib spoke out strongly for the distinction between Iraq and the Hijaz, going so far as to say: "I would rather a thousand times have the Turks back in the 'Iraq than see the Sharif or his sons installed here"; yet in the next breath he excluded himself from consideration as a political head of state.[16] By April, 1921, however, anxious over the growing evidence of British support for Faysal, the Naqib appeared ready to reverse his previously unalterable position. Upon his return to Cairo, Sir Percy Cox had a long conversation with the Naqib, who denied any thought of becoming king of Mesopotamia or of having any active ambition. He would not exert himself in any way to bring about such a denouement, but, if he were to find himself spontaneously elected by the free unfettered will of the people, he was not prepared to say that he would not as a patriot of Iraq accept the responsibility.[17] The Naqib unquestionably possessed the character, prestige, and respect desired of a leading candidate; he lacked only the dynamism and ambition necessary to keep Faysal from the throne.

These very qualities were conspicuous in the person of Sayyid Talib, however. His personal ambition had been known to the British for many years but had not prevented their utilizing him during the 1920 disorders to serve their interests. Even his foremost supporter, H. St. John Philby, who was acting as British adviser to the Ministry of the Interior, characterized him as "quite obviously the outstanding man in 'Iraq in intellect and strength, but . . . quite unscrupulous, and for that he was feared by all and hated by most."[18] What made him tolerable was his frequently stated conviction that the welfare of Mesopotamia depended upon acceptance of the British mandate.

Consequently, while agreed as to Talib's ability and disabilities, British officials involved in Mesopotamian affairs differed over the role he was to play. Writing in October, 1920, Cornwallis rejected Talib as a

16. "Self-Determination in Mesopotamia," memorandum no. S-24, 22 February 1919, app. 1, "Political Views of the Naqib of Baghdad," British Museum.
17. Cox to Churchill, 11 April 1921, "Future Ruler of Mesopotamia," in 17873 of C.O. 730/1.
18. Philby, *Arabian Days*, p. 189. Miss Bell, one of Talib's most implacable foes, termed his career innocuous and opportunistic in her "Review of the Civil Administration of Mesopotamia," Cmd. 1061, p. 2.

candidate: ". . . the previous career of Seyyid Taleb is sufficiently lurid to debar him from serious consideration . . . except in the improbable event of there being a strong and universal popular demand for him."[19] By contrast, A. T. Wilson had at one time suggested Talib as head of the Arab state. Interestingly, at the height of the Mesopotamian wave of violence, Montagu had proposed that the support of the pro-British nationalists be secured through two possible leaders, Faysal and Talib, and that "possibly we may run both, Saiyab [sic] Talib as Governor of Basrah and Feisal as Arab 'king' at Baghdad."[20] Philby saw Talib as "director of the destinies of an independent 'Iraq for years to come"[21] and devoted himself to fulfilling the vision. Sir Percy Cox preferred instead to satisfy Talib's desire for power by entrusting him with responsibility as minister of the interior.

The danger inherent in giving Talib power within the government became real when the question of a monarch was reopened and Talib began to campaign in earnest. He found one source of support in his official adviser, Philby, and another in the opportunity to appoint local district officials loyal to himself. Further, his position enabled him to travel extensively throughout the country. British plans were therefore disrupted in March by news that the Naqib of Baghdad and Sayyid Talib apparently had agreed to concert their efforts. The first confirmation was received at Cairo when Bonham Carter cabled on the 18th: ". . . resignation of the Naqib who undoubtedly now entertains hopes of being elected must be reckoned on, and the active opposition of Talib, who I am informed, has agreed to support him on the condition that the position is not hereditary."[22]

With the Naqib thus lending his name and prestige, Sayyid Talib set off on what was termed a tour of inspection. In meetings with tribal leaders and in public speeches he put forth the slogan *al-'Iraq li'l-'Iraqiyin*, "Iraq for the Iraqis," an obvious reference to the Arabian origin of Faysal and his family. At the same time Talib was careful to moderate his words by emphasizing once again the imperative need for cooperation with Great Britain. During March reports reached Cairo and Lon-

19. 18 October 1920, in E12756 of F.O. 371/5231.
20. E10440, F.O. 371/5229, circulated as C.P. 1790 on 25 August 1920.
21. Philby, *Arabian Days*, p. 189.
22. Bonham Carter to Cox, no. 50, 18 March 1921, in 21451 of C.O. 730/14.

don telling of Talib's being accorded "a magnificent reception everywhere."[23] Alarm increased when word came that the pro-Turkish party and Ibn Saʿud were also exerting their influence covertly on behalf of the Naqib in opposition to a sharifian candidate.

The growing threat posed by the Naqib-Talib coalition prompted Cox to hasten back from Cairo. Having disposed of the minor problem of the *shaykh* of Muhammara, he turned to the far more serious threat. Confronting the Naqib on 11 April, Cox detected a change of attitude, particularly with regard to the prospects of his accepting a popular draft. Referring to the many rumors of British support for Faysal, the Naqib sought assurance that Britain would refrain from becoming active on behalf of any individual candidate. He did concede, however, the need for His Majesty's Government to be satisfied that the individual desired or elected was an Anglophile and acceptable from the point of view of British interests. Such assurance was approved by both Churchill and Cox.[24]

Less than a week later the backbone of resistance to the Cairo decision on behalf of Faysal was shattered by one decisive act. On 17 April Cox issued a communiqué to the people of Iraq informing them that Sayyid Talib had been removed from Baghdad "in the interest of law and order and good Government" after having delivered a speech containing "an unseemly threat of recourse to armed force against His Majesty's Government."[25]

Events between Cox's meeting with the Naqib and the enforced exile of Sayyid Talib to Ceylon are unclear, and several aspects of the episode

23. See Mesopotamian Intelligence Report no. 9, 15 March 1921, in 20750 of C.O. 730/1; see also Khayrī al-ʿAmrī, "al-Ṣirāʿu al-Siyāsiyu hawla al-ʿArsh al-ʿIrāqi, 1920–1921," in *Dirāsāt Arabīyya*, February, 1967, pp. 35–36.
24. 17873, C.O. 730/1. Cox's efforts at dissuading the Naqib are striking when compared with a note written by him from Baghdad on 22 April 1918; it reads in part: "If it is decided that we should have a nominal headpiece . . . I think . . . that it would be possible to find a local candidate, and I cannot see the least justification or necessity for introducing one of the family of the Sherif of Mecca to play this role. . . . In my opinion, we have in the Naqib of Baghdad and his family a dynastic element which would carry the necessary moral sanction . . . in Iraq as a whole" (Political Department memoranda, B. 284, I.O.).
25. Cox to Churchill, 17 April 1921, "Saiyid Talib: Removal from Government," in 18628 of C.O. 730/1; see also *Report on ʿIraq Administration, October, 1920–March, 1922*, pp. 10–11, 126.

are subject to controversy. What does emerge from the official papers is the following:

On the evening of 13 April, as part of the open campaign to project himself as an independent, national figure, Sayyid Talib invited the French consul, the Persian consul general, several tribal leaders, and a number of other persons to a private dinner in honor of Percival Landon, correspondent of the *Daily Telegraph*. In the course of the evening he complained that the British officials were not entirely neutral in regard to the selection of a ruler, whereas the people of Iraq were determined to have freedom of choice. Here Talib allegedly pointed to the Arab chiefs and cautioned that they and their armed tribesmen would ask why the professed British policy of impartiality was not being carried out. He went on to say that at any sign of Great Britain's taking sides the Naqib was prepared to appeal to the Islamic world for support.[26]

If, as alleged, the speech was so inflammatory, there is no explanation why Sir Percy Cox was not informed of its contents earlier than the 16th. Nor is there any adequate explanation of why he responded so sharply, except to illustrate the uneasiness which the Naqib-Talib movement occasioned among the British. Nevertheless, Cox accepted as accurate the secondary report given him by Miss Bell, who was admittedly hostile to Talib and dedicated to the sharifian cause, as related to her by a Mr. Tod, manager of the Mesopotamian-Persian Corporation, who knew Arabic, and by Mr. Landon, who did not.

After a brief consultation with General Haldane, the plan for removing Talib from the political scene was quickly put into effect. According to Philby, Sayyid Talib had had a long-standing invitation to afternoon tea at the Residency on the 16th. To avoid implication, Cox excused himself with apologies. Upon leaving the house, Talib's car was blocked by British lorries just beyond the driveway and he was seized by a Major Bovill and a Captain Cox. He was carried off in an armored car to a launch waiting downstream to take him to Basra, and from there was conveyed to Ceylon, where he was joined by his family.[27] The official

---

26. This account is the one given Churchill by Cox on 16 April 1921, in 18676 of C.O. 730/1.
27. Philby, *Arabian Days*, pp. 198–99; see also Burgoyne, *Gertrude Bell*, p. 214.

version, however, merely notes that he "was successfully arrested in a public thoroughfare."[28]

In explaining his action to Churchill, Cox offered as justification the fact that none of the leaders of the 1920 uprising had said anything that came as close to threatening a recourse to force as had Sayyid Talib. An additional factor was the high official position held by Talib, which made his remarks, admitted to be indiscreet even by Philby, "quite intolerable" to Cox.[29] Yet the possibility that the deportation might be condemned as a trick to remove a constant rival of Britain's favorite candidate had to be reckoned with, and Cox advised the colonial secretary that the best approach would be to cite Talib's earlier self-denial of his candidacy. Thus reassured, Churchill wired his approval on 20 April.

Whatever its damage to British protestations of impartiality, and however it might be construed in Mesopotamia itself, the deportation of Sayyid Talib in effect swept the field clear of any potential rival to Amir Faysal. This was gradually acknowledged in London, where the news was met with relief. Reader Bullard, in minuting a related file, expressed the view that there was no thought of forcing an amir on Iraq, "but we could hardly be criticised for exercising a right of veto if a man with whom we felt we could not work seemed likely to succeed in the elections."[30] Perhaps the most candid admission of the fortuitous nature of the event came from Shuckburgh at the year's end, when Faysal was already safely installed. "Saiyid Talib's removal from Iraq was essential to the success of the Sherifian policy, and his own intemperate behaviour afforded clear justification for the drastic steps that were taken."[31] As related by Hubert Young, Churchill lightheartedly concluded that "one advantage of being under the Colonial Office . . . is that it has an almost unlimited selection of salubrious spots for the planting out of objectionable people."[32]

But in Mesopotamia the impact was of a more somber nature. De-

28. 18676, C.O. 730/1; see also a critical, somewhat belated account of the "kidnapping" in *The Times*, "Mesopotamian Mystery," 28 and 29 December 1921.
29. See H. St. John Philby, *Forty Years in the Wilderness* (London: Robert Hale, 1957), p. 76, and Cox, 18676, C.O. 730/1.
30. File 19484, minuted on 18 April 1921, C.O. 730/1.
31. Interoffice note, dated 24 December 1921, in 61359 of C.O. 730/10.
32. Young to Deedes, 28 April 1921, in 20546 of C.O. 733/17A.

prived of its actual leader, the anti-sharifian movement collapsed. Anxious to vindicate himself, on 21 April Cox informed London that there were many expressions of satisfaction, relief, and even congratulation rather than any signs of dissatisfaction or resentment. The only slightly discordant note was a remark by the French consul that what Talib had said seemed to be no more than what he had said many times before.

In condemning Talib, Cox, mindful of the important function still being fulfilled by the Naqib, studiously avoided implicating him; consequently, the Naqib accepted the deportation with "complete loyalty." By 1 May Miss Bell was reporting that, while the Naqib had in no way withdrawn his candidacy, he showed signs of relaxing his determined opposition to the sharifians "to the extent of saying that the country will do best to follow the wishes of His Majesty's Government whatever they may be."[33] An air of resignation prevailed in the country as well.

By virtue of Cox's drastic action, Mesopotamian politics were no longer dominated by personalities, or rather were dominated by the single personality of Amir Faysal. Such opposition as remained was based instead on issues, such as the form of government appropriate to Mesopotamia. Much to the consternation of the British officials who had committed themselves to a sharifian monarch, there arose a sentiment in favor of the continuance of the existing regime under control of a high commissioner. Propaganda was also expressed for treatment of Basra on separate lines, for creation of a republic, and for importation of a Turkish prince.[34] All four suggestions were debated by the public as alternatives to a monarchy under Faysal. Cox, however, felt confident that Faysal's actual presence in the country would shift the balance decisively in favor of a monarchy, and he devoted himself to preparing for the amir's arrival. What hampered him throughout the three phases leading to the enthronement—competition, campaigning, and election— was the constant need to have British actions approximate British statements, to exert influence, and, if necessary, to bring pressure, without openly violating the promise of impartiality.

A useful indication of British intent appeared in the instructions presented to Cox when he became high commissioner. His orders read:

33. Mesopotamian Intelligence Report no. 12, 1 May 1921, in 29462 of C.O. 730/2.
34. Cox to Churchill (no. 171), 9 June 1921, in 28897 of *ibid.*; see also al-'Amrī, "al-Sirā'u al-Siyāsiyu," pp. 44–46, for Iraqi press comment.

"Suffice it to say:—That the precise form of the Government to be created, in which the sovereignty of the Arab State will be vested, will be a matter for the free choice of the peoples of Mesopotamia, whose wishes you will endeavour to ascertain by whatever means you think fit. Similarly the choice of a ruler (if they decide in favour of a monarchy) will be left to them."[35] But this was superseded by the Cairo Conference and its decision on Faysal's behalf. Even there, in the heady atmosphere of pro-sharifian support, the tactical dilemma could not be overlooked. As Churchill explained it:

Both Cox and Miss Bell agree that if procedure is followed, appearance of Feisal in Mesopotamia will lead to his general adoption. But this will be partly because the mere fact that we have allowed him to return will universally be interpreted as if it were a coupon election candidature. On the other hand, anything less than this course may lead to an incoherent verdict by a small majority in favour of an unsuitable candidate at elections scarcely worthy of name in so scattered and primitive a community.[36]

Therefore, what Churchill sought and received, and what Cox gave the broadest interpretation, was the "liberty to do our best in unostentatious ways"[37] in order to secure the adoption of Faysal. Thus, at the same time that assurances of neutrality toward the possible candidates were being given, contradictory actions were being taken, whether in removing other candidates through a combination of persuasion and force, or in assisting Faysal by means of a detailed timetable.

Mesopotamian leaders, like the Naqib, were told of Britain's intention to refrain from becoming active on behalf of any individual candidate. In his Commons speech of 14 June, Churchill told the nation, and indirectly the people of Mesopotamia, that Faysal had been informed of his suitability as a candidate and that, "if he is chosen, he will receive the countenance and support of Great Britain."[38] To those officials within the High Commission who advised against too direct an involvement, Cox steadfastly maintained that Great Britain had no such intention.

35. Revised draft from the India Office, with Cabinet approval, 28 August 1920, in E10758 of F.O. 371/5229.
36. Churchill to the Prime Minister, 18 March 1921, F.O. 371/6342. For the procedure see Churchill's proposals of 14 March 1921, pp. 108–9 above.
37. Churchill to the Prime Minister, 21 March 1921, F.O. 371/6342.
38. *Parliamentary Debates* (Commons), 5th ser., 143 (14 June 1921) : 275.

Philby, anxious about the prospects of his protégé, referred to repeated denials by Cox after Cairo of any British assistance to Faysal.[39] The advice of Bonham Carter, who advocated "benevolent neutrality" as opposed to support for either Faysal or Talib, was consciously rejected by the conferees at Cairo. He had pleaded on 18 March: "I would represent most emphatically that any attempt to impose a particular candidate on the country is most undesirable and may defeat its object, and that any pronouncement that may be interpreted to that effect should be avoided. It follows that at this stage at least our officers should maintain an attitude of neutrality."[40] Mere lip service was paid to such protestations in the succeeding crucial months.

Vigorous denials or circumspect diplomatic notes were also used to allay French fears. As early as August, 1920, the French chargé d'affaires warned that Faysal's enthronement would be regarded as "un acte peu amical vis à vis de la France." Responsibility for deflecting French opposition fell to the Foreign Office. Lord Hardinge told General Gouraud in December that there was no foundation whatsoever to newspaper reports of Faysal's having been designated ruler of Mesopotamia. By January, 1921, however, Sir Eyre Crowe was careful to avoid replying directly when Count de Saint-Aulaire raised the issue and expressed French objections to Faysal personally.

The impressions of a direct relationship between Faysal and Great Britain which prevailed in France were summed up by *Paris-Midi* on 20 March when it referred derisively to Faysal as "*l'élégant émir de* Berkeley square."[41] Yet British officials continued to issue formal denials. On 23 March, in another of his direct confrontations with the French ambassador, Lord Curzon claimed that since Faysal's arrival in England "no official communication" had been made to him regarding Mesopotamia and that "no plot existed between us on the matter"—this only a day after the Cabinet had approved the Cairo recommendations. Equally frank, if less devious, in his reply, the French ambassador said that whatever justification Britain might have, or whatever explanation might be given, nothing would alter the conviction of the French that there was a definite plan for installing Faysal and thereby rendering

39. Philby, *Arabian Days*, pp. 196 and 200.
40. Telegram from Bonham Carter to Cox (Cairo), no. 50, 18 March 1921, in 21451 of C.O. 730/14.
41. E3644, F.O. 371/6350.

France's position in Syria more difficult.[42] As the plan moved toward fulfillment, the French reaction, like that of the Mesopotamians to Talib's deportation, surprised the British government in its mildness.

Having committed everything to Faysal's success, Cox and the Colonial Office worked to coordinate their efforts on his behalf from April to July. On 28 March Faysal used the Foreign Office wireless to send his father a telegram reporting the message from Lawrence to start at once for Mecca. Faysal, mentioning a report he had sent to Husayn on 1 March concerning the favorable turn in his conversations in London, offered congratulations on the "return of confidence between Great Britain and your Majesty as it was during most critical circumstances."[43] Calling again at the Foreign Office on the 31st, prior to his departure, the amir was received by Mr. Lindsay, through whom he assured the British government of his intention to avoid "any action that could embroil the British and the French authorities."[44] He then sailed on the steamship *Malwa*, arriving at Port Said on 13 April.

When the Colonial Office suggested that Lawrence accompany him from there to Jidda, the Foreign Office objected and re-emphasized the very delicate nature of the British undertaking. Curzon earnestly hoped that Churchill would not take any step which might confirm the French government in its impression that Britain had broken faith with France, not only by deliberately planning the amir's candidacy but also by doing her utmost to further it at each stage.

The Colonial Office then contented itself with having Lawrence confer secretly with the amir at Port Said, where Faysal was given further instructions on the procedure to be followed. Faysal expressed appreciation of Britain's general policy and reiterated his intention to do all in his power to make it work; but he unexpectedly insisted as a condition of his proceeding that a British adviser, preferably Colonel Cornwallis, be assigned to his personal staff to accompany him on his fateful trip.

Catching the British by surprise, Faysal's precondition led to a flurry of cables between London and Baghdad. Churchill was initially reluctant, reasoning that to attach a British official to Faysal at that point

42. Curzon to Hardinge, 23 March 1921, in C6427/2740/18 of F.O. 406/45.
43. Curzon to Major Batten (Jidda), for Husayn, 28 March 1921, in E3703/8/91 of F.O. 406/45.
44. Foreign Office to Colonial Office (confidential), 6 April 1921, in E4075/4/91 of F.O. 406/46.

British Policy in the Arab World

would compromise British assurances of neutrality. But by then it was difficult to counter Shuckburgh's logic: "We are staking everything on Feisal 'making good' in Mesopotamia. It would be folly to allow minor difficulties to deprive him of the officer whom he has asked for and without whom he may be unwilling to embark on his great adventure."[45] Despite the strong opposition of Sir Percy Cox, Churchill approved the temporary transfer of Cornwallis from Egypt to the staff of the high commissioner of Mesopotamia, regarding it as "so vital to [the] success of our policy that technical difficulties cannot be allowed to stand in the way."[46] Having extracted this concession, which later served as a precedent, Faysal took leave of Lawrence and continued aboard the khedivial mail boat *Tantah* to Jidda.

Faysal reached the Hijaz on 25 April. More than five years had elapsed since he had first set out to capture Damascus from the Turks. If he was hesitant to be reunited with his highly critical father, such fears were unfounded, for Husayn traveled from Mecca to greet him, gave a luncheon party in his honor, and, more important, took the occasion to assure the British consul that, "although my patience is almost exhausted, I will try to keep patient while I see what is going to happen."[47] Further, King Husayn asked that a message be communicated on his behalf to the British government: "As already stated, I am prepared to carry out the wishes of HMG, especially in the matter of which Feisal has informed me, and I have received from the people of Mesopotamia telegraphs asking for one of my sons. I am awaiting news of date of Feisal's departure in order to notify Mesopotamians. . . ."[48]

While Faysal sojourned at Jidda, there was evidence of uneasiness in Mesopotamia and London. Intelligence reports referred to murmuring among the natives that Faysal was too "English," and the long visit to

---

45. Minute, 19 May 1921, in 24324 of C.O. 730/2.
46. Churchill to Cox, 19 May 1921 (clear the line, personal and private), *ibid*. Cox's objections and other factors in the question of Cornwallis being assigned to Faysal, and in what capacity, are found in files 24324, 25982, and 26706 of *ibid*. Only on 28 May did Cox agree to the deputation of Cornwallis and his coming to Mesopotamia; on the 31st Churchill initiated the complex procedure of asking the Foreign Office to instruct Lord Allenby to press the Egyptian government strongly to spare Cornwallis for a leave period of three months.
47. A description of Faysal's stay is found in the Jidda report for the period 21–30 April in E5784/455/91 (Marshall to Curzon, no. 35, secret), F.O. 406/46.
48. Marshall to Curzon, 21 May 1921 (no. 52, telegram), in E5872/100/93, *ibid*.

England was being cited as proof of his having become a foreigner. The Naqib as yet was keeping counsel only with himself regarding his own intentions. In London, as late as 29 May, General Haddad told a correspondent for the *Basrah Times* he was not aware that unofficial proposals had been made to Faysal concerning the throne of Mesopotamia.[49] The high commissioner's staff was divided over the principle of monarchy, Faysal's candidacy, and the nature of the British role in these important matters, and even Sir Percy Cox, preoccupied with orchestrating all of the movements, showed signs of strain. On 21 May he informed Churchill that it had been necessary to carry out bombing operations against two tribes as an example to the six different sections of the Nasiriya Division which had been deliberately defying the authority of the Arab government.[50] He professed to having no doubt that a general conflagration would otherwise have resulted. This show of strength, of course, demonstrated to the entire country Great Britain's intention to remain in complete control, and it proved effective. As if to compensate for the use of force, Cox issued a general amnesty the following week to all political offenders since the 1920 uprisings.[51]

Faysal, his reunion with the head of the sharifians a success, left Jidda on 12 June. He had obtained his father's initial support for the Cairo program and of his own claim to the Mesopotamian throne. His attention therefore turned to the future and the reception awaiting him in Iraq. With accomodations provided on the *Northbrook* and travel expenses paid by Great Britain,[52] Faysal and his retinue sailed for Basra, arriving there on the evening of 24 June.

49. *Basrah Times*, 29 May 1921, p. 3.
50. Extract from telegram from Cox to the Secretary of State for the Colonies, no. 124, 21 May 1921, in 27278 of C.O. 730/2. There does not seem to have been any prior notification by Cox of the situation developing in these areas nor of any request for permission to carry out the bombings.
51. Text in the *Basrah Times* of 30 May 1921, p. 3. On the 31st, editorializing on the amnesty, the paper also commented on the rumor about Faysal: "It seems to us that no better choice could be made."
52. In a secret note to the War Office on 23 June, Shuckburgh confirmed the undertaking already described verbally to the director of transports and shipping, Board of Trade, that the cost of diverting the *Northbrook* from her direct voyage from Suez to Bombay would be borne by the Colonial Office (29704, C.O. 730/12). See also approval by the lords commissioners of His Majesty's Treasury in 29916, *ibid.*, and 28897, C.O. 730/2.

Cox had laid the foundation for an impressive welcome. Mindful of the importance of public opinion and of the Naqib's central position, he had persuaded the elderly president of the Provisional Council to partici- pate in welcoming the distinguished visitor to Iraq. Thus Faysal had received a private message from the Naqib while aboard ship. Addressed to "the Light of the Candle of the Family of the Prophet, the Pearly Star in the heaven of honour," it read: "I have received with respect Your Highness's telegram which proves Your Hashimid sentiments towards me and gives me the happy news of your arrival. Our hearts have been filled with pleasure. We thank you and pray for your speedy and safe arrival. The Ministers and the nation welcome you."[53] Then, in a meeting of the Council of Ministers on 16 June, at the Naqib's initiative a resolu- tion had been adopted that Faysal should be the guest of the national government and that all fitting hospitality was to be extended to him.[54] Accordingly, on the 24th representatives of the high commissioner went aboard to welcome Faysal, acompanied by Philby, Ja'far Pasha, the governor of Basra, and about 120 notables.[55]

The amir then disembarked and plunged into two days of activity. He rode in an automobile procession through the decorated streets of Basra, which were lined with crowds applauding and shouting welcome. The following day he received successive delegations from the nobility, no- tables, and guilds of Basra. In replying to several complimentary speeches, he thanked his adherents for their invitation and the reception committee for the cordial welcome given him. At a tea party and recep- tion later that evening he emphasized his humility and patriotism by saying: "As for myself I call Allah to witness that I come with no per-

53. Texts of telegrams exchanged between the Naqib and Faysal were printed in al-ʿIrāq, no. 326, 24 June 1921 (41687 of C.O. 730/3). Faysal had initiated contact with the Naqib at Cox's urging; see 30117 of C.O. 730/2.
54. 30471, ibid. Churchill, noting that the attitude of the Naqib, "which is greatly to his credit, is most gratifying," inquired of Cox: "Would it, in your opinion, please him to receive British decoration?" Apparently thinking along the same lines, Cox responded: "Decoration I had in mind for Naqib . . . was K.C.M.G. or perhaps even a G.C.M.G." The resolution appeared in print on 18 June 1921 in the Baghdad Times, p. 2.
55. Cox to Churchill (no. 234, personal), received 27 June 1921, in 32181 of C.O. 730/2; see also the Basrah Times of 26 June 1921, p. 2, and Muḥammad ʿAbd al-Husain, Dhikrā Faysal al-ʾAwwal (Baghdad, 1933), pp. 14–25.

sonal ambition but simply for purpose of serving my country. I swear also by tombs of my ancestors that I am fully prepared to render loyalty to man whom nation shall choose. . . ."[56]

On 29 June Faysal reached Baghdad, where he was enthusiastically received at the train station. Once again there was the inevitable procession through the main streets followed by several smaller banquets, a visit to a Shi'ite shrine, and an open-air banquet. At all these functions addresses were given which alluded to Faysal as "the King elect of 'Iraq" and which were received with acclamation by the local audience. Conspicuously missing, however, was the Naqib, "whose infirmity prevents him from leaving the house." On the 30th Faysal went personally to the Naqib's house to see him.

Despite these warm receptions, Faysal joined Cornwallis in telling Cox that there had been "a certain amount of lukewarmness and suspicion . . . apparent in Basrah and but little cordiality . . . shown at Kerbela or Najaf."[57] Faysal tended to attribute such mild greetings to Philby's less than enthusiastic attitude toward him. These complaints elicited a dual response from the high commissioner. He first reprimanded Faysal for his inclination to take the line that he had been sent as a candidate by the British and that it was therefore up to them "to do his business for him." While assuring him that it would daily become easier for Britain to come into the open and render all possible help, Cox explained to Faysal why it was essential that he should pose primarily as the candidate of the people with British support, and not the converse.

In addition, Cox considered as "highly improper" remarks made by Philby to the amir in favor of a republic and against Britain's handling of the Talib episode. He was cognizant of Faysal's being very bitter toward the junior officer and wished to avoid further friction. There was one more consideration: "Philby as Adviser in charge of Ministry of the Interior was obviously in a position in which his pronounced personal views must inevitably exercise some influence over Arab and British officials serving under him and thus even influence our elections. Therefore I consider it incompatible with the interests of HMG that he

---

56. Description provided by Cox in his telegram of 28 June 1921, in 3244 of C.O. 730/2.
57. Cox to Churchill, 1 July 1921 (no. 250), in 33044 of C.O. 730/3.

should retain his post."[58] Confronting Philby early in July, the high commissioner instructed him to relinquish his duties immediately, a decision which Churchill deemed wise in view of Philby's "anti-Sherifian tendencies."[59]

As a result of Cox's firm administrative action the situation improved. In an almost imperceptible shift in status from visitor to campaigner, Faysal began actively to seek native support. He made a series of speeches and forays into the countryside, in addition to receiving tribal *shaykhs* who came to the high commissioner to pay their respects.

One such occasion was described vividly by Miss Bell, who accompanied the amir on his visit to the Dulaim tribe at Ramadi. When Faysal had concluded his speech the *shaykhs* told him, "We swear allegiance to you because you are acceptable to the British Government." As Miss Bell wrote: "Faisal was a little surprised. He looked quickly round to me smiling and then he said, 'No one can doubt what my relations are to the British, but we must settle our affairs together.' He looked at me again, and I held out my two hands, clasped together as a symbol of the Union of the Arab and British Governments."[60] She undoubtedly expressed the feelings of Cox, Ja'far, Nuri, Cornwallis, and Faysal when she wrote on 30 June, "One is straining every nerve all the time to pull the matter forward; talking, persuading, writing, I find myself carrying on the argument even in my sleep."[61] But the effort was bearing fruit. Churchill, capturing the note of renewed optimism in his cable of 9 July, repeated his confidence in Sir Percy Cox. "I am very anxious not to

---

58. Cox to Churchill, 7 July 1921, paraphrase telegram no. 270 (clear the line), in 33926 of C.O. 537/822.
59. Churchill to Cox (air mail), 6 August 1921, in 37171 of C.O. 730/3. At Faysal's suggestion Cornwallis eventually filled the vacant post. Philby's account of his meeting with Cox is found in his *Arabian Days*, p. 204. He maintained that he had merely been carrying out Cox's earlier orders that the elections were to be free and that British officials were not to give active support. Refusing to "rig the elections," he tendered his resignation, which Cox calmly accepted: "Thank you, Philby. I'm sorry you can't see your way to continue helping us."
60. Lady Bell, *The Letters of Gertrude Bell*, p. 615, letter of 31 July 1921. Her official accounts apparently were even more vivid, for Bullard felt obliged to suggest that the wording be toned down a little before publication. "The celebrations seem to have gone to the Oriental Secretary's head" (28 July 1921, in 37879 of C.O. 730/3).
61. Lady Bell, *The Letters of Gertrude Bell*, 2:607.

burden you with rigid instructions but to support you in every way in the difficult task you are discharging with a measure of success which is increasing."[62]

As the situation improved and Faysal impressed his audiences, success confronted Cox and the British government with the need to make yet another important decision; at no time had there been an explicit understanding of just how Faysal was to be confirmed in his designated position.

Beginning at the Cairo Conference, a certain ambiguity on the subject of Faysal's ratification had developed. The original proposal in advance of the conference had called for the "selection" of an Arab ruler by the Council of State, providing Cox could ensure that the council would indeed select Faysal. Once assembled in Cairo the experts had perpetuated this imprecision. While subscribing to the need for the prior formation of a local government of "real prestige and authority," for a monarchy, and for Faysal as the first ruler, they stopped short of defining actual procedure. As Churchill informed the prime minister on 14 March, "Method of choice will require careful study in order to avoid confused or meaningless expression of Mesopotamian opinion."[63] Cox suggested that a national assembly be convened which would select a monarch from among the candidates, and he promised that, if necessary, the assembly could be ready to meet and vote within six weeks of his return. But the attention of the conference was diverted by Miss Bell and Colonel Lawrence, both of whom assumed that Faysal would be received with unanimous approval, thus precluding the need for formal machinery. Point eight of the "Suggested Programme and Time-Table for Mesopotamia" therefore read: "It is expected that Faisal's announcement, followed by his arrival in the country, would result in such a definite expression of public feeling on his behalf as would make it unnecessary for us to ask the Congress to discuss the question of the ruler; they would simply confirm directly or indirectly his nomination."[64] A striking feature of the conference minutes, as well as of the Cairo-London telegrams and replies, is their variegated phraseology. The word "se-

62. Churchill to Cox, 9 July 1921 (priority A, secret and personal), in 33549 of C.O. 730/3.
63. F.O. 371/6342, p. 1.
64. F.O. 371/6343, p. 59; see also p. 109 above and Churchill to Lloyd George, F.O. 371/6342, p. 4.

lection" appears quite frequently, in preference to "election," as do the equally neutral terms "adoption" and "accepted."[65]

If anything seems obvious it is that elections were deemed inappropriate by all those involved in the conference. Cox had volunteered in December, 1920, that, "as regards the people of this country, I am doubtful if the Congress will ever reach a result on the question of the ruler, and believe that majority would prefer to have the question decided for them. . . ."[66] Shuckburgh, concerned about French opinion, candidly told a Colonial Office colleague on 17 March: "We could no doubt so arrange matters as to make it appear that Mesopotamia was voting of its own free will for a particular ruler; but this would not deceive the French for a moment. It would be camouflage. . . ."[67] Again, in a memo to the Cabinet, he wrote that a genuine plebiscite was an impossibility in a country like Mesopotamia, citing the inconclusive effort made along such lines shortly after the armistice.[68] Churchill also objected to an election. Stressing technical difficulties and a traditional assumption of imperialist logic, he made reference to the scattered and primitive population of Mesopotamia. Yet after his return to Baghdad, Cox, in a surprising reversal, became the champion of the electoral method.

A gap in communications, so typical of Britain's pre-Cairo policy in the Middle East, seemed to reappear during the tense and fluid summer months in Iraq. Expressing Colonial Office understanding of the plan, Shuckburgh wrote in June that the election of an Arab ruler for Mesopotamia was not contemplated. All indications leaned toward the election to the national assembly of a large proportion of pro-sharifian members who would then merely confirm an offer of the crown to Faysal.[69] Then, on 5 July Churchill, writing to Cox, urged "striking while the iron is hot." He thought that perhaps Faysal, given his reported cordial reception, could be declared amir of Iraq, after which the pro-

65. F.O. 371/6342, pp. 8 and 9, and F.O. 371/6343, p. 3. In a secret paper submitted on 17 February on "the Proposed Kingdom of Mesopotamia," the General Staff employed such terminology as "appointment," "accession," "nomination," "proclaimed," "selection," "make" Faysal king, or "Feisal becoming King"; no use was made of the word "election" (10368, C.O. 730/12).
66. Cox to Montagu (telegram 123S), 26 December 1920, in E100 of F.O. 371/6349.
67. Shuckburgh to Mr. Marsh, 17 March 1921, in 14449 of C.O. 730/9.
68. 19 March 1921, *ibid.;* see also Cmd. 1061, p. 127, on earlier experience, and E3315 of F.O. 371/6379.
69. Note by Shuckburgh, June (undated), in 27506 of C.O. 732/5.

spective assembly would confirm the decision. In short, the desire for a *fait accompli* suggested abandonment of a complicated, lengthy process of first electing an assembly which would only then select Faysal.

At that point Cox stressed the importance of surface appearances. Rather than consent fully to the call for haste emanating from London, he drew attention to the need for "carefully safeguarding our own proceedings vis-à-vis public constitutional correctness" in order to avoid accusation from any quarter.[70] Once again seizing the initiative, and without waiting for a full hearing in London, he sought a compromise: election of a national assembly would be replaced by a national election of Iraq's first monarch. Accordingly, on 9 July he informed Churchill of his intended reply to the Council of Ministers on why issuance of the promised electoral law was being delayed. He would express regret at the unavoidable delay arising from the difficulty in providing the Kurdish communities with the special safeguards to which they were entitled under the Treaty of Sèvres. He then told of the need to devise more speedy machinery to obtain an early decision since there was now "an insistent demand on the part of [the] public for [an] immediate opportunity to decide who should be their ruler."[71]

On 11 July, the Council of Ministers passed a unanimous resolution declaring Amir Faysal king of Iraq, provided that the resulting regime "shall be a constitutional, representative and democratic Government limited by law." On 16 July the council authorized a plebiscite. That same day Cox issued a communiqué which read: "Whereas this resolution of Council has come to me for confirmation and whereas I have little doubt that it reflects the prevailing views of people, yet without fortifying myself with a specific expression of assent of people I do not feel justified in confirming it, and I am accordingly asking Council to authorise Minister of Interior to take requisite steps in order that such expression may be obtained."[72] Perhaps the most plausible explanation of this *volte face* by Cox lay in the collapse of all meaningful opposition to Faysal's candidacy, which permitted the luxury and innovation of a

---

70. Cox to Churchill (no. 280, personal and private), 9 July 1921, in 34418 of F.O. 371/6352.
71. Cox to Churchill (no. 281), received 9 July 1921, *ibid*.
72. Cox to Churchill (no. 294), 12 July 1921, in 34963 of C.O. 730/3. In a clear indication of the distinction he made between reality and the impression given, Cox added that, his reference to the Ministry of the Interior notwithstanding, "Feisal, myself and Naqib will discuss and decide on the precise nature of steps to be taken."

national expression on behalf of the amir. In any case, Churchill had little choice but to continue his trust in the high commissioner; on 15 July he wired: "Your action has my entire approval."

"Less centralised and more expeditious machinery" was hastily improvised. The Ministry of the Interior issued instructions requiring that representative committees of the inhabitants record their opinion on the council resolution in favor of Faysal. Provincial governors were then entrusted with the ballots and forwarded them to Baghdad. The declarations were simple in form, wording, and connotation.

We, the undersigned, residents of Nahiya/Mahallah _____, in Qadha/Town of _____, in the Liwah of _____, have heard, understood and fully considered the above Resolution of the Council of State: and it results that _____ express themselves in agreement therewith, and profess their allegiance to Amir Faisal, while have signified their dissent _____.[73]

Although it was not until 18 August that the Ministry of the Interior announced that "an overwhelming majority of the people of the country" had supported the council's choice of Faysal, Cox cabled Churchill on 31 July, "Results of referendum from most places have already reached me and no doubt remains as to issue."[74] The remainder of his

73. Intelligence Report no. 18, 1 August 1921, in 44326 of C.O. 730/4.
74. Despite a thorough investigation of Colonial Office documents, the present author was unable to discover detailed figures on the election results. And it would appear that London never received specific totals, for as late as 9 March 1922 Churchill, when asked in Parliament how many votes there had been, replied: "I cannot say. There were quite a large number, several hundreds of thousands" (*Parliamentary Debates* [Commons], 5th ser., 151 [1922]:1544).

The only statistics provided by the high commissioner's office are contained in Intelligence Report no. 19, 15 August 1921. While in no way corresponding to the claim of balloting in the thousands, they do indicate the absence of a choice.

Liwah	Madhbatahs in Favor of Faysal	Against
Baghdad	157 (68 on condition that Iraq be fully sovereign)	—
Dulaim	26	—
Basrah	47	—
Diyalah	41	—
Hillah	41	—
Karbala	28	—
Amarah	7 (5 on condition that British Mandate will continue)	—
Mosul	68	—
Kirkuk	20	21
Muntafiq	(Madhbatahs not yet received)	

Iraq   161 telegram looked to the future: an early coronation, recognition of the monarchy by other of the Great Powers, and the nature of the formal British-Iraqi relationship.

With Faysal's victory all but assured, Churchill and Cox anticipated no further obstacles to the full implementation of the Cairo decisions on Mesopotamia. But on the eve of the coronation still another challenge arose, and from the least expected source—Faysal himself. Having dutifully complied with British instructions and advice for half a year, he suddenly expressed dissent, insisting upon a revision, prior to enthronement, of the relationship with his patrons based on the principle of Mesopotamian sovereignty. This brief episode, while showing the mutual, sometimes embarrassing commitment of the two parties to each other, also offers a preview of the central issue which was to dominate Anglo-Iraqi relations in the future.

The Middle East Department had suggested that, as the second item on its agenda, the Cairo Conference discuss proposals for readjusting relations between His Majesty's Government and the Mesopotamian government that would shortly come into being. In particular, the necessity for retaining control of Mesopotamia's foreign relations and responsibility for her external defense were underlined. A division of authority was foreseen whereby Great Britain would be responsible for the diplomatic and military protection of Mesopotamia against attack from overseas or from French Syria, Turkey, Persia, or Muhammara. Although a number of related political questions were prepared for discussion, the conference did not delve into the subject directly, neglecting

---

See 46069 of C.O. 730/4.

On 29 July the *Times of Mesopotamia* carried a report of the voting in Basra Province, where not a single vote against Faysal was recorded, and suggested the electors deemed it advisable to be politically "in the swim." Writing in 1924, H. W. V. Temperley questioned the degree of enthusiasm for Faysal, particularly in Basra, where direct British rule was preferred in order to secure commercial stability; see his *History of the Peace Conference of Paris*, 6:186. Intelligence Report no. 20, of 1 September 1921, told of the "overwhelming majority" but did not provide statistical confirmation; see file 48631 of C.O. 730/4.

Cox's cable to Churchill (no. 351, clear the line) is in 38479 of C.O. 730/3. Churchill later excused irregularities when he described the election, which "whatever its shortcomings to Western standards, has certainly been the freest election ever held in any Oriental country" (Churchill, "Mesopotamia and the New Government," p. 696).

it in favor of the more pressing financial and military aspects and the timetable for installing Faysal.

Consequently, when Lawrence met Faysal for consultation at Port Said, he was authorized only to assure the amir that "in [your] first public statement in Iraq [you] will be allowed to say that His Majesty's Government have agreed that after ratification of the Organic Law, modifications in the mandate may be made by negotiations" between Britain and the duly constituted government.[75] Yet Faysal later claimed to have departed from that meeting with a different impression—that a treaty would replace the mandate.

The subject next surfaced in August when Churchill advised Cox that a treaty would be inserted into the future Organic Law. In the meantime, he warned, "the situation cannot be defined and Feisal cannot exercise plenary sovereign functions."[76] Cox then discussed the subject at length with Faysal. The results were as unsatisfactory as they were disconcerting. The monarch-designate declared himself altogether unable to accept the throne on the basis indicated by London. Further, he asked that arrangements for his coronation be deferred until a satisfactory solution could be reached.[77]

Churchill, visibly angered by the crisis, sent an immediate and authoritative reply on 15 August. Cox was instructed to advise Faysal that whether under a mandatory or treaty arrangement Britain expected to be consulted "so long as we are meeting heavy financial charges in Mesopotamia." Acknowledging the promise to convert the mandate into a treaty, he stated it would be done only after the new government was duly constituted. Churchill then admonished the amir, advising that he show himself capable of maintaining peace and order unaided before becoming full sovereign, and "this will certainly take some time." Conscious of the necessity to have Faysal crowned without delay, Churchill sought to end his message in a somewhat more conciliatory tone. Faysal

75. Churchill to Lawrence, 19 April 1921 (clear the line), E4700, F.O. 371/6365.
76. Churchill to Cox, 9 August 1921 (clear the line), 38479, C.O. 730/3. The colonial secretary candidly advised Cox of the intended British position: "In the Organic Law it will be necessary to incorporate some modus vivendi which will leave the power with you in the last resort even in internal affairs, HMG remaining solely responsible for foreign affairs."
77. Cox to Churchill (no. 390), 14 August 1921, in 40704 of C.O. 730/4. Faysal also insisted that the Kurdish areas be incorporated under his rule.

was to be told that Britain regarded as binding his promise, made apparently to Lawrence, to accept the mandate system. For her part, Britain proposed to go further than her undertaking and to make the treaty arrangement as soon as possible. Cox was urged to keep London appraised but, at the same time, not to delay taking any necessary action.

The impasse was broken and the crisis ended for the moment when Faysal capitulated upon receipt of Churchill's message. With a sense of relief, the high commissioner notified the Colonial Office on 16 August that Faysal, despite his displeasure, felt it would be highly prejudicial to the interests of all parties if any further delay occurred. The fact that Faysal already saw himself in an unenviable, even impossible, position is apparent from Cox's report on their most recent conversation. "Speaking generally he [Faysal] feels his accession must be marked by some (? definite) outward sign of change. If impression is given that he is merely a puppet in hands of British his influence will be (? weak) and he will not be able to recover it. He is convinced it would be far better for British interests if everything possible is done to strengthen him in eyes of people."[78] Churchill was insisting upon a definite provision for safeguarding the authority of the high commissioner; Faysal asked that the relationship be founded on a "cordiality of co-operation" between the amir and the high commissioner and a readiness on the part of the former to accept advice from the latter. Cox admitted that he was moved by the amir's logic and even felt inclined "to take our courage in both hands and give Feisal position he presses for."[79]

On 19 August the "Committee on the Proposed Treaty with the Emir Feisal" met at the Colonial Office to discuss the issues raised in the challenge from Faysal. Churchill, Curzon, and Montagu, attended by their legal advisers, reached two conclusions: (1) Faysal's accession should take place as scheduled, with the treaty being drafted subsequently; (2) a complete statement of the way in which the British government had carried out the mandate for Mesopotamia, and of the political developments which led to the proposal to exercise the mandate by means of a treaty with Faysal, should be prepared for the League of Nations.[80]

78. Cox to Churchill (no. 396), 16 August 1921, in 41499 of C.O. 730/4.
79. Cox to Churchill (no. 397), 17 August 1921, in 41616, *ibid*.
80. CAB 23/27, vol. 9; see also 42372 of C.O. 730/15 and E9786 of F.O. 371/6352.

Churchill accordingly provided Sir Percy Cox with the text of a declaration which Faysal was expected to incorporate into his speech from the throne. This was accompanied by a reassertion of the previous position that, while no doubt existed as to the two parties "working together quite easily and happily in practice," a formal guarantee of the British role was essential. For the British, it was suggested, "must be in a position to show that in making the treaty we are still legally in position to discharge and are not seeking to evade the responsibilities we have assumed towards League of Nations. It is essential that we be able to show that we have acted honourably before the nations of the world and in true interests of Iraq."[81] Faysal was then induced to sign an *ad interim* statement, drafted by Cox, which recognized the international and mandate obligations of Great Britain; the statement would suffice until Churchill could telegraph more precise details about these obligations. Although the amir conformed to the demand, he added, ". . . it would be very much more satisfactory to me to have fuller information as to sort of obligations that are meant and I beg you to ask meanwhile for a fuller explanation if you have no objection."[82]

Assurances having been extracted, the path was cleared finally for the accession ceremony. And on 23 August, in a show of pageantry which, in the words of the high commissioner, "passed off brilliantly," Faysal was installed as the first monarch of Iraq. At this historic ceremony the new king spoke warmly of Great Britain and looked to a future of close cooperation and of consultation with Sir Percy Cox, whom he referred to glowingly as having "proved his friendship to the Arabs in a manner which will ever live in their affectionate memory. . . ."[83]

With Faysal's accession a new era in the history of the country was inaugurated, and steps were taken to institutionalize the transition. On the following Friday, the name of Faysal ibn Husayn was inserted in the *khutba*, or religious sermon. The word "Iraq" replaced "Mesopotamia" in all official correspondence. Faysal called upon the Naqib to serve as prime minister, and on 10 September the formation of a new

---

81. Churchill to Cox (personal and secret), 20 August 1921, in 41616 of C.O. 730/4.
82. Cox to Churchill (no. 427), 25 August 1921, in 42913, *ibid.*; see also E9854, F.O. 371/6352.
83. Cox communicated the accession speech to London, hailing it as "very satisfactory" in his cable of 25 August 1921; see 42935 of C.O. 730/4. See also his report of the ceremony on 23 August 1921, in 42642, *ibid.*

cabinet was announced. In an interview with Lord Hardinge on 15 September, M. Briand, speaking in conciliatory terms, "saw no reason why, in the course of time, there should not be perfectly satisfactory relations" between King Faysal and the French authorities in Syria.[84] And by 3 November enough progress had been evidenced to justify the next phase of British troop withdrawal in fulfillment of the hope expressed at Cairo.

Beneath this surface of progress through cooperation, however, Faysal's original demand for a greater degree of independence continued to strain British relations with the monarchy. The secretary of state for the colonies, while professing to understand the king's reluctance to commit himself unduly, nevertheless was disappointed by the lack of trust. Yet he still refused to specify the exact obligations which Faysal would be expected to assist in fulfilling, calling the task of specification "difficult if not impossible." He ended on a note of resolve to work with and through the king, since "we are determined not to allow our faith in him to be shaken by his reluctance to take action which might prejudice his position in the country."[85] In a very real sense each became a prisoner of the other.

The end of 1921 found Churchill in an irritable state of mind, a result of the disturbing news that was arriving almost daily from various parts of the Arab world. A draft of a proposed telegram to Cox, although never sent, reveals his brusque attitude toward Faysal. In a note to Shuckburgh on 24 November he wrote:

I am getting tired of all these lengthy telegrams about Feisal and his state of mind. There is too much of it. Six months ago we were paying his hotel bill in London, and now I am forced to read day after day 800-word messages on questions of his status and his relations with foreign Powers. Has he not got some wives to keep him quiet? He seems to be in a state of perpetual ferment, and Cox is much too ready to pass it on here. . . . Let him learn to so develop his country that he can pay his own way, and then will be the time for him to take an interest in all these constitutional and foreign questions.[86]

Faysal's desire to act as an independent ruler therefore diverted the at-

84. Hardinge (Paris) to Curzon, 15 September 1921, in E10437 of F.O. 371/6353.
85. Churchill to Cox (no. 365, clear the line), 3 September 1921, in 42913 of C.O. 730/4.
86. File 59435, C.O. 732/16.

tention of the dynamic, ambitious colonial secretary from other affairs, such as the Irish Rebellion, while inadvertently conspiring with other forces to jeopardize the accomplishments at Cairo.

Responsibility to the League of Nations, Kurdish unrest, and the protracted failure to reach a compromise with the nationalist Turks were three additional matters affecting Iraq and, by extension, engaging the concern of the Colonial Office. Preoccupied with affairs in the Arab regions, Churchill underplayed British accountability before the League, at one point noting disparagingly: "There is also too much talk about 'Mandates', 'Mandatories' and things like that. All this obsolescent rigamarole is not worth telegraphing about. It is quite possible that in a year or two there will be no mandates and no League of Nations."[87] But Lord Balfour, chief British delegate at Geneva, cautioned that decisions toward Iraq could not be taken unilaterally and without reference to the League. This was particularly true of any treaty with Faysal which was intended to replace or even to revise the mandate. As Sir Cecil J. B. Hurst pointed out to Balfour in a memorandum on 25 October: the sovereignty of Mesopotamia was technically Turkish; Great Britain was merely a military occupant until her position was regularized by the issue and ratification of a mandate; consequently, Britain had no *locus standi* for entering into a treaty which embodied provisions of indefinite duration.[88]

In the first instance, Churchill used this legal brief to justify procrastinating on the treaty promised to Faysal. However, he did for a time give greater attention to explaining British conduct and aims as mandatory over Iraq; on 17 November a full statement prepared by the Colonial Office was presented to the Council of the League of Nations. After reviewing recent developments, the statement assured that the proposed treaty was not intended as a substitute for the mandate. Rather, it was viewed as a more satisfactory instrument for defining relations between the mandatory power and the mandated state. Four assurances were also given that the treaty would secure: (1) British control over the foreign relations of Iraq; (2) due fulfillment of the international obligations incurred by His Majesty's Government; (3) such measure of financial control as was deemed necessary; (4) while

87. Churchill to Shuckburgh, 9 July 1921, in 33549 of C.O. 730/3.
88. Hurst to Balfour, E11847, F.O. 371/6380.

Iraq   167

in no way contravening either the spirit or the letter of the League covenant. The statement was received by the Council without comment, and Churchill interpreted this as a vindication of past measures as well as authorization to continue taking practical steps which the situation might require from time to time.

An inconclusive, if temporarily expedient, policy toward the Kurds was also pursued. At the end of May, Cox took it upon himself to ascertain the wishes of the Kurds, suggesting as a solution that they remain an integral part of Iraq, provided they could retain the existing degree of local autonomy in domestic affairs and were directly ruled through the high commissioner rather than by the government of Iraq. Both Young and Lawrence recalled that the balance of opinion at Cairo had favored a separatist policy in Kurdistan, but Cox's action now made this extremely hard to pursue. Churchill took issue with Cox, favoring a policy of setting up a Kurdish buffer between the Arabs and Turks as originally contemplated at Cairo.[89] During a visit to Iraq in October, Young frankly told King Faysal that British policy was aimed at the "encouragement of Arab nationalism not Arab imperialism."

Iraqi claims to the Kurdish areas were never retracted, nor was the Cairo decision implemented. This tension between the narrower nationalism of the Kurds and the wider Iraqi perspective therefore persisted throughout the interwar period and beyond.

A very serious problem, and one most prejudicial to British plans for Iraq, was the enduring enmity between Great Britain and the Kemalists, which led to the threat of a Turkish invasion and reconquest of the former imperial territory. Churchill saw the danger and its full implications but was unable to affect the outcome directly since Turkish affairs remained under Foreign Office control. His fear that the Turks' anti-British activities on the frontiers of Iraq might prevent the scheduled troop reductions recommended at Cairo was fully shared by Cox. Indeed, the Cairo decisions had been premised upon improved relations with the Turks; yet the opposite was true. The London Conference at the end of February had been a disappointment. Turkish military strength, and hence pressure, was on the increase. In addition, Kemalist diplomacy had achieved a series of triumphs, topped by the treaty of friendship and collaboration with the Bolsheviks signed in Moscow on 16

89. Churchill to Cox (no. 162), 13 June 1921, in 30932 of C.O. 730/2.

March and the Franklin-Bouillon agreement between Ankara and Paris of 20 October.

Despite Churchill's entreaties that Lord Curzon alter his policy and enter into direct negotiations with Mustafa Kemal, the foreign secretary remained adamant. In desperation Churchill suggested in May that as an alternative Faysal be permitted to approach Kemal informally on the matter of Turkish intrigue along the Iraqi border. In reply Curzon preferred to express no definite opinion for the present, asking that the matter be brought up again when an Iraqi king had become a reality.[90] When the suggestion was submitted a second time, after Faysal's accession, a conference of ministers met on 21 December and decided that there was no objection to Faysal's communicating with Naji Bey, a Kemalist agent, provided it was clearly understood that this was with the object not of entering into negotiations with Kemal, but rather of discovering his attitude toward Iraq.[91]

Thus, at the end of 1921, Churchill in London and Sir Percy Cox in Baghdad could reflect with satisfaction upon the "harmonious march of events" stimulated and given direction by the Cairo Conference, while looking confidently to the future. As a result of their skillful engineering of events and personalities the chaos of 1920 had been replaced by a new sense of stability and progress. Iraqi development—social, economic, and political—was provided with an able leader and a central institution, while Iraqi nationalism was temporarily appeased. Simultaneously, British interests in the area were guaranteed, even while public demands for immediate military and financial reductions were being satisfied.

The fact that Faysal and the monarchy would be compromised by close identification with a foreign, imperial power, that a rising generation of nationalists would not long suffer a limitation, however indirect, upon their sovereignty—these and other challenges could not be foreseen, nor their gravity appreciated, in 1921. The future, as always, would have to take care of itself. In terms of 1921, suffice it for Churchill, Cox, Faysal, and all the participants in the Cairo discussions on Mesopotamia to read with satisfaction the statement by Sir Arnold T. Wilson to the *Times of Mesopotamia:* "For two years after the Armistice

90. Their exchange of memos is in C.O. 730/9.
91. E14079, F.O. 371/6369.

we in Mesopotamia waited for a decision as regards policy. Mr. Winston Churchill gave us one in as many months. Sir Percy Cox, with the help of his staff, has done in twelve months what I thought it would take five years to accomplish. Under his guidance the people of Mesopotamia seem to have achieved unity."[92]

92. Interview given in Calcutta, *Times of Mesopotamia*, 8 September 1921, p. 3.

CHAPTER 8

Palestine

> *Palestinians demand the abolition of the principle of the creation of a National Home for the Jews in Palestine.*
> —Palestine Arab delegation to the League of Nations, September, 1921

> *We, the Zionist Organisation, have the firm belief ... in the steadfastness and continuance of that wise and far-sighted policy of Great Britain that found its expression in Mr. Balfour's declaration ... and upon this policy ... we build our whole future.*—Dr. Weizmann to Sir Herbert Samuel, March, 1921

> *... It will be a difficult and delicate task and we must be prepared to resist pressure from both sides at every stage. ...*—Sir John Shuckburgh to Winston Churchill on the Palestine mandate, 10 June 1921

Two factors were efficacious for the British position in Mesopotamia throughout 1921. In the first instance, the Colonial Office had as its representative an individual who, using power effectively, was able to remain in control of events from the initial stage of formulating a new policy at Cairo to the progressive realization of that policy in Baghdad. He was aided, in turn, by the passivity of the local population. The masses and their leaders were either unwilling, or as yet unable, to test the authority of Sir Percy Cox and ultimately that of the mandatory power. In the case of Palestine during this same period both features were lacking, and with fateful results.

But the absence of these two factors began to be apparent only after May, 1921; the first four months of the year gave little cause for alarm. A residue of good will still remained from Sir Herbert Samuel's arrival the previous July, and both he and his staff had assiduously cultivated relations with spokesmen for the Arab and Jewish communities in Palestine. Cultural and economic projects were drawn up and awaited only League approval of the mandate in order to be initiated. Although a fundamental disparity existed between Arab and Jewish nationalism, neither movement was capable of speaking with one voice; nor were they implacable toward each other, as evidenced by their joint participation on the high commissioner's Advisory Council. Furthermore, on the level of daily contact the two communities lived in comparative harmony, even if not in full accord. Thus the unpleasant disturbance of April, 1920, was not viewed as a precedent for the future.

Sir Herbert Samuel had occasion to express this optimism regarding the future when on 8 January 1921 he submitted a lengthy appreciation of the finances of the country.[1] Aware of the sentiment in England against the continued use of British troops in Palestine, he predicted that within a year or two only a very moderate military force, paid for from local revenues, would be necessary. What concerned him was the anarchic situation across the Jordan River, not the presently satisfactory political situation within Palestine. The absence of any comprehensive evaluation of policy in Jerusalem or in London during the latter part of 1920 and into 1921 gave further indication of Foreign Office satisfaction or, conversely, preoccupation with Mesopotamia and Transjordan. Indeed, during this period greater attention was given to the external status of Palestine—its boundaries with French Syria and its international character as a mandated territory—than to its domestic affairs.[2]

No serious effort was made to answer such questions as how to reconcile the Zionist idea of Palestine with that of the Arab nationalists, how to introduce representative government, or how to balance Arab majority and Jewish minority rights. One difficulty with the Balfour Declaration as a statement of principle had been its vagueness for both sides; delay in clarifying its meaning and intent served only to heighten Arab and Zionist uneasiness. Nowhere in the Middle East was the British policy of drift more apparent than in Palestine at the start of 1921.

As has been shown, the motivating force behind both the transfer of authority to the Colonial Office and the resultant Cairo Conference was the need for change, drastic and immediate. Mesopotamia, Arabia, Transjordan, troop deployment, and general expenditures—all necessitated positive action. Of all the major agenda topics, Palestine alone did

1. Samuel to Curzon (no. 11), E1062/401/88 of F.O. 406/45.
2. On the complicated issue of the northern boundary, see H. F. Frischwasser-Ra'anan, *The Frontiers of a Nation* (London: The Batchworth Press, 1955).

not appear to require any major departure from the policy of the recent past. To Churchill, coming as he did to his new position from the War Office, Palestine, except for the worrisome situation across the Jordan, represented an excellent opportunity for satisfying the public clamor for demobilization. The draft agenda for the conference therefore stressed discussion of Transjordan, its status relative to the Palestine mandate, and the composition of the permanent garrison until 1925.[3] A special subject for possible consideration was the anticipated relationship between the Advisory Council and elected Arab and Jewish assemblies, should the latter materialize in the future. Otherwise, the "general policy of the Palestine Administration calls for no observations. It is in strict accordance with the Mandate, and has been attended by the happiest results."[4]

Consequently, at Cairo, and again at Government House in Jerusalem, discussion centered on a policy for creating a defense force and on Palestine's financial contribution toward the upkeep of the force. This also enabled Churchill to concentrate his energies on impressing the plans of the Middle East Department for Mesopotamia and Transjordan first upon the conferees, then upon the prime minister and Cabinet. In short, Palestine lacked any sense of immediacy for Great Britain in March. Yet by June the situation had deteriorated so badly that Churchill, referring to Palestine, had to tell Parliament and the nation that "here, at the present time, the problem is more acute than in Mesopotamia."[5] The events of this brief intervening period—as well as the British, Arab, and Zionist reactions to them—are of importance both because they dominated the remainder of 1921 and because they may constitute a microcosm for studying the entire period of the British mandate.

The first indication of a crisis in Palestine came on 2 May. Sir Herbert Samuel informed London by cable of a "serious affray" between Jews and Muslims the previous day during a labor meeting in Jaffa.[6] No details were provided other than a rough estimate of the casualties: about

3. Under the heading "Palestine," the first paragraph of the conference summary read: "The outstanding question to be discussed was the policy to be adopted with regard to Trans-Jordania, and its effect upon the strength of the Imperial garrison in Palestine" (F.O. 371/6343, p. 7).
4. *Ibid.*, p. 31.
5. *Parliamentary Debates* (Commons), 5th ser., 143 (14 June 1921) : 283.
6. Samuel to Churchill, 2 May 1921, in 21723 of C.O. 733/3.

40 persons killed, 179 in hospital, and 48 treated and discharged. But reassurance was given that it had not been found necessary to proclaim martial law; so, too, the rest of the country was declared to be quiet.

But as the rioting continued the high commissioner had no alternative but to declare a state of martial law on 3 May. He also requested General Congreve in Egypt not to remove from Palestine some of the units which were about to leave. Reading of this, Churchill sensed for the first time the disastrous implications for his timetable of reductions and savings. That same day, at the eighth meeting of the Advisory Council, Samuel appeared in person and promised that the instigators would be punished. After expressions of sympathy from several members, the Council, as if in a political vacuum, resumed its discussion of the condition of the roads in the country. Only by strenuous efforts and the use of British troops were the riots contained. As the eventful week drew to a close, actual disturbances of the peace ended, except for raids against Hadera and four other Jewish colonies. Public unrest, however, remained acute.

Given this lull, on 7 May Samuel was able to direct a commission to inquire into and report on the recent disturbances in the neighborhood of Jaffa and elsewhere in Palestine. Samuel was certainly the first British official to grasp the magnitude of the riots, linking them to the fundamental political questions so long unanswered and ignored even at such a comprehensive discussion of the Middle East as that held in Cairo. "Whatever may be found by the Commission to have been the proximate causes of the outbreak," he wrote to Churchill on 8 May, "it is clear that its continuance for three days at Jaffa, the conflicts that have taken place, or that have been narrowly averted, elsewhere, and the character of the agitation that has prevailed, indicate that there are deep-seated causes at work, and that these are to be found in the political questions that have been disturbing the minds of large sections of the people."[7]

The Commission of Inquiry, under the chief justice of Palestine, Sir Thomas Haycraft, took somewhat longer to reach essentially the same conclusions, submitting its report on 10 August. The Jaffa riots, as described and supplemented by Colonial Office files, began on the morning

7. High Commissioner (Palestine) to Secretary of State for the Colonies (dispatch no. 82, confidential), in 24660 of *ibid.*

of Sunday, 1 May, when, oddly enough, two Jewish groups—the Achdut ha-Avodah labor party and a revolutionary group attempting to link Jewish labor parties in Palestine to the principles of the Communist Third International—clashed in rival labor demonstrations on the outskirts of Tel Aviv. Arabs of the Manshiah district of Jaffa began to collect at a distance to observe what was happening. Thereafter, the commission had to content itself with a general narrative, the precise sequence of events being uncertain because of conflicting, often unreliable evidence.[8] The situation grew critical when neither side was willing to return to its own quarter before the other did. Shots were heard in the Manshiah quarter, thereby alarming the two sides, which then came to blows. The few local police officers, Jewish and Arab, lost control of the situation. Looting of Jewish shops in Jaffa took place as mob rule asserted itself in defiance of pacification efforts by the mayor of Jaffa and other Arab notables.

Events took a decided turn for the worse that afternoon when an angry crowd of Arabs broke into Immigration House, used as a shelter for newly arrived immigrants. Despite resistance from those inside, the toll of dead and wounded in this "gruesome episode" was thirteen Jews killed or mortally wounded and twenty-four wounded, one Arab killed and four wounded. Fighting and looting continued unabated until late that day; the arrival of British troops from the nearby Sarafand base and from Jerusalem put an end to the riots for the time being, and the night passed quietly. But in succeeding days, despite British reinforcements, martial law, disarming of the local populace, and the occupation of Jaffa by British soldiers, incidents of hostility continued to be reported. As of 6 May there were 95 confirmed deaths—48 Arabs and 47 Jews—and 219 wounded.

On 14 May the high commissioner issued an order under his general authority confirming the temporary prohibition of Jewish immigration. Although this measure was acclaimed by the Arab population, it was the first of several actions by Samuel which led to Zionist alienation from him. On 16 May seven Arabs were placed under preventive arrest and removed to Jerusalem, to be followed on the 18th by three Jews;

8. "Palestine Disturbances in May, 1921: Reports of the Commission of Inquiry with Correspondence Relating Thereto" (Cmd. 1540) ; hereinafter cited as Cmd. 1540.

all ten were believed responsible for the reciprocal boycott in Tel Aviv and Jaffa. Soon shops began to open and daily life was restored to a semblance of normalcy. In the course of the month the government arrested members of the extremist Jewish labor group, and fifteen recent arrivals, convicted of having belonged to the group, were deported from Palestine. Regardless, passions did not subside for a much longer time, and all parties looked to the government for some distinct declaration of policy. In terms of actual physical violence, however, the peak had been reached on 6 May; thereafter, the general situation began to improve.

In probing into the deeper causes of the riots, the Haycraft commission explained the state of exasperation among the Arabs in terms of six principal grievances put before it in the course of its inquiry. Politically, the Palestinian Arabs saw Great Britain being influenced by the Zionists to adopt a policy directed toward a Jewish national home and not toward the equal benefit of all Palestinians; they pointed to the Zionist Commission, official advisory body to the government and described by the Arabs as an *imperium in imperio,* as proof of their suspicions. They also claimed that there was an undue proportion of Jews in the government service (perhaps an indirect reference to Samuel, but more specifically one to the legal secretary, Norman Bentwich). Economically, Arab witnesses expressed alarm at the influx of European Jews who possessed greater commercial and organizing experience than themselves and could be expected eventually to dominate the entire economy. These immigrants, it was claimed, constituted an economic danger because of their competition and the alleged favorable position accorded them by the government. Culturally, the Jewish pioneers were charged with offending Arab sensitivities by their arrogance and disrespect for Arab social attitudes, while insufficient precautions allowed Bolshevik immigrants to enter the country and to promote social strife.

Thus the report concluded that although the direct cause of the riots had been the Jewish labor disturbance, the fundamental cause was "a feeling among the Arabs of discontent with, and hostility to, the Jews" for the reasons mentioned above.[9] Once the disturbance had begun, "an already acute anti-Jewish feeling extended it into an anti-Jewish riot."

9. *Ibid.,* p. 59.

Never before had British representatives delved into the underlying causes of unrest in Palestine so penetratingly nor emerged with such ominous conclusions. As long as Arab and Jewish differences remained unreconciled the possibility would always be present of further, even more deadly confrontations.

Despite the shock of the May Day riots there had been prior evidence of mounting tension, partially revolving around Churchill's brief visit after the Cairo Conference. Both communities within Palestine had welcomed the opportunity in March to present their respective cases before a distinguished member of the British government.

News of Churchill's impending trip caused considerable excitement. The Arab community raised money for a delegation chosen by the Arab-Palestinian Executive Committee in Haifa, engaged in heightened political debate, and sought peaceful demonstrations. The deputation left for Egypt on 12 March, disregarding a suggestion by the administration to wait for Churchill to come to Jerusalem. They were received by the colonial secretary on the 22d and told that he could not discuss political questions with them but would be pleased to see them again in Jerusalem on the 28th.[10] The meeting did eventually take place, the delegation dutifully presenting its memorandum and receiving a straightforward reply from Churchill.[11]

That very day in Haifa a demonstration occurred in disregard of a ban by the governor; it resulted in a clash, the death of one Christian boy and one Muslim, and injury to one Christian, ten Jews, and five policemen. Disappointed first with Samuel and then with Churchill, the Arabs now determined to send a second delegation to Europe, believing in the chance of an eleventh-hour change in British policy and that a direct appeal would influence a British public ignorant of affairs in Palestine. Perhaps the strongest indictment of Churchill's visit was provided by Captain C. D. Brunton, of General Staff Intelligence, in his evaluation of the causes of the May violence. Referring to the gradual development of bitter and widespread hostility toward the Zionists and resentment of the British, Brunton said the visit "put the final touch to the picture" since Churchill "upheld the Zionist cause and treated the

10. "Report on the Political Situation in Palestine and Trans-Jordania for the Month of March 1921," 21698 in C.O. 733/2.
11. See pp. 127–28 above.

Arab demands like those of a negligible opposition to be put off by a few political phrases and treated like bad children."[12]

By contrast the Zionists had reason to be pleased with the visit, particularly because of their original anxiety. New fears had been aroused in Jewish circles in Palestine by the transfer of the mandate administration from the Foreign Office to the Colonial Office.[13] In London, however, Weizmann assessed both the transfer of power and Churchill's expected trip more calmly. Interpreting these actions as evidence of the colonial secretary's desire to study conditions on the spot, to give "serious attention to the safeguarding of the newly established arrangements in that part of the world," and to clear away all obstacles, he wrote to Sir Herbert Samuel on 7 March that "Mr. Churchill's journey fills us with great hope."[14]

Not content to rely solely on hope, the Zionist Organisation took steps to increase contacts with Churchill. Early in March Nahum Sokolow sent a personal note expressing confidence that Churchill would use his good offices "to assist in the great work of rebuilding Palestine" and wishing him a pleasant and successful journey.[15] At the first meeting of the Zionist Executive on 2 March, Weizmann reported an unsuccessful effort to have Leonard Stein accompany Churchill and proposed instead to send Mr. James de Rothschild. When the latter said he would not go as a representative of the Zionist Organisation but would as that of the Economic Council for Palestine, the Executive decided on the 4th to send Sokolow as well "in order to safeguard the interests of the Zionist Organization during Mr. Churchill's stay in Palestine."[16] Memoranda were prepared on the mandate, the eastern-frontier question, and the

12. Supplement to the secret memorandum ("The Situation in Palestine") submitted by the secretary of state for the colonies on 9 June 1921, C.P. 3030, CAB 24/125.
13. Cf. the *Zionist Review* of February, 1921, with that of May, 1921.
14. Weizmann to Samuel, 7 March 1921, in 16994 of C.O. 733/16.
15. File A18/43/4, C.Z.A.
16. Minutes of the several meetings of the Executive at the beginning of March devoted to the Cairo Conference are found in the Weizmann Archives. I am grateful to Mr. Eli Mizrachi of the Israel State Archives for evidence of Rothschild's close contact with Churchill during the journey, as seen in the visitor's book of Government House in Jerusalem. Its entry for 29 March 1921 contains Churchill's signature followed by those of his wife and James de Rothschild.

military garrison. On the 10th Weizmann wrote Samuel that Pinchas Rutenberg, a young engineer with ambitious plans for developing Palestine, would be coming; he also asked Samuel to see that Churchill came into contact with the *chalutzim*, or pioneers, in order to get an accurate view and to dispel the rumor of the pioneers' Bolshevik tendencies.[17] Whether because of Churchill's prior sympathetic view of the utility of Zionism, the influence upon him of Rothschild, Sokolow, Rutenberg, and Samuel, or the moderate memorandum presented to him by the Zionist delegation in contrast with that of the Arab delegation, the colonial secretary's reply gave the Zionists considerable satisfaction, and his appearance at a Zionist function in Jerusalem was reported with elation: "perfect order, beautiful day, wonderful impression."[18]

The net effect of Churchill's visit to Palestine therefore was a mixed one. At first heartened, the Arabs emerged disappointed, if not insulted, from their meeting with the colonial secretary. Their frustration led to two developments: the outburst on 1 May and the dispatch of a delegation to Europe. The opposite was true of the Zionists. Initially reserved in their view of the new colonial secretary, they came away pleased at his sympathetic approach. Their renewed confidence led in turn to greater cooperation with the British government and an inflexibility toward the Arabs which also contributed to the Jaffa riots. On balance, Churchill, like others before him, failed to provide a basis of confidence in Palestine, and in some ways his visit contributed to the increasing tension which shortly thereafter found release in a resort to arms rather than words.

In the wake of the riots, attempts were made to understand their implications and, if possible, to repair the damage. In May and in subsequent months one conclusion emerged above all others: the effects of the riots were far-reaching; in one stroke they had rudely shaken the foundation of British administration in Palestine only one month after Churchill confidently returned to England. The two pillars of this foundation had been understood to be first, a respect by both communities for British authority, and second, a willingness by both Arab and Jew to live together, albeit with uneasiness and suspicion. Instead, British

17. Weizmann to Samuel, W. A.
18. Zionicom Press cable to Zioniburo London, 30 March 1921, *ibid.*

authority had been directly challenged and the gap between the two communities widened.[19]

The latter effect is exemplified by the retraction of plans for a combined defense force, long cherished by Samuel as a means of reducing British expenditures through local cooperation. At Cairo and Jerusalem, supported by Captain Peake and Mr. Deedes, Samuel had successfully defended the project for a mixed force of Arabs and Jews instructed and led by British officers. He was making final preparations for recruitment when the riots broke out. The Haycraft commission issued a strong indictment of the mixed police force already in existence, whose members had failed to subordinate their racial and religious prejudices to their sense of duty; cases were cited of police who had participated in or had actually led the violence.[20] Subsequently, it would be too dangerous to train and equip natives, who could be expected to take sides in any future clash. Bowing to this reality, Samuel abandoned the project. In its place a British gendarmerie of five hundred men, most of whom had been in the celebrated Black and Tan Brigade in Ireland, was brought to Palestine.

The challenge to British authority was most evident with regard to the person symbolizing that authority—the high commissioner. Because of his sincere dedication and firm conviction in the righteousness of the British role as beneficent, impartial mandatory in Palestine, Sir Herbert Samuel was deeply shaken by the riots. That confidence which he had labored so diligently to create was shattered in a few hours on 1 May. As unaccustomed to violence as he was committed to rational discussion, Samuel reacted cautiously, to the displeasure of both sides.

His most controversial action was the order forbidding any further immigration as of 14 May. Although initially taken to avoid harm to Jewish immigrants arriving in Jaffa, the measure struck at the heart of the Zionist program with its emphasis upon immigration, investment,

19. A useful description of the contrasting communities is provided in *Great Britain and Palestine, 1915–1945*, Information Papers no. 20, published in 1946 by the Royal Institute of International Affairs, pp. 17–37, and in J. C. Hurewitz, *The Struggle for Palestine* (New York: W. W. Norton & Co., 1950).

20. Cmd. 1540, pp. 47–50, 59. The Colonial Office's military adviser, Colonel Meinertzhagen, noted on the 13th that no force, if composed of Jews and Muslims, could be relied upon to deal with internal disturbances, which could only take the form of a conflict between Jew and Arab. His alternative of a purely Jewish force was quickly dismissed. See 23739 of C.O. 537/826.

and settlement. Samuel's action was therefore seen as a capitulation to Arab pressure: what had been denied by Churchill to the Arab delegation slightly more than a month earlier—an end to immigration—was now achieved through force.[21] Of importance for understanding Samuel's difficulties is the fact that this concession, while alienating his fellow Jews, still did not gain for him the confidence or support of the Arabs, who persisted in demanding nothing less than that Britain repudiate the Balfour Declaration in its entirety.

Thus caught between the two sides, the high commissioner was also subjected to pressures from England. The riots had been described there as Bolshevik inspired, arousing the fear that Palestine was being subverted by Russian Jews. On 3 May the Executive Committee of the Arab Palestinian Congress sent letters to the pope, the king of England, the House of Lords, and the British, French, Italian, American, and Spanish foreign secretaries warning of the danger to Palestine posed by Bolshevik infiltration:

The nation has, in vain, repeatedly protested against this unfortunate [Balfour] Declaration and policy; and now, at the time when the fire of Bolshevism is consuming one of our most important cities, and its red flag is openly flaunted in our streets, while its revolutionary publications are being freely and assiduously distributed broadcast [sic] in the land, we come again to request that this Declaration and policy be abolished before the spirit of Bolshevism is too widely spread, and any attempt on our part to help the Government to extinguish it prove in vain.[22]

Given the fear of bolshevism still current in Europe, and Churchill's personal detestation of that movement, such interpretations had a definite impact in shaping British reaction to the riots.

The colonial secretary sent a personal message to his high commissioner on 12 May expressing confidence that "only grave anxiety would I feel have induced you to suspend immigration." He indirectly reprimanded Samuel and exonerated himself from responsibility by adding: "You will recollect that during my visit I told you that my information from several quarters led me to the conclusion that atmosphere was be-

---

21. Weizmann expressed this opinion in a memorandum to Lloyd George on 21 July 1921; see E/86/8/2, Lloyd George Papers. The *Jewish Chronicle* on 20 May 1921 frankly called the action "a bad blunder" (p. 5).
22. The Foreign Office copy is found in 23918 of C.O. 733/16.

coming electric." Yet rather than argue over the past, Churchill, believing that Britain should certainly persevere, addressed himself to the future by suggesting that Samuel ". . . at once endeavour to purge Jewish Colonies and newcomers of communist elements and without hesitation or delay have all those who are guilty of subversive agitation expelled from the country."[23]

Samuel accepted the suggestion, approving the deportation of several recent arrivals known to be Bolsheviks, but went even further. In his telegram of 12 May he submitted four proposals which he intended to announce in a forthcoming speech: placing the Advisory Council as well as municipalities on an elective rather than selective basis; strictly limiting immigration to those who could be employed immediately; enforcing more stringent conditions with a view to preventing the entry of "political undesirables"; and postponing the formation of a local defense force while substituting an effective police reserve.[24]

In further correspondence Samuel offered an insight into his interpretation of the Balfour Declaration in light of recent events as well as into what prompted him to take the initiative in these proposals.

What it means is that Jewish people scattered throughout the world but whose hearts always turn to Palestine should be enabled to found here a spiritual centre and that some of them within the limits fixed by numbers and the interests of present population should be allowed to come help by capital labour and intelligence to develop country to advantage of all inhabitants. If any methods have been adopted which depart or even appear [to] depart from those principles they must be changed. If in order to convince Moslems and Christians their rights are really safe any measures are needed they must be taken.[25]

Although Churchill approved most of the proposed text of Samuel's speech, he was concerned by the restricted definition given and offered more preferable wording, "as the announcement of any paraphrase of the words National Home would lead to the impression that as a result of the recent disturbances the policy of His Majesty's Government has been altered."[26]

23. Churchill to Samuel, 12 May 1921 (personal), in 23742 of C.O. 733/13.
24. Samuel to Churchill (no. 151), 12 May 1921, in 23678 of C.O. 733/3.
25. Samuel to Churchill (no. 271, clear the line), 27 May 1921, in 26711 of ibid.
26. Churchill to Samuel (no. 122, clear the line), 2 June 1921, ibid. The text of the speech is in E7350 of F.O. 371/6375.

When the high commissioner delivered his speech to an assembly of notables on 3 June, it was strongly condemned by the Zionists. In an editorial of 10 June the *Jewish Chronicle* warned that Eastern peoples could never be pacified by gaining their contempt, noted that Samuel "had nothing to say in denunciation of the wild outrage" at Jaffa, and feared that the speech "is really the presage of what will form one of the blackest instances of political betrayal recorded throughout all history."[27] Even Weizmann was so shocked that in his memorandum to the prime minister more than a month later he wrote bitterly of the speech: "Its form and spirit are throughout timid and apologetic."[28]

The impact of Samuel's speech is most apparent in Palestinian immigration statistics for 1921.[29] The total number of Jewish immigrants in January was 706, 50 per cent below the number for December, 1920. In February the number dropped to 547, only to rise to new peaks in March and April—1,219 and 1,619 respectively. Thereafter, as a result of Samuel's measures the totals dropped to 184 in May and 90 in June but rose to 815 by October. Whereas 10,061 immigrants had entered Palestine during the eight months ending 30 April 1921, from 3 June, when immigration was restricted by conditions linking influx to absorptive capacity, to 31 December only 4,861 visas were issued.[30]

By midyear it had become apparent that the riots and their aftermath were producing additional transformations in the Palestinian triangle. For Great Britain there arose an opportunity to relinquish the troublesome mandate, citing the new climate of animosity and the failure of the League as yet to actually approve the draft mandate. But if this was a real possibility it received little support either in London or Jerusalem.

Wyndham Deedes, writing from his post in Jerusalem on 18 May, interpreted the riots as an aberration in which "reason went to the winds"—but only temporarily. It was his thesis that the local politicians had raised forces which, when set in motion, they found themselves unable to control. Similarly, his premise was that the demonstrators and rioters had been universally anti-Jewish and definitely not anti-British.

27. *Jewish Chronicle,* 10 June 1921, "Is It the End?" pp. 7–8.
28. F/86/8/2, Lloyd George Papers.
29. These statistics are drawn from monthly statements by the Palestine administration contained throughout F.O. 371/6382.
30. *Report on Palestine Administration, July, 1920–December, 1921* (London, 1922), p. 127.

Assuming these two assertions to be true, he proposed a tough approach: in the event that disorder should break out again the most vigorous measures, including the use of troops, should be taken. He concluded, however, that "the real remedy is to adopt a policy which will be acceptable to all sections of the Community. That this can be done without departing in any respect from the principles of HMG's policy as embodied in the Mandate is my firm conviction."[31] As examples he advocated: (1) a clear statement of British policy and of the meaning given the Balfour Declaration; (2) greater care in handling immigration, since to the Arab it is "the tangible, visible evidence of Zionism"; and (3) instituting representative bodies.

Hubert Young of the Colonial Office took a somewhat different view only to arrive at the same conclusion. Was Britain prepared to acknowledge that she could carry her Zionist policy into effect only to the extent that a local representative body, its majority Arab, agreed with it? Or was the only solution for her to fulfill the pledge in spite of local opposition? This was the British dilemma, and Young's view was that if local opinion was indeed incurably anti-Zionist "we should throw over not only Zionist policy but also the mandate."[32] Nevertheless, he did not believe local opinion to be unanimous in its hostility to Zionism and consequently felt that a compromise was possible.

The most realistic confirmation that Britain's future prospects were understood already in 1921 to be anything but encouraging came from the colonial secretary himself. On 9 June in a secret memorandum, "The Situation in Palestine," Churchill so informed the Cabinet: "There is no doubt we are in a situation of increasing danger which may at any time involve us in serious military embarrassments with consequent heavy expenditure. Besides this, we shall no doubt be exposed to the bitter resentment of the Zionists for not doing more to help their cause and for not protecting them better."[33] Gone was that air of optimism and certainty which had inspired Churchill during the Cairo Conference; "with the resources at my disposal I am doing all in my power, but I do not think things are going to get better in this part of the world, but rather worse." Yet his decision had been given without

31. Deedes to Young, 18 May 1921, in 26735 of C.O. 733/17A.
32. Comment of 10 June 1921 on Dispatch no. 124, in 28358 of C.O. 733/3.
33. C.P. 3030 in CAB 24/125.

hesitation: "we should certainly persevere." And in his speech before Parliament Churchill vigorously championed the British role in Palestine; the task would lie in persuading both Arab and Zionist to compromise their demands "by keeping a reasonable margin of force available in order to ensure the acceptance of the position by both parties."[34] Despite the setback, Great Britain, in the person of Mr. Churchill, stiffened her will to persevere in Palestine at whatever cost.

In the case of Mesopotamia such determination sufficed to gain victory and compliance; in Palestine it did not. During this same period (May through July) the Zionists and the Arabs also resolved to pursue maximum gains. Although they eschewed violence, their most articulate leaders intensified efforts to seek full satisfaction through firmness and through all available means of influencing British policy.

The Zionists' first indication of their continuing dependence upon British support came in internal debate over Sir Herbert Samuel and his actions. Because of his long identification with their cause, the series of decisions made by the high commissioner in May was all the more disappointing: his suspension of immigration, regarded as insensitive and unwarranted;[35] his failure to condemn the Arab attacks on Jaffa and surrounding settlements; the appointment of Haj Amin al-Husayni, convicted for inciting the brief riot in 1920, as grand mufti of Jerusalem;[36] Samuel's speech of 3 June; and, in general, his eagerness to satisfy Arab demands. These actions, indicative of Samuel's divergence over the priorities and means of the Zionist program, raised the question of whether or not he should be openly criticized.

By June this question was under serious discussion among the Zionists. Weizmann staked out his position quite clearly. No one was more disappointed than he. As late as June, 1922, he called Samuel "meek

34. *Parliamentary Debates* (Commons), 5th ser., 143 (14 June 1921) : 287.
35. On 16 May S. Landman of the Zionist Office spoke to Young on the plight of people already en route to Palestine to whom entry would be forbidden. Young thought that Samuel could have arranged for them to come in quietly via Kantara. On 19 May Churchill took it upon himself to ask if Samuel would announce in his speech that parties temporarily held up at Constantinople and Trieste would be allowed to proceed. For details see 24067 of C.O. 733/16.
36. In April, under pressure from pro-Husayni supporters, Samuel and Ronald Storrs visited Haj Amin to discuss the possible appointment. He declared his earnest desire to cooperate with the government and to maintain tranquility in Jerusalem. See Pol 2287, I.S.A.

and mild and timid"; but his practical bent compelled him to admit: "Still he is with all that the best we can have under the circumstances."[37] Landman, the general secretary of the Zionist Organisation, reflected the consensus in London when on 16 June 1921 he argued that it would be fatal to bring about the resignation of the high commissioner. An alternative strategy was prepared: "We think it would be useful to drive a wedge between him and those members of the Administration who are unfriendly to the Balfour policy."[38] Consequently, a decision was made and carried out, not to attack the high commissioner either publicly or officially.

Weizmann reflected the ambivalence in Zionist thinking. In a letter to "My dear Sir Herbert" on 27 June he reported in detail on his trip to the United States. He used this opportunity to reassure the high commissioner: "We realize your difficulties so much and I shall bend all energies to get to work."[39] Yet he followed up with a remarkable letter on 19 July which began: "It is not easy for me to write these lines to you, and I am doing so in my private capacity as one who has been honoured by your friendship and by a long standing intimate association in the work for Zionism. I would not like to add to your many burdens and I can understand only too well how worried you must be and what you must have gone through in these dark days of the Jaffa riots."[40] Replying to Samuel's claim that the political pronouncements of May and June had gone a long way toward quietening public opinion, Weizmann then volunteered that, at the same time, they had gone a long way toward inflicting serious damage on the Zionist cause. "It seems that everything in Palestinian life is now revolving round one central problem—how to satisfy 'and to pacify' the Arabs." Consequently, he reasoned, "Zionism is being gradually, systematically, and relentlessly 'reduced,' " so that, in his opinion, the situation was very critical indeed. Hopes for the reconstruction of Palestine had been shattered, Weizmann felt, by the turn that the situation suddenly took and by "the rapid, almost panic-stricken legislation" that accompanied it. "It is an article of faith with us that Palestine will be ours some day,

37. Weizmann to Eder (Jerusalem), 3 June 1922, S25/4785, C.Z.A.
38. Landman to Eder, 16 June 1921, Z4/480, C.Z.A.
39. Weizmann to Samuel, 27 June 1921, W.A.
40. Weizmann to Samuel, 19 July 1921, copy to prime minister, in F/86/8/1 of Lloyd George Papers.

but for the present it seems as if everything is conspiring to render our task almost impossible." The letter ended on a conciliatory note as the Zionist leader assured the high commissioner that "we are all anxious to help you in your difficult task, but we must be given a fair chance."

Samuel did not reply to these two letters until 10 August, when he sent a personal and private letter thanking Weizmann for his frankness. He recalled warning Weizmann as early as 1920 that the importance of the Arab problem had been underestimated by the Zionist movement, an observation only reconfirmed by his year of administration. Fearing that Weizmann and his colleagues were under serious delusion in thinking that their difficulties were due "to bias of this or that Administrator or to the lack of understanding of the Zionist Movement by the officials generally," he warned: "Unless there is very careful steering it is upon the Arab rock that the Zionist ship may be wrecked."

Samuel made it clear that he saw himself in the vital role of helmsman. "I have been from the beginning quite aware that this Policy [since May] must inevitably disappoint many, and indeed most, of my Zionist friends, and seriously diminish the satisfaction which was so cordially expressed at the time of my appointment. Nevertheless it is the only policy to be pursued, and in the long run it will be realised that it is in the best interests of the Zionist Cause."[41] If generated in England by further riots, debate over Palestine, Zionism, and the British burden could only harm the Zionists' cause, he believed, and thus he justified the policy of soothing the Arabs. In this manner a coolness developed in the relations of these two men as their different primary responsibilities—Samuel to His Majesty's Government, Weizmann "to the Jewish masses who have trusted me hitherto"—and different conceptions of the best means for achieving ultimate success were forced into sharp contrast by the events of May and June.

Because of this estrangement, Weizmann and the Zionist strategists in London—Landman, Leonard Stein, and Sokolow—made a second procedural decision. If, by common consent, there was no alternative to Sir Herbert Samuel, then two courses ought to be pursued. On the one hand, they should endeavor "to replace some of those who surround the High Commissioner and who have largely inspired his Arab policy by men of larger experience, of more open minds, and of more

41. Samuel to Weizmann, 10 August 1921, W.A.

sanguine temperaments."[42] But at the same time the high commissioner should be passed over in favor of personal contacts with his superiors in London, particularly Churchill and members of the Middle East Department. Weizmann corresponded periodically with Wyndham Deedes, Samuel's deputy in Jerusalem and an individual regarded as sympathetic, while Colonel Richard Meinertzhagen, Churchill's military adviser, was frequently consulted, and offered advice as well as information.[43]

Weizmann also had access to the leaders of the British government. Desiring to arrange a high level conference, he asked Balfour to intercede on his behalf, and the meeting was scheduled for 22 July at Balfour's home. Weizmann first met with the colonial secretary (at Churchill's request) on 10 July, and according to Weizmann they had "a very long argument." As he described the meeting: "I went to him and in quite clear terms pointed out to him the vicious circle into which the attitude of the Palestine Administration, and of the Government, is placing us. On the one hand, they complain about Zionism being the burden of the British taxpayer, and when we desire to lighten this burden by developing Palestine and so increasing the wealth and productiveness of the country, they refuse to let us go on with our work because they are fearing an Arab outburst."[44]

In attendance at the meeting on 22 July were Lloyd George, Churchill, Balfour, and the influential Cabinet secretary Maurice Hankey. According to the confidential notes of the meeting,[45] Weizmann explained that his mission to the United States—to raise funds for the development of Palestine—had been vitiated by events in Palestine, specifically by Samuel's speech, which was "a negation of the Balfour Declaration." Churchill alone demurred at this interpretation of the speech, while Bal-

---

42. Report by Leonard Stein to the Zionist Organization on "The Situation in Palestine," made upon his return in August, 1921. Two copies were sent to Shuckburgh on 19 October. See 52260 of C.O. 733/16.

43. This is apparent from Meinertzhagen's *Middle East Diary* and is supported by Weizmann's calendar for 1921.

44. Weizmann to Dr. Schmarya Levin (New York), 15 July 1921 (confidential), W.A.

45. Transcript in Weizmann Archives, text largely reproduced in Meinertzhagen, *Middle East Diary*, pp. 103–6. In a personal and private letter, to "My Dearest Friend" (Deedes) dated 31 July, Weizmann provided a slightly different verbatim account of portions. The carbon copy is in the Weizmann Archives.

four and the prime minister both said that by the declaration they had always meant the eventual founding of a Jewish state.

There followed a brief exchange about the project for representative government. In its defense Churchill cited similar plans being effected in Mesopotamia and Transjordan. To this Weizmann replied: "You will not convince me that self-government has been given to these two lands because you think it right, it has only been done because you must." All three British leaders agreed and then the prime minister spoke.

MR. LLOYD GEORGE: Frankly speaking you want to know whether we are going to keep our pledges?

DR. WEIZMANN: Yes. (*Mr. Balfour nodded.*)

MR. LLOYD GEORGE: You must do a lot of propaganda. Samuel is rather weak.

The discussion lasted for over an hour, and after the prime minister departed Balfour said: "It was a satisfactory conversation and action will follow." Then he added: "It is alright. The Prime Minister is very keen on the affair, has a high regard for you, and understands your difficult position."

Even with this encouragement, Weizmann's depression continued. In a letter to Deedes nine days later he wrote of his intention to resign at the next Zionist congress because of his deep disappointment over the present state of affairs in Palestine. "Our lives, our honour are not safe there, our prestige is being ruined, British public opinion which three years ago was distinctly in our favour is being systematically poisoned against us and I fear chiefly by those '9/10'. Of the Balfour Declaration nothing is left but mere lip service. The rock on which policy has been built up is shattered."[46] Yet from the depths of despair he concluded philosophically: "But out of this present terrible crisis, the Jewish idea will emerge triumphantly after much tribulation, because we are indestructible. . . . Ukraine, Poland, Bolshevism—all that is not enough. We must be pogromed in Palestine, submitted there to restrictions and difficulties. Such are the ways of Providence, and I believe faithfully, that

46. Weizmann to Deedes, 31 July 1921, W.A. His reference to "9/10" stemmed from the meeting of 22 July where Churchill, in describing the difficulties of fulfilling the Balfour Declaration, claimed that nine-tenths of the British officials on the spot sided with the Arabs in opposition to it.

it is all for the good in the end." In this state of mind the leading Zionist spokesman prepared to meet with the Palestine Arab delegation, scheduled to arrive in London during the early part of August.

No less anxious to influence the British government, the Arabs of Palestine used the lull after 1 May to evaluate the strengths and weaknesses of their cause. Their direct appeal to Churchill having failed, and with Samuel regarded at worst as a Zionist sympathizer, at best as an official taking his orders ultimately from London, they decided to send a delegation to Europe. Another consideration was the important advantage of the Zionists in being able to influence British policy directly, at its source in London rather than necessarily from Palestine; the very origin of the Balfour Declaration attested to this.

In 1921 the Palestinian Arab community was still fragmented. The most organized group was the Palestinian Arab Congress, with Musa Kazim Pasha al-Husayni as its president; the British administration refused to recognize it, however, challenging the representative character of the congress. Nevertheless, a fourth congress was convened at Jerusalem on 29 May with eighty-seven delegates—both Christian and Muslim, the majority of them of the landowner class—participating. Discussion centered on the Jaffa riots and the desired reaction to them. Accordingly, two decisions were taken. First, because the administration had officially recognized that the Bolsheviks were at the bottom of the disturbances, the congress should accept this contention and make it the basis of its brief. Second, the delegation to Europe and London should consist of the following: Musa Kazim Pasha (president), Haj Tawfik Hammad (vice-president), Mr. Shibly Jamal (secretary), and Muwin Bay al-Madi, Amin Bay al-Tamimi, and Ibrahim Effendi Shammas (members).[47]

Sir Herbert Samuel retracted his previous opposition to the congress and approved its decision to send these delegates. In comprehending the country's political situation after his speech of 3 June, Samuel noted an important change in the Arab community. While confirming the "public dissatisfaction of the Jews," he emphasized a general interest in public affairs stimulated by the riots and noted that the classes now were not only more race-conscious but "impressed by the power which

47. Intelligence report on the Fourth Arab Congress, in 30956 of C.O. 733/13.

they find that they possess to resist and obstruct the Government."[48] Believing that these factors did not augur well for the maintenance of good order and tranquility, the high commissioner concluded that a serious attempt had to be made to arrive at an understanding with the opponents to the Zionist policy, "even at the cost of considerable sacrifice." The only alternative would be a policy of coercion. In his mind, therefore, the Arab delegation's journey to London offered at least the opportunity for arriving at such an understanding away from the high emotional state of both communities in Palestine.

Prospects for an understanding seemed ripe. Many, perhaps a majority, of the Arabs and Jews in Palestine had been appalled by the violence and its disruptions. Similarly, the riots had alerted the administration and the British government to the serious problems inherent in the Palestine mandate. Thus, while the Arab delegation remained extreme in its demands—insisting upon abrogation of the Balfour pledge, an end to Jewish immigration, and the beginning of representative government—it was moderate in terms of its approach. Sharing fully in the need to resent and to oppose the idea of transforming Palestine into a home for the Jews, the delegation saw its role in striving through diplomacy, political pressure, and propaganda rather than by force and bloodshed.

As the delegation completed its preparations, Sir Herbert Samuel took the opportunity to once again impress upon the Colonial Office the urgency of the situation as well as the implications of either success or failure in the impending negotiations. Evaluating the Arab delegates as being well disposed, he was inclined to think that their visit offered the best prospect of a solution to the difficulties that the British were likely to have in Palestine. As regards their strategy, he felt that in the first place they would ask for the entire abandonment of the Balfour Declaration, even though they really did not expect to secure it. Churchill was likely to find that they would then be willing to come to an arrangement more or less on the lines indicated in the high commissioner's speech of 3 June. Samuel also took pains to warn of the consequences of failure. "If, on the other hand, no accommodation is reached and they return embittered by a sense of failure, they have it in their power to cause

48. Samuel to Churchill (dispatch no. 160), 13 June 1921, in 31760 of C.O. 733/3.

very great trouble. We should in that event be faced by a formidable movement, which, while the leaders will maintain a form of constitutional action, will, in fact, result in underground manoeuvres giving rise to disturbances, probably of a widespread character."[49]

On the eve of departure the delegation reinforced Samuel's impression of its being moderate by issuing a manifesto appealing to the inhabitants "to stand by their rights, with head high, and to await the results of the efforts of the Delegation. . . . Heaven will bring success."[50] Consequently, during the following months Palestine remained quiet as British, Zionist, and Arab interests, in a rare instance of correlation, dictated that the initiative be transferred from violence in the Holy Land to diplomacy in London.

The delegation left Palestine on 19 July, making its first stop in Rome on the 27th. On the following day the delegation was received by the pope in a brief audience, after which four members left for Paris and two for Geneva.[51] Meanwhile, the Colonial Office discussed its own options. On 6 July Major Young expressed what would become part of a twofold strategy. Contacts between the delegation and the Zionist Organisation were to be stressed since "there is some prospect of both sides being reasonable." As far as direct approaches by the mission to the Middle East Department were concerned, Shuckburgh saw "no reason why we should not listen to their views and discuss frankly with them any points they may have to raise" while inviting them to formulate any concrete proposals that they may have to make.[52]

Thus prepared, Churchill and Young met the delegation for the first time on 12 August. Throughout the interview the Arabs asked repeatedly what His Majesty's Government meant by a "Jewish National Home." The colonial secretary deflected such inquiries by asking the Arabs to get down to specifics and by urging them to meet with the Zionists. The fact that the differences evident in Jerusalem had hardly changed is reflected in the following exchange.

49. Samuel to Churchill, 18 July 1921, in F/9/3/72, Lloyd George Papers.
50. This manifesto is part of file 38169 of C.O. 733/16; it was published in *Doar Hayom* on 29 July 1921.
51. The delegation was kept under close surveillance by British embassies in each of the cities visited; see F.O. 371/6396.
52. Memorandum of 25 July 1921, in 37529 of C.O. 733/13.

MR. CHURCHILL: What I must tell you is this. I want you to see Dr. Weizmann.

MR. SHIBLY JAMAL: The Pasha says we do not recognise Dr. Weizmann. We recognise the British Government. We like our argument to be with the Government, because it has the power that can give or take away from us. The people of the country do not wish us to parlay with them.[53]

In repeating his insistence, Churchill revealed his primary concern: to achieve not a lasting settlement but a temporary accommodation. "I want you to try to come to some form of working arrangement. Instead of looking forward to what will happen, or may happen hundreds of years hence, let us think about what will happen in the next five years, and let us see if we cannot carry on a partnership for the next five years which could be reviewed at a later date." The meeting, however, ended with a hardening of positions by both sides and a mutual reluctance to speak in specifics.

Churchill, perhaps conscious of Samuel's earlier admonition that the fate of the British enterprise might well depend on his efforts, consented to meet for a second time with the delegation on 22 August and sought to be more conciliatory in tone. The Arabs believed that they would get nothing more out of the Palestine administration, hence their presence in England; the Colonial Office continued to view them as an unofficial body. The Arabs insisted that they did not see how the two parts of the Balfour Declaration could be harmonized; the colonial secretary appealed to them to be reasonable.

Churchill wanted to see both sides dwelling in Palestine in peace and amity. He would be the opponent of whoever tried to oppress the Arab. Could they not work hand in hand? Could they not reassure their people? Take up their share in the government of the country and give the Jews their chance? If this did not work, they would have plenty of time in the future to make their complaints. The Jews, after all, faced a far more difficult task than did the Arabs.[54] But his efforts failed. In a letter dated 1 September Musa Kazim Pasha informed him that the Palestine Arab delegation most sincerely regretted its inability to re-

53. Verbatim report of the interview, in 41298 of C.O. 733/17B.
54. Minutes in 42762 of C.O. 733/14.

move or modify the difference which existed between its point of view
and that of the government with regard to the policy of the government
in Palestine.[55]

Despite this early impasse, the British and the Arab delegation agreed
that the mission definitely should not be terminated, though for different
reasons. As Shuckburgh cautioned, "The return of the Delegation empty-
handed might well be the signal for renewed disturbances, and I know
that the S. of S. is anxious to keep them on in England for the present. . . ."[56] For their part, the Arabs were intent upon remaining and
renewed their efforts on a broader scale. Writing to a supporter in the
United States, the secretary of the delegation, Shibly Jamal, described
its activities.

Concerning publicity we are using every means to give our cause the adver-
tisement it deserves. We have engaged the services of an advertising and
Press Agency which not only distributes our circulars, statements and articles to all the Press in England both urban and provincial, but also employs
other means, such as engaging halls for speeches, advertising on the street,
etc. etc. We hope soon to be able to put the cause of Palestine in a nutshell
before the man on the street, as well as penetrate into the homes of the rich
and influential men in this country.[57]

The delegation was in almost daily contact with several members of the
House of Lords and the Commons who were in sympathy with the Arab
cause. Indicating that "on the whole . . . we are all satisfied with the
work so far," Jamal cautioned that "it may take months before we succeed in changing the present current of thought in the Government and
in the Press."

Having received sympathetic reactions from the pope, the archbishop
of Paris, and the archbishop of Canterbury, the delegates pressed their
case before the League of Nations. Two official letters were submitted,
on 2 September and again on the 10th, informing the Council that the
Palestinians demanded the abolition of the principle of the creation of a
national home for the Jews in Palestine and rejected any mandate over

55. See 44017 of C.O. 733/16.
56. Memorandum of 2 October 1921, in 48808 of C.O. 733/6.
57. Jamal to Dr. F. I. Shatara of the Palestine National Society in Brooklyn, New
   York; a duplicate is in the Weizmann Archives.

the country.[58] On 29 September, in an interview with Mr. Fisher, head of the British delegation in Geneva, the Arabs reiterated their opposition to the importation of what they termed "undesirable Jews" and the denial not so much of self-government as of the right to it.[59] Commenting on Faysal's enthronement in Iraq, they viewed it as partial redemption, though still not sufficient, of the British wartime pledge and urged that Britain pay closer attention to the grievances of the Arab peoples in Syria and Palestine. This revival of the call for a larger, united Syria stemmed from the fact that, while in Geneva, several of the delegates also participated in a conference of Syrian exiles in order to push their claims.

Upon its return to London the delegation relented somewhat and consented to meet with Zionist representatives. The British government, anxious to facilitate some form of Arab-Jewish rapprochement, applied pressure on both sides. On 12 November Shuckburgh informed the delegation and Dr. Weizmann that Mr. Churchill was now in a position to make a statement of policy in Palestine and would be glad to receive them on the 16th. On the day fixed for the meeting both parties received telephone calls that the colonial secretary was ill and that the meeting could not take place. Weizmann was subsequently informed that Churchill had changed his mind and was not prepared to make a statement. Instead, another meeting was called for 29 November, at which Churchill would not preside, delegating this duty to Shuckburgh, who was not empowered to make a clear statement.[60]

The meeting, which took place at the Colonial Office, lasted for more than two hours and was, on the whole, conducted with good temper on both sides. Dr. Weizmann offered to enter into direct discussion on the two main points raised by Shuckburgh: limitation of Jewish immigration and constitutional safeguards against Jewish political ascendancy. The Arabs did not accept this offer, although Shuckburgh appealed to them to do so. Weizmann assured his listeners that the Zionist movement

58. Letters dated 2 and 10 September 1921, from the Palestine Arab Delegation; see E11029 of F.O. 371/6380 and 50371 of C.O. 733/11.
59. Memorandum of the interview with the "Delegation from Syria and Palestine," in 49739 of C.O. 732/5.
60. Weizmann's diary, however, indicates that on 28 November he had a meeting with Churchill just prior to the conference with the Arabs.

did not mean to enroach on the legitimate political aspirations of the indigenous Arabs; nor would it concentrate on measures designed to effect a partition of Palestine, preferring to see the two nations live in political harmony in the future. The Arab delegates in turn directed their criticism primarily at the British government, maintaining that it did not understand the meaning of the Balfour Declaration. "Why could not His Britannic Majesty's Government give a clear interpretation so that Arabs might know where they were? In the present circumstances they were unable to discuss anything at all since they knew not what to discuss."[61]

With the Zionists standing firmly on the draft mandate, which incorporated the Balfour Declaration, with the Arabs calling the draft "quite repugnant" and regarding revocation of the declaration as the proper solution to the problem, and with the British again unwilling to set forth a clear statement of official policy, the meeting proved inconclusive. Each party was left to draw its own conclusions. In the years that followed, the respective Arab and Zionist positions hardened, just as the frequency of their dialogue diminished.

Groping for a straw of hope, Shuckburgh wrote of his fear that the results of the meeting were rather negative in character but that at least it was something to have brought the two parties together. He contributed to the policy of temporization which in later phases of the Palestine problem would be followed by Great Britain, the United States, and the international community by concluding: "I do not think that we need be in a great hurry to reach the next stage. Doctor Weizmann is just off to America and until he comes back further joint discussions are not likely to do much good. I think also that there may be some advantage in allowing the parties to kick their heels a little."[62]

Another British participant to the meeting, Mr. Mills, Palestine government officer at the Colonial Office, laid the blame for the failure directly at the feet of Weizmann, criticizing not so much his remarks as their presentation. "Dr. Weizmann, while his speech was conciliatory, adopted an unfortunate manner in delivering it. His attitude was of the nature of a conqueror handing to beaten foes the terms of peace. Also

61. "Note on a meeting between the Arab Delegation and the Zionist Organisation" (secret), in C.O. 537/855.
62. *Ibid.*

I think he despises the members of the Delegation as not worthy protagonists—that it is a little derogatory to him to expect him to meet them
on the same ground."[63]

Weizmann, for his part, was critical of the British position. "Before
any progress can be made, it is essential that the Delegation should
realise that the Mandate is regarded by His Majesty's Government as
chose jugée. . . . Faced with an unambiguous intimation to this effect,
the Delegation . . . will doubtless see the expediency of descending into
the region of practical politics."[64]

The Arab delegation, never having put great faith in talks with the
Zionists, returned to its primary objective of influencing the British
government, directly or indirectly, through "practical politics."

When dialogue with the delegation proved sterile, the Zionists cast
about for an alternative, seeking an Arab leader, at once influential and
willing to accept the Zionist program, with whom to negotiate. For by
this time the Zionist leadership in Palestine and in London fully understood the necessity of repairing the breach in relations with the Arab
community. To be sure, voices of moderation did exist among the Arabs.
In an interview published during November in an Arab newspaper,
General Haddad Pasha, in Egypt on his way to Amman, voiced his
opinion that the Arabs could not ask Great Britain to withdraw the
Balfour Declaration, because they would not care to have British pledges
to themselves annulled.[65] In December Dr. Eder, director of the Zionist
Commission in Jerusalem, was instructed to meet with the mufti of
Jerusalem and other members of the Husayni family. He reported that
the Arabs were willing to accept the Balfour Declaration and government control over immigration in return for an elected legislative assembly.[66] One member of the Arab delegation, Muwin Bay al-Madi, was
described as conciliatory in his talks with Weizmann. Furthermore, the

63. *Ibid.* Weizmann's true feelings must have been obvious, for on 10 August he
had written of the Arab delegation, "Happily they are fifth rate people but they
can make a stink and they are supported by an anti-semitic clique . . ." (letter to
a colleague in America, W.A.).
64. Weizmann to Shuckburgh, 1 December 1921, in 59977 of C.O. 733/16.
65. Interview in *Mokattam*, commented on in the *Near East*, 10 November 1921, p.
590.
66. Eder to Weizmann, 14 December 1921, W.A. On 8 December Weizmann had
urged him to work at "forming another party and this Delegation [in England]
will lose its importance" (*ibid.*).

Zionists were in continuous contact with Amir Abdullah in Transjordan.[67] At Rosh Pinna, in Galilee, Chaim Kalvarisky continued his individual efforts to arrive at a settlement with notables of the area.

The main hope of the Zionists at the end of 1921, however, was a young Syrian nationalist, Riad al-Sulh, who was later, in 1943, to serve as premier of Lebanon. At the time, al-Sulh was in exile in Europe, having been secretary of the interior in the first Syrian cabinet under Ali Rida al-Rikabi. He fled along with many others after Maysalun and had been court-martialed *in absentia* by the French. He was currently a member of the Executive Committee of the Arab Nationalist Congress, which had recently met in Geneva.

Riad al-Sulh apparently had been introduced to Weizmann for the first time in London during October, and Weizmann had found him sympathetic, despite the tendency of Deedes to regard him as "a very slippery customer."[68] Consequently, on 8 November a secret meeting took place at the home of Mr. James de Rothschild. Present were Rothschild, Weizmann, Leonard Stein, a Mr. Wolfenson, Ittamar Ben-Avi, and Riad al-Sulh. A "Draft Basis for Discussion of Arab-Jewish Entente" was discussed in detail.[69] The draft had resulted from a resolution passed by the Twelfth Zionist Congress (held in Carlsbad, Czechoslovakia, during October) which called for efforts to "secure an honourable entente" with the Arabs "on terms of concord and mutual respect." The draft accordingly stressed the following points: insuring minority rights; Jews and Arabs were to be regarded as "living side by side on a footing of perfect equality in all matters"; there would be limited immigration based on capacity; most non-Palestinian officials were to be replaced gradually by natives; Jews would support the demand for development of self-governing institutions on a representative basis; and Zionist leaders and Palestine Jews would, "in general, cooperate whole-heartedly with the Arab people in its efforts to realise its legitimate national aspirations" by giving all possible moral and ma-

67. Weizmann to Eder, 8 December 1921, *ibid.*
68. A record of the talk is part of the minutes of the fifth meeting of the Zionist Executive on 24 and 25 October 1921. Eder reported the view of Deedes on 27 November. Both accounts are in the Weizmann Archives.
69. At Weizmann's request Stein sent a note on the meeting to Shuckburgh on 8 November (56020 of C.O. 733/16); see also file A18/43/6 in C.Z.A.

terial support. In many ways it was reminiscent of Weizmann's agreement with Faysal in 1919.

Riad al-Sulh agreed to most of the clauses and promised to give further consideration to the draft and also to formulate counterproposals on objectionable parts. In December, while on a mission for the Arab Nationalist Congress to Palestine, Transjordan, and Egypt, he visited Sir Herbert Samuel and related to him his activities in London. Although Riad al-Sulh continued to negotiate with the Zionists throughout 1922,[70] nothing came of this secondary effort to achieve an understanding. Instead it was but one more setback during the year which led Weizmann to refer to 1921 as "this terrible year ever."

In several respects 1921 ended with all parties disillusioned and sharing Weizmann's personal exasperation over prospects for peace and development. First, the Zionists—and none more so than their leader, Dr. Weizmann—regarded the year as a setback. Among the reversals that could be listed were: differences with the "Zionist" high commissioner; a decline in support among the British public; insecurity and the fear of further violence inside Palestine; a policy of immigration linked to absorptive capacity while the economy was stagnating; the continued delay in gaining League approval for the mandate; and the failure to remove Arab opposition. Indeed, it was apparent from the nature of the discussions in London that a regression of sorts was taking place. Samuel's speech of 3 June and the Arab delegations's strategy opened to question the validity and intent of a declaration obtained from Balfour and the British government four years earlier.

Weizmann's letters of November and December, 1921, reflect his fear that the Zionist cause was in jeopardy. In a letter to Shuckburgh on 16 November, Weizmann, the individual who would always be identified and attacked as an enthusiast of Zionist success through dependence upon Great Britain, wrote: "For years I have used every endeavour to cooperate loyally with the Administration of Palestine to impress upon my own followers the need of patience and carefulness—but I can see how every effort is being systematically thwarted and the chances of

---

70. For an account of these later negotiations, see Ascher Saphir, *Unity, or Partition! An Historical Survey of Judaeo-Arab Negotiations for the Recognition of Jewish Rights in Palestine* (Jerusalem, 1937).

success ruined."[71] This he attributed to political sabotage by "definite forces working in the dark," whose interest was to render the Palestine problem acute. Without specifying the nature and composition of these forces, he ended with an even broader, if ultimately objective, assessment of guilt. "We are all condoning a state of affairs for which some day we shall be called to book by the people of this country, when the whole sad story of Palestine becomes known."

In late November Weizmann proposed to write to Churchill as well. Although the letter was never sent, the draft offers further insight into the Palestine situation as seen from the narrower perspective of Zionist interests.[72] The writer wished to reaffirm his belief that there was "a natural alliance, almost an identity of interest," between Zionism and England in Palestine based on the fact of "Jewish Nationalism as a powerful world-force." Then, in a shift of emphasis, he requested that the colonial secretary strengthen the hand of Sir Herbert Samuel; for the real mind of the high commissioner, Weizmann maintained, was expressed not in the policy announced on 3 June but in a speech delivered on 2 November 1919 in which he adhered to the dream of Palestine's becoming "a purely self-governing Commonwealth under the auspices of an established Jewish majority." The trouble, he suggested, was that the conditions had not been created for Samuel to become "an effectual managing trustee of the British and Zionist interests." These conditions were an operative mandate, purging the Palestine civil service of every insubordinate who would not work for the mandate, and making Palestine independent in its military organization from the "headquarters in Egypt which are definitely anti-Zionist." Still, according to Weizmann, the main fault was with the government for not making its policy so plain that it would be impossible for any official to oppose it and still keep his position.

Weizmann, feeling his own standing among Zionists endangered, wrote along similar lines to Wyndham Deedes on 13 December. He did not miss the opportunity to repeat his contention that the real cause of all the evil was the attitude of the majority of the British in Palestine, which accounted for the "negative and obstructive" posture of the Arab

71. Weizmann to Shuckburgh (private and personal), 16 November 1921, W.A.
72. The draft, typed on Zionist Organisation stationery, has survived as part of Weizmann's papers, W.A.

delegation and for the disappointing state of Palestine during 1921. Two recent developments were offered as evidence. The first was a luncheon given by the Arab delegation on 15 November at which Lord Sydenham delivered a speech, entitled "Zionist Aggression in Palestine," wherein he denounced the Balfour Declaration and any right of the Jews to Palestine.[73] What Weizmann objected to, in addition to the speech itself, was the countenance given it by political officers and generals lately a part of the British administration in Palestine.

The second incident alluded to by Weizmann was a circular issued by General Congreve, commander of British troops in Palestine, in late October. It read, in part:

... Whilst the Army officially is supposed to have no politics, it is recognised that there are certain problems such as those of Ireland and Palestine, in which the sympathies of the Army are on one side or the other.

In the case of Palestine these sympathies are rather obviously with the Arabs, who have hitherto appeared to the disinterested observer to have been the victims of the unjust policy forced upon them by the British Government.[74]

In another context Weizmann commented: "I think that of all the wicked things that have been done to us in the last six months, this is about the worst," the most exasperating feature being that Samuel had allowed the circular to be issued without protesting it.[75]

Such evidence of opposition notwithstanding, Weizmann concluded his letter to Deedes, and thus the year, with renewed determination to persevere. "It is quite true that the Zionist ideals may have upset some

73. See a report on the affair in *The Times*, 16 November 1921, p. 12. Among those in attendance were: Lord Raglan, the former Major Somerset, just returned from his post in Transjordan; General Costello, late commander of the defunct Palestine Defense Force; General Palin, former commander of troops in Palestine; Colonel Gabriel, late financial adviser to the Palestine administration; and Colonel Waters-Taylor, until recently chief of staff to the chief administrator in Palestine. The speech was subsequently printed and distributed in England, a copy being found also in the Weizmann Archives.
74. The text is in F/86/8/4 of the Lloyd George Papers. General Congreve told Young on 10 October that he and his officers were certainly under the impression that His Majesty's Government was in the hands of the Zionist Organisation; see 56586 in C.O. 733/17B.
75. Weizmann to Eder, 13 December 1921, in S25/4785, C.Z.A.

Arabs and British anti-Semites, but these are the very ideals which have been sanctified by thousands of years of martyrdom. . . . Take them away, or water them down, and Zionism ceases to exist. That is why I cannot endorse the speech of June 3rd, though I have no intention of entering into a public controversy on the subject." To the Zionists the Cairo Conference had passed Palestine by. The order of priority for 1922, therefore, was for all parties to "speak perfectly clearly about fundamental matters."

The Arabs also reflected upon 1921 with misgivings. The immigration of Jews continued, threatening the traditional way of life and the Arabs' majority status. Some concessions had been granted as a result of the riots, but at a heavy cost of disruption and recourse to violence. The fear that the events of May had indeed established an ominous precedent was confirmed for Arab moderates by a further, milder outbreak on 2 November in which forty-two arrests were made, thirty-six people were wounded, and eight persons died—five Jews and three Muslims.[76] Meanwhile, in Europe, apparently sharing British concern that the return of the mission to Palestine without tangible evidence of success would only strengthen the extremists, the Arab delegation continued its efforts.

Members of the delegation lingered in England throughout the first half of 1922, engaging in sporadic correspondence with the Colonial Office. When allowed to see the draft of a proposed Palestine Order in Council, which embodied a scheme of government, they saw enough justification for rejecting it, primarily on the grounds that it fell short of giving the people of Palestine full control of their own affairs.[77] Expressing continued confidence in the justice of the British government and its sense of fair play, the delegation awaited a new initiative from Churchill. This took the form of a statement of the existing political situation in Palestine, which has since become known as the Churchill White Paper.[78]

---

76. The clash began in Jerusalem with protestations and demonstrations by Arabs on the fourth anniversary of the Balfour Declaration. Relevant material is found in file 2108 at the Israel State Archives and in Samuel's report of 29 December 1921, in 1641 of C.O. 733/8.
77. Letter dated 21 February 1922.
78. "Palestine: Correspondence with the Palestine Arab Delegation and the Zionist Organisation" (Cmd. 1700), 1922.

The statement contained nine points: (1) the declaration of November, 1917, was reaffirmed by the government and declared to be not susceptible to change; (2) a Jewish national home would be founded with the Jewish people there "as of right and not on sufferance"; (3) no disappearance or subordination of Arab population, language, or culture was contemplated; (4) all citizens would have the status of Palestinians; (5) Britain intended to foster a full measure of self-government —but gradually; (6) the Zionist Executive would not share in the government of the country; (7) immigration would not exceed economic capacity and (8) would be regulated by the legislative assembly in consultation with the administration; (9) any religious community or "considerable section of population" which claimed that terms of the mandate were not being fulfilled would have the right to appeal to the League of Nations.

The Executive of the Zionist Organisation resolved on 18 June 1922 to conduct activities in conformity with this new statement of policy. The reply from the Arab delegation, dated 17 June, was in the negative, given the fact that "His Majesty's Government has placed itself in the position of a partisan in Palestine of a certain policy which the Arab cannot accept because it means his extinction sooner or later." In short the Palestinian Arab community, as represented by the delegation, persisted in expecting Great Britain to sever her tie to the Balfour Declaration as the precondition for negotiation.

As for the members, civilian and military, of the administration in Palestine, they could not agree on any single priority after the confusing, divisive events of 1921. Uncertain as to Great Britain's purpose in Palestine, and eventually identifying with either the Arabs or Zionists, individual officials also differed over specific measures and responses adopted by the high commissioner. Nor did Samuel, unlike Sir Percy Cox, control his staff to the extent of removing dissenters. Rather, for Samuel the "absolute necessity" was securing settlement of the mandate question. A constitution and municipal elective system, adoption of a nationality law, appointment of a holy places commission, a Palestinian currency, the development of mineral resources, private enterprise and investment—all these were in abeyance pending issuance of the mandate and a regularization of the British position. Such a contrast between inactivity and the hopes which initially had been entertained of development under British rule, Samuel believed, combined to cause "a general feeling of uncertainty, which is a direct incentive to agitation,"[79] and therefore inimical to peace.

In effect, while the Zionists, the Arabs, and the high commissioner could find precious little upon which to agree during 1921, their respective priorities—defining policy, revising it, and securing the mandate—did coincide in requiring that the major initiative come from London. But circumstances were such that the Middle East Department offered little indication of assuming such a task. It had been hoped that through the Cairo Conference stability would be restored to the Fertile Crescent. The Palestinian riots in May, coming so soon after the conference, had had a naturally disheartening effect, particularly when taken in conjunction with the tension involved in securing Faysal in Iraq and the unsatisfactory state of affairs in Transjordan. In addition, Churchill apparently lost interest in the Middle East, and especially in the frustrating Palestine issue, toward the end of the year, preferring to direct his energies to such challenges as the Irish Rebellion. Thus, as early as 16 November 1921, Meinertzhagen noted: "Winston does not care two pins, and does not want to be bothered about it. He is reconciled to a policy of drift. He is too wrapped up in Home Politics."[80]

Not prepared to assert its full influence on both nationalist movements in Palestine, the British government favored quiet and, in essence, inaction as the prudent approach. This was to endure throughout the mandatory period. Another feature of British rule which began in 1921 was the tendency of Great Britain to accept responsibility for Palestine, yet with a strange air of resignation and even cynicism. Commenting on French diplomatic maneuvers on 20 December, Sir John Shuckburgh wrote: "The French are not such fools as to wish to become responsible for setting up the National Home."[81] Great Britain would persist, conscious of the heavy and thankless burden, and aware that virtually no progress had been made in the year of the Cairo Conference toward answering the political questions that disturbed the minds of so many people—whether Arab, Jew, or Englishman.

79. Samuel to Churchill, 14 October 1921, in 52954 of C.O. 733/6.
80. Meinertzhagen, *Middle East Diary*, p. 112.
81. Shuckburgh to Sir James Masterton Smith, 20 December 1921, in 63608 of C.O. 733/11.

CHAPTER 9 Transjordan

> ... *I have had enough of this wilderness of Trans-*
> *Jordania where I am surrounded by these hateful*
> *Syrians who think of themselves only. . . .* —Amir
> Abdullah, August, 1921

The year 1921, already memorable for the genesis of monarchy in Iraq and the atmosphere of intransigence and violence in Palestine, also marks the beginning of Jordan's history. Amir Abdullah began his long reign, and the territory took its first, hesitant strides toward eventual statehood and sovereignty, both on the basis of a firm relationship with Great Britain.

At the start of the year the status of Transjordan remained unsettled, a condition which had persisted during the latter half of 1920, much to the discomfiture of the Foreign and War offices and to the anxiety of the British high commissioner for Palestine. In January, disregarding the official rebuff to his plea for a direct occupation the previous autumn, Sir Herbert Samuel renewed efforts along those same lines. On 7 January, in correspondence with Foreign Secretary Curzon, he enclosed a general report from the 'Ajlun area, where the British representative on the spot warned that Syrian immigrants from the north were posing a serious problem. The mere presence of these individuals, described as extreme nationalists, persons condemned by the French, discharged officers and officials, adventurers and criminals, most of them penniless, was felt to be "both a burden and a danger."[1]

Again, on 8 January, writing from Jerusalem, Samuel contended that events in Transjordan were having an immediate influence on Palestine and, in particular, on efforts at reducing the British garrison.

If there is no effective administration there, if lawless bands are able to terrorise the settled population, if trade is hampered, or stopped altogether, and life and property are insecure, the effects will straightway be felt here. The raids which have been launched from that quarter periodically will recommence. The supplies of food will be curtailed or cease, and the people of Palestine will become aggrieved at the higher cost of living that will result. The whole territory having been placed under British influences, such a state of affairs will discredit British administration. . . .[2]

These considerations, plus the likelihood that Transjordan would become a center for propaganda hostile to the Palestine administration, led Samuel to suggest as a preventive measure the stationing of 500 men of the British army at Amman. Such an action, requiring perhaps 30,000 Egyptian pounds, would still allow for reduced expenditures by obviating the necessity for positioning a much larger force in the Jordan valley and as a reserve in central Palestine.

On 1 February Samuel informed London that sharifian propaganda and preparations for attack on the French were continuing uninterrupted and that the local governments, established after his earlier visit to Salt, were finding it increasingly difficult to maintain authority and collect taxes.[3] A week later he elaborated: three women from Damascus had arrived at Maʻan to serve as nurses; an anti-French recruiting drive was under way in Amman; two sharifian officers and a small party had left for the north intent upon destroying the railway north of Daraa. Sharifian influence in general was increasing steadily at Maʻan under the direction of Abdullah and under his lieutenant, one Sharif Ali ibn Husayn, in Transjordan proper, while British prestige and authority were declining.[4]

1. "General Report on Ajloun Area," enclosure by Samuel to Curzon, 7 January 1921, in E1064/31/88 (no. 13), F.O. 406/45, p. 169.
2. Samuel to Curzon, 8 January 1921, in E1062/401/88 (no. 11), *ibid.*
3. Samuel to the Foreign Office, 1 February 1921, in E1515 (no. 45) of F.O. 371/ 6371.
4. Samuel to the Foreign Office, 10 February 1921, in E1868 (no. 57) of *ibid.*

The bankruptcy of British policy east of the Jordan at this time is reflected by comments from within the Foreign Office. R. C. Lindsay confessed on 11 February that he could not think of "any temporary expedient" for dealing with the situation. Hubert Young, recalling General Haddad Pasha's comment the previous evening that Britain had only herself to blame—not for refusing to dispatch troops, but for allowing such a long period of chaos and anarchy to persist—tended to agree and felt that the sooner "we can select an Arab ruler, take guarantees from him, and let it be known that as long as he fulfils them he will have our support" the better. By contrast Lord Curzon showed a penchant for dwelling on the past record, claiming to have constantly advocated British troops and an Arab Transjordan, only to meet opposition from other sources, particularly the War Office—that is, Churchill. But as the administration of the Middle East was presently being transferred to the Colonial Office, the consensus was to maintain the status quo as well in Transjordan until Britain had decided on her whole future policy in the Arab countries.

Sharifian pressure, however, did not abate, nor did it respect the British moratorium on decision-making. On 12 February Samuel had a long conversation with Auni Abdul Hadi, reputed to be in close touch with Husayn and his sons, Faysal and Abdullah.[5] The Arab emissary first sought some expression of approval for the movements in Transjordan against the French, but when the high commissioner gave him friendly advice not to pursue it further he then dwelt on the deep disappointment of the Arabs generally, and of the sharifians in particular. It was impossible, he maintained, for them to sit still and accept the present situation in Syria. Samuel in turn relieved himself of his grievance that sharifian activity had introduced confusion into the minds of the people of Transjordan and was therefore undermining the British position. The two men then parted, neither having made any form of commitment.

Perhaps because of the inconclusive nature of this conversation, Wyndham Deedes several days later voiced the feeling in Jerusalem that, in default of the permanent location of British troops in Transjordan, a route march ought to be carried out.[6] A portion of the troops in Palestine would parade the flag that spring, starting from Semakh

5. Samuel to Curzon, 12 February 1921, in E2354/35/88 (no. 83) of F.O. 406/45.
6. Deedes to R. C. Lindsay, 18 February 1921, in 12555 of C.O. 733/9.

through Irbid, 'Ajlun, Jerash, Salt, Amman, and Kerak. Such a gesture, though obviously transitory, might nevertheless strengthen the authority of the local governments while constituting an overt sign of British interest in Transjordan.

The suggested route march also was tabled because of the imminent Cairo Conference, where a fundamental decision would have to be reached as to the degree of responsibility and control to be exercised by His Majesty's Government in Transjordan. In the midst of the conference preparations, further alarm was occasioned by news from Samuel that Abdullah was expected to enter Amman shortly. This initiative, which ended the brief British experiment in local administration, ran contrary to assurances given by Faysal in London, Husayn in the Hijaz, and Auni Abdul Hadi in Jerusalem. In one decisive action Abdullah had upset the uneasy equilibrium, placing Great Britain on the defensive and increasing the prospects of a frontal assault against the French in Syria. The latter was reconfirmed by reports from Consul Palmer in Damascus that Arab raiders under Ahmad Muraywad, a former supporter of Faysal, had penetrated Syrian territory and blown up an important railway bridge.[7] Palmer subsequently added that in the course of their expedition the marauders had persuaded the fourteen gendarmes on guard at the bridge to join Abdullah and had even driven off some French troops that were in pursuit.

This bold act of defiance, while never traced directly to Abdullah, enhanced the amir's prestige. On 7 March Palmer wired that many volunteers and ex-officers from the Damascus state were flocking to the sharifian camp and that consequently "an attack by him is considered imminent."[8] Finally, on 14 March, with the Cairo Conference already in session, Palmer submitted a more detailed report based on information from Druze sources.[9] It was confirmed that Abdullah was in Amman, where he was joined by most of the local *shaykhs*. His forces were estimated at 8,000 armed men, including cavalry, while seventeen guns and ten airplanes of the Hijazi army were said to be moving up slowly.

---

7. Palmer (Damascus) to Curzon, 23 and 25 February 1921, in E3108 (no. 10) and E3142 (no. 11) of F.O. 406/45.
8. Palmer to Curzon, 7 March 1921, in E3513/117/89 (no. 19) of *ibid.*; see also *The Times*, "Arabs Make Trouble in Syria" (dated Cairo, 24 February 1921), 28 February 1921.
9. Palmer to Curzon, 14 March 1921, in E3810/31/88 (no. 26) of F.O. 406/45.

Many Druze and natives of the Hauran could be expected to side with Abdullah if he were successful at the outset. The amir also had sent letters to former officials of the Damascus government seeking volunteers and had contracted for 4,000 uniforms to be supplied through Jerusalem. Meanwhile, Abdullah was not giving any regular pay to his followers, but made them a daily largess from his personal funds and promised to reward them with the spoils of Damascus.

When the authorities who had gathered at Cairo learned of these developments—which constituted open defiance of Great Britain—they reacted sharply, for Abdullah's action possessed grave implications for British policy in the Middle East. Not only did it restore Transjordan to its chaotic condition, but it jeopardized the fragile tranquility in Palestine as well. Even more serious, it threatened to renew violence in Syria and to reopen the prospect of an effective French presence, by retaliation, near Arabia and on a second border of both Mesopotamia and Palestine. Moreover, a war between France and the sharifians would vitiate a constant of Foreign Office policy since 1918: to avoid the necessity of choosing between the French and the Arabs.

With the stakes so high, even Churchill favored Samuel's renewed plan for occupying Transjordan immediately, using British troops from Palestine. The Palestine Political and Military Committee so moved on 17 March.[10] Churchill cabled the prime minister accordingly the following day and received hesitant Cabinet approval on the 22d as he prepared to confront Amir Abdullah personally in Jerusalem.[11] Because this recommendation depended for its success on the attitude adopted by the amir, the colonial secretary placed great emphasis on this meeting.

Meanwhile, Abdullah arrived at Amman on 2 March, offering as an explanation for his coming the need for a change of air, necessitated by a severe attack of jaundice.[12] Accompanying him were about 30 officers and 200 Hijazi Bedouin. On the 21st he received an invitation from Samuel to come to Government House on the 27th to meet Churchill.

10. Minutes of the discussion are contained on pp. 97–106 of the official report, F.O. 371/6343.
11. Prime Minister to Churchill, F.O. 371/6342, p. 9.
12. Samuel to Churchill, "Report on the Political Situation in Palestine and Trans-Jordania for the month of March 1921" (Dispatch no. 32), 8 April 1921, in 21698 of C.O. 733/2.

Between the Cairo recommendation and Abdullah's entry into Amman and the Abdullah-Churchill conversations, both men had mellowed. The colonial secretary, while bellicose at Cairo, realized the need for accommodation with Abdullah and the utility of incorporating Transjordan into the sharifian solution. Also, the overriding desire to achieve demobilization and economy—as well as the setback Britain's occupation of Transjordan would imply—reasserted itself as the central element in Churchill's thinking as he traveled to Jerusalem.

Abdullah, on the other hand, was described as "much concerned" to hear the news of the French settlement with the Kemalists. As well he might, for it made any ambition to regain Syria by external force a hollow dream. There is serious doubt as to whether Abdullah ever really intended to carry out his threat to seize Syria, either for himself or for Faysal. Lawrence, for one, claimed to have advised Churchill: "I know Abdulla, you won't have a shot fired."[13] A halt in the Franco-Turkish fighting ended the possibility of any Kemalist-sharifian concert and thus enabled General Gouraud to deal forcefully with Abdullah should he dare to cross into Syria. The amir's attitude, once he reached Amman, was "just to wait and see what happens."[14] He must have traveled from there to Jerusalem in a somewhat chastened mood.

As a result of these considerations the Jerusalem talks were conducted amicably by both sides.[15] At their conclusion Abdullah was entrusted with control over Transjordan for a six-month period. Thus he would not be forced to lose face by either challenging France or withdrawing to the Hijaz, while Churchill and Great Britain might yet succeed in avoiding military intervention and direct control in Transjordan.

The Abdullah-Churchill agreement provided for the permanent constitution of Transjordan as an Arab province within Palestine under the ultimate supervision of the British high commissioner for Palestine. On 2 April Churchill cabled instructions to Samuel to make an immediate advance of £5,000 to Abdullah from the Palestine treasury for his per-

13. Graves and Hart, *T. E. Lawrence to His Biographers*, p. 131.
14. Sir Alec Kirkbride to the present author, 13 December 1967. Asked to characterize Abdullah, the former British minister to Jordan and long-time confidant of the amir described him as always a gambler. See Kirkbride, *A Crackle of Thorns*, pp. 25–26, for an account of their initial meeting upon Abdullah's arrival in Amman.
15. See pp. 129–32 above; for the official record, see F.O. 371/6343, pp. 107–14.

sonal expenses, quite apart from administrative or military expenditures. A chief political officer was to be appointed shortly to advise Abdullah during the interim administration. In the meantime, at the request of Sir Herbert Samuel, Colonel Lawrence would rejoin the amir early in April at Amman.[16]

In his first dispatch, dated 10 April, Lawrence provided a picture of Abdullah's unenviable position. Judging the situation to be "fairly satisfactory" at the outset, he noted that the

financial position of Abdullah is more difficult than he gave us to expect. He has about 500 men with him, soldiers, irregular cavalry and camel corps. They are in arrears of pay. Further he has to entertain all comers, and deputations of 2 or 3 hundred are a daily matter, his living expenses are very great. His account for last month totalled nearly £10,000. No estimate of financial position of Trans-Jordania has as yet been made by his staff who are framing wild projects of complete armies and administrations.[17]

The British therefore felt obliged to do whatever was necessary to assist the amir. On 11 April Samuel notified Churchill, by now back in London, that the appointment of Mr. Abramson, of the high commissioner's office, as chief political officer in Transjordan would be welcomed by Abdullah, and Churchill consented on the 14th. Samuel, accompanied by Deedes, Lawrence, and Abramson, then spent three days (17–19 April) in Amman in consultation with the amir and members of his embryonic administration. Upon his return to Jerusalem he wired a favorable appraisal of the situation to Churchill. "Attitude of cordial friendship he adopted at Jerusalem is maintained by Abdullah. In his abandonment of attacks against French he is sincere and has impressed this policy upon his followers, to many of whom it is unwelcome. However, his influence has not been impaired and our cooperation with him undoubtedly is a satisfaction to whole population."[18]

Defense had been the main topic of discussion, since Lawrence in his earlier visit had alerted the Middle East Department to Abdullah's inability, even with his good intentions, to maintain effective internal se-

16. Lawrence to Shuckburgh, via Jerusalem, 1 April 1921, in 16308 of C.O. 732/1.
17. Lawrence to Churchill, via Jerusalem (no. 72), 10 April 1921, in 17941 of C.O. 733/2.
18. Samuel to Churchill (paraphrase telegram no. 93, pt. 1), 21 April 1921, in 19801 of *ibid.*

curity. Churchill's temporary arrangement with Abdullah had post-poned the placing of a British garrison at Amman, leaving only the Arab soldiers—many of whom retained their desire to raid Syria—and the Royal Air Force to support the local government. Lawrence thought a detachment of two armored cars at Amman would be most useful to control the tribes.

Shortly after the Abdullah experiment began, Sir Herbert Samuel dismissed the local government headed by Rashid Tali' as "more of a picnic than an administration"; however, its very weakness in fulfilling the minimal task of maintaining order increasingly disturbed British leaders. With their hopes for stability centered on Abdullah, Churchill and his associates in London could see no alternative to extending their commitment when pressure came from within Transjordan and then from French Syria.

The fragility of Abdullah's position was certainly apparent by the end of April. An intertribal dispute occurred in the neighborhood of Madayba and became a challenge to the authority of the incipient amir-ate when important *shaykhs,* sent by Abdullah to settle the matter, were killed. Abdullah then asked Samuel to support his authority by commit-ting British airplanes and armored cars to crush the revolt. Abramson, having taken up his post at Amman, urged such action, and Samuel con-curred. Samuel's request for authorization was answered in a telegram from the War Office on 18 April in which permission was granted for the armored cars (there were two) to be employed in general support of measures taken by the Royal Air Force "for maintenance of order . . . and not only for immediate purpose of reconnaissance."[19] Only by such assistance was Abdullah able to suppress this early, minor insurrection; in the process, he established a precedent for dependence upon Great Britain in order to survive.

Even so, his presence remained tenuous, for he became the center of renewed controversy between Britain and France. As Abdullah himself put it during a visit to Jerusalem late in May, he was obliged both to curb the ambitions of his Syrian entourage and to satisfy his father, who was following a course "tending to an end which was to be com-

19. For the exchange of telegrams, see 21527 of *ibid.* On 1 June Samuel informed Abramson that air force activities on Abdullah's behalf might include demonstra-tion, bombing action, or combined operations with the local forces.

pared to a mirage," namely, the reconquest of Syria.[20] He might have added two further handicaps: agitators in and around Syria could boast of having his sympathy, while the French, with their long-standing suspicion of the sharifians, were only too willing to implicate him in the Syrian unrest.

Indeed, by May there were reports of renewed raids against trains between Beirut and Aleppo, and French authorities, anticipating an attack and a native revolt, redoubled their military precautions. Coincidental or not, the French government simultaneously made a series of strong representations to the British Foreign Office. The first was delivered by Count de Saint-Aulaire on 25 March, even before Churchill's return from the Middle East. Calling Lord Curzon's attention to an earlier belligerent proclamation made by Abdullah to the *shaykhs* of Transjordan—which was regarded in Paris as *"très violent en la forme, injurieux et véhément à l'égard de la France"*—the ambassador challenged the wisdom of the imminent meeting between the colonial secretary and Abdullah.[21] He feared it would have immediate repercussions on native opinion in Syria and the Hauran. But it was obvious that the protest was too late and insufficient in itself to deter Churchill from working out as satisfactory a solution as possible with Abdullah.

The French, however, persisted. On 5 April a letter from Count de Saint-Aulaire arrived at the Foreign Office, addressed to Sir Eyre Crowe. It reaffirmed the French conviction that Abdullah's presence in Transjordan was aimed against Syria, had already inspired acts of violence, and might oblige French officials to react vigorously against the sharifians. This official *démarche* included several documents, allegedly written by Abdullah, as proof of his hostility, none of which was conclusive, however, since all were dated prior to the Cairo Conference. The letter also noted that French opinion regarded Churchill's visit to the Middle East as having been too brief for him to acquire a full comprehension of "the difficulties and misunderstandings" plaguing the French and British in that region.[22]

This protestation gained the French ambassador an immediate hearing with Lord Curzon, in the midst of speculation over the Cairo Con-

20. Samuel to Churchill (no. 129), 28 May 1921, in 29398 of C.O. 733/3.
21. The text of the French communication is in E3935/31/88 of F.O. 406/45.
22. See E4027/31/88 of F.O. 406/46.

ference and its decisions.[23] Count de Saint-Aulaire began by warning that, if Faysal and Abdullah actually were chosen as rulers, France would believe that these decisions had been taken on the special ground that they were enemies of France. Curzon protested vehemently against this "unwarrantable inference," and there ensued a discussion of earlier attitudes and dealings with Faysal and his family. When de Saint-Aulaire promised that France would never forgive Faysal for having shed the blood of Frenchmen, Curzon could not resist pointing out that this consideration had hardly deterred France from reaching an agreement with Mustafa Kemal. The meeting having ended inconclusively, de Saint-Aulaire sent a formal note on the following day, 7 April, advising Curzon of the enduring difference of view toward the sharifians held by the two countries: *"notre opinion publique considérait Feysal et même Abdallah, non pas comme d'anciens alliés, mais comme des adversaires."*[24]

During May an exchange of visits between the highest officials of Great Britain and France in the Middle East afforded another opportunity for intense dialogue but yielded essentially the same results. From 17 to 20 May General Gouraud visited Egypt as the guest of Lord Allenby, to whom he expressed alarm at what in his opinion were the aims being pursued by Faysal and Abdullah. Sir Herbert Samuel, in his visit to Beirut from 27 to 29 May, spoke at great length with both Gouraud and his aide, M. de Caix, about Transjordan. Here, too, it was apparent that Abdullah suffered from his relationship to Faysal. When Samuel attempted to promote an understanding between Abdullah and France, he was rebuffed by de Caix, who utilized a new argument; while Britain seemed to regard independence for Damascus, Homs, Hama, and Aleppo as a promise made specifically to the sharifians and for their advantage, France regarded it as a promise made to the Arabs generally. Except for this objection to Abdullah's entrenchment in Transjordan, the meetings proved amicable. Conclusions were reached jointly on a number of matters: a boundary commission, administration of the Lake Huleh district, trains from Haifa to Nasib, the waters of the Upper Jordan and Yarmuk rivers, the Hijazi railway, and extradition procedures.[25]

23. Curzon to Hardinge, 6 April 1921, in E4164/3816/65 (no. 990) of *ibid.*
24. De Saint-Aulaire to Curzon, 7 April 1921, in E4267/3816/65 of *ibid.*
25. Samuel to Churchill, 2 June 1921, in E7234/117/98 (no. 113) of *ibid.*

One incident, however, threatened to destroy this working arrangement, together with the entire makeshift policy toward Abdullah and Transjordan. On 25 June Churchill received a cable from Samuel informing him of an assassination attempt against General Gouraud on the 23d near Kunaytra. Gouraud's party had been ambushed by four men disguised as gendarmes, and an officer with him had been killed. Samuel added ruefully: "It is on the Transjordanians that suspicion falls."[26] Although Samuel acted quickly to forestall a possible crisis by instructing police and military authorities in Palestine, as well as Abramson in Amman, to do everything possible to apprehend the guilty persons if they had taken refuge in the British zone, and by sending a personal telegram to Gouraud, the French would not be placated. A protest, stressing such "grave and inexcusable acts," was made against "the intrigues of the Syrian political refugees residing in territory under a British mandate" and against the tolerance they were receiving from the British and *"leur client hachémite."*[27] Then, on 18 July, Gouraud canceled his intended visit to Jerusalem because of "plots laid by certain Arab persons against [the] French mandate in Syria." In succeeding months Damascus and Paris insisted upon satisfaction through the arrest of Gouraud's assailants.

Negative developments such as these, showing the inability of Abdullah to control affairs in Transjordan, added urgency to an issue already under discussion in London. As mentioned above, the understanding arrived at between Churchill and Abdullah had been of a temporary nature, covering a period of only six months. Consequently, following his return from the Middle East, Churchill had to give consideration to the future of Abdullah and the political status of Transjordan beyond December, 1921. In his letter to General Gouraud on 31 March, the colonial secretary had formulated an early standard for evaluating Abdullah's performance.

. . . I have made an arrangement with Abdullah of an informal and temporary character whereby he is to use his whole influence to prevent any disturbances in the French zone arising out of Transjordania. . . .

---

26. See E7395/7255/89 (no. 236), *ibid.,* and Palmer (Damascus) to Curzon, 24 June 1921, in E7260/7255/89 (no. 7) of *ibid.*
27. For the French account of the attack and the subsequent formal complaint, see Catroux, *Deux missions en Moyen-Orient,* pp. 106–12, 116.

Undoubtedly the Emir Abdullah in the existing situation has power to create considerable disturbances. It remains to be seen whether he will have equal power to prevent them. It is by his success or failure in this respect that he must be judged.[28]

Individuals within the Middle East Department, the Foreign and War offices, and the Palestine administration, however, evaluated Abdullah's record differently in terms of this "indispensable stipulation."

Curzon, critical of Colonial Office actions since its reorganization, and under constant diplomatic pressure from France regarding the new sharifian policy, observed on 5 May: "I see that Abdullah has already become 'His Majesty'. I venture to think that much trouble is in store in the Arab world."[29] By contrast, somewhat before the Gouraud incident, Churchill reported favorably to the Cabinet on the amir, describing him as amenable to reason and to keeping faith.[30] The colonial secretary also hinted for the first time that Abdullah might remain into 1922, assuming that this was acceptable to both His Majesty's Government and the sharifians.

On 13 June Samuel expressed his dissatisfaction with Abdullah, recalling that Churchill and he had hoped that Abdullah would herald a more settled state of affairs. Instead, it now appeared that the people were far from content under the new regime, that tax-collecting was subject to much the same difficulties as before, and that public security left much to be desired.[31] Samuel attributed this, in the first instance, to Abdullah personally, accusing him of being "preoccupied to some extent with ideas of wider bearing and greater ambition" in Mesopotamia and Syria. But he also felt that the Syrian entourage surrounding Abdullah was a cause of embarrassment, being disliked by the native Transjordanians and regarded by them as expensive and incompetent.

In reply Churchill confessed that he too was not quite happy about the situation and was giving serious thought to inviting Abdullah to London in September. "While Abdulla is here I might be able to suggest to him that he should go straight from London to Mecca and later

28. Curzon to Hardinge, 15 September 1921, enclosure, in E10247/7250/89 (no. 2448) of F.O. 406/47.
29. E5789, F.O. 371/6372.
30. Cabinet meeting of 31 May 1921, Cab. 45 (21), E6408/533/65, F.O. 371/6342.
31. Samuel to Churchill, 13 June 1921, in 31760 (no. 160) of C.O. 733/3.

on be employed by his father in negotiating with the Imam and Idrisi."[32] Yet, in his speech before the Commons the following day, Churchill had nothing but praise for Abdullah, referring to him as "a very agreeable, intelligent, and civilised Arab prince" who was maintaining an "absolutely correct attitude" toward both England and France.[33] Moreover, he implied that the initiative resided with Abdullah; "should he find it necessary to lay down the charge which we have persuaded him to assume," then Britain would have to find a suitable replacement.

But within the Middle East Department the emphasis was rather upon whether to force Abdullah to withdraw, and appraisals of him were far from laudatory. From his vantage point in Cairo, General Congreve wrote to Young on 16 June: "in Trans-Jordania Abdulla is a fraud. . . . If anything is to be made of him he must be given a good strong Englishman who will run him entirely and British troops to back him up."[34] Even Abdullah's principal supporter, Colonel Lawrence, and to a lesser extent Shuckburgh, defended the existing arrangement on grounds other than efficiency. As Lawrence put it on 29 June, "We asked Abdulla only to keep peace with his neighbours, not to run a good administration." Taking issue with Samuel's analysis of 13 June, Lawrence applied completely different reasoning: "His total cost to us is less than a battalion; his regime prejudices us in no way, whatever eventual solution we wish to carry out, provided that it is not too popular and not too efficient."[35] Shuckburgh concurred, noting on 1 July: "With regard to Trans-Jordania, I do not think we need trouble ourselves unduly over the inefficiency of Abdulla's administration, so long as he fulfills our main object by keeping the peace with his neighbours. If we want efficient administration we should have to pay for it, and that is what we cannot afford to do."[36] In short, Samuel, the administrator and official most immediately responsible for Transjordan and Palestine, emphasized the narrower need for efficiency, while Lawrence represented those taking into consideration larger political factors.

The Gouraud incident, however, severely damaged the case for retaining Abdullah, and throughout July sentiment within the British gov-

32. Churchill to Samuel, 11 July 1921, no. 188, *ibid.*
33. *Parliamentary Debates* (Commons), 5th ser., 143 (14 June 1921) : 289.
34. See 32297 of C.O. 733/17A.
35. *Ibid.*
36. *Ibid.*

ernment was almost unanimously opposed to any renewal of the status quo in Transjordan. Foreign Secretary Curzon took particular satisfaction in criticizing the arrangement. Upon reading Samuel's dispatch no. 160 of 13 June, I. Murray, a member of the Foreign Office, commented: "The situation in Palestine is gloomy; that in Transjordania is still darker." When the file reached Curzon's desk on 2 July he added a notation: "The famous Cairo Conference seems to be a little shaky."[37] He held Abdullah at fault for not being able to assert authority and for tolerating officials bent on a war of revenge against the French.

On 6 July, replying to Congreve's analysis of 16 June, Major Young defended the personal decision originally taken by Churchill in Jerusalem. "As a matter of fact we never hoped that Abdulla would be able to rule strongly, nor did we anticipate that he would be able to collect much money during his provisional six months. As you will remember I was personally opposed to putting him into Trans-Jordania at all for various reasons, but as it was quite impossible to get him out I think we did the right thing in leaving him there."[38] Nevertheless, Young advised Congreve that the Middle East Department was giving thought to replacing Abramson, who was regarded as too weak to control Abdullah, and that it had plans for Transjordan which were still very much in embryo. Meanwhile, Deedes, reporting on his recent tour of the amirate, claimed that Abdullah himself had little desire to remain. "His Highness's participation in the affairs of the Administration is a somewhat languid one. Apart from a temperamental disinclination to great exertion of any kind he does not conceal the fact that his interest in Trans-Jordania is but a fleeting one and is due to the particular circumstances in which he finds himself."[39] It was believed, Deedes continued, that Abdullah still thought the British government would be instrumental in assisting him to get Damascus, and this could explain his remaining in a position "so little palatable to him." Concluding that the situation would have to get worse before it could get better, Deedes predicted that when Abdullah reached the stage of retiring to another sphere, more likely a southern than a northern one, "any illusions that may in any quarter have been entertained as to the blessings of a Shereefian

37. E7438, F.O. 371/6372.
38. 32297 of C.O. 733/17A.
39. Part of a confidential dispatch from Samuel to Churchill, 11 July 1921, in 36252 of C.O. 733/4.

Government will have disappeared." A steady reaction favoring a British administration would set in; and then the "ultimate formation of something in the nature of a union" between Palestine and Transjordan could be anticipated. On 18 July Young assured Deedes of the similar reasoning in London: Abdullah "made an admirable stop-gap, but he would not do as a permanency at all."[40]

Churchill allowed the debate to continue, and in the middle of July the two protagonists, Samuel and Lawrence, had occasion to amplify their respective viewpoints. In a cable addressed to Lawrence at Jidda and dated 23 July, the high commissioner reported Abdullah to be impatient and demanding a definite solution at the end of the probationary period. Samuel ruled out the two solutions of either moving Abdullah to Syria or linking the Hijaz with Transjordan, the latter option being contrary to the mandate for Palestine; therefore, "an exit must be found which will . . . save his face." He ended by predicting the unlikelihood of Abdullah's accepting a continuation of the existing arrangement after six months. In any case, continuation would merely perpetuate administrative confusion in Transjordan and accentuate political complications with the French.[41]

Lawrence wasted no time in replying. On 25 July he wired Samuel concurring in the opinion that union with Palestine was the best future for Transjordan. However, with the lack of self-government in one and chaotic administration in the other, such a union was presently undesirable by both populations. Consequently, according to Lawrence, it was advisable to continue the temporary system. "I should therefore deprecate such alteration in the present system as would involve us and our forces in the responsibility of seeing that effect was given to the decisions [at Cairo]. That could only be done if we had real military control. It is said that battalion at Amman would give us this. I consider that four battalions would not."[42]

Young remained unimpressed by such logic, for he concluded that the sharifian regime had proved a failure; he also confessed that Abramson was not the right man to be with Abdullah, and that Abdullah himself was only a *pis-aller*, a last resort. Nevertheless, Lawrence's presentation, with its stress on the military factor, did impress Churchill.

40. See 32297 of C.O. 733/17A.
41. Samuel to Churchill, for Lawrence, 23 July 1921, in 37118 of C.O. 733/4.
42. Lawrence, for Samuel, to the Colonial Office, 25 July 1921, in 37473 of *ibid.*

Abramson, the British official closest to Abdullah, entered the debate on 1 August by complaining of the attitude and conduct of the amir, who, in his opinion, continued to show neither an interest in administration nor an inclination to rid himself of the Syrians surrounding him, despite their being an obstacle in any effort at a rapprochement with the French and an anathema to the natives. Believing that Britain could never settle the Bedouin with a "Bedu Emir" [sic] as the head of government, "besides which Trans-Jordania cannot support an Emir," Abramson suggested what Churchill had at one point contemplated— a trip by Abdullah to London as a means of saving face.[43]

Beyond his general administrative ineptitude, what particularly annoyed the British about Abdullah was his refusal to take prompt and effective action following the attack on General Gouraud. At first the amir promised to do his best to seize the criminals. While repudiating the attack, he also protested against French representations and communiqués implicating him personally in the plot. By 12 August Deedes had instructed Abramson to express to Abdullah his extreme dissatisfaction at this procrastination in arresting two of the suspected assassins, Ahmad Muraywad and Ibrahim Hananu, both of whom were known to have sought refuge inside Transjordan. Fearing a further deterioration in Anglo-French relations in the region, Deedes insisted that pressure be applied to make Abdullah carry out his promise to Churchill in letter as well as in spirit; in the Middle East Department, however, Mr. Clauson was ready to conclude from this that Abdullah's elimination seemed to become more urgently necessary with every passing day.[44]

Abramson complied in urging Abdullah to make the arrests, to which the amir pleaded: "I understood that there was a good chance of means being found by the end of the six months to install me in Damascus. I have now lost everything and you want me to lose the little that is left, namely the good-will of the Arabs which I shall lose if I do anything to hand over the men who have taken refuge with me, that is to say in

43. Deedes, for the high commissioner, to the Colonial Office (secret), containing report no. 6, dated 1 August 1921, from the chief British representative at Amman; see 41683 of C.O. 733/5. Young appended: "We must try to remove Abdullah."
44. Deedes to Churchill, 12 August 1921, in C.O. 537/850.

my province."[45] Having "had enough of this wilderness," the amir much preferred to travel to London as a pretext for retiring gracefully from Transjordan. But while the British weighed this possibility, Abdullah, caught in such a compromising position, continued to procrastinate. As late as 22 November the British member of the Anglo-French boundary commission to delimit the border between the Syrian and Palestinian mandates, Colonel Newcombe, complained that his difficulties, certainly as regards General Gouraud, were "much increased by the non-arrest of his would-be assassins who are still walking freely in Transjordania."[46]

A new French complaint was presented to Lord Hardinge on 23 August. The note reported of an agent of Abdullah's, Asad al-Atrash, riding into Suwayda, capital of Jabal Druze and within the French sphere, raising the sharifian flag, and claiming possession of the area in the name of Abdullah. Citing once again the Gouraud episode, the note concluded with a strong warning that the British government would not be able to avoid a certain responsibility for the acts of Abdullah, "this British protégé," and should put an end to them.[47]

Hubert Young, assigned to draft a reply, informed the Foreign Office that in Mr. Churchill's opinion the exploits of Asad al-Atrash did not necessarily constitute a breach of faith on the part of the amir. Indeed, if Abdullah had thrown in his lot with the Syrian extremists, a far more unsatisfactory situation would exist at present, especially since the French had not accepted the suggestion, made by Churchill in March, to declare a general amnesty. Then, for the information of Lord Curzon, Young revealed that Churchill did not propose to give any guarantee that Abdullah's cooperation would be dispensed with at the end of the six-month probationary period.[48] Instead, Curzon's approval was sought for having Lawrence proceed from the Hijaz (where he was conferring

45. Abramson to Deedes, 29 August 1921, in 49096 of C.O. 733/6. Abdullah earlier had asked Abramson to provide Hananu with a note of introduction to Deedes, which Abdullah took as an assurance of safe conduct. When Hananu was seized in Jerusalem, Abdullah became furious with Abramson and the British, and an anti-British demonstration took place in Amman. See also Vatikiotis, *Politics and the Military in Jordan*, pp. 64–68, on Abdullah's difficulties.
46. Newcombe to the Colonial Office, 22 November 1921, in 60774 of C.O. 733/17B.
47. Hardinge to Curzon, 23 August 1921, in E9673/117/89 (no. 2378) of F.O. 406/47.
48. Young, for Shuckburgh, to the Foreign Office, 30 August 1921, in 42681 of C.O. 732/2.

with King Husayn while on temporary loan to the Foreign Office) to Jerusalem to examine the situation at first hand. Lawrence would then be able to recommend steps either to ensure the amir's authority in Transjordan or to permit him to retire gracefully. Curzon's comment of 1 August that "the present experiment is doomed to a well deserved failure" was beginning to seem premature.

Yet, in the absence of a final decision, the debate continued. Abramson detected a change of attitude in Abdullah, who, with the vacant throne at Damascus still in mind, now promised to remove all the undesirable Syrians as a gesture to the French.[49] On 20 September, Lancelot Oliphant wrote to Shuckburgh on Curzon's behalf that, as far as King Husayn was concerned, the coronation of Faysal, the prospective conclusion of a treaty by the Hijaz with Great Britain, and the subsidy payment should suffice to counterbalance the ill-effects of any setback to sharifian aspirations caused by Abdullah's failure.[50] Mr. Clauson believed that if the amir was not invited to London, "it is quite possible that he may disappear sulkily down the Hejaz Railway, which if not perhaps the best would be at any rate the cheapest solution!"[51] And Colonel Meinertzhagen asked on 18 October: "When is this mountebank administration to stop?"[52] Yet such speculation and debate were meaningless, except as they reflected sentiment in London. The decision itself was being taken in Jerusalem, where Lawrence, Abramson, and Samuel, joined by Hubert Young, were meeting to discuss the merits and demerits of maintaining or dispensing with Abdullah's services.

On the surface the setting was conducive to a decision to release Abdullah from his earlier undertaking. Abramson, Samuel, and Young all had expressed dissatisfaction with the amir's performance at various times during the long debate. Only Churchill remained unconvinced either way. Abdullah himself had asked to be relieved. Moreover, the French continued to apply pressure against Abdullah as part of their general anti-sharifian policy. But at this decisive stage T. E. Lawrence proved to be the determining factor on Abdullah's behalf, coming to Amman from the Hijaz early in November. During the previous four

49. Abramson's report no. 7, 1 September 1921, submitted by Samuel on the 19th, in 49095 of C.O. 733/6.
50. Urgent, 20 September 1921, in 47205 of C.O. 733/11.
51. 21 September 1921, *ibid.*
52. See 50933 of C.O. 733/6.

months he had been a roving ambassador in the Middle East to secure the success of those several decisions originating in Cairo, a campaign which caused Curzon to remark: "These movements are beyond me." On 7 July he was empowered to negotiate a treaty, already in draft form, with King Husayn; it would give the latter a regular subsidy in return for his recognition of the mandate principle.

By 7 August Lawrence reported acceptance by Husayn of virtually all articles of the proposed treaty except the main one recognizing the mandates over Palestine and Mesopotamia; he concluded: "It has been a bad week for both of us." On the 15th he left for Aden, returning at the end of the month to resume the discussions. On 6 September he reviewed the most recent stage of the difficult negotiations, in which Husayn had imposed new demands, including his right to appoint all qadis and muftis in Arabia, Palestine, and Mesopotamia, as well as his supremacy over rulers everywhere in the Arab world. With the negotiations thus stalemated, Lawrence learned on 16 September that his presence was required in Transjordan as soon as possible to decide future policy there.[53] Leaving the Hijaz and an angry Husayn on the 29th, Lawrence proceeded directly to Jerusalem.

Before Lawrence intervened, Young had participated in initial discussions with Samuel, Deedes, and Abramson. Of these he kept Shuckburgh informed, as on 30 September: "What we have got to face is either continued expenditure on Abdullah, whose influence has gone down almost to vanishing point, and who is no longer a substitute for even a section of Infantry, or to take our courage in both hands and send a small force over, if only temporarily, in order to set Revenue Collection on a proper footing, and to make sure of getting rid of the Syrians and Hedjazis."[54] The best alternative would be for Lawrence to persuade Abdullah to fulfill these tasks and then appoint a suitable regent to take his place. The worst prospect was that Abdullah might refuse to comply. But even then Young saw little choice but to remove him and

53. The reports filed by Lawrence, as well as the text of the draft treaty, are found primarily in F.O. 406/47. Munīb al-Māḍī and Suleiman Mūsā, *Tārīkh al-'Urdun fī'l Qarn al-'Ishrīn* [A history of Jordan in the twentieth century] (Beirut, 1959), provide a second reason for Lawrence's trip to Transjordan, claiming that he was encouraged by the amirs Ali and Zayd, Haddad Pasha, and Fu'ad al-Khatib, the Hijazi foreign secretary, to discuss the treaty with Abdullah after Husayn showed himself to be so adamant; see p. 173.
54. Young to Shuckburgh, 30 September 1921, in 56584 of C.O. 733/17B.

appoint in his place an Arab governor on the lines originally proposed at Cairo.

Young obviously favored the first alternative, as did Lawrence apparently, for on 7 October, after their conversation, Young reported that Lawrence was "still pretty confident that he will be able to get rid of Abdullah or 'Sunny Jim' as he is called locally, and I hope he has not over-estimated his power of persuasion." Young had in mind a very recent precedent, for, as he wrote, "one cannot lose sight of the fact that all the plans that were made in Cairo in March about Trans-Jordania were upset when Abdullah himself was consulted, and it is possible that the same thing may happen again."[55] Again on the 7th, he advised Shuckburgh to expect concrete proposals in a day or two which probably would contemplate immediate removal of Abdullah and his Syrian officers and their replacement by an administration under a local Arab official.

Young then introduced a new idea: not only should Abramson be removed as chief British representative, but "what is really required is someone of [the] calibre of Philby." The idea readily appealed to Churchill, for it found employment for Philby, who was no longer *persona grata* in Iraq, and meant that a "good strong Englishman," urged by General Congreve, would take up residence in Transjordan. Nevertheless, because of Philby's argumentative reputation, Churchill approved the appointment only tentatively. He immediately gained the consent of Sir Percy Cox and instructed Philby to proceed to Amman, ostensibly to discuss Sa'udi-Hijazi relations in light of Lawrence's mission to Jidda, but really to have Samuel, who would be his superior, observe him. Philby then traveled to London to meet Churchill personally, at which time the appointment was offered to him. On 4 November Samuel was informed of Philby's acceptance and of his understanding that the "question of retention or otherwise of Abdullah is an open one" and would remain so until Philby had had an opportunity to consider matters on the spot.[56] Philby assumed his new position on 28 Novem-

55. Young to Shuckburgh, 7 October 1921, in 56585 of *ibid*.
56. Churchill to Samuel (no. 338, personal and private), 4 November 1921, in 58211 of C.O. 733/15. Shuckburgh sent an informal letter on 9 November to Sir Arthur Hirtzel of the India Office about "the great Philby," writing: "I imagine that the Government of India will not shed many tears over the indefinite postponement of Philby's return. We really want him in Trans-Jordania, and he is delighted at the prospect of going there."

ber, finding himself "in charge of a chaos which was called an office,"[57] and began to exercise an important influence on Abdullah and Transjordan.

The main problem, that of Abdullah's future, still remained, however, although in retrospect the appointment of Philby, a strong administrator, did affect the discussion. This was reflected in the next dispatch from Young on 15 October, which cited factors other than Abdullah as being responsible for the deplorable—and dangerous—state of affairs. While admitting that the prestige of the amir had almost vanished, Young believed the blame was partially Samuel's and Abramson's for keeping the Middle East Department "rather in the dark about what is going on here" and for not taking a stronger line.[58] In short, the fact of Abdullah's weakness "was very largely due to our being unable to give him even the limited support we had intended to give." As proof of this Young pointed to there being only two armored cars instead of the intended four, neither of which had stirred out of camp in three months for lack of spare parts or tires, while the reserve force, nearly six hundred strong, had no rifles, little or no ammunition, and no machine guns. Whatever the cause, Young concluded, "it is clearly necessary for Lawrence to take the whole thing in hand at once."

The first direct report from Lawrence came on 24 October. Beginning on a note of optimism, it predicted a less bleak future, but without addressing itself to the central question.[59] Instead, it urged secondary measures, such as improving the roads; increasing the usefulness of the reserve force, "the only unarmed body of men in the country," under Peake Pasha; and making the armored cars operational, since the existing crew "can drive the car forward but is not good at reversing."

This report was accompanied by a note prepared in the secretariat of the high commissioner for Palestine which, taking issue point by point with Lawrence's view, gave an entirely different appraisal of the situation. It explained the noticeable difference between the tone of this

57. Philby to Samuel, 18 April 1922, in 21848 of C.O. 733/21.
58. Young to Shuckburgh, 15 October 1921, in 53454 of C.O. 733/7.
59. "Report by Colonel Lawrence on the Situation in Trans-Jordania," sent to Samuel on 24 October 1921 and relayed to the Colonial Office on 4 November as a secret dispatch; see 57016 of *ibid.* In passing, Lawrence did drop a hint of Abdullah's retention when he wrote: "If Abdullah stays till March at £1,000 a month that will cost £7,000."

report and those previously submitted by Mr. Abramson as reflecting "a difference in the temperament, in outlook, in administrative aims or ideals and in interpretation of facts rather than as indicating the discovery of any new facts" in the situation. Continuing to reproach Lawrence, the secretariat noted that he had confined himself to Amman, where he was subjected to the influence of, if not indeed swayed by, the Syrians surrounding the amir; warned of a further drift toward the complete political separation of Palestine and Transjordan; and maintained that the saving of Transjordan and its development through a local government, in the opinion of those having more than a passing familiarity with Transjordan (an obvious inference to Lawrence), "can best be brought about by the elimination of the Emir Abdullah."

The worst fears of the secretariat were confirmed by Samuel, also on 24 October, when he advised Churchill that Lawrence had discovered that Abdullah did not now want to leave Transjordan. Inquiries by Lawrence therefore pointed to the desirability of the following policy: (1) Abdullah's administration of Transjordan would continue for the present, but without any official announcement to that effect; (2) his personal subsidy would be reduced from £5,000 a month to £2,000 for October and to £1,000 per month thereafter; (3) certain Syrian officials would be removed from office; (4) a statement would be made in London and republished in Transjordan that application of the Zionist provisions of the Palestine mandate was not contemplated; (5) Abdullah would be pressed to secure the arrest of Gouraud's assailants; and (6) Abdullah would be invited to London after the winter.[60] Once Lawrence had spoken, Churchill was willing to abide by his recommendations. Thus Hubert Young's premonition that history might repeat itself, as in the agreement of March, to the benefit of Abdullah was fulfilled.

Most puzzling in this episode is the willingness of Abdullah to extend the original arrangement after such a difficult and unpleasant experimental period. Some insight is provided, however, by a message from Consul Palmer in Damascus that Abdullah was in touch with the French, presumably to discuss a rapprochement, through two individuals, Ahmed al-Ba'sh and Ghalib al-Sha'lan.[61] Corroboration came a

60. Samuel, for Lawrence, to Churchill (private and personal), 24 October 1921, in 53454 of *ibid.*
61. Palmer to Curzon, 21 October 1921, in E12064 of F.O. 371/6373.

week later in Dr. Eder's letter to Dr. Weizmann, with a copy going to Colonel Meinertzhagen, which told of Abdullah's renewed confidence in the possibility of his being placed in Damascus by the French.[62] Abdullah considered as favorable to his candidacy the French anxiety to find some peaceful solution which would warrant a troop withdrawal and their difficulty in finding any other suitable candidate; the chance that Gouraud and de Caix, his main critics, might be replaced; his belief that Britain would not object; and the fact that he had not really shown himself in any way hostile to France and was prepared to work with her in Syria. It is perhaps no mere coincidence that Abdullah's change of heart came while Lawrence, who had reportedly justified the amirate in March as a peaceful steppingstone to Syria, was residing in Amman.

As for Lawrence, there might have been an additional consideration. Arriving in Transjordan after his unsuccessful visit to the Hijaz, he may have viewed a bargain with Abdullah as the key to salvaging his entire mission. In fact, on 8 December an Anglo-Hashimite treaty, the same as that rejected by Husayn, was signed in Amman by Lawrence and Abdullah.[63] By showing this willingness to cooperate with Great Britain, even at the risk of opposing his father, Abdullah strengthened the conclusion which Lawrence had been forced to make that this was the best alternative for Great Britain in Transjordan.

The actual outcome of these numerous events found Abdullah's position reconfirmed in Transjordan at the end of 1921. Believing it necessary to explain his decision to accept the offer from Lawrence, Abdullah told Samuel that in reality he wished to leave but felt it his duty not to unless some other personal link with the sharifian movement were to replace him.[64] On 24 November Samuel indicated a general consensus within his administration that the machinery of government would work better without the amir. But he was either unable or unwilling to resist the determined Lawrence, and after the last round of discussions among Lawrence, Philby, Abdullah, and himself, Samuel informed Churchill of the amir's desire to continue the administration of Transjordan and of their approval.[65] The colonial secretary, involved in other affairs,

62. Eder to Weizmann, 30 October 1921, W.A.
63. The text is in E930/248/91 of F.O. 406/48.
64. Samuel to Churchill (confidential), 24 November 1921, in 60892 of C.O. 733/7.
65. Samuel to Churchill (confidential), 19 December 1921, in 261 of C.O. 733/8.

summed up his own position two months later: "I do not want to change Abdulla or the policy followed during the last 9 months."[66]

During the latter half of 1921 the legal question of the status of Transjordan was no less perplexing to the British government than the political question of Abdullah's personal role beyond December. At issue was the relationship between Transjordan and Palestine, one aspect of the larger problem for Great Britain—to gain the League of Nations' approval of her Middle Eastern mandates.

By the beginning of 1921 there was an obvious need for clarification of this relationship. But British leaders, Churchill included, chose instead to procrastinate. This resulted in Transjordan's evolving over the next two decades from a territory with an independent administration under the Palestine mandate to a Hashimite, or sharifian, kingdom, fully independent and sovereign in theory, but in fact artificial and dependent upon external assistance, whether from Britain, the United States, or fellow Arab countries.

In September, 1920, Lord Curzon had instructed his representatives in Paris to leave the eastern boundary of Palestine for subsequent definition. While treating Transjordan as a separate entity from the Damascus state, formed by the French after Maysalun, the foreign secretary wished to avoid any "definite connection" between it and Palestine, thus leaving the way open for the establishment there, "should it become advisable," of some form of independent Arab government.[67] In November Hubert Young maintained that Great Britain would have difficulty refuting the contention that in 1915 Sir Henry McMahon had pledged to acknowledge the independence of the Arabs in Transjordan, although Palestine had been intentionally excluded.[68] The Zionists, how-

66. 2 February 1922, *ibid*. Churchill also added an emphatic "Yes" to Shuckburgh's question "Do we or do we not wish to see Abdullah settle himself firmly in the Trans-Jordanian saddle," leaving unanswered the latter half, "and come to be regarded as the permanent sovereign of the country?" See Meinertzhagen, *Middle East Diary*, pp. 33–34.

67. Curzon to Vansittart (Paris), 30 September 1920, in E11698/4164/44 (no. 157), *Documents*, 13:351.

68. Young, "Memorandum on Possible Negotiations with the Hedjaz," 29 November 1920 (confidential), in E14959/9/44 of C.O. 732/3. At the request of John Shuckburgh, Sir Henry McMahon submitted the following letter to the Colonial Office on 12 March 1922 for use in discussions with the Palestine Arab delegation:

ever, simultaneously argued for the incorporation of Transjordan into Palestine. On 28 October Associate Justice of the United States Supreme Court Louis Brandeis had cabled Lord Balfour, warning that "depriving Palestine of the use of Litany [River] and the watershed of the Hermon-Yarmuk valley and the Transjordanian plains of Hauran and Jaulon would cripple Jewish homeland project, rendering impossible and futile attempts at reclamation, resettlement, and any reasonable immigration."[69]

As for the natives of the territory, who were accustomed to decentralized authority, Sir Herbert Samuel described them at the end of 1920 as devoid of any pro-French, pro-sharifian, or Arab nationalist feeling. Nor were they anxious or ready to come directly under the Palestine government, for it was, to their minds, "too much of a Government" and under Zionist influence.[70] They feared an influx of Jews who, by settling on land purchased in Transjordan, would eventually dominate the area. However, Samuel personally was of the opinion that the territory required a direct British presence. The Foreign Office, pre-

---

With reference to our conversation on Friday (10th) I write you these few lines to place on record the fact that in my letter of the 25th October 1915 to the Sherif of Mecca, it was my intention to exclude Palestine from independent Arabia, and I hoped that I had so worded the letter as to make this sufficiently clear for all practical purposes.

My reasons for restricting myself to specific mention of Damascus, Hama, Homs and Aleppo in that connection in my letter were (1) that these were places to which the Arabs attached vital importance and (2) that there was no place I could think of at the time of sufficient importance for purposes of definition further South of the above.

It was as fully my intention to exclude Palestine as it was to exclude the more Northern coastal tracts of Syria.

I did not make use of the Jordan to define the limits of the Southern area because I thought it might possibly be considered desirable at some later stage of negotiations to find some more suitable frontier line east of the Jordan and between that river and the Hejaz Railway. At that moment moreover any detailed definitions did not seem called for.

I may mention that I have no recollection of ever hearing anything from the Sherif of Mecca, by letter or message, to make me suppose that he did not also understand Palestine to be excluded from independent Arabia.

I trust that I have made my intention clear. [See 384 of C.O. 733/35.]

69. E13614, F.O. 371/5247; see also Weizmann's letter to Churchill of 1 March 1921, Appendix G of this volume.

70. Deedes, for Samuel, to the Foreign Office, 5 December 1920, in E16167/13556/44 of F.O. 406/44.

---

sented with these contradictory views, continued to table the matter, especially since the re-allocation of responsibility for the Middle East was so imminent.

The occasion of the Cairo Conference offered an opportunity to clarify the matter. As Lloyd George and Churchill both agreed, the solution consisted of treating Transjordan as "an Arab province or adjunct of Palestine" while at the same time "preserving [the] Arab character of the area and administration."[71] This immediately posed several legal questions regarding the Palestine mandate, which Churchill referred to legal experts in London. Despite the objection from Eric Forbes Adam in the Middle East Department that it was better not to raise the question of different treatment publicly by suggesting new amendments or additions to the mandates, the legal officers of the Colonial and Foreign offices, meeting on 21 March 1921, deemed it advisable, as a matter of prudence, to insert in advance general clauses giving the mandatory "certain discretionary powers" in applying the Palestine and Mesopotamia mandates to Transjordan and Kurdistan respectively.[72] After further interoffice correspondence it was agreed to introduce Article 25 into the Palestine mandate, which would entitle Great Britain "to postpone or withhold" application of certain unsuitable provisions and to provide local administration for Transjordan.

Reactions and interpretations varied. In his meeting with Lawrence on 15 April, Faysal recognized the necessity for the political subordination of Amman to Jerusalem but stressed Amman's administrative independence.[73] Within the Colonial Office, Forbes Adam understood Article 25 to mean that Britain could act provisionally, on the assumption that Transjordan was to be a province of Palestine, though an

71. Prime Minister to Churchill, 22 March 1921, and Churchill to the Prime Minister, 23 March 1921, both in F.O. 371/6342.
72. These clauses were Articles 16 and 25 respectively of the Mesopotamia and Palestine mandates; see p. 123 above. The debates resulting from Churchill's request for legal consideration are found in file 13896 of C.O. 732/5. Curzon approved the additions on 31 March. These discussions occurred at a delicate moment, for Parliament was insisting on the right of prior scrutiny before the mandates could be binding upon Great Britain, viewing this as "a constitution principle of the first importance." As *The Times* of 24 March 1921 editorialized: "Is Mr. Churchill a servant of the League of Nations or the British Nation?" See also *The Times* of 22 March and *Parliamentary Debates* (Lords), 5th ser., 44 (1921) : 502–42.
73. Lawrence to Churchill, 15 April 1921, in E4509/100/93 of F.O. 406/46.

Arab one; Shuckburgh concurred.[74] By contrast, Meinertzhagen saw the article as severing Transjordan from Palestine and believed that Abdullah had been placated at the expense of the Jewish national home; this view was shared by Sir Alec Kirkbride, who later wrote: "In due course the remarkable discovery was made that the clauses of the mandate relating to the establishment of a National Home for the Jews had never been intended to apply to the mandated territory east of the river."[75] Even Abdullah acknowledged this when, years later, he recalled his success in creating the government of Transjordan "by having it separated from the Balfour Declaration."[76]

Yet in 1921 the Zionists were strangely reticent in questioning the validity of this distinction between Palestine and Transjordan. On 25 April three Zionist leaders—Cowen, Jabotinsky, and Landman—were summoned to the Colonial Office to be informed of the addition of Article 25 to the mandate, news which they accepted without comment. One explanation, however, might be found in an editorial in *Palestine* on 30 April: "The appointment of Abdullah east of the Jordan does not necessarily imply separation from the rest of Palestine, and in any arrangement that may be made the essential oneness of Palestine should be recognised. . . ."[77] It was perhaps not yet appreciated that administrative independence might be the prelude to a separate national entity in the future.

His Majesty's Government, having avoided any strong internal opposition to Article 25, next turned to the broader problem of gaining League approval for the draft mandates as a whole. At British and American urging, the council had agreed on 22 February to postpone further discussion of all the "A" mandates—Syria, Palestine, and Mesopotamia—until its next session in June.

---

74. See 15612 of C.O. 733/9, minuted on 5 and 8 April 1921.
75. Meinertzhagen, *Middle East Diary*, pp. 99–100, and Kirkbride, *A Crackle of Thorns*, p. 27.
76. King 'Abdallāh of Jordan, *My Memoirs Completed [al Takmilah]*, trans. Harold Glidden (Washington, D.C.: American Council of Learned Societies, 1954), p. 97.
77. *Palestine* 9, no. 7 (30 April 1921) : 50. Similarly, at the Carlsbad congress later in the year, the political report of the Zionist Executive was content to note merely that "Zionists have thought, and still think, that Transjordania falls under the provisions of the Palestine Mandate" (The Zionist Organisation, *Reports of the Executive of the Zionist Organisation to the XII Zionist Congress* [London, 1921], p. 38).

On 1 June a meeting was held in Lord Curzon's office, attended by Balfour, Churchill, Curzon, Sir Cecil Hurst of the Foreign Office, H. A. L. Fisher of the British delegation, and Sir Eric Drummond, secretary-general of the League of Nations.[78] A consensus was achieved in favor of making every effort to get the mandates passed immediately, since delay would prejudice the British position in both Palestine and Mesopotamia and withdrawal would only "hand those countries over to anarchy." The Middle East Department, in particular, urged the need for prompt League approval, regardless of the expected American and French opposition. Conscious of higher diplomatic implications, however, the Cabinet decided not to press for a decision at the meeting of the League on 17 June.[79] While the very right of Great Britain to take any action at all in the mandated territories thus remained open to question, Churchill and all the officials under him proceeded, with not a little uneasiness, to take the many steps necessary for implementing the decisions of the Cairo Conference.

In terms of Transjordan specifically, this further delay in establishing the validity of Article 25—indeed, of the entire Palestine mandate—permitted additional debate. Lawrence wrote in July that union with Palestine was Transjordan's best future, while on 19 August Major Somerset raised doubt as to the advisability of encouraging the natives of the area "to form a small nation."[80]

A more serious challenge to the reasoning behind Article 25 came in early November from the French. Crediting London with the intention of detaching Transjordan in order "to convert it into a more or less separate dependency" under Abdullah, they stated that such a change would be viewed with great apprehension.[81] The internal reaction of the Middle East Department to this statement reflects Transjordan's uncertain status in government circles toward the end of the year. Mr. Clauson volunteered, "It is rather awkward to be asked our intentions in T.J. [sic] at the moment for we hardly know ourselves what they

78. Secret minutes in 32958 of C.O. 732/5.
79. Cab. 49 (21), 14 June 1921, CAB 23/26.
80. Samuel to Churchill, 25 July 1921, in 37473 of C.O. 733/4; and Somerset to the Colonial Office, 19 August 1921, in 41846 of C.O. 733/14.
81. De Saint-Aulaire to Sir William Tyrrell, 4 November 1921, in 56061 of C.O. 733/11.

are," and Shuckburgh confessed, "The position is a little difficult." At Churchill's instruction, the reply to the French was therefore "well-guarded" and "colourless," assuring that Britain was constantly pre-occupied with the affairs of Transjordan and would prevent French interests from being "injuriously affected."

The Zionists gradually awoke to the possible larger implications of Article 25. In his letter to Deedes of 13 December reviewing events of 1921 in Palestine, Weizmann charged that every possible obstacle had been put in the way of a Jewish company which desired to do some business in Transjordan. Deedes, in commenting on this letter to Shuck-burgh, said, much like Lawrence, that union ultimately was the desired goal, although "it is but elementary prudence to wait until the people of the country are in a frame of mind to look at the matter"[82]—Jewish immigration, Jewish enterprise, and a single government for both Palestine and Transjordan—reasonably.

So as to forestall further criticism, Young, Lawrence, Meinertzhagen, Shuckburgh, and Vernon met during January, 1922, and their discussion revealed a wide divergence of opinion on the broad question of policy in Transjordan. Their conclusion, as summed up by Shuckburgh, was not to allow Zionism in Transjordan for the present ("certainly not"—Churchill), but not to bar the door against it for all time.[83] Rather than clarify the complex issue, Shuckburgh believed that "the less we say publicly on the subject the better."

This approach received explicit endorsement from Churchill a week later when, after giving the political future of Transjordan his most careful consideration, he wrote: "It seems undesirable that any attempt should be made at the present juncture to alter the status quo in the direction of a closer assimilation to Palestine."[84] He preferred to allow matters in Transjordan "to pursue their present course" while also having Philby refrain from any action likely to give the impression of a change in British policy in the direction of perpetuating the existing temporary arrangements. In addition to countervailing Zionist aspirations by fostering Transjordanian distinctiveness, Churchill also con-

82. Weizmann's letter and the comments by Deedes are contained in C.O. 537/854.
83. Shuckburgh to Sir James Masterton Smith, 31 January 1922, in 261 of C.O. 733/8.
84. This confidential reply by Churchill is dated 7 February 1922; see *ibid.*

tributed to the tradition of official silence by declaring, "I am averse from making further public pronouncements upon matters which must inevitably arouse controversy."

Finally, on 1 July 1922 the British government transmitted the revised final draft of the Palestine mandate to the secretary-general of the League of Nations and it was formally approved on 22 July. Shortly thereafter, on 16 September 1922, the Council of the League received from the British representative a memorandum about Article 25 which invited the Council to pass a resolution that several provisions of the mandate pertaining to the Zionists would not be applicable to "the territory known as Trans-Jordan." The latter was defined as "all territory lying to the east of a line drawn from a point two miles west of the town of Akaba on the Gulf of that name up the centre of the Wady Araba, Dead Sea and River Jordan to its junction with the River Yarmuk; thence up the centre of that river to the Syrian Frontier."[85] The Council complied by approving the memorandum, which became the operative document governing Britain's latitude in supervising affairs in Transjordan. Despite sporadic complaints from the Permanent Mandates Commission at the lack of information on conditions inside that territory,[86] Great Britain continued to regard herself as having independence of action. And in December, 1922, following a visit by Abdullah to London, His Majesty's Government entered into an agreement whereby "the existence of an independent constitutional Government in Trans-Jordan under the rule of His Excellency the Emir Abdullah ibn Hussein" was recognized.[87]

Progressive separation from Palestine received a new impetus in 1928 when a second agreement was signed in Jerusalem on 20 February.[88] It confirmed Britain's authority in the area by virtue of the mandate, especially in matters affecting her international obligations, while recogniz-

85. "Mandate for Palestine, together with a Note by the Secretary-General Relating to its Application to the Territory Known as Trans-Jordan, under the provisions of Article 25" (Cmd. 1785), 1923.
86. League of Nations, *Records of the Permanent Mandates Commission* (C.341. M.99, minutes of the thirteenth session), 1928, p. 43.
87. This agreement, together with the British refusal at the time to accept Abdullah's request for complete sovereignty and admission to the League, is found in F.O. 406/50.
88. "Agreement between the United Kingdom and Trans-Jordan" (Cmd. 3069), 1928.

ing the existence of an independent government, under "His Highness" Abdullah, entrusted with powers of legislation and administration. For the first time "Palestine" was defined in its new, restricted sense as the area west of the Jordan. Although Transjordan still remained dependent upon Great Britain in practical terms, from a legal standpoint the agreement represented a mutual undertaking by two equal contracting parties. This agreement of 1928 remained in force until it was superseded in 1946 by a treaty of alliance recognizing Transjordan as "a fully independent State" and Abdullah as its sovereign ruler.[89]

From a historical perspective, the treaty of 1946 constituted the logical climax to a process initiated, or at least catalyzed, by the events of 1921, and in particular by the decision at the end of the year to retain Abdullah in Amman, essentially for the lack of a better alternative. The separation of Transjordan from Palestine also had indirect, yet significant, implications for Britain's Palestine problem in its more acute stage. In 1936, and again in 1947, partition was formally suggested as a possible solution to the definite impasse, first by the British Peel Commission and later by the United Nations. One can only speculate as to whether the prospect of a larger Arab Palestine both to the east and west of the Jordan, rather than mere enclaves, might not have had greater appeal and cogency for Palestinian nationalists.

Abdullah, by daring to proceed northward to Amman in March; the Cairo Conference, by recommending an impractical policy of occupation; Churchill, by his independent decision to avoid occupation through an undertaking with Abdullah; Lawrence, by emphasizing political factors other than administrative efficiency; the Zionists, by not challenging the arrangement; the French, by not strenuously opposing Abdullah's continued presence; the League of Nations, by deferring to Great Britain as the responsible mandatory power; and lastly the natives, who gradually coalesced around Abdullah—all contributed to the emergence of the Hashimite kingdom of Jordan, perhaps the most enduring, yet fragile, creation of the Cairo Conference.

89. "Treaty of Alliance: Britain and Transjordan" (Cmd. 6916), 1946.

CHAPTER 10 **Perspective and Conclusions**

*A hidden pitfall in historiography is disregard for the fact
that conditions within the nations and races change with
the change of periods and the passing of days. This is a
sore affliction and is deeply hidden, becoming noticeable
only after a long time, so that rarely do more than a few
individuals become aware of it.*—Ibn Khaldun, *The
Muqaddimah* (14th century)

*. . . It thus often happens that the opening chapters of a
society's tragic decline are popularly hailed as the
culminating chapters of a magnificent growth.*
—Arnold J. Toynbee, *A Study of History*

The stability of the Arab world after 1921 must have been gratifying to
those individuals associated in some capacity with the Middle East Department of the Colonial Office. From positions in Aden, Amman, Baghdad, Beirut or Damascus, Cairo, Jidda, and Jerusalem, or from offices
in Whitehall and Downing Street, they could survey the region with a
sense of relief and accomplishment, contrasting it with the atmosphere
of crisis which had prevailed during 1920 and the greater part of 1921.
For then the prestige of Great Britain had been shaken, her will to persevere questioned, and her imperial interests, developed over many
years and at great cost, jeopardized. Now the general area under the
jurisdiction of the Middle East Department was tranquil, at least on the
surface, compared with the persisting Near Eastern problems of the
Foreign Office.

Winston Churchill, architect of Britain's new Arab policy, offered
the House of Commons a full report on conditions prevailing within the
individual countries on 9 March 1922, the first anniversary of the Cairo
Conference.[1] Britain, having found an answer to the question of

1. *Parliamentary Debates* (Commons), 5th ser., 151 (9 March 1922) : 1538–52.

237

"whether gold makes a better weapon than steel or lead," was unchallenged on the Arabian peninsula. An equilibrium was being maintained among the several rival chieftains of the peninsula through the careful use of subsidies. King Faysal, benefiting from the counsel of Sir Percy Cox, was working to create a viable, responsible monarchy in Iraq as well as a sense of Iraqi nationalism. Arab-Zionist differences still hindered the smooth administration of the mandate in Palestine, but there had been no repetition of violence on the scale of the Jaffa riots. Churchill happily told his audience that in Transjordan Abdullah "has fulfilled our expectations of last year." These conditions had combined to produce a saving of £5,000,000 in the current year alone, while troop reductions were also continuing. Thus vindicated, the colonial secretary, attempting to silence his critics, asked: could all the previous investment be thrown away for nothing, "just at the moment when it may well be that satisfactory results are at hand"? Great Britain would stand firm in the Middle East on the basis of those governing principles enunciated and acted upon at Cairo.

This dissimilarity between 1920 and 1922 could not help but affect early evaluations of the Cairo Conference and Britain's resultant Middle Eastern policy. On 18 July 1921 Hubert Young had confessed: "The whole performance is a desperate gamble and we hop from razor's edge without any definite prospect of reaching firm ground anywhere. I suppose we shall muddle through somehow."[2] In ending his speech on 9 March 1922 Churchill revealed his more mature appreciation of the Arab world and his respect for its complexities by prudently offering a caveat. "I cannot guarantee that the future will be unclouded or that no misfortune will arise; I cannot at all promise that either in Iraq or in Palestine. I can only say that I believe the course we are taking is the best we can take in the circumstances."[3] As events both within and beyond the Arab world solidified the British position there, Churchill became more assured in his judgment of the Cairo policy. By 1923 he pointed with pride to the fact that "our difficulties and our expenses have diminished with every month that has passed. Our influence has grown, while our armies have departed."[4]

2. See 20546 of C.O. 733/17A.
3. *Parliamentary Debates* (Commons), 5th ser., 151 (9 March 1922) : 1552.
4. Churchill, "Mesopotamia and the New Government," pp. 696–97.

Writing again in 1929, Churchill felt even safer in assigning prominence to the accomplishments of 1921, basing his opinion, as always, on the three criteria of lower troop figures, monetary savings, and relative tranquility. Reductions in the first two categories were impressive indeed. Whereas at the beginning of 1921 the number of infantry battalions in Iraq had stood at thirty-two, by 1929 it had reached a new low of two. As for their cost, the 1927/28 estimates showed a figure of £1,648,038, a notable decline from the 1921/22 sum of £20,097,684. These figures led Churchill in 1929 to offer a final appraisal of the policy inaugurated in 1921 and "continued up to the present time. . . . Like other policies, it has had its ups and downs. There have been moments of difficulty and of danger. In spite of these, however, it has been steadily pursued, often in face of fierce and unscrupulous press criticism at home, and has achieved a measure of success which few of us thought at all probable eight years ago."[5] Churchill correctly maintained that as a direct result of the Cairo Conference Great Britain and her empire had been able to weather the storm in the Arab world.

Press criticism, alluded to by Churchill, had been more immediate and less complimentary in evaluating the Cairo Conference. As early as 9 May 1921 the *Daily Mail* condemned Churchill editorially as having "never conceived any scheme as ruinous and so fatal as his projected Middle Eastern Empire. . . . Should he be allowed to pursue his course

5. Churchill, "Memorandum Upon the Pacification of the Middle East," *The World Crisis, 1918–1928: The Aftermath*, pp. 491–96. Subsequent evaluations by other Britishers have been even more enthusiastic. The Cairo Conference has been termed "a brilliant settlement" (Virginia Cowles, *Winston Churchill: The Era and the Man* [London: Hamish Hamilton, 1953]) ; "a magnificent affair in its way," short and decisive, "a species of Privy Council" with Churchill as monarch and "pro-consuls, chiefs, and bearers of great names giving him the light of their opinions" (J. M. N. Jeffries, *Palestine: The Reality* [London: Longmans, Green & Co., 1939]) ; "British imperial statesmanship at its best" (John Marlowe, *Rebellion in Palestine* [London: The Cresset Press, 1962]). T. E. Lawrence, however, who resigned as Arab adviser to the colonial secretary on 4 July 1922, was hesitant, initially foreseeing the trip to Cairo as "a new page in the loosening of the Empire tradition," and afterwards, on 21 May 1921, admitting uncertainty: "On paper it isn't virtuous, but in flesh and blood? I wish I knew" (Graves and Hart, *T. E. Lawrence to His Biographers*, pp. 12 and 13). By contrast, Arab historians have taken a critical view of the conference and its achievements. Amīn Saʻīd accused Churchill of deception, while George Antonius believed that the 1921 solutions "fulfilled neither the letter nor the spirit" of the wartime promises made to the Arabs.

unchecked, he will exhaust the resources of these impoverished islands just as surely as Rome used up her strength in the same sinister regions. His plan contains the germs of the destruction of the old British Empire."[6] The *Spectator,* offering a nostalgic picture of the management of the empire in former times, took issue with procedural aspects of the conference, particularly its haste. In the nineteenth century there had been very few blunders. "Our policy was slow, cumbrous, timid, and often without much foresight or insight, but at any rate we did not plunge. We took a long while to decide upon any sort of change or development." Citing Cairo as an example, the *Spectator* concluded: "We now plunge light-heartedly into all sorts of action fraught with tremendous consequences and trust to luck to get us out."[7] At the end of 1921 a lengthy critique of Arab policy, published in *The Times,* urged: "We must evacuate Mesopotamia while we can, and now is the moment"; otherwise, Churchill's hopes of saving millions of British pounds sterling would most likely prove illusory. Disparaging the logic of imperialism, the series in *The Times* ended with a prediction and a policy recommendation contrary to that of the Cairo Conference. "So long as we stay there will ever be a fresh reason for staying, and a fresh reason for spending. Let us arise and go."[8]

Thus there were two opposing interpretations of the Cairo policy. Churchill chose to underline its immediate realization of economies and its compromise with Arab—as equated with sharifian—ambitions, which enabled Britain to retain her prominent position in the region through less direct means while satisfying the outcry in England for savings. Critics of the policy preferred instead to emphasize the sins of omission stemming from the fundamental decision neither to relinquish the mandates nor to withdraw from the Fertile Crescent.

Churchill, the Colonial Office, and those in England who favored standing firm in the Arab world did benefit indirectly from other factors leading to reduced tension in the Middle East. Bolshevik and Turkish revolutionary activity began to recede in 1921. Russia's leaders, adopting the New Economic Policy (NEP), addressed themselves in the first

6. Lovat Fraser, "How to Destroy the Empire," *Daily Mail,* 9 May 1921, p. 6.
7. *Spectator,* 25 June 1921, pp. 803–4.
8. *The Times,* in its issues of 27, 28, and 29 December 1921, printed a series of three articles by its special correspondent at Teheran reviewing unfavorably the train of events in the Middle East during 1921.

instance to domestic problems and to consolidating the revolution at home. An Anglo-Russian trade agreement was signed in 1921, and by January, 1924, full diplomatic relations had been restored between Great Britain and Soviet Russia. Similarly, Mustafa Kemal employed his energies in directing his people along the path of national development. On 20 October 1921 the Franklin-Bouillon agreement terminated Kemalist hostilities with France. In a speech delivered on 1 November Kemal urged his countrymen to renounce larger ambitions based on Pan-Islamism. "Rather than run after ideas which we did not and could not realise and thus increase the number of our enemies and the pressure upon us, let us return to our national, legitimate limits. And let us know our limits."[9]

Although Britain began to negotiate with the Kemalists in November, 1922, agreement was not reached at Lausanne until 24 July 1923. But just as Bolshevik and Turkish forces had contributed to the general unrest in the Fertile Crescent in 1920 and 1921, so did they serve to lessen tension thereafter. India was safe, her land and access routes secure. In addition, no European or Asian power—France, Germany, Italy, Russia, or Turkey—was capable of seriously intervening in the region, and the United States, if she possessed the capability, lacked the desire. Consequently, British primacy was insured for the succeeding two decades.

Another factor no less conducive to British security and renewed confidence originated within the Arab world itself, where, in the 1920's, extremism—the use of force, the demand for immediate, full independence and an end to any European presence, direct or otherwise—waned. In February, 1921, Reza Khan had staged a coup in Persia, ending a long period of chaos and regaining independence for Iran. On 28 February 1922 the British government unilaterally proclaimed Egypt's independence. When the Anglo-Iraqi treaty was concluded on 10 October 1922 Iraqi nationalists viewed it as a definite rejection of mandatory status and as the first stride toward complete independence. A majority of them rallied around the person of King Faysal, the institution of monarchy, and the concept of nationhood. In Palestine the two communities, still persisting in their mutually exclusive demands, drew further apart, with Britain interposed between them, each becoming more dis-

9. Ismet Pasa Inonu, *Inonu'nun Soylev ve Demecleri* (Istanbul, 1946), 1:193, quoted in Bernard Lewis, *The Emergence of Modern Turkey*, pp. 346–47.

tinct and self-contained. Given the strong British military presence, violence was avoided for the time being. In Transjordan, although the dream remained, the prospect of reaching Damascus gradually receded. As a result, Abdullah and his supporters concentrated on enhancing their personal positions and that of the modest amirate. In short, nationalism was satisfied in Turkey and Persia, appeased in Egypt, and suppressed in Syria, while in the Fertile Crescent, under the Cairo policy, it was either largely diverted or constricted.

A useful standard for evaluating the effectiveness of the Cairo policy might be found in those four objectives set forth by Winston Churchill just prior to the conference: to realize economies, to uphold the honor and vital interests of Great Britain, and to reduce commitments. Whatever degree of success was achieved during the interwar period must be attributed to two characteristics of British policy. First, a clear decision was made as to priorities. By withdrawing from Persia and Turkey, the British in effect gained strength to deal with the Arabs—an insight which was derived perhaps from the precedent of France's choice in 1920 between Turkey and Syria in favor of the latter. Second, once the choice had been made, the successful use of the military made it possible to apply the Cairo decisions. Self-imposed limitations as to ends and means thus were given greater definition than at any other time either before or after 1921.

With regard to the primary objective of realizing economies, there is little question but that the policy succeeded in the immediate sense, although Great Britain would be called on in later years to incur expenses, as in Transjordan, and to supply troops, as in Palestine. Similarly, British strategic interests—Iraqi oil fields, the Transjordanian air route, the reserve base near the Suez Canal in Palestine, the secure water route to India, and, more generally, diverse cultural and economic investments—were upheld throughout the interwar period.

Somewhat harder to assess is the extent to which British honor was upheld after 1921. Honor, in the sense of abiding by contractual and treaty commitments, was maintained as successive British governments bound themselves to the Husayn promise and to the Balfour Declaration, to the League mandates and to the series of Iraqi and Transjordanian treaties. These commitments continued until each was either superseded by changing circumstances or unilaterally abrogated by the force of Arab nationalism. But British honor, in the sense of high esteem, was compromised by the Cairo policy. In the eyes of the Arabs Britain's reputation declined thereafter as she became the focus for nationalist resentment in each of the countries of the Fertile Crescent. This resulted partly from the fact that honor and interest are not synonymous. Whenever the two could not readily be equated in their Middle Eastern context British statesmen tended to choose interests over honor. Yet, precisely because British intentions were progressively discredited by the Arabs, and in Palestine by the Jews, British interests also suffered, if not before, then certainly after, World War II.

The cause of democracy also was weakened through association with Britain and the West. Those tenets and institutions introduced with the mandates gradually were overthrown as disillusionment with Europe led to a rejection of its forms of government. Equality and freedom were viewed as incompatible in the framework of Arab politics. Representative government, parliamentary bodies, political parties—these were abused and eventually repudiated. Barriers against intervention by the military were torn down in country after country by those very armies brought into existence by Great Britain in the 1920's.

The emphasis at Cairo had been upon introducing political reform from the top, mainly through individual monarchs and their British advisers and closest political associates. But even Faysal, with his dedication and ability to command respect, was unable to overcome the strong particularistic and therefore divisive forces existing in Iraq at the lower levels of society. His untimely death in 1933 deprived the country of a source of stability; the first military *coup d'état* in the Arab world took place in Iraq in 1936.

In Transjordan Abdullah relied on British-trained army and police units to exercise his personal command and to force the tribes into submission. Britain was hardly any more successful in Arabia, where first King Husayn and later King Ibn Sa'ud were very slow in accepting political reforms. In Palestine, where both communities actively sought political responsibilities, the British in many ways actually prevented any progress toward that goal of self-government implicit in the mandate.

While financial and military savings were a major achievement of the Cairo policy, our larger historical perspective indicates that an inaccurate assessment of the Arab milieu constituted its principal failing. The authorities who gathered at Cairo, as servants of the British Empire, recoiled from the embarrassment and confusion of 1920 and sought, above all, stability. They, together with Churchill, who described his task as "pacification" of the Middle East, blended such palliatives as Abdullah, subsidies, air power, and the status quo in Palestine with the fixed principle of political support for the sharifians and reference to the League mandates as legal justification for any degree of control. The abandonment of imperial interests in the Arab world was as alien to them as the idea of a permanent British presence became to a younger generation of Arab nationalists.

Upon reflection, however, later British difficulties resulted from the tacit agreement at Cairo to appease rather than to satisfy Arab nationalism. At best, through their ties to the sharifians the British gained an alliance only with the moderate, conservative nationalists—Faysal, Abdullah, Nuri al-Sa'id, and others. This insufficient attention to nationalism was acknowledged in mid-1922 when the Inter-Departmental Committee on Eastern Unrest cautioned that "the principal cause of unrest prevalent throughout the East is an intense nationalism," sincere, unique to each country, and uncentralized, which gave no indication of subsiding. The implications for Great Britain also were underlined: "Owing to her preponderating position in the East, Great Britain is looked upon as the greatest obstacle to the fulfilment of national aspirations. . . . Whilst individually the various factors causing unrest do not constitute an immediate danger to the Empire, and India in particular, their cumulative effect is undermining our prestige, and is a source of real danger if allowed to develop without restraint."[10] Because the Arab world thereafter did not occasion any sense of immediacy—a tribute in part to Colonial Office success in restoring stability and British confidence—and because the Cairo Conference did not become a precedent for comprehensive review and consultation, this original deficiency in assessing Arab sentiment remained an enduring characteristic of Britain's Middle Eastern policy.

As a result, the Cairo policy, rather than effecting the fourth of Churchill's objectives—reducing commitments—contributed to their increase. It succeeded only to the extent that the presence of Great Britain became less direct, less conspicuous. Her representatives, working

10. "Report of the Inter-Departmental Committee on Eastern Unrest" (most secret), completed on 17 August 1922, C.O. 537/835.

through native institutions and agents, continued to promote distinctly British interests. Despite such indirect rule, or because of it, the original commitments endured and Britain's involvement increased: as a mandatory power and protector of the Arab world; as a mediator in Palestine and founder of Transjordan; as an ally of the sharifians; and as an arbiter in Arabia. This trend toward greater involvement has been reversed in the years since World War II, essentially by an involuntary process: the abandonment of Palestine in 1948, the dismissal of Glubb Pasha from Jordan and the evacuation of the Suez Canal area in 1956, the violent overthrow of the Iraqi monarchy in 1958, and withdrawal from Aden in 1967. The intended departure from the Persian Gulf area, scheduled for 1971, will have brought the British recessional from the Middle East to its ultimate conclusion fifty years after the Cairo Conference.

A fixed tenet of Great Britain's relationship to the Arabs throughout the interwar period, what Elizabeth Monroe has described as "the years of good management," was the sharifian policy. Yet it became a source of increasing embarrassment for both the British and the sharifians. From the outset the Middle East Department regarded the intended policy as a gamble, one major risk being the association between the two parties. Nor was the implication lost upon Faysal, who on 17 August 1921 perceived that "His Majesty's Government and I are in [the] same boat and must sink or swim together."[11]

Husayn refused to endorse the relationship and was unable to resist the Sa'udis alone. His sons, Faysal and Abdullah, conformed to the principle of working in conjunction with Britain and succeeded. Yet in their very success both compromised their prestige in the Arab world by too great a dependence on Great Britain. The amirs and their successors and supporters became the medium by which the British were able to exert their influence in the region, directly affecting both the style and pace of development—social, economic, legal, political, institutional—in each Arab country during those critical years of widening political consciousness.

11. Cox to the Colonial Office (paraphrase telegram, no. 397), 17 August 1921, in 41616 of C.O. 730/4; see also Shuckburgh's comparable assessment on 17 March in 14449 of C.O. 730/9. On 30 December 1921 *The Times* editorialized: "Feisal owes his throne to British bayonets—a great pity for him and for Britain" (see p. 11).

In their different personalities, tactics, and reputations, Faysal and Abdullah offer an interesting study of Arab leadership. Faysal professed to be guided by a desire to serve in the cause of Arab unity, although his very success in Baghdad constituted a setback. Nevertheless, he is held in high regard by Arab historians, perhaps because of his early demise. Less noble motives were imparted, by contrast, to Abdullah. His initiative in entering Transjordan has often been ascribed to personal ambition, the fear of being left without any prominent position under the final British arrangement. Yet from his modest throne he endeavored constantly to inspire a larger political union—of course under his rule. As a result of this partisan maneuvering his stature is somewhat lower than that of his brother's. Whereas Faysal gained his throne by patient cultivation of British ties and through an emphasis on tact and diplomacy, Abdullah secured his position through the bold, direct defiance of British desires.

With the passing of time, however, the sharifians, and with them the foundation of Britain's presence, were supplanted by Arabs less compromising and more determined in their insistence upon full, immediate independence and in their dedication to Arab unity. Only the Hashimite kingdom of Jordan remains, precariously, as a vestige of sharifian ambitions and misplaced British hopes and as a testimony to the historical insight of Ibn Khaldun, who wrote, "When a dynasty is overrun from the center"—as was the Hijaz in 1924—"it is of no avail to it that the outlying areas remain intact."

Conversely, after 1921 the British government found itself bound to the sharifians by both interest and honor. Having staked so much on the sharifian principle and having permitted this to constitute a vested interest, it became progressively harder to break with tradition, even in view of the ascendance of new Arab forces. A related failing was the notion that the Arabs of the Fertile Crescent would be satisfied merely with the forms, rather than the substance, of independence.

In summary, the policy which emerged from the Cairo Conference was insufficient for the times. It underestimated the Arabs and the extent of their political awakening. It deprecated their desire for independence and unity and their determination to achieve these even at the price of British support. At a time when Britain's resolve in administering her empire and in bearing the "white man's burden" had begun to falter, the conference deliberated in an atmosphere of lingering self-confidence. It was also marked by expediency, for as Churchill explained: "We must have some friends, we cannot possibly carry on in these countries with a dwindling military force at an enormous expense, and no friends of any sort or kind. You must pick some out of the scrimmage and have them on your side."[12] This imperative led to an *alliance de convenance* which soon proved fraught with inconvenience for both sides.

The Cairo Conference, in short, was perhaps too ambitious, grafting monarchies and seeking to project the sharifians onto the entire Arab world, only to find that they were neither powerful nor respected enough to lead the Arabs. Leaders, like ideas, proved vulnerable and obsolete in the transitional Middle East.

The fact that British policy was conducted along these lines and on the basis of these premises was due in no small measure to Winston Churchill's influence upon the decision-making processes before, during, and after the Cairo Conference. What had recommended him to Lloyd George in January, 1921, aside from his increasing concern with the military and financial implications of Middle Eastern affairs, were his known qualities of assertiveness and dynamism. "Clear leadership, violent action, rigid decisions one way or the other," Churchill was later to write, "form the only path not only of victory, but of safety and even of mercy."[13] His skill as a technician, as an articulate proponent and able leader, was already apparent at this intermediate stage of his career. But three other traits cast doubt about his competence in this specific instance: his unfamiliarity with the Arabs, dedication to the empire idea, and restlessness.

Lord Milner, Churchill's predecessor at the Colonial Office, wrote of him: "His weakness is that he is too apt to make up his mind without sufficient knowledge."[14] Because of insufficient knowledge of the Arab world Churchill adopted a simplistic approach to the Palestine problem at the outset, transferred to the Arabs his preconceived notions about

12. Churchill in a speech delivered before the Imperial Conference on 22 June 1921, Imperial Meetings, 1921, vol. 1 (secret), CAB 32/2, p. 9.
13. Churchill, *The World Crisis, 1911–1918*, pt. 1, p. 239. Lord Clement Attlee later wrote of Churchill, "Energy rather than wisdom, practical judgment or vision, was his supreme qualification" (*The Observer, Churchill by His Contemporaries* [London: Hodder & Stoughton, 1965], p. 35).
14. Bowle, *Viscount Samuel*, pp. 212–13.

the relationship of an imperial power to its subject peoples, and relied heavily upon the advice of T. E. Lawrence.[15] Then, after the conference, as conditions changed and the Cairo policy needed unceasing supervision, Churchill, regarding the Middle East as pacified and his major objectives as accomplished, became absorbed in other, non-Arab matters. On 19 October 1922 the Coalition government, headed by Lloyd George, fell, thus ending the brief, though significant, period of Churchill's involvement in Arab affairs. He was succeeded as secretary of state for the colonies by the duke of Devonshire.

T. E. Lawrence imparted to Churchill the "imagination and courage" to make a "fresh departure" and a knowledge of political procedure which enabled him to put "his political revolution" into operation in the Middle East and in London, peacefully.[16] To be sure, the Cairo Conference and policy were not entirely fresh departures and certainly not a political revolution. As we have seen, the basic elements of that policy had been either in effect or under consideration before the conference. Adhering to the Balfour Declaration, pursuing British interests through less direct forms of control, and creating native political institutions, for example, had been part of established British policy in 1920. Similarly, the possibility of employing the air force to control dispersed tribal groupings and of using subsidies in Arabia to balance rival forces had been tabled before the Cabinet, while the utility of the sharifians in general, and of Faysal in particular, had been the subject of memoranda within the several ministries well in advance of the conference.

Rather, the conference's contribution, and Churchill's, was to momentarily arrest the process of drift which had hindered Great Britain in the Fertile Crescent since World War I. It integrated the ideas brought to it in order to form a comprehensive policy and a durable foundation. Yet the new policy, a combination of tradition and innovation, was in turn subjected to inertia, enduring until it was repudiated

15. Cf. 58211 of C.O. 733/15 and Meinertzhagen, *Middle East Diary*, p. 33, on the Lawrence-Churchill relationship. Churchill, speaking of Iraq in June, 1921, said: "There is no doubt that these turbulent people are apt to get extremely bored if they are subjected to a higher form of justice and more efficient administration than those to which they have for centuries been accustomed. At any rate we have reverted perforce, and by the teaching of experience, to more primitive methods" (speech before the Imperial Conference, Imperial Meetings, 1921, vol. 1, CAB 32/2, p. 8).

16. Cited in Graves and Hart, *T. E. Lawrence to His Biographers*, pp. 112–13.

by the major shock of World War II and the dissolution of the British Empire.

From a different perspective the events of 1921 had a mixed effect on the Middle East region. Partition of the Fertile Crescent, an idea initially subscribed to by the European Powers in 1915, was taken for granted at Cairo. In one case, Transjordan, the events of 1921 actually surpassed earlier estimates of the number of possible political units. But if these arrangements appeased the territorial and strategic imperatives of England and France, they definitely compounded administrative difficulties thereafter. In addition to creating artificial entities, arbitrary and therefore illogical boundaries, and narrow national loyalties, partition also provided a basic obstacle for the later struggle on behalf of the ideal of Arab unity.

Much of inter-Arab politics in the period between the two world wars can be characterized as a clash of rival plans for confederation or consolidation, and of contenders for leadership of the Arab world. Abdullah never abandoned his dream of ruling Syria or, alternatively, of uniting Palestine and Transjordan. Egypt gradually assumed a more prominent role in Arab affairs, first under King Farouk and, after 1952, under Gamal Abdul Nasser. Nuri al-Sa'id, once in power in Iraq, became very active in promoting his "Greater Syria" plan, which called for the unification of Syria, Iraq and Transjordan under a common Hashimite crown. Lebanon, because of her unique ethnic composition, always opposed such schemes, while Syrians were often divided over the issue of separateness as a nation or submergence in a larger entity. The permanent division of geographical Syria into Lebanon, Syria, and Palestine and the separation of Transjordan from Palestine thus have proved to be serious obstacles to the more recent efforts of the 1960's to achieve a unified Arab world. At the same time, the Zionists, belatedly viewing Transjordan as the product of partition,[17] held Britain accountable for this reduction of "historical Palestine."

17. Not until the end of the 1920's did Vladimir Jabotinsky demand a Jewish state on both sides of the Jordan, making this a cardinal tenet of his Revisionist party. Dr. Weizmann did not object publicly to the arrangement in Transjordan until 1930; see his article in the *Week-End Review* 2, no. 34 (1 November 1930): 611–12. For additional Zionist criticism of the loss of Transjordan, see Jewish Agency for Palestine, *Memorandum Submitted to His Majesty's Government* (May, 1930), p. 66, and *Memorandum to the Palestine Royal Commission* (November, 1936), pp. 210–13.

Leopold Amery, a former colonial secretary, told the House of Commons on

It may be added that 1921 also influenced significantly the course of the Palestine problem. Events tested the will of each of the three parties involved and left each more determined to persist.

The Jaffa riots, followed by the stationing of a permanent garrison of British troops in Palestine and the publicized mission of the Arab delegation to Europe, stimulated intense debate in England. The relative merits of the Zionist and Arab claims were analyzed at length until English society split in supporting one or the other of the two competing national groups. Even more debatable was the fundamental question of what Britain conceived her role to be in Palestine. Could Britain (or, for that matter, any other power) do justice to what was becoming an ever more difficult, emotional, and costly issue? What benefits or interests were so overriding as to warrant retention of this onerous chore of policing the mandate?

Yet the fact remains that Britain, despite her awareness of the difficulties and her encounters with obstacles and resistance along the way, did not yield the Palestine mandate for another twenty-five years, thereby challenging historians and political scientists to offer adequate explanation for such seemingly irrational political behavior. It was surely not pure humanitarianism or an inflexible sense of honor, as moralists would have us believe, that compelled His Majesty's Government to persist. But neither can those twenty-five years be explained solely in terms of self-interest as advocates of power politics might argue, for by the 1930's Palestine was becoming less of an asset and more of a liability to the British Empire. It is more likely that Britain's tenacity resulted from a blend of both aspects: a willingness to bear the responsibilities that attach to great-power status, and a respect for undertakings which manifested itself frequently and forcefully under the *Pax Britannica*. Empire determined strategy, and strategy dictated the retention of Palestine.

Doubt and factionalism also appeared within the Zionist camp. Dr. Weizmann, it is now clear, had deep misgivings about British intentions

22 May 1939 that 1921–22 had "marked the drastic scaling down of Jewish hopes. It began by taking out of Palestine the larger and better half, the half more suitable to large-scale colonisation, namely Transjordan. That was the first partition" (Jewish Agency for Palestine, *Book of Documents Submitted to the General Assembly of the United Nations Relating to the Establishment of the National Home for the Jewish People* [May, 1947], p. 37).

and the utility of dependence upon Great Britain as sponsor of the Zionist program. This was many years before his anguish over the British White Paper of 1939, which restricted Jewish immigration into Palestine at the height of nazi persecution in Europe. Yet he, too, found little room for flexibility in the absence of any alternative great power inclined to support Zionism. Identification with Great Britain subjected Weizmann to criticism from his colleagues. Vladimir Jabotinsky expressed anger over the loss of Transjordan and the failure to present an appropriate official Zionist demurrer. David Ben-Gurion and other members of the *Yishuv* in Palestine objected to Weizmann's patience with London.

The fact that moderation was losing ground among the Zionists was perhaps due in part to the estrangement which developed between its two foremost proponents: Dr. Weizmann and Sir Herbert Samuel. Although they shared the hope for a Jewish commonwealth in Palestine, the two men differed over the means to its realization. Weizmann was responsible to his constituency, the Zionist membership; Samuel was a British public servant responsible to the Colonial Office and, ultimately, to the Cabinet. Weizmann in his own way applied pressure on British leaders for tangible evidence of support, particularly the right to promote immigration and land settlement even in the face of Arab opposition. By contrast, charged with maintaining order, Samuel feared that such direct pressure would only alienate the British public, while neglect of Arab sensitivities would assure success only at the expense of Arab-Jewish understanding and cooperation. In short, Weizmann stressed the need for support from the international community, whereas Samuel urged that greater attention be given to gaining some sort of accommodation with the native Palestinian Arabs. While history has vindicated Weizmann in his preoccupation with world support for Jewish statehood, it also has confirmed Samuel in his fear that the very fact of statehood might be vitiated if gained at the expense of the Arabs—indeed, imperiled by their intense opposition.

The Arabs of Palestine, last component of this triangle, also shared in affecting the subsequent pattern. Having failed to impress Churchill or to gain the support of British leaders, the Palestinian community, in its relations with the mandatory and with the *Yishuv* was characterized by bitterness and, above all, by negativism. The Arabs boycotted institutions premised on joint Arab-Jewish activity and refused to cooperate with the mandate. While the Zionists welcomed every opportunity to gain experience in government, the Arabs did not create viable political institutions as a preparatory stage for any future transition to self-rule. Nor did they provide responsible local leaders.

If the Zionists were guilty of paying too little attention to the Arabs, the latter compounded this by not presenting individuals of stature or authority with whom the Zionists might have negotiated. Prior to 1921 the Palestinian Arab community had been spoken for by outsiders such as the Sublime Porte, Husayn, Faysal, or the Syrian nationalists. It failed to take the initiative when given the opportunity for independent expression, becoming involved instead in family rivalries, in clashes of personality and ambition. Consequently, control of Palestinian interests passed gradually, often involuntarily, to the neighboring Arab countries. Forty-nine years later the Palestinian Arabs are still struggling to fully regain their rightful status as one of the two parties directly involved in the most recent form of the Palestine problem. In truth, therefore, partition was an actuality in Palestine long before Great Britain, and in 1947 the United Nations General Assembly, regarded it as a political solution. In the absence of moderation, of a meaningful dialogue between the two resident communities, and of an unmistakable British statement of intent, violence alone remained to compound the tragedy of earlier lost opportunities.

Britain's interwar policy toward the Middle East, with its recourse to balances and compromises, reflected the primary emphasis in London upon immediate advantage and short-term interests. By localizing and deflecting regional discontent, by appeasing Arab nationalism only when compelled to do so under pressure, and by supporting conservative leaders and classes, the British succeeded in fostering an impression of imperial order and calm throughout the Arab world in the period 1922–39, only to delude themselves.

Within this context, and under British protection, the United States was able to establish and broaden contacts in the region, deriving benefits without commensurate responsibilities. In time these largely private American enterprises, charitable institutions, and interest groups increased their investments, and these became permanent interests. By 1945 the investments were acknowledged in Washington as major official commitments. As the United States assumed joint and primary responsibility for the Middle East in the initial stage of the cold war,

American policy was grafted onto the earlier foundations of British policy. These foundations—embodying interests and situations, assumptions and attitudes, individual leaders and social groups—thus became part of Britain's dubious legacy both to the United States government and to the inhabitants of the Middle East.

In 1915 the peoples of the Middle East looked to Great Britain as their redeemer from Turkish domination. Within the brief span of twenty-five years, however, British prestige declined to such an extent that by 1939 many Arab circles had turned to Germany in hopes of ridding the region of Britain's presence. Unsuccessful, they then turned to the United States and, most recently, to the Soviet Union. Yet the transformation of the Arab world during this same period—to a considerable degree the result of British policy—is no less impressive. Whereas in 1915 Sharif Husayn of Mecca was seen as the principal spokesman for the Arab cause, by 1939 not even the pretense of Arab solidarity remained. King Farouk of Egypt, Nuri al-Sa'id in Iraq, King Ibn Sa'ud in Arabia, the grand mufti of Palestine, and King Abdullah in Transjordan rivaled each other for that elusive role of voice of the Arabs.

Yet Great Britain concurrently did encourage a sense of unity, albeit indirectly. The Arab world was dealt with administratively as a single unit through the Middle East Department of the Colonial Office. All parts of the region were linked by a network of air, sea, oil pipeline, and motor routes. For strategic purposes the area was considered as an integrated whole, and the peoples of these countries were exposed collectively to the technology of modernization and to the culture of the West.

Precisely because of the numerous forces initiated, strengthened, or suppressed in 1921, the relationship between the British Empire and the Arab world was modified substantially when Winston Churchill returned to Cairo as prime minister of Great Britain in November and December, 1943, to construct a new, less ambitious foundation for British foreign policy there. As a forum for evaluating both the problems and prospects of the Arab world, the Cairo Conference of 1921 was therefore unprecedented in the long history of British relations with that region. And in its recognition of the importance of the Middle East for any global power and for world politics it has not been equaled since, not by Great Britain nor by the United States.

APPENDIX A **De Bunsen Committee Maps**

Map 1. First Scheme of Annexation, Including Alexandretta in British Territory

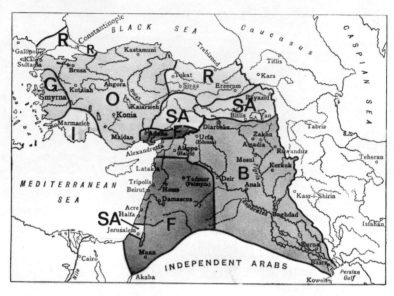

Map 2. Second Scheme of Annexation, with Haifa Replacing Alexandretta

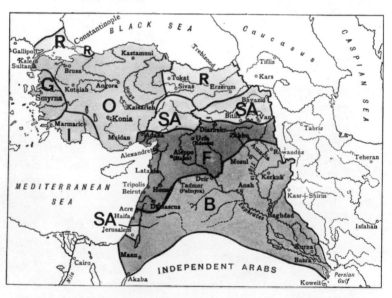

Appendix A

Map 3. Zones of Interest

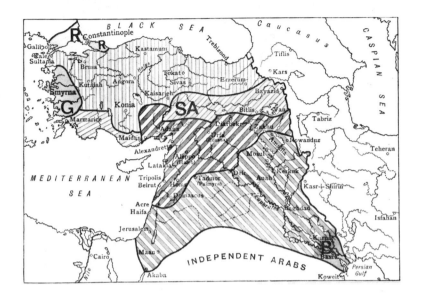

Map 4. Ottoman Independence

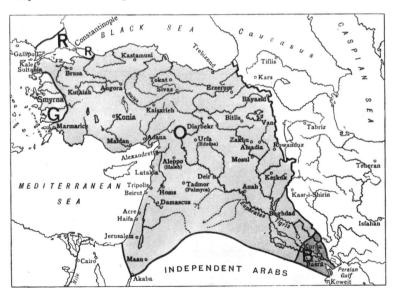

Map 5. Ottoman Devolutionary Scheme

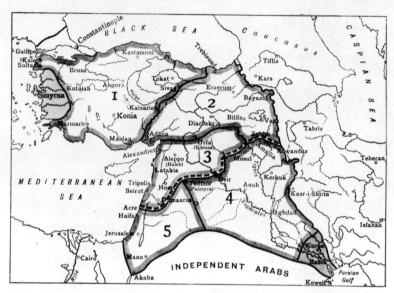

Map showing the areas of the five ayalets: *(1) Anatolia, (2) Armenia, (3) Syria, (4) Jazirah-Irak, and (5) Palestine. Broken line marks northern boundary of British sphere of enterprise.*

British	B	
French	F	
Greek (possible)	G	
Italian (possible)	I	
Ottoman	O	
Russian	R	
Special Administration	SA	SA

Deputation of Executive Committee of the
Haifa Congress Received by the Secretary of
State for the Colonies at Government House,
Monday, 28 March 1921

President of the Haifa Congress, Musa Kazim Pasha, presented the following memorandum:

When Palestine emerged from the Great War she found herself tied down
and her adversary, sword in hand, bending over her. She found herself, too,
separated from her surrounding Arab sisters by vast distances which she
had covered by running after an imaginary friend. But she found no friend,
she found an enemy, rather.

This is the story of Palestine, land of miracles and the supernatural, and
the cradle of religions. She neither complained nor was unfaithful to her
first friend, but when sorrow filled her breast she breathed a sigh and
dropped a tear, and, lo, the Third Arab Palestine Congress was born. This
congress, therefore, is a true representative of Palestine, her mouthpiece. In
it all classes are legally represented. Town, village, factory and farm—in
fact, all the live aspects of the nation—acknowledged its leadership. . . .

Confident in the justice of their cause, the Arabs are convinced that this
unnatural partitioning of their lands must one day disappear. It would be a
grand task for England—the traditional friend of the Arab—to accomplish
this reunion, and thereby gain the Arabs. For the Arabs are the key to the
East, and they possess its doors and passes. Arabia, on the Red Sea and the

Persian Gulf, is the way to India, and Palestine, on the Mediterranean, holds to-day the balance between the Powers.

Fleets and armies cannot conquer the heart of a nation. England could have conquered the Arabs' hearts by safeguarding their country's integrity. Then all these huge millions required for the upkeep of her large armies would be saved to her and her taxpayer.

The relation of Turk to Arab should teach England a lesson. Submitting to the Turk from necessity, the moment the Great War started the Arab seized his opportunity and threw off the yoke. To-day the Arab's belief in England is not what it was. This is to be deplored, for the Arab is noble and large-hearted; he is also vengeful, and never forgets an ill-deed. If England does not take up the cause of the Arabs, other Powers will. From India, Mesopotamia, the Hedjaz and Palestine the cry goes up to England now. If she does not listen, then perhaps Russia will take up their call some day, or perhaps even Germany. For though to-day Russia's voice is not heard in the councils of the nations, yet the time must come when it will assert itself.

In the interests of universal peace, therefore, if not for love of the Arab, England should refrain from taking this false step. Zionists can never be true to her, as they can be true to no one, and to this their mischievous work in Austria, Germany and Russia can testify. They have one and only [one] aim in life, from which nothing can divert them. . . .

Had Zionists come to Palestine simply as visitors, or had matters remained as before the war, there would be no question of Jew or non-Jew. It is the idea of transforming Palestine into a home for the Jews that Arabs resent and fight against. The fact that a Jew is a Jew has never prejudiced the Arab against him. Before the war Jews enjoyed all the privileges and rights of citizenship. The question is not a religious one. For we see that Christian and Moslem alike, whose religions are not similar, unite in their hatred of Zionists. . . .

We will now proceed to dissect the Balfour Declaration, and to show how to the Arab, the Palestinian and the Britisher it is strongly prejudicial.

a. *From a Legal Point of View*

1. Before drawing a contract with Zionists for the sale of Palestine, England had drawn a contract with King Hussein by virtue of which he was to be given Arab lands. Consequently the contract with King Hussein annuls that with the Jews. In the eye of the Jew the first is valid and the second is not. Shall it go down to history then, that England was false to her plighted word through Mr. Balfour, and was it not for the sake of a plighted word to the Belgians that she unsheathed her sword in the Great War?

2. King Hussein paid a price for his contract by rising against the Turks. This was his part of the contract. England's contract with the Jews, therefore, can have no legal value as long as King Hussein is ignorant of it. So far, then, as the Arabs are concerned the Balfour Declaration is not valid.

Besides, there were understandings with France and Russia before this declaration was made; consequently, though France was influenced to include it in the mandate, international law cannot give it a legal status.

3. Countries with their civic and other rights and privileges are the property of their inhabitants and constitute an heirloom of the nation, handed down from father to son. Now the people of Palestine inherited this country from their ancestors, as these did from those who had gone before them. Palestine, therefore, with its air, water, lands and roads, commerce, industry and agriculture, is in inalienable possession of the nation, and neither England nor any other Power can bring a foreigner in to share this inheritance. But Palestinians are gradually losing their birthright through Jewish immigration, and thanks to Mr. Balfour's Declaration, which was denounced in the press, from the pulpit and before the American Commission.

But it might be argued that Mr. Balfour spoke on behalf of the British Cabinet of which he is a member. But even this does not give his declaration any legal validity, since Great Britain, though occupying the country, does not possess it. Putting aside for one moment Mr. Wilson's Fourteen Points and the repeated assertions of the Allies that they were not out in this war for colonisation or self-aggrandisement, we find in international law that a conquering people can lay hands only on the personal possessions of the defeated Power and on its rights and privileges, but that it has no right to touch anything that belongs to private persons.

In the light of international law, then, Mr. Balfour's declaration is an act of modern Bolshevism, pure and simple.

4. One of the great laws governing international treaties is that the two parties should possess the quality of government. A treaty between a governing Power and an individual cannot have international force.

Now the contract between Great Britain and Zionists over Palestine is one between a Great Power and a company of men who are neither a Power nor a nation. In fact, it is a contract between England and a collection of history, imagination and ideals existing only in the brains of Zionists who are a company, a commission but not a nation. Is it right or just, then, that a treaty concluded with King Hussein should be made null and void by one made with Zionists?

For thousands of years Jews have been scattered over the earth, and have become nationals of the various nations amongst whom they settled. They have no separate political or lingual existence. In Germany they are Germans, in France Frenchmen, and in England Englishmen. Religion and language are their only tie. But Hebrew is a dead language and might be discarded. How then could England conclude a treaty with a religion and register it in the League of Nations? Nay, rather, how could the Jews themselves agree to this treaty? For if there exists a Jewish Power and a Jewish nation, what is the status, amongst others, of those high Jewish officials who are serving England to-day? Are they Jewish nationals or English nationals, for it is obvious they cannot be both at the same time?

Sir Herbert Samuel and Lord Reading are Englishmen and Jews. Now if Jew-ism is a nationality what about their English-ism? One -ism must be sacrificed for the other, but which for which?

Besides, this promise was made long before British troops came into possession of Palestine, and since this victory was an Allied one, France, Italy and the Arabs have taken active parts in it, the consent of all should be secured before any gift is made. But the Arabs have not been consulted, and never will consent, and Russia, when it wakes up, will have a word to say.

5. There can be no question that Palestine belongs legally to the Arabs. They inherited it from their ancestors and have been occupying it for more than twenty centuries. The Jews saw, knew and accepted this fact. Now, had they any right to own Palestine they would have contested our occupation of it long ago, or at least, lodged a protest against us. But they did nothing of the kind, knowing full well they had nothing to claim.

Moreover, in the days of the Turks, the Jews, the great majority of whom were nationals of European Governments and consequently protected by the Capitulations, could have used their privileges and the weakness of the Turkish Government to extort at least some official recognition of their claim to Palestine. In fact, some European Powers would have abetted and encouraged them in their demands. But no claim was made, and native Palestinians remained undisturbed in the possession of their country.

After all this can anyone doubt that Palestine belongs to the Arabs, and that the Balfour Declaration is a gross injustice?

b. *Historical Point of View*

Zionists and Great Britain appeal to history in confirmation of their claim. Because at one period of history the Jews conquered this land and lived in it, hence, it is argued, they possess it for ever.

The argument contains more of poetry in it than logic. According to it the Arabs should claim Spain since once upon a time they conquered it and there developed a high civilisation. Why then should Palestine be given back to the Jews and Spain remain in the hands of Spaniards? The Turks too, at one time conquered all the Balkan States right up to Vienna, why does Europe then keep these back from them?

Even while in possession of Palestine for about 4,000 years the Jews' right to it was always contested by their neighbours. Wars, revolts, religious and political agitations and internal troubles filled the whole period; and it was only during the reign of King Soloman that peace prevailed. But the Arabs' reign in Palestine was undisturbed for a long time until the Crusaders arrived, and then they bought the country again, for the second time, after having once bought it from the Romans, by shedding rivers of blood. Besides, they were always at peace with their neighbours—an achievement which the Israelites cannot claim.

It might be argued, too, that the Jews' claim to Palestine rests on the monuments and buildings which their ancestors built and left behind them. As a matter of fact, no nation in history has left less behind it than the Jews; and those temples and monuments established by them in their golden age disappeared before the nation was scattered.

But if ancient monuments establish a claim, what about Arab and Turkish monuments in Europe to-day; and does not every ruin in Palestine bespeak Arab origin.

It is surprising to think that students of ancient Jewish history interest themselves in the religion and kingly glory of this people and neglect that other part of it dealing with revolts, mutinies, internal troubles, and those wars with their neighbours which finally led to their expulsion from the land. Have statesmen ever found out the reason why the Israelites could not get on with their neighbours, or why they were so detested by all surrounding tribes? We believe that such a study would reveal points that may prove very helpful to modern diplomacy and statecraft.

Arabs, on the other hand, have lived here for centuries at peace with all their neighbours, and even the very long reign of the Turks was not able to change the character of the land or to Turkify its inhabitants.

c. *Moral Point of View*

Jews have been amongst the most active advocates of destruction in many lands, especially where their influential positions have enabled them to do more harm. It is well known that the disintegration of Russia was wholly or in great part brought about by the Jews, and a large proportion of the defeat of Germany and Austria must also be put at their door. When the star of the

Central Powers was in the ascendant Jews flattered them, but the moment the scale turned in favour of the Allies Jews withdrew their support from Germany, opened their coffers to the Allies, and received in return that most uncommon promise.

We have seen a book entitled *"The Jewish Peril"* which should be read by everyone who still doubts the pernicious motives of the Jews towards the Powers that be and towards civilisation. It is a collection of the minutes of a secret society of prominent Jews who meet from time to time to discuss world affairs in relation to Judaism. The book is replete with an overflowing hatred of mankind, and Christendom in particular. It points out in detail ways and means for upsetting the present order of things, so that out of the ensuing chaos Jews might come out masters of the world.

Looking into the ranks of socialism, we find Jewish names such as Carl Marx, Becknin and Trotsky topping the list, besides a host of others as pernicious, if not as renowned.

The Jew, moreover, is clannish and unneighbourly, and cannot mix with those who live about him. He will enjoy the privileges and benefits of a country, but will give nothing in return. The Jew is a Jew all the world over. He amasses the wealth of a country and then leads its people, whom he has already impoverished, where he chooses. He encourages wars when self-interest dictates, and thus uses the armies of the nations to do his bidding.

Palestine suffers in this manner from her Jewish colonies. Wherever these exist the surrounding peasant population has had to sell out and migrate. Because of their clannishness Jews will, as far as they can help it, not employ a native, or buy at his store or benefit him in any way; on the contrary, they will watch every opportunity to harm him if this can be done with impunity.

In commerce and finance they are pitiless foes. Since Palestine opened its doors to them its trade has gradually drifted into their hands. They depreciate the value of land and property, and at the same time manipulate a financial crisis in order that landlords, under the stress of need, should sell out at ruinous prices.

Can Europe then expect the Arab to live and work with such a neighbour? Had not England better find a country for them in the vast uninhabited regions of her great Empire?

If Russia and Poland, with their spacious countries, were unable to tolerate them, how could Europe expect Palestine to welcome them? Can the Arabs carry the burden which Europe is unable to support; or will the Jew, on coming to Palestine, change his skin and lose all those qualities which have hitherto made him an object of dislike to the nations?

Appendix B

d. *Economic Point of View*

1. But there are economic difficulties in Mr. Balfour's declaration which render it valueless in our view.

Under Turkish rule the whole Empire was one big field for the trade of the Palestinian. From Constantinople to Mesopotamia and from the Red Sea to the Indian Ocean there was one system of customs, passports and coinage. To-day all this has changed. Goods sent to Damascus or Beyrout are charged double customs, merchants going north or east must have passports, which entail delays, expense and worry. All this is bad for business.

Now the Palestinian merchant is comparatively poor, while Zionists have wealth; consequently, they will be able soon to compete with him, crush and drive him out of the market. This done, they will turn on the consumer and force him to accept their prices. To say trade is free does not help matters. In Europe Governments endeavour by laws and taxation to protect their trade; why does not the Government here do likewise?

2. Palestine is an agricultural country, and depends largely on her export of cereals for a living. Now Jewish immigration has raised the cost of living, and the Government, in order to keep prices down in the interest of the Jewish consumer, has prohibited the export of certain cereals, with the result that the granaries of the land are stocked with products, and merchants cannot find an outlet for their trade. Consequently, a financial crisis set in and hundreds of merchants were bankrupt. Now, if this is the policy of Zionists while they still form a small minority, what will it be when they become more numerous?

Again, Palestine was ruined by the war, and is in dire need of money. The Jews started their campaign of advancing money on land and property. This can have one and only one conclusion; Jews will finally buy up these mortgaged lands, oust the owners, and rule in their places.

3. Again, in order to bring Palestine up to the level of European countries, the Government, in spite of the poverty of the people, has started a series of innovations and improvements which, though useful, are not so keenly needed at the present moment. It has opened up new unnecessary roads, repaired old ones which fully served their purposes, widened some railway lines, and created new gardens. The poor taxpayer has been burdened with costs. On the other hand, needs of more vital importance, such as public education have been grudged their due budgets. Recognising the benefits of these improvements, we would like our Treasury not to exceed its financial capacity, but to go slow, putting what is vital and essential before that which is a comparative luxury.

The above-mentioned works, too, are undertaken more in order to give employment to the thousands of Jewish immigrants than because they are immediate necessities. The Jewish labourer on these works is paid double the amount given to the native, though he does less work.

Ever since the High Commissioner took the reins of office he has been considering the floating of a loan for public works, or, in other words, he wants to borrow money in the name of the native taxpayer in order to help out Jewish immigrants. Is it not enough that the highest posts with fat salaries are given to the Jews, while the native official, who is more conversant with local needs, is neglected to a third-class position, with a salary too little for his needs and out of all proportion with his work?

e. *Expense to the British Government*

Thanks to the back-sliding efforts of Zionists, the Government has come to consider natives as enemies with whom she should always be on her guard. Consequently, a huge army is maintained in order to keep them quiet. Seven millions a year have been quoted as a moderate estimate for this army. Who is to pay? Certainly not the Palestine Treasury, as its whole income does not come up to one-third of this amount. Is it to be accumulated as a debt on the country to be paid when better days set in? We do not think the British Government would ever do such a thing. But if England pays what would her taxpayer say? If Zionists lent this amount the interest on the money would be enormous. The British taxpayer would hardly be expected to pay willingly seven millions a year for something which is valueless to him.

Yes, the British army in Palestine is of immense value to the Jews, and it is to their interest and safety that it is kept.

f. *Political Effects*

We would call the attention of Great Britain to the following three points:
1. Zionists are ambitious. If to-day they accept the mandate of England they may not do so to-morrow. Their one aim is to establish a Jewish kingdom, bring back the glory of Israel in the "Land of Promise," and gradually control the world. This ideal is expressed by their leader, Mr. Herzl, and by other Jewish writers. Already they complain that England has given them less than she promised. Here is their first word of ingratitude. They propose that a Jewish army be created to take the place of British troops. In this we have a foretaste of what is to come, for once they are strong enough, they will turn their backs on England as they did on Germany and Russia.

2. If England goes out of Egypt, how would she like to see the keeping of the eastern side of the Suez Canal in the hands of a Jewish State.

3. Egypt, India, Mesopotamia, Arabia, and Palestine, all these countries are a chain in the East; what takes place in the one finds an echo in them all, since not only have they similar customs and habits, but also the same religion. Now, as soon as this National Home is realised, there will migrate into Palestine the undesirables of Russia and Poland—men and women imbued with Bolshevism, poor and uneducated. As soon as Zionists cease to aid these they will revolt against them, against the Government and against society.

Economic troubles in which natives of Palestine were invited to take part have actually occurred many a time already, and it was only through the assistance of the Government that they were not allowed to spread. Now, if such things can happen to-day, when the number of immigrants is small, how will it be when they number hundreds of thousands, and who can guarantee that during some future trouble the natives, who are poor and ignorant, will again refuse to join.

Once Bolshevism spreads in Palestine it will quickly extend to other Arab peoples, who are free and democratic by nature, and who possess little more than their swords and emotions.

Will England, who should be the greatest foe of Bolshevism, be pleased to see it grow in Palestine and from it spread into Arab lands? . . .

For all the above reasons, we ask in the name of justice and right that—

First: The principle of a National Home for the Jews be abolished.

Second: A National Government be created, which shall be responsible to a Parliament elected by the Palestinian people who existed in Palestine before the war.

Third: A stop be put to Jewish immigration until such a time as a National Government is formed.

Fourth: Laws and regulations before the war be still carried out and all others framed after the British occupation be annulled, and no new laws be created until a National Government comes into being.

Fifth: Palestine should not be separated from her sister States.

> For the Executive Committee of the Arab Palestine Congress:
> [Signed]   MOUSA KAZEM EL-HUSSAINI, President

Churchill's Reply to the Palestine Arab
Deputation

Let me make it clear in the first place why it is I am receiving you here.
I came out to Cairo to hold a conference mainly about Mesopotamia, and my
friend Sir Herbert Samuel invited me, as I was so close, to come on up and
pay him a visit in Palestine, so as to be able to see something of the country
and to discuss with him some of its problems on the spot. You must not suppose that my coming here in any way supersedes him. He is the responsible
representative of the Crown in Palestine, and any direction which I may give
in the name of His Majesty's Government I shall send by despatches from
London in the usual way after full consideration with my other advisors at
home. But as I was here in the country some of you asked to come to see me,
and at the request of the High Commissioner I have done so as a matter of
courtesy and of goodwill and not in any sense as a formal conference.

Now I think it always best to be as plain as possible in everything that is
said, so that there cannot possibly be any misunderstanding. In the very
able paper which you have read, there are a great many statements of fact
which we do not think are true, and I think everyone of you knows in his
heart that it must be taken as a partisan statement and one side of the case
rather than as a calm judicial summing up of what is best for us all to do in
the difficult circumstances in which we find ourselves. But still, as you have

said all that you feel you ought to say, you will, I am sure, wish me to reply with equal candour. The great thing is to know exactly where we are.

You have asked me in the first place to repudiate the Balfour Declaration and to veto immigration of Jews into Palestine. It is not in my power to do so, nor, if it were in my power, would it be my wish. The British Government have passed their word, by the mouth of Mr. Balfour, that they will view with favour the establishment of a National Home for Jews in Palestine, and that inevitably involves the immigration of Jews into the country. This declaration of Mr. Balfour and of the British Government has been ratified by the Allied Powers who have been victorious in the Great War; and it was a declaration made while the war was still in progress, while victory and defeat hung in the balance. It must therefore be regarded as one of the facts definitely established by the triumphant conclusion of the Great War. It is upon this basis that the mandate has been undertaken by Great Britain, it is upon this basis that the mandate will be discharged; I have no doubt that it is on this basis that the mandate will be accepted by the Council of the League of Nations, which is to meet again shortly.

Moreover, it is manifestly right that the Jews, who are scattered all over the world, should have a national centre and a National Home where some of them may be reunited. And where else could that be but in this land of Palestine, with which for more than 3,000 years they have been intimately and profoundly associated? We think it will be good for the world, good for the Jews and good for the British Empire. But we also think it will be good for the Arabs who dwell in Palestine, and we intend that it shall be good for them, and that they shall not be sufferers or supplanted in the country in which they dwell or denied their share in all that makes for its progress and prosperity. And here I would draw your attention to the second part of the Balfour Declaration, which solemnly and explicitly promises to the inhabitants of Palestine the fullest protection of their civil and political rights. I was sorry to hear in the paper which you have just read that you do not regard that promise as of value. It seems to be a vital matter for you and one to which you should hold most firmly and for the exact fulfilment of which you should claim. If the one promise stands, so does the other; and we shall be judged as we faithfully fulfil both.

After all, the British Government has a view of its own in this matter, and we have right to such a view. Our position in this country is based upon the events of the war, ratified, as they have been, by the treaties signed by the victorious Powers. I thought, when listening to your statements, that it seemed that the Arabs of Palestine had overthrown the Turkish Government. That is the reverse of the true facts. It has been the armies of Britain which have liberated these regions. You had only to look on your road here this afternoon to see the graveyard of over 2,000 British soldiers, and there are many other graveyards, some even larger, that are scattered about in this land. The position of Great Britain in Palestine is one of trust, but it is also one of right. For the discharge of that trust and for the high purposes we have in view, supreme sacrifices were made by all these soldiers of the British Empire, who gave up their lives and their blood. Therefore I beg you to realise that we shall strive to be loyal to the promises we have made both to the Arab and to the Jewish people, and that we shall fail neither in the one nor in the other.

I would also draw your attention to the very careful and exact nature of the words which were used by Mr. Balfour. He spoke of "the establishment in Palestine of *a* National Home for the Jews." He did not say he would make Palestine *the* National Home for the Jews. There is a difference between the two which is of great importance. The fact that Palestine shall contain a National Home for the Jews does not mean that it will cease to be the National Home of other people, or that a Jewish Government will be set up to dominate the Arab people. On the contrary, the British Government is well disposed towards the Arabs in Palestine, and indeed, cherish a strong friendship and desire for co-operation with the Arab race as a whole. That is what you would expect from the British Empire, which is the greatest of all the Moslem States in the world, and which must never cease to study the needs and wishes of its Moslem subjects and allies; and surely you have found that—at any rate I have been assured on this point by many Moslems since my arrival here—in the daily contact with the officers of this Administration in Palestine; that they make no distinction as between Arab and Jew, and that they endeavour in every way to render impartial, even-handed justice.

We regard this matter of such importance that we moved His Majesty the King to appoint Sir Herbert Samuel as High Commissioner. He has held very high office in our own country, and he has many years experience in our Parliamentary and Cabinet life. Therefore in selecting him we knew we had a trained and experienced man who would understand what ought to be done and what the full meaning and purpose of British policy was. Moreover, he is himself a Jew, and therefore we knew that in holding the balance even and securing fair treatment for all he could not be reproached for being hostile to his own people, and he would be believed by them when he said that he was only doing what was just and fair; and I think this appointment has been vindicated and justified not only by what has been done but by its results.

I do not think you have any need to feel alarmed or troubled in your minds about the future. The British Government have promised that what is called the Zionist movement shall have a fair chance in this country, and the British Government will do what is necessary to secure that fair chance. But after all it is only upon its merits that Zionism can succeed. We cannot tolerate the expropriation of one set of people by another or the violent trampling down of one set of national ideals for the sake of erecting another. If a National Home for the Jews is to be established in Palestine, as we hope to see it established, it can only be by a process which at every stage wins its way on its merits and carries with it increasing benefits and prosperity and happiness to the people of the country as a whole. And why should this not be so? Why should this not be possible? You can see with your own eyes in many parts of this country the work which has already been done by Jewish colonies; how sandy wastes have been reclaimed and thriving farms and orangeries planted in their stead. It is quite true that they have been helped by money from outside, whereas your people have not had a similar advantage, but surely these funds of money largely coming from outside and being devoted to the increase of the general prosperity of Palestine is one of the very reasons which should lead you to take a wise and tolerant view of the Zionist movement. The paper which you have just read painted a golden picture of the delightful state of affairs in Palestine under the Turkish rule. Every man did everything he pleased; taxation was light; justice was prompt and impartial; trade, commerce, education, the arts all flourished. It was a wonderful picture. But it had no relation whatever to the truth, for otherwise why did the Arab race rebel against this heavenly condition? Obviously the picture has been overdrawn. And what is the truth?

This country has been very much neglected in the past and starved and even mutilated by Turkish misgovernment. There is no reason why Palestine should not support a larger number of people than it does at present, and all of those in a higher condition of prosperity.

But you will say to me, are we to be led by the hopes of material gain into letting ourselves be dispossessed in our own house by enormous numbers of strangers brought together across the seas from all over the world? My answer is; no, that will not be, that will never be. Jewish immigration into Palestine can only come as it makes a place for itself by legitimate and honourable means; as it provides the means by which it is to be supported. The task before the Zionists is one of extraordinary difficulty. The present form of government will continue for many years, and step by step we shall develop representative institutions leading up to full self-government. All of us here to-day will have passed away from the earth and also our children and our children's children before it is fully achieved. The Jews will need the help of the Arabs at every stage, and I think you would be wise to give them your help and your aid and encourage them in their difficulties. They may fail. If they are not guided by wisdom and goodwill, if they do not tread the path of justice and tolerance and neighbourliness, if the class of men who come in are not worthy of the Jewish race, then they will fail and there will be an end of the experiment. But on the other hand, if they succeed, and in proportion as they do succeed year by year, such success can only be accompanied by a general diffusion of wealth and well-being among all the dwellers in Palestine and by an advance in the social, scientific and cultural life of the people as a whole.

These are the words which I speak to you with great belief in their truth. I am sure if you take my advice you will not find in the future any difference in the life you have led in the past, or in the part you have played in your country, except an improvement. There will be more food, there will be more freedom, there will be more people, there will be more health among the people, there will be more knowledge, the fruits of toil will be more securely enjoyed, and the harvests will be more fully reaped by those who have sown them. Above all there will be a complete respect for everyone's religious faith. Although the Arabs are in a large majority in Palestine and although the British Empire has accepted the mandate for Palestine, yet in a certain wider sense Palestine belongs to all the world. This city of Jerusalem itself is almost equally sacred to Moslem, Christian and Jew—not only those who dwell in this land, but those of these three religions who all over the world look to what is the holy centre of their faith. The Arabs of Palestine have therefore a great trust which we look to them to discharge and to help us (the British Government) in discharging, and just as in the spiritual sphere the profession of one faith does not mean the exclusion of another, so in the material world there is room for all. If instead of sharing miseries through quarrels you will share blessings through co-operations, a bright and tranquil future lies before your country. The earth is a generous mother. She will produce in plentiful abundance for all her children if they will but cultivate her soil in justice and in peace.

APPENDIX D Deputation of Representatives of the Jewish
Community Received by the Secretary of
State for the Colonies on Monday,
28 March 1921

The deputation presented the following memorandum:

The Jewish National Council of Palestine, a body representative of the
Jews of this country and elected by the Jewish National Assembly convened
on the basis of general elections of the whole of the Palestine adult Jewish
population, desire to express to you the deep feeling of gratitude of the Jewish population of Palestine towards the British Government, which was the
first to declare its readiness to assist in the rebuilding of the Jewish National
Home in Palestine.

The Jewish people has during the long years of its exile from its land always kept alive the love of the country of its glorious past. The belief that
one day the people would return to its ancient land has kept it alive under
the most trying circumstances in all parts of the world, and Great Britain's
promise to assist in rebuilding the National Home of Israel has filled every
Jewish heart with gratitude.

The Jewish people are under a further obligation of gratitude to Great
Britain for accepting the mandate for Palestine, and the mission of re-estab-
lishing the Jewish National Home here in pursuance of the decision of the
League of Nations. We trust that the realisation of this decision will be made

possible by giving Palestine its historical frontiers and by adjusting them to the needs of its full and independent economic development, which is based on the water-power and the granaries of North and East.

The Palestine Jews, and with them the Jewish people in all countries, recognise in the appointment of the Right Hon. Sir Herbert Samuel, a brother Jew, as the High Commissioner to our historical country, the first practical step towards the realisation of the declaration of the British Government given through Mr. Balfour on the 2nd November, 1917, and towards the fulfilment of the decision of the Allied Powers at San Remo on the 24th April, 1920.

Sir Herbert Samuel, during the eight months he has been fulfilling the responsible task of governing Palestine, has shown not only that he is an administrator of rare distinction, but that he appreciates to the full that he is the bearer of a lofty historic mission, rooted alike in the fundamental ideas of the Jewish people and in British traditions of liberty and progress. In protecting the rights of all inhabitants of the country and in furthering the interests of the whole population, the High Commissioner fulfils Mr. Balfour's declaration in its integrity.

It is our constant endeavour to assist the High Commissioner in establishing cordial relations between all sections of the population, and our Jewish and Zionist programme lays special stress on the establishing of sincere friendship between ourselves and the Arabs. The Jewish people returning, after 2,000 years of exile and persecution to its own homeland, cannot suffer the suspicion that it wishes to deny to another nation its rights.

The Jewish people have full understanding of the aspirations of the Arabs with regard to a national revival, but we know that by our efforts to rebuild the Jewish National Home in Palestine, which is but a small area in comparison with all the Arab lands, we do not deprive them of their legitimate rights. On the contrary, we are convinced that a Jewish renaissance in this country can only have a strong and invigorating influence upon the Arab nation. Our kinship in language, race, character and history give the assurance that we shall in due course come to a complete understanding with them.

The two brother nations, Jews and Arabs, working together in peace and harmony, are destined to bring about the cultural and economic revival of the awakening peoples of the Near and Middle East.

The history of Jewish colonisation in Palestine is a proof of the great advantages which Jewish work has brought to the inhabitants of the country. The colonies established by Jews in the course of the last forty years have changed waste areas into flourishing gardens; sandy plains, which were not or were only to a very small degree cultivated have been turned into fertile fields and colonies, the orchards and gardens of which are now worth millions of pounds and give work and food to many people. These areas, in which formerly only the herds of the wandering Bedouins grazed, and then only during a few weeks of the year, have now become closely populated settlements with factories and industries. They embrace already a population of about 15,000 people, and will be able to absorb after special technical improvements a further similar number of new settlers in the near future. Through these colonies many thousands of non-Jews of the neighbourhood earn a living. Experts in all branches of science and industries are devoting their energy, their experience, and their knowledge to the development of the land, and their methods are being copied by their neighbours. Swamps which formerly bred disease and which played havoc with the first Jewish pioneers have now been changed into flourishing settlements. Industries which were unknown in this country have been established and introduced by Jews, such as iron works, cement works, factories for building materials, furniture and joinery, machinery, mills, wine cellars and soap works, printing houses. New towns have been built according to modern ideas and taste. The commerce of the country has been greatly developed, and its branches have spread and widened. Parallel with the great influx of Jewish immigrants, non-Jewish production has been developed and the standard of agriculture has been raised. The tax revenue can be taken as an illustration of this change. Forty years ago the taxes of the Rishon-le-Zion area, for instance, amounted to only a few medjidiehs (1 medjidieh = 20 piastres), collected for some water mellons which the Bedouin has sown: now the taxes of this area amount to 5,000 £P. Land has increased in value to an extent formerly unknown, and the greatest part of the sums invested by Jews, which amount to millions of pounds, have remained in the hands of the local inhabitants. Sums which would cover the educational budgets of fully-developed countries have been spent by the Jews to realise modern ideas of education and civilisation. More than 100,000 £P were spent by the Zionist organisation for their school work the last year. Our example is being followed by the Arabs.

The work for the revival of the country is being continued. Besides persons of means who are building and establishing factories and developing commerce and industry, there are thousands of young men who have fled from their ruined houses in Eastern Europe to devote their strength and energy to their own country. They include teachers, physicians, students and clerks, the majority of them in the prime of life. They are labouring hard on roads and in draining marshes in order to take their part in building up the country.

The Jews are anxious to take their part in the defence of their Motherland.

They have proved already their readiness for sacrifice when they enlisted in thousands during the great war, from Palestine and other countries, into the Jewish battalions which fought with the British army for the liberation of Palestine. As the economic development of Palestine progresses with Jewish immigration, Jewish capital and Jewish devotion—the capacity of the country for self-defence will correspondingly expand.

For the rebirth of this country and the restoration of all its ancient glory, all the living forces of Jewry throughout the world must be united in a ceaseless effort. The Jewish people is ready to come forward and bring the necessary sacrifices for the great cause of its regeneration. Quickened by the belief that the foundations of its National Home have been already laid by the declaration of the British Government and the decision of San Remo, the Jewish people feels sure that the facts of daily life in Palestine will go further and further to prove that the Jewish National Home is becoming a living factor. In the recognition of the world Zionist organisation by the Mandatory Power as the representative of the Jewish people for the building of its National Home and in the recognition of Hebrew as an official language of the country, the first steps for embodying the principles of the historic declaration find their expression. And infinite trust fills the hearts of Jewry that the continuation of the work of the Mandatory Power in Palestine will bring each day nearer the realisation of the Jewish National Home in the Jews' ancient country.

It must be accepted as a basic principle in considering the present and the future of the Jewish National Home, that the Jewish people throughout the world are inseparably connected with Palestine and its future. Among the practical measures of the Mandatory Power for hastening the development of the Jewish National Home we would suggest the adoption of a policy of close land settlement; the improvement of the sanitary conditions of the country; the introduction of an improved system of roads and other means of communication; and charging the Jewish people with the development of State lands and such other lands as are uncultivated and have no private owners and with the development of the natural resources of the country.

The historic task of Great Britain in hastening and protecting the rebirth of the Jewish people in its ancient land would then be assured a great future, and the Jewish and Arab peoples will, under the guidance of Great Britain, faithfully collaborate in building up this country of a glorious past and of an ever-promising future.

Churchill's Reply to the Palestine Jewish
Deputation

I have just finished receiving a deputation representing some of the Moslem inhabitants in this country, and I have told them quite plainly that there can be no question of our departing from the principles enunciated by Mr. Balfour in his declaration. I pointed out to them that these principles are two-fold: in the first place, the British Government will favour the establishment of a Jewish National Home in Palestine; in the second place that process will take place without prejudice or unfairness to the existing Arab and Christian inhabitants of the country, who together are of course in an overwhelming majority. I am myself perfectly convinced that the cause of Zionism is one which carries with it much that is good for the whole world, and not only for the Jewish people, but that it will also bring with it prosperity and contentment and advancement to the Arab population of this country, and I shall do my best to help my friend Sir Herbert Samuel in carrying out the policy already declared by the British Government. But I must not conceal from you, indeed you probably know it yourselves, that there is a great deal of alarm felt by the Moslem population of Palestine lest they should be dispossessed of their lands and property and supplanted from their rights in this country in which they dwell, and put under the rule of those who are now in a minority, but who will be re-inforced by large numbers of strangers coming from over the seas. I have pointed out to them that Zionism can only succeed by a process which confers benefits upon the whole country, and which at each stage provides the means for supporting by industry or agriculture the newcomers who come in. They have also expressed alarm at the character of some of the immigrants whom they accuse of bringing Bolshevik doctrines. Whatever we may think of these fears, it is your labour to dispel them and do your very utmost to promote a spirit of peace and goodwill in the country. This I know is your wish and intention. I know it is the intention and policy of my Right hon. friend.

I have just been making a statement to the Moslem deputation which I am afraid was not very agreeable to them. They will not expect me to make a statement to you which will be very agreeable to you. It is my duty to try to reassure and encourage both. We intend to do our best to secure a fair chance for the Zionist cause and movement, but we shall need all the help we can get, and not only help in the way of enthusiasm and energy, though that is very necessary, but also help in the still harder quality to display, especially in conjunction with enthusiasm, restraint and forbearance.

When I go back to London, I have no doubt I shall be told that but for the Zionist movement there would be no need to keep up such a large British garrison, at so great an expense in this country. You must provide me with the means, and the Jewish community all over the world must provide me with the means of answering all adverse criticism. I wish to be able to say that a great event is taking place here, a great event in the world's destiny. It is taking place without injury or injustice to anyone; it is transforming waste places into fertile; it is planting trees and developing agriculture in desert lands; it is making for an increase in wealth and of cultivation; it is making two blades of grass grow where one grew before, and the people of the country who are in a great majority, are deriving great benefit, sharing in the general improvement and advancement. There is co-operation and fraternity between the religions and the races; the Jews who are being brought in from Europe and elsewhere are worthy representatives of Jewry and of the cause of Zionism, and the Zionists are taking every step to secure that that shall be so. The pioneers in a matter of this sort must be picked men, worthy in every way of the greatness of the ideal and of the cause for which they are striving, and in that way you will give me the means of answering effectively those who wish to prevent this experiment and cause from having its fair chance. It would be easier for me to speak in terms of ardent enthusiasm of the cause which you have at heart, but I should only be speaking to those who are already convinced. It is more important for me in these words which I address to you to counsel prudence and patience, and to endeavour to strike a note which will make your path more easy, while allaying the alarm, however unjustified, of others. I earnestly hope that your cause may be carried to success. I know how great the energy is and how serious are the difficulties at every stage and you have my warmest sympathy in the efforts you are making to overcome them. If I did not believe that you were animated by the very highest spirit of justice and idealism, and that your work would in fact confer blessings upon the whole country, I should not have the high hopes which I have that eventually your work will be accomplished.

I think we have given it its best chance of accomplishment by the appointment which His Majesty has made of Sir Herbert Samuel. He is, I know, animated by strong principles of liberal and impartial justice and by an affection for all the people of the country over whom he has been set, and no-one can accuse him of not also being devoted to the cause which you have at heart. With his prudence, experience and guidance, I trust that the difficult years of beginning may be passed through and that in a few years' time there will be a feeling of greater well-being among the people of Palestine, and that things will be better for everyone and that the fears which are honestly entertained, mistaken if you will, by the Mohammedan inhabitants of the country will be proved to have been without any foundation.

I thank you very much for coming to see me. I am much honoured by the trouble you have taken. I have read with great interest and sympathy the paper you have prepared, and I shall lay it before the British Cabinet on my return. They will see the case presented with so much force on both sides, and I shall do what I can to assist his Excellency in the task which the British Government has given him.

Churchill's Speech at the Hebrew
University Site

Chief Rabbis, Mr. Sokolov, Ladies and Gentlemen. I thank the honourable Rabbis for the precious gift you have presented to me, the scroll of the Law, which, as you have said, contains all the truth which has been accepted by the greater part of the enlightened world, and which is the heritage of Christians and Jews alike. I shall treasure this present in my family and hand it down to my children after me. I repeated yesterday the promise which Mr. Balfour made in the name of His Majesty's Government. Great Britain always keeps her promises and honours the scraps of paper on which they are written. This time, too, we shall do all we can to fulfil our engagements.

Personally, my heart is full of sympathy for Zionism. This sympathy has existed for a long time, since twelve years ago, when I was in contact with the Manchester Jews. I believe that the establishment of a Jewish National Home in Palestine will be a blessing to the whole world, a blessing to the Jewish race scattered all over the world, and a blessing to Great Britain. I firmly believe that it will be a blessing also to all the inhabitants of this country without distinction of race and religion. This last blessing depends greatly upon you. Our promise was a double one. On the one hand, we promised to give our help to Zionism, and on the other, we assured the non-Jewish inhabitants that they should not suffer in consequence. Every step you take should therefore be also for moral and material benefit of all Palestinians. If you do this, Palestine will be happy and prosperous, and peace and concord will always reign; it will turn into a paradise, and will become, as is written in the scriptures you have just presented to me, a land flowing with milk and honey, in which sufferings of all races and religions will find a rest from their sufferings. You Jews of Palestine have a very great responsibility; you are the representatives of the Jewish nation all over the world, and your conduct should provide an example for, and do honour to, Jews in all countries.

The hope of your race for so many centuries will be gradually realised here, not only for your own good but for the good of all the world.

Once more I thank you for the present you have given me, and for the kind reception you have organised in my honour.

I am now going to plant a tree, and I hope that in its shadow peace and prosperity may return once more to Palestine.

APPENDIX G **Weizmann's Letter to Churchill Regarding Transjordan, 1 March 1921**

Dear Sir,

May I bring to your attention a matter of vital importance to the economic future of Palestine and the upbuilding of the Jewish National Home. It is the question of the eastern and southern frontiers. The question has become especially critical in view of the agreement reached with France regarding the northern boundary which cut Palestine off from access to the Litani, deprived her of possession of the Upper Jordan and the Yarmuk and took from her the fertile plains east of Lake Tiberias which had heretofore been regarded as one of the most promising outlets for Jewish settlement on a large scale.

During the discussions with the French, it may be recalled, very little was said specifically about the eastern boundary south of the Yarmuk. It was for practical purposes assumed that so far as the territory in the east was brought within the British sphere, the needs of the Jewish National Home would be fully satisfied. Were this not the case, of course, there would have been little purpose in the struggle to secure for Palestine the right to use the Yarmuk, as the rights secured would be in large part valueless if the territory to the south also were to be taken from her jurisdiction and control. That territory must, it is clear, be settled with a fixed population in order to give physical security and economic value to the extensive engineering works contemplated.

It must be confessed, however, that certain parts of the address delivered to the Sheikhs assembled at Es Salt last August, by His Majesty's High Commissioner, which might perhaps be interpreted as suggesting the possible separation of Trans-Jordania from Cis-Jordania were the cause of some misgiving, but it was taken for granted that those remarks were not intended to foreshadow a fundamental change in the policy of His Majesty's Government and that they were not meant to do more than adumbrate the possible division of the country for administrative purposes into two parts—Western and Eastern Palestine. It was, none the less, expected that even should this eventuate, Trans-Jordania would still fall under the general provisions of the Palestine Mandate. It is quite appreciated, however, that the administrative control of the mandatory might assume a looser form in Trans-Jordania than in Cis-Jordania, and that the local customs and institutions might be modified gradually as Zionist colonisation proceeded. The Jewish colonists, moreover, could not expect the same security for life and property in Eastern Palestine as in Western Palestine. They would, like pioneers in all countries, be expected to defend their settlements from raids and local disturbances. The opening of Eastern Palestine to Jewish colonisation would consequently, far from aggravating the military burden of the mandatory, offer the most promising prospect of its gradual reduction and ultimate surcease, for it is only through a permanent settlement of a peaceful population upon the Trans-Jordanian plateaux that the problem of the defence of the whole Jordan Valley can be satisfactorily solved.

Zionists have, of course, always recognised the special Moslem interests in the Hedjaz Railway. It was for that reason that in our original proposals to the Peace Conference—which proposals the Emir Feisal publicly stated he considered to be moderate and proper—it was suggested that the Eastern frontier be drawn close to, but west of the railway. At that time the French were not yet in Damascus, and it was thought desirable that a small corridor be provided along the railway, so as to connect the Hedjaz Kingdom with Damascus. In view of the French occupation of Damascus, His Majesty's Government may now consider that the reason for the corridor no longer exists and that it would be better for the present at least, to draw no definite eastern frontier short of the desert but simply to provide special safeguards for the Moslem interests in the Hedjaz Railway.

But if it is thought advisable to provide a corridor between Palestine and the desert, it should none the less be clearly recognised that the fields of Gilead, Moab and Edom, with the rivers Arnon and Jabbok, to say nothing of the Yarmuk, the use of which is guaranteed under the recently signed convention, are historically and geographically and economically linked to Palestine, and that it is upon these fields, now that the rich plains to the north have been taken from Palestine and given to France, that the success of the Jewish National Home must largely rest. Trans-Jordania has from earliest times been an integral and vital part of Palestine. There the tribes of Reuben, Gad and Manasseh first pitched their tents and pastured their flocks. And while Eastern Palestine may probably never have the same religious and historic significance as Western Palestine, it may bulk much larger in the economic future of the Jewish National Home. Apart from the Negeb in the south, Western Palestine has no large stretches of unoccupied land where Jewish colonisation can take place on a large scale. The beautiful Trans-Jordanian plateaux, on the other hand, lie neglected and uninhabited save for a few scattered settlements and a few roaming Beduin tribes. The total population of the regions within the British sphere is considerably less than 200,000 and on the average there are fewer than 50 inhabitants per square mile. The only settled communities of any size are those about Maan, Es Salt and Kerak. Maan is not claimed for Palestine. The inhabitants of Es Salt and Kerak are chiefly Christian who desire to be linked with Palestine rather than with the Hedjaz.

The climate of Trans-Jordania is invigorating; the soil is rich; irrigation would be easy; and the hills are covered with forests. There Jewish settlement could proceed on a large scale without friction with the local population. The economic progress of Cis-Jordania itself is dependent upon the development of these Trans-Jordanian plains, for they form the natural granary of all Palestine and without them Palestine can never become a self-sustaining, economic unit and a real National Home. The evidence of competent and impartial authorities collected in the attached memorandum gives abundant proof of this. The linking of Trans-Jordania with the Hedjaz Kingdom would prove disastrous to the future of Eastern Palestine as well as Western Palestine and would in the end be of little or no value to the Hedjaz.

It is fully realised that His Majesty's Government must consider their pledges to the Arab people and the means of satisfying their legitimate aspirations. But the taking from Palestine of a few thousand square miles, scarcely inhabited and long derelict, would be scant satisfaction to Arab Nationalism, while it would go far to frustrate the entire policy of His Majesty's Government regarding the Jewish National Home. Nothing need be said of the land stretching southwestwards from Maan. That, it is assumed, will be either incorporated in or allied to the Hedjaz Kingdom. But it is clear that apart from a small corridor along the Hedjaz Railway, there is no concession north of Maan, short of Damascus, to which Arab nationalism could attach any real or permanent value. The aspirations of Arab nationalism centre about Damascus and Bagdad and do not lie in Trans-Jordania.

It is confidently hoped, therefore, that there will be no thought of any further diminution of the legitimate claims of Palestine when the eastern and southern frontiers come under discussion. The unsatisfactory character of the settlement on the north makes it all the more vital that the Jewish National Home be generously dealt with on the east and south.

I am, Sir, Your most obedient humble servant, Ch. Weizmann.

Selected Bibliography

UNPUBLISHED DOCUMENTS *(Public Record Office and India Office, London)*

CABINET OFFICE

Allied and International Conferences on the Terms of Peace and Related Subjects, 1920–21	CAB 29/90–92
Committees: General Series, 1915	27/1
Imperial Conferences, June–August, 1921	32/2–3
Memoranda	24/93, 99, 100, 103–7, 121–23, 125–27
Minutes	23/23–27
Registered Files	21/186, 202

COLONIAL OFFICE

Iraq: Government Gazettes, 1921–25	C.O. 813
Original Correspondence, 1921	730/1–18
Supplementary Correspondence	537/819–25

Middle East: Confidential Print, 1921   935/1
     Original Correspondence, 1921   732/1–5
     Supplementary Correspondence   537/826–35
Palestine: Acts   765/1
     Government Gazettes, 1919–22   742/1
     Original Correspondence, 1921   733/1–18
     Sessional Papers, 1921–25   814/1
     Supplementary Correspondence   537/848–58

FOREIGN OFFICE

Confidential Prints, Eastern Affairs,
     Iraq, 1920–22   F.O. 406/43–50
General Correspondence, Political
     (Eastern) : General, 1921   371/6342–45
         Mesopotamia, 1921   371/6346–69
         Palestine, 1921   371/6370–98
         Peace Conferences of 1919–20   608/84, 96,98–99,
         Syria, 1921   371/6453–63
         Turkey, 1920   371/5065, 5124,
                              5228–31, 5245,
                              5247

INDIA OFFICE

Memoranda, 1920
Political and Secret Department, 1920–21

WAR OFFICE

Correspondence and Papers, 1920–21   W.O. 106/195–210

PUBLISHED DOCUMENTS *(Her Majesty's Stationery Office, London)*

ADMIRALTY

A Handbook of Arabia. 2 vols. 1916.
A Handbook of Mesopotamia. 4 vols. 1918.
A Handbook of Syria (including Palestine). 1920.
British and Foreign State Papers, 1920–22.

COLONIAL OFFICE

Report on Palestine Administration, July, 1920–December, 1921. 1922.
Report on Palestine Administration, 1922. 1923.

Report by His Britannic Majesty's Government on the Palestine Administration, 1923 (Colonial no. 9). First annual report to the Council of the League of Nations, 1925.

Report of the High Commissioner on the Administration of Palestine, 1920–1925 (Colonial no. 15). 1925.

Report on 'Iraq Administration, October, 1920–March, 1922 (n.d.).

FOREIGN OFFICE

Arabia (Peace Handbook no. 61). Originally prepared in the spring of 1917. 1920.

Mesopotamia (Peace Handbook no. 63). 1920.

Syria and Palestine (Peace Handbook no. 60). 1920.

PARLIAMENT

Parliamentary Debates (Commons). 5th ser. Vols. 130–56 (1920–22).

Parliamentary Debates (Lords). 5th ser. Vols. 40–44 (1920–21).

Parliamentary Papers

Cmd. 565: "Memorandum of the Secretary of State for War Relating to the Army Estimates for 1920–21." 1920, vol. 28.

Cmd. 964: "Treaty of Peace with Turkey" (signed at Sèvres on August 10, 1920). 1920, vol. 51.

Cmd. 1061: "Review of the Civil Administration of Mesopotamia." 1920, vol. 51.

Cmd. 1070: "Memorandum of the Secretary of State for War Relating to the Army Supplementary Estimate for 1920–21." 1920, vol. 28.

Cmd. 1176: "Draft Mandates for Mesopotamia and Palestine as Submitted for the Approval of the League of Nations." 1921, vol. 43.

Cmd. 1195: "Franco-British Convention of December 23, 1920, on Certain Points Connected with the Mandates for Syria and the Lebanon, Palestine, and Mesopotamia." 1921, vol. 42.

Cmd. 1226: "Correspondence Between His Majesty's Government and the United States Ambassador Respecting Economic Rights in Mandated Territories." 1921, vol. 43.

Cmd. 1499: "An Interim Report on the Civil Administration of Palestine during the period 1st July, 1920–30th June, 1921." 1921, vol. 15.

Cmd. 1500: "Final Drafts of the Mandates for Mesopotamia and Palestine for the Approval of the Council of the League of Nations." 1921, vol. 43.

Cmd. 1540: "Palestine Disturbances in May, 1921: Reports of the Commission of Inquiry with Correspondence Relating Thereto." 1921, vol. 15.

Cmd. 1570: "Correspondence Between His Majesty's Government and the French Government Respecting the Angora Agreement of October 20, 1921." 1922, vol. 23.

Cmd. 1700: "Correspondence with the Palestine Arab Delegation and the Zionist Organisation." 1922, vol. 23.

Cmd. 1785: "Mandate for Palestine, together with a Note by the Secretary General Relating to its Application to the Territory Known as Trans-Jordan, under the Provisions of Article 25." 1923, vol. 25.

Cmd. 5957: "Correspondence between Sir Henry McMahon, His Majesty's High Commissioner at Cairo, and The Sherif Hussein of Mecca, July 1915–March, 1916." 1939, vol. 27.

Cmd. 5964: "Statements made on behalf of His Majesty's Government during the year 1918 in regard to the Future Status of certain parts of the Ottoman Empire." 1939, miscellaneous no. 4.

DOCUMENTARY COLLECTIONS

Degras, Jane, ed. *Soviet Documents on Foreign Policy*. Vol. 2: *1917–1924*. London: Oxford University Press, 1951.

Gooch, G. P., and Temperley, Harold, eds. *British Documents on the Origins of the War*. Vols. 5 and 10. London: His Majesty's Stationery Office, 1928 and 1936.

Hurewitz, J. C. *Diplomacy in the Near and Middle East*. Vol. 2. Princeton: D. Van Nostrand Co., 1956.

Jerusalem. Central Zionist Archives.

Jerusalem. Israel State Archives.

League of Nations. *Records of the Permanent Mandates Commission*. Geneva, 1920–21 and 1928.

Rossi, Ettore. *Documenti Sull' Origine e Gli Sviluppi della Questione Araba (1875–1944)*. Rome: Instituto per l'Oriente, 1944.

Seton, C. R. W. *Legislation of Transjordan, 1918–1930*. London: The Crown Agents for the Colonies, 1931.

Shapiro, Leonard, ed. *Soviet Treaty Series*. Vol. 1: *1917–1928*. Washington, D.C.: The Georgetown University Press, 1950.

Woodward, E. L., and Butler, Rohan, eds. *Documents on British Foreign Policy, 1919–1939*. 1st ser. Vols. 4, 8, and 13. London: Her Majesty's Stationery Office, 1952, 1958, and 1963.

MEMOIRS

Amery, Leopold S. *My Political Life*. Vol. 2: *War and Peace, 1914–1929*. London: Hutchinson & Co., 1953.

Ataturk, Mustafa Kemal. *A Speech Delivered by Ghazi Mustapha Kemal* (October, 1927). Leipzig: K. F. Koehler, 1929.

Beaverbrook, Lord. *Politicians and the War, 1914–1916.* London: Oldbourne Book Co., 1960.

Bell, Lady. *The Letters of Gertrude Bell.* Vol. 2. London: Ernest Benn, 1927.

Bentwich, Norman and Helen. *Mandate Memories, 1918–1948.* London: The Hogarth Press, 1965.

Bowman, Humphrey. *Middle-East Window.* London: Longmans, Green & Co., 1942.

Bullard, Sir Reader. *The Camels Must Go.* London: Faber & Faber, 1961.

Burgoyne, Elizabeth. *Gertrude Bell: From Her Personal Papers, 1914–1926.* London: Ernest Benn, 1961.

Catroux, General. *Deux missions en Moyen-Orient, 1919–1922.* Paris: Librairie Plon, 1958.

Churchill, Winston S. *The World Crisis, 1911–1918.* 3 vols. New York: Charles Scribner's Sons, 1931.

———. *The World Crisis, 1918–1928: The Aftermath.* New York: Charles Scribner's Sons, 1929.

Garnett, David, ed. *The Letters of T. E. Lawrence.* New York: Doubleday, Doran & Co., 1939.

Graves, Philip P., trans. *Memoirs of King Abdullah.* London: Jonathan Cape, 1951.

Graves, Sir Robert. *Storm Centres of the Near East: Personal Memories, 1879–1929.* London: Hutchinson & Co., 1933.

Haldane, General Sir Aylmer L. *The Insurrection in Mesopotamia, 1920.* London: William Blackwood & Sons, 1922.

———. *A Soldier's Saga.* London: William Blackwood & Sons, 1948.

Hardinge, Lord, of Penhurst. *Old Diplomacy: The Reminiscences of Lord Hardinge of Penhurst.* London: John Murray, 1947.

al-Ḥuṣrī, Sāṭi'. *Day of Maysalun.* Translated from the Arabic by Sidney Glazer. Washington, D.C.: The Middle East Institute, 1966.

King 'Abdallāh of Jordan. *My Memoirs Completed [al Takmilah].* Translated by Harold Glidden. Washington, D.C.: American Council of Learned Societies, 1954.

Kirkbride, Alec. *A Crackle of Thorns.* London: John Murray, 1956.

Lawrence, T. E. *Seven Pillars of Wisdom.* New York: Doubleday, Doran & Co., 1935.

Lloyd George, David. *The Truth About the Peace Treaties.* Vol. 2. London: Victor Gollancz, 1938.

Meinertzhagen, Richard. *Middle East Diary, 1917–1956.* London: The Cresset Press, 1959.

Nicolson, Harold. *Peacemaking, 1919.* London: Methuen & Co., 1964.

Philby, H. St. John. *Arabian Days.* London: Robert Hale, 1948.

———. *Forty Years in the Wilderness.* London: Robert Hale, 1957.

Riddell, G. A. *Lord Riddell's Intimate Diary of the Peace Conference and After, 1918–1923*. London: Victor Gollancz, 1933.

Samuel, Viscount Herbert. *Grooves of Change*. New York: Bobbs-Merrill Co., 1946.

Steed, Wickham H. *Through Thirty Years, 1892–1922*. Vol. 2. London: William Heinemann, 1924.

Storrs, Sir Ronald. *Orientations*. London: Nicholson & Watson, 1937.

Weizmann, Chaim. *Trial and Error*. New York: Harper & Brothers, 1949.

Wilson, Sir A. T. *Mesopotamia, 1917–1920: A Clash of Loyalities*. 2 vols. London: Oxford University Press, 1930–31.

Young, Hubert. *The Independent Arab*. London: John Murray, 1933.

PRIVATE PAPERS

Jerusalem. Israel State Archives. Herbert Samuel Papers.

London. The Beaverbrook Library. David Lloyd George Papers.

London. The British Museum. Arthur James Balfour Papers.

London. The British Museum. Arnold T. Wilson Papers.

London. Library of the House of Lords. Herbert Samuel Papers.

Oxford. Bodleian Library, New College, Oxford University. Alfred Milner Papers. By permission of the librarian.

Oxford. St. Antony's College, Oxford University. Collection of private papers, including those of Major the Honorable F. R. Somerset.

Rechovot, Israel. Weizmann Archives. Dr. Chaim Weizmann Papers.

INTERVIEWS

Professor Norman Bentwich (attorney general of Palestine, 1920–1931), December 15, 1967.

Sir Alec Kirkbride (British representative at Salt, Transjordan, 1921, and minister to Jordan, 1946), December 13, 1967.

BIOGRAPHIES

Bowle, John. *Viscount Samuel*. London: Victor Gollancz, 1957.

Churchill, Winston S. *Great Contemporaries*. London: Thornton Butterworth, 1937.

Erskine, Mrs. Steuart. *King Faisal of 'Iraq*. London: Hutchinson & Co., 1933.

Graves, Philip P. *The Life of Sir Percy Cox*. London: Hutchinson & Co., n.d.

Graves, Robert, and Hart, Liddell. *T. E. Lawrence to His Biographers*. London: Cassell, 1963.

Hart, Liddell. *T. E. Lawrence*. London: Jonathan Cape, 1934.

James, Robert Rhodes. *Churchill: A Study in Failure, 1900–1939*. London:

Weidenfeld & Nicolson, 1970.

Jarvis, C. S. *Arab Command: The Biography of Lieutenant Colonel F. G. Peake Pasha*. London: Hutchinson & Co., 1943.

Lawrence, A. W., ed. *T. E. Lawrence By His Friends*. London: Jonathan Cape, 1954.

Marlowe, John. *Late Victorian: The Life of Sir Arnold Talbot Wilson*. London: The Cresset Press, 1967.

Morris, James. *The Hashemite Kings*. London: Faber and Faber, 1959.

Mosley, Leonard. *Curzon: The End of an Epoch*. London: Longmans, Green & Co., 1960.

Mousa, Suleiman. *T. E. Lawrence: An Arab View*. London: Oxford University Press, 1966.

Nicolson, Harold. *Curzon: The Last Phase, 1919–1925*. New York: Harcourt, Brace & Co., 1939.

The Observer. Churchill by His Contemporaries. London: Hodder & Stoughton, 1965.

al-Rayḥānī, Amīn. *Fayṣal al-Awwal* [King Faysal I]. Beirut, 1934.

Ronaldshay, The Earl of. *The Life of Lord Curzon*. 3 vols. London: Ernest Benn, 1928.

Stitt, George. *A Prince of Arabia: The Emir Shereef Ali Haider*. London: George Allen & Unwin, 1948.

Waley, S. D. *Edwin Montagu*. London: Asia Publishing House, 1964.

Wavell, Field-Marshal Viscount A. P. W. *Allenby in Egypt*. London: George G. Harrap & Co., 1943.

Wrench, John Evelyn. *Alfred Lord Milner*. London: Eyre & Spottiswoode, 1958.

GENERAL WORKS

Antonius, George. *The Arab Awakening*. Philadelphia: Lippincott, 1939.

al-Bazzāz, abd al-Rahman. *al-'Irāq min al-'Ihtilāl hatta al-'Istiqlāl* ['Iraq: From Occupation to Independence]. Cairo, 1960.

Bentwich, Norman. *England in Palestine*. London: Kegan Paul, Trench, Trubner & Co., 1932.

Berkes, Niyazi. *The Development of Secularism in Turkey*. Montreal: McGill University Press, 1964.

Browne, Brigadier J. Gilbert. *The Iraq Levies, 1915–1932*. London: The Royal United Service Institution, 1932.

Buchanan, Sir George. *The Tragedy of Mesopotamia*. London: William Blackwood & Sons, 1938.

Bullard, Sir Reader. *Britain and the Middle East*. London: Hutchinson University Library, 1964.

Cumming, Harry H. *Franco-British Rivalry in the Post-War Near East*. London: Oxford University Press, 1938.

Darwazah, Muhammad 'Izzat. *al-Waḥḍah al-Arabīyya* [Arab Unity]. Beirut, 1957.

De Novo, John A. *American Interests and Policies in the Middle East, 1900–1939.* Minneapolis: The University of Minnesota Press, 1963.

Earle, Edward M. *Turkey, the Great Powers, and the Bagdad Railway.* New York: Macmillan Co., 1924.

ESCO Foundation for Palestine, Inc. *Palestine: A Study of Jewish, Arab, and British Policies.* 2 vols. New Haven, Conn.: Yale University Press, 1947.

Evans, Laurence. *United States Policy and the Partition of Turkey, 1914–1924.* Baltimore, Md.: The Johns Hopkins Press, 1965.

Fitzsimons, M. A. *Empire by Treaty: Britain and the Middle East in the Twentieth Century.* Notre Dame, Ind.: University of Notre Dame Press, 1964.

Foster, Henry A. *The Making of Modern Iraq: A Product of World Forces.* London: Williams & Norgate, 1936.

Frischwasser-Ra'anan, H. F. *The Frontiers of a Nation.* London: The Batchworth Press, 1955.

Glubb, Sir John Bagot. *Britain and the Arabs.* London: Hodder & Stoughton, 1958.

Gottlieb, W. W. *Studies in Secret Diplomacy.* London: George Allen & Unwin, 1957.

Graves, Philip. *Palestine: The Land of Three Faiths.* London: Jonathan Cape, 1923.

Hanna, Paul L. *British Policy in Palestine.* Washington, D.C.: American Council on Public Affairs, 1942.

Haut-Commissariat de la République Française en Syrie et au Liban. *La Syrie et le Liban en 1921.* Paris, 1922.

Hogarth, D. G. *The Nearer East.* London: William Heinemann, 1902.

Hourani, Albert H. *Great Britain and the Arab World.* London: John Murray, 1945.

———. *Syria and Lebanon.* London: Oxford University Press, 1946.

Howard, Harry N. *The King-Crane Commission.* Beirut: Khayats, 1963.

———. *The Partition of Turkey: A Diplomatic History, 1913–1923.* Norman: University of Oklahoma Press, 1931.

Hurewitz, J. C. *The Struggle for Palestine.* New York: W. W. Norton & Co., 1950.

'Abd al-Husain, Muḥammad. *Dhikrā Fayṣal al-'Awwal* [Recollection of Faysal I]. Baghdad, 1933.

Ireland, P. W. *Iraq: A Study in Political Development.* London: Jonathan Cape, 1937.

Jeffries, J. M. N. *Palestine: The Reality.* London: Longmans, Green & Co., 1939.

Kedourie, Elie. *England and the Middle East.* London: Bowes & Bowes, 1956.

Khadduri, Majid. *Independent Iraq*. 2d ed. London: Oxford University Press, 1960.

Kohn, Hans. *Nationalism and Imperialism in the Hither East*. New York: Harcourt, Brace & Co., 1932.

———. *Western Civilization in the Near East*. London: George Routledge & Sons, 1936.

Loder, John De Vere. *The Truth About Mesopotamia, Palestine, and Syria*. London: George Allen & Unwin, 1923.

Longrigg, Stephen H. *Oil in the Middle East*. London: Oxford University Press, 1961.

———. *Syria and Lebanon Under French Mandate*. London: Oxford University Press, 1958.

al-Māḍī, Munīb, and Mūsā, Suleiman. *Tārīkh al-'Urdun fi'l Qarn al-'Ishrīn* [A History of Jordan in the Twentieth Century]. Beirut, 1959.

Marlowe, John. *The Persian Gulf in the Twentieth Century*. London: Oxford University Press, 1958.

———. *Rebellion in Palestine*. London: The Cresset Press, 1962.

Marriott, Sir John A. R. *The Eastern Question: An Historical Study in European Diplomacy*. London: Oxford University Press, 1940.

Medzini, M. *Eser Shanim shel Mediniut AretzYisraelite* [Ten years of Palestinian politics]. Tel Aviv, 1928.

Miller, David Hunter. *My Diary at the Conference of Paris, with Documents*. 22 vols. New York: Appeal Printing Co., 1928.

Monroe, Elizabeth. *Britain's Moment in the Middle East, 1914–1956*. Baltimore, Md.: The Johns Hopkins Press, 1963.

Mowat, Charles Loch. *Britain Between the Wars, 1918–1940*. London: Methuen & Co., 1955.

Nevakivi, Jukka. *Britain, France and the Arab Middle East 1914–1920*. London: The Athlone Press, 1969.

Northedge, F. S. *The Troubled Giant: Britain Among the Great Powers, 1916–1939*. New York: Frederick A. Praeger, 1966.

Peake, F. G. *A History of Jordan and Its Tribes*. Coral Gables, Fla.: University of Miami Press, 1958.

Pichon, Jean. *Le Partage du Proche-Orient*. Paris, 1938.

Ramazani, Rouhallah K. *The Foreign Policy of Iran*. Charlottesville: The University Press of Virginia, 1966.

Royal Institute of International Affairs. *British Interests in the Mediterranean and Middle East*. London: Oxford University Press, 1958.

———. *Great Britain and Egypt, 1914–1951*. Information Papers no. 19. London, 1952.

———. *Great Britain and Palestine, 1915–1945*. Information Papers no. 20. London, 1946.

———. *The Political and Strategic Interests of the United Kingdom*. London: Oxford University Press, 1939.

Sacher, Harry, ed. *Zionism and the Jewish Future*. London: John Murray, 1917.

———. *Zionist Portraits and Other Essays*. London: Anthony Blond, 1959.

Saʿīd, Amīn. *Al-Thawra al ʿArabīyya al-Kubra*. 3 vols. Cairo, n.d.

Ṣāyigh, ʾAnīs. *al-Hāshimīyūn wa al-Thawra al-ʿArabīyya al-Kubra* [The Hashimites and the Arab revolt]. Beirut, 1966.

al-Sayyid, Afaf Lutfi. *Egypt and Cromer: A Study in Anglo-Egyptian Relations*. London: John Murray, 1968.

Seton-Williams, M. V. *Britain and the Arab States: A Survey of Anglo-Arab Relations, 1920–1948*. London: Luzac & Co., 1948.

Smith, George Adam. *The Historical Geography of the Holy Land*. London: Hodder & Stoughton, 1894.

———. *Syria and the Holy Land*. London: Hodder & Stoughton, 1918.

Spector, Ivar. *The Soviet Union and the Muslim World, 1917–1958*. Seattle: University of Washington Press, 1959.

Stein, Leonard. *The Balfour Declaration*. London: Valentine-Mitchell, 1961.

Stoyanovsky, J. *The Mandate for Palestine*. London: Longmans, Green & Co., 1928.

Sykes, Christopher. *Crossroads to Israel*. Cleveland: World Publishing Co., 1965.

Temperley, H. W. V., ed. *A History of the Peace Conference of Paris*. Vol. 6. London: Henry Frowde, Hodder & Stoughton, 1924.

———. *England and the Near East*. London: Frank Cass & Co., 1964.

Toynbee, Arnold J. *Survey of International Affairs, 1920–1923*. London: Oxford University Press, 1927.

———. *Survey of International Affairs, 1925*. Vol. 1: *The Islamic World Since the Peace Settlement*. London: Oxford University Press, 1927.

———. *The World After the Peace Conference*. London: Oxford University Press, 1926.

Trumpener, Ulrich. *Germany and the Ottoman Empire, 1914–1918*. Princeton: Princeton University Press, 1968.

Vatikiotis, P. J. *Politics and the Military in Jordan*. London: Frank Cass & Co., 1967.

Wahbah, Ḥāfiz. *Jazīrat al-ʿArab fiʾl Qarn al-ʿIshrīn* [Arabia in the twentieth century]. Cairo, 1935.

Wolfers, Arnold. *Britain and France Between Two Wars*. New York: W. W. Norton & Co., 1966.

Woodhouse, C. M. *Britain and the Middle East*. Geneva: Publications de l'Institut Universitaire de Hautes Études Internationales, no. 30, 1959.

Wright, Quincy. *Mandates Under the League of Nations*. Chicago: University of Chicago Press, 1930.

Yahyā, Jalāl. *al-Thawra al-ʿArabīyya* [The Arab revolt]. Cairo, 1959.

al-Ziriklī, Khayr al-Dīn. *ʿĀmān fi ʿAmmān* [Two years in Amman]. Cairo, 1925.

Zayid, Mahmud. *Egypt's Struggle for Independence.* Beirut, 1965.
Zeine, Zeine N. *The Struggle for Arab Independence: Western Diplomacy and the Rise and Fall of Faisal's Kingdom in Syria.* Beirut, 1960.

ARTICLES, PAMPHLETS, AND PERIODICALS

al-'Amrī, Khayrī. "al-Sirā'u al-Siyāsiyu hawla al-'Arsh al-'Irāqi (1920–1921)." *Dirāsāt Arabīyya,* February, 1967, pp. 31–54.
Baghdad Times, May–December, 1921.
Basrah Times, April–December, 1921.
Canaan, Tewfik. *Conflict in the Land of Peace.* Jerusalem, 1936.
"The Changing East." *Round Table,* no. 40 (September, 1920), pp. 756–72.
Churchill, Winston S. "Mesopotamia and the New Government." *Empire Review* 38, no. 270 (July, 1923): 691–98.
———. *The Position Abroad and at Home.* Speech delivered at Dundee on 14 February 1920. London: Harrison & Sons, 1920.
———. *Reason and Reality.* Speech delivered at Sunderland on 3 January 1920. London: Harrison & Sons, 1920.
Cohen, Stephen P. "Issue, Role, and Personality: The Kitchener-Curzon Dispute." *Comparative Studies in Society and History* 10, no. 3 (April, 1968): 337–55.
Cunningham, Allan. "The Wrong Horse?—A Study of Anglo-Turkish Relations before the First World War." *St. Antony's Papers,* no. 17 (Middle Eastern Affairs no. 4), pp. 56–76. London: Oxford University Press, 1965.
Daily Telegraph, 1921.
Dann, Uriel. "The Beginnings of the Arab Legion." *Middle Eastern Studies* 5, no. 3 (October, 1969): 181–91.
Dawn, C. Ernest. "The Amir of Mecca al-Husayn ibn 'Ali and the Origin of the Arab Revolt." *Proceedings of the American Philosophical Society* 104, no. 1 (February, 1960): 11–34.
Gauvain, August. "Five Years of French Policy in the Near East," *Foreign Affairs* 3, no. 2 (December 15, 1924): 276–92.
Graubard, Stephen R. "Military Demobilization in Great Britain." *Journal of Modern History* 19, no. 4 (December, 1947): 297–311.
Hogarth, Commander D. G. "Present Discontents in the Near and Middle East." *Quarterly Review* 234, no. 465 (October, 1920): 411–23.
Jewish Chronicle, 1921.
Kedourie, Elie. "Britain, France, and the Last Phase of the Eastern Question." In *Soviet-American Rivalry in the Middle East,* edited by J. C. Hurewitz, *Proceedings of The Academy of Political Science* 29, no. 3 (1969): 189–97.
———. "Sir Herbert Samuel and the Government of Palestine." *Middle Eastern Studies* 5, no. 1 (January, 1969): 44–68.

Khadduri, Majid. " 'Azīz 'Alī Miṣrī and the Arab Nationalist Movement."
    St. Antony's Papers, no. 17 (Middle Eastern Affairs no. 4), pp. 140–63.
    London: Oxford University Press, 1965.
Kohn, Hans. "Die staats- und verfassungsrechtliche Entwicklung des Emir-
    ats Transjordanien." *Archiv des öffentlichen Rechts* (Tübingen), 1929,
    pp. 238–67.
"The Last of the Peace Treaties." *Round Table*, no. 39 (June, 1920), pp.
    493–519.
The League of Zionists-Revisionists. *What Revisionism Stands For*. New
    York, 1926.
Louis, William Roger. "The United Kingdom and the Beginning of the Man-
    dates System, 1919–1922." *International Organization* 23, no. 1 (Winter,
    1969) : pp. 73–96.
Luntz, Yosef. "Diplomatic Contacts between the Zionist Movement and the
    Arab National Movement at the Close of the First World War." *Hamiz-
    rach Hehadash [The New East]* 12, no. 3 [47] (1962) : 212–29.
Mahan, Captain A. T. "The Persian Gulf and International Relations." *Na-
    tional Review*, September, 1902, pp. 27–45.
Manuel, Frank E. "The Palestine Question in Italian Diplomacy, 1917–
    1920." *Journal of Modern History* 27, no. 3 (September, 1955) : 263–80.
"Mr. Churchill in Palestine." *Zionist Review* 5, no. 1 (May, 1921) : 4.
Morning Post, 1921.
Near East. A weekly review of the politics and commerce of the Balkan
    peninsula, Egypt and the Sudan, Morocco, Asia Minor, Arabia, Mesopo-
    tamia, Persia, and India. 1919–21.
Noel, Major E. W. C. *Note on the Kurdish Question*. Baghdad: Office of Civil
    Commissioner in Mesopotamia, 1919.
"The Northern Boundary of Palestine." *Zionist Review* 4, no. 9 (January,
    1921) : 159–60.
Oriente Moderno. Rome: Instituto per l'oriente, 1921.
Ormsby Gore, Captain Hon. "The Organization of British Responsibilities in
    the Middle East." *Journal of the Central Asian Society* 7, pt. 3 (1920) :
    83–105.
"The Outlook of the Middle East." *Round Table*, no. 37 (December, 1919),
    pp. 55–97.
Palestine. The organ of the British Palestine Committee. 1917–24.
"Palestine and its Neighbours." *Zionist Review* 7, no. 2 (June, 1923) : 1.
Palestine Arab Delegation. *Report on the State of Palestine Submitted to
    His Excellency the High Commissioner for Palestine by the Executive
    Committee of the Palestine Arab Congress on the 13th of October, 1925*.
    Jerusalem, 1925.
"The Palestine Blunder." *Spectator*, June 25, 1921, pp. 803–4.
"Palestine Under the Colonial Office." *Zionist Review* 4, no. 10 (February,
    1921) : 178.

Pearlmann, Moshe. "Chapters of Arab-Jewish Diplomacy, 1918–1922." *Jewish Social Studies* 6, no. 2 (April, 1944) : 123–54.

Philby, H. St. John. "Trans-Jordan." *Journal of the Central Asian Society* 11, pt. 4 (1924) : 296–312.

Rappard, W. E. "The Practical Working of the Mandates System." *Journal of the British Institute of International Affairs* 4, no. 5 (September, 1925) : 205–26.

Saphir, Ascher. *Unity, or Partition! An Historical Survey of Judaeo-Arab Negotiations for the Recognition of Jewish Rights in Palestine.* Jerusalem, 1937.

Sayigh, Rosemary. "The Profession of an Arab-Lover." *Middle East Forum* 38, no. 2 (February, 1962) : 41–42.

Sforza, Count. "Panarabism and Zionism." *Contemporary Review* 148, no. 836 (August, 1935) : 208–12.

Slater, S. H. "Iraq." *The Nineteenth Century and After* 99 (April, 1926) : 479–94.

Stein, Leonard. *Weizmann and England.* London: W. H. Allen, 1964.

Sunday Times, 1920–22.

La Syrie et Le Liban sous l'occupation et le Mandat français, 1919–1927. Berger-Levrault, eds. Paris, 1929.

Tibawi, A. L. "Syria From the Peace Conference to the Fall of Damascus." *Islamic Quarterly* 11, nos. 3 and 4 (July and December 1967) : 77–122.

The Times, 1920–22.

Times of Mesopotamia, July–December, 1921.

Tolkowsky, S. *The Jewish Colonisation in Palestine: Its History and Its Prospects.* London: The Zionist Organisation, n.d. (*ca.* 1918).

Toynbee, Arnold J. "Great Britain and France in the East." *Contemporary Review* 121 (January, 1922) : 23–31.

U.S., Department of State, Division of Near Eastern Affairs. *Mandate for Palestine.* Washington, D.C.: Government Printing Office, 1927.

Verete, M. "Ha-Masa ve Ha-Matan Ha-Tzioni-Aravi bi Aviv 1919 ve Ha-Mediniut Ha-Anglit" [Zionist-Arab-British Relations and the Inter-Allied Commission]. *Zion* (quarterly for research in Jewish history), nos. 1 and 2 (1967), pp. 76–115.

Weizmann, Chaim. *The Jewish People and Palestine.* Statement made before the Palestine Royal Commission in Jerusalem on 25 November 1936. Jerusalem: The Zionist Organisation, 1936.

———. "The Palestine White Paper." *The Week-end Review* 2, no. 34 (November 1, 1930) : 611–12.

The Zionist Organisation. *Reports of the Executive of the Zionist Organisation to the XIIth Zionist Congress* (Political Report). London, 1921.

Biographical Sketches

Abdul Hadi, Auni

    1919   Member of the Hijazi delegation to Paris
    1921   Accompanied Abdullah in meetings with Churchill
    1936   Secretary of the Arab Higher Committee in Palestine

Abdullah ibn Husayn (1882–1951)

    Confirmed as ruler (amir) of Transjordan in March, 1921
    Monarch of the Hashimite Kingdom of Jordan from 26 April 1949, until
      assassinated in Jerusalem on 20 July 1951

Allenby, Field Marshal Sir Edmund, 1st viscount of Megiddo (1861–1936)

    1917–1919   Commander-in-chief of Egyptian Expeditionary Force
    1919–1925   High commissioner for Egypt

al-'Askari, Ja'far Pasha

    Saw military service in World War I, first under the Turks and then un-
      der Faysal
    Military governor of Aleppo, 1919
    Minister for defense in Iraq's Council of State, October, 1920

Prime minister of Iraq, 1923–24 and 1926–28
Killed in a *coup d'état* in Iraq, October, 1936

Asquith, Herbert Henry, 1st earl of Oxford and Asquith (1852–1928)

1908–16   Prime minister and first lord of the treasury
1920–21   Leader of the Opposition

Ataturk, Mustafa Kemal (1881–1938)

1919   Began struggle against imposed Allied settlement
Founder of modern Turkey and her first president (1923–38)

Balfour, Arthur James, 1st earl of Balfour (1848–1930)

1902–5   Prime minister
1916–19   Foreign secretary
1919–22   President of the Council of State

Bell, Gertrude (1868–1926)

1916   Military intelligence staff, Mesopotamian Expeditionary Force
Served as Oriental secretary to the British administration of Iraq in
   Baghdad from 1916 until her death

Berthelot, Philippe (1866–1934)

French diplomat at the Quai d'Orsay, 1904–23 and 1925–32
General secretary of the foreign ministry in 1920

Bonham-Carter, Sir Edgar (1870–1956)

1919–21   Judicial adviser, Mesopotamia

Bullard, Sir Reader (1885–)

1920   Governor of Baghdad
1921   Member of the Middle East Department of the Colonial Office
1923–25   British agent and consul, Jidda
1939–46   Minister (later ambassador) at Teheran

Cambon, Paul (1843–1924)

1898–1920   French ambassador to London

Churchill, Winston Spencer (1874–1965)

1919–21   Secretary of state for war and air
1921–October, 1922   Secretary of state for the colonies

1940–45   Prime minister, first lord of the treasury, and minister of defense

Clemenceau, Georges (1841–1929)

1917–20   Premier of France

Congreve, General Sir Walter (1862–1927)

1921   General officer commanding troops in Egypt and Palestine

Cornwallis, Sir Kinahan (1883–1959)

1916–20   Director of the Arab Bureau, Cairo
1921   Seconded to Iraqi government as personal adviser to Amir Faysal
1921–35   Adviser to the ministry of interior, Iraq
1941–45   Ambassador to Baghdad

Cox, Major General Sir Percy Z. (1864–1937)

1914–18   Chief political officer, Indian Expeditionary Force
1918–20   Acting British minister to Persia
1920–23   High commissioner in Mesopotamia

Crowe, Sir Eyre (1864–1925)

1920–25   Permanent undersecretary of state for foreign affairs

Curzon, George Nathaniel, 1st marquess of Kedleston (1859–1925)

1891–92   Undersecretary of state for India
1919–24   Secretary of state for foreign affairs

de Bunsen, Sir Maurice (1852–1932)

1877   Entered diplomatic service
1906–13   Ambassador to Lisbon
1913–14   Ambassador to Vienna
1915   Chairman of committee appointed to define British desiderata in Asiatic Turkey

de Caix, M. Robert

1920   Accompanied General Gouraud to Syria as his secretary general
Held office until 1923 and thereafter remained a principal French spokesman, notably at Geneva, on Syrian affairs

Deedes, Brigadier General Sir Wyndham (1883–1956)

1918–19   Military attaché, Constantinople
1919–20   Director general of public security in Egypt
1920–23   Chief secretary to the British administration in Palestine

de Saint Aulaire, Count

1921   French ambassador to London

Faysal ibn Husayn (1885–1933)

1916–18   Commander of the Hijazi army in the Middle Eastern theater
of operations
1919   Represented the Hijaz at Paris Peace Conference
1918–20   Head of British administration in Syria
23 August 1921   Proclaimed king of Iraq

al-Gaylani, 'Abd al-Rahman

1920   Naqib of Baghdad and president of the first Council of State
1921   First prime minister under King Faysal until his resignation in
1922

Georges-Picot, M. F.

1915–16   An ex-consul general in Syria, he represented France in negotiations with Great Britain on the future of the Arab regions
1917   Accompanied General Allenby to Palestine to uphold French
claims
French high commissioner in Beirut until relieved by General Gouraud
in 1920

Gouraud, General Henri (1867–1946)

1920–22   Commanded French forces in the Levant as high commissioner
for Syria
1923–37   Military governor of Paris

Grey, Sir Edward, 1st viscount of Fallodon (1862–1933)

1905–16   Secretary of state for foreign affairs
1919   Temporary ambassador to the United States
1928–33   Chancellor of Oxford University

Haldane, General Sir Aylmer (1862–1950)

1904–5   Military attaché with the Japanese Army in the Russo-Japanese
War
1914–19   Served in European theater of war

1920–22   Commander of British forces in Mesopotamia

Hananu, Ibrahim

1921   Accused of assassination attempt against the French high commissioner for Syria; took refuge in Transjordan
1928   Founder of the National Bloc (*Kutla*) in Syria

Hardinge of Penhurst, Charles Lord (1858–1944)

1910–16   Viceroy of India
1916–20   Permanent undersecretary of state for foreign affairs
1920–23   British ambassador to Paris

Hirtzel, Sir Arthur (1870–1937)

1894   Entered India Office
1917–21   Assistant undersecretary of state for India
1921–24   Deputy undersecretary of state for India

Hogarth, David George (1862–1927)

Noted Orientalist and director of the Ashmolean Museum, Oxford
1916   Director of the Arab Bureau, Cairo
1919   Nominated as a member of the proposed interallied investigating commission to the Middle East (King-Crane commission)

al-Husayni, Musa Kazim

Dismissed as mayor of Jerusalem after the disturbances of 1920
1921   Leader of the Arab delegation to London

Husayn ibn Ali (1856–1931)

A sharifian (descendant of the Prophet Muhammed) of the family of Hashim; father of Abdullah of Transjordan and Faysal of Iraq
Appointed amir of Mecca in 1908 by Sultan Abdul Hamid
Proclaimed himself "King of the Arab Countries" in 1916 and Caliph after expulsion of the last incumbent by Kemalists in 1924
3 October 1924   Abdicated as ruler of the Hijaz and went into exile in Cyprus
1931   Died on visit to Amman

Ibn Sa'ud, Abdul Aziz (1880–1953)
23 December 1924   Captured Jidda from the sharifians
8 January 1926   King of the Hijaz and Sultan of Nejd and dependencies, uniting a major part of the Arabian peninsula
18 September 1932   Proclaimed king of Saudi Arabia

Imam Yahya (1868–1948)

Ruler of Yemen, faithful to Turkey in World War I
Assassinated in 1948

Kirkbride, Sir Alec (1897–)

1920–21 British military representative, Es Salt, Transjordan
1939 British Resident in Transjordan
1946 Minister to the Hashimite Kingdom of Jordan

Kitchener, Field Marshal H. H., 1st earl of Khartoum (1850–1916)

1911–14 British agent and consul general in Egypt
1914 Secretary of state for war

Lawrence, T. E. (Thomas Edward Shaw) (1888–1935)

1917 Major in British army, attached to staff of the Hijazi Expeditionary Force
1918 Transferred to General Allenby's staff
1919 Member of the British delegation to the Paris Peace Conference
and then Research Fellow of All Souls College, Oxford
1921–22 Adviser on Arab affairs, Middle East Department of the Colonial Office

Leyguès, Georges (1857–1933)

1920 Premier of France

Lindsay, Sir Ronald C. (1877–1945)

1920–21 Minister plenipotentiary in Paris
1921–24 Undersecretary at the Foreign Office
Ambassador to Constantinople (1925–26), Berlin (1926–28), Washington (1930–39)

Lloyd George, David (1863–1945)

1915–16 Minister of munitions
1916 Secretary of state for war
1916–22 Prime minister and first lord of the treasury

Masterton Smith, Sir James (1878–1938)

1919–20 Assistant secretary at the War Office and air ministry
January, 1921 Chairman of committee to reorganize the Colonial Office
and to establish within it a Middle East Department

1921–24   Permanent undersecretary of state for the colonies

McMahon, Colonel Sir Henry (1862–1949)

1914–16   First high commissioner for Egypt; representative of Great Britain in correspondence with Sharif Husayn of Mecca
1919   Proposed as a member of the interallied investigating commission to the Middle East (King-Crane commission)
1920   Created officer of the first class of the Order of El Nahda by the king of the Hijaz
1920–25   Member of Board of British Empire Exhibition

Meinertzhagen, Colonel Richard (1878–1967)

1919–20   Chief political officer in Palestine and Syria
1921–24   Military adviser in the Middle East Department, Colonial Office

Millerand, Alexandre (1859–1943)

January, 1920   Succeeded Clemenceau as premier and took charge of foreign affairs
1920–24   President of France

Milner, Viscount Lord Alfred (1854–1925)

1916–18   Member of the War Cabinet (minister without portfolio)
1918–19   Secretary of state for war
1919–21   Secretary of state for the colonies

Montagu, Edwin (1879–1924)

1917–22   Secretary of state for India

Peake, Frederick G. (1886–1970)

Inspector general of gendarmerie, Transjordan (1921) and director of public security (1923)
Raised the Arab Legion, 1922
Replaced in 1939 by Major John Bagot Glubb

Philby, H. St. John B. (1885–1960)

1920–21   Adviser to the ministry of interior, Mesopotamia
1921–24   Chief British representative in Transjordan
1926–46   Resident director of Sharqieh Ltd., Jidda
Explorer and scholar of the Arab world

Rumbold, Sir Horace (1869–1941)

1920–24 High commissioner and ambassador to Constantinople
24 July 1923 Signed Lausanne agreement for Britain
1936–37 Member, Royal Commission on Palestine (Peel commission)

al-Sa'id, Nuri (1888–1958)

1920 Chief of staff of Iraqi army
1922–30 Minister of defense of Iraq
1933–36 and 1936–41 Minister of foreign affairs
Prime minister, 1930–32 and frequently thereafter
1958 Killed in Iraqi revolution

Salmond, Air Chief Marshal Sir Geoffrey (1878–1939)

1916–21 Served in the R.A.F. in the Middle East
1927–31 Air officer commanding the R.A.F. in India

Samuel, Herbert, 1st viscount of Mount Carmel and Toxteth (1870–1963)

1914–15 President of the Local Government Board
1920–25 High commissioner of Palestine
1931–35 Leader of the Liberal Parliamentary party

Shuckburgh, Sir John (1877–1953)

1917–21 Secretary in the Political Department, India Office
1921–31 Assistant undersecretary of state, Colonial Office
1931–42 Deputy undersecretary of state, Colonial Office
1939 Appointed governor of Nigeria but, because of the war, did not assume office

Sokolow, Nahum (1860–1936)

1920–31 Chairman of the Zionist Executive
Author of *History of Zionism, 1600–1918*

al-Sulh, Riad

An Arab nationalist exiled from Syria by the French, he was in contact with leading Zionists in 1921.
Prime minister of Lebanon, 1943–51; assassinated while on a visit to Jordan

Sykes, Lieutenant Colonel Sir Mark (1879–1919)

1911 Elected to House of Commons
1915 Member of de Bunsen committee

Biographical Sketches

1916   British representative in negotiations with France over partition
        of the Middle East
1916   Chief adviser to the Foreign Office on Near Eastern policy

Talib, Sayyid

Member of noted family from Basra and an Iraqi nationalist
1920   Minister of the interior in the Council of State
Candidate for head of state in Iraq, but deported to Ceylon in April, 1921
Died in Munich, Germany, in 1929

Trenchard, Marshal Hugh (1873–1956)

1919   Air Marshal of the R.A.F.
1922   Air Chief Marshal of the R.A.F.
1927   Marshal of the R.A.F.

Weizmann, Dr. Chaim (1874–1952)

President, World Zionist Organisation and Jewish Agency for Palestine,
    1921–31 and 1935–46
First president of the state of Israel

Wilson, Lieutenant Colonel Sir Arnold T. (1884–1940)

1909   Member, Political Department, India Office
1916   Deputy civil commissioner of Mesopotamia
1918–20 Acting civil commissioner and Resident for the Persian Gulf
1921–32 With Anglo-Persian Oil Co.

Wilson, Field Marshal Sir Henry (1864–1922)

1918–22 Chief of Imperial General Staff

Young, Major Sir Hubert (1885–1950)

1915–17 Assistant political officer, Mesopotamia
1919–21 Foreign Office staff
1921–27 Assistant secretary, Middle East Department, Colonial Office
October–November, 1932 Envoy extraordinary and minister plenipoten-
    tiary in Baghdad
Governor and Commander-in-chief of Nyasaland (1932–34), of Northern
    Rhodesia (1934–38), and of Trinidad and Tobago (1938–42)

Zaghlul, Sa'd (1860–1927)

Emerged as leader of the Nationalist (*Wafd*) party after World War I

Index

establishes Middle East Department, 93; expresses goals, 94–96, 242; favors *détente* with Turkey, 169; and Faysal, 152–53, 163–64, 166; fear of Bolsheviks, 82, 181; idea for a conference at Cairo, 93–94; impact on Middle Eastern politics, 244–47; informed on Mesopotamian candidates, 141–49; at Jerusalem, 127–33, 177, 207; later appraisal of Cairo policy, 237–40; and League of Nations, 167–68; loses interest in Middle East, 204; meets Abdullah, 129–32, 210, 215–16; opposes occupation of Transjordan, 72; on Palestine, 173–79, 182, 184–85; Palestine Arabs disappointed with, 177, 179, 190, 192–94, 251; pleased at success in Iraq, 157–62, 169; praised for policy, 169–70; procedure for confirming Faysal, 141–42, 150, 158–59; reports to Cabinet, 133–34; role evaluated, 247–49; secretary of state for war, 29, 83, 85, 95; and sharifian solution, 102, 114, 120, 124, 136; speech to Commons, 134–38, 150; and Transjordan, 209, 228, 230, 232–34; White Paper, 202–3; and Zionists, 178–79, 188–89, 200

Churchill White Paper (1922), 202–3

Cilicia, 36, 39–41, 49

Clauson, Gerard, 220, 222, 232–33

Clayton, Sir Gilbert, 64, 96

Clemenceau, Georges, 26, 34–35, 37, 39, 41–42, 46, 48–49, 62

Colonial Office: affected by administrative reorganization, 87–93, 172; consulted on Transjordan and subsidies, 123, 125; and French interests, 132–33; Lawrence dispatched to Egypt by, 152–53; and League of Nations, 167–68, 230; return of Churchill to, 133–34, 137; and treaty with Faysal, 164–65; wisdom of Cairo policy, 240, 253. *See also* Churchill; Middle East Department

Congreve, General Sir Walter, 69, 72, 105, 119, 174, 201, 217–18, 224

Constantinople, 3, 5, 11, 20, 40, 117

Cornwallis, Colonel Kinahan: 59, 98, 101–2; accompanies Faysal, 144–45, 152–53, 156–57

Cox, Sir Percy: and Anglo-Persian treaty, 59, 77–78; appointed high commissioner, 59–62; Churchill wishes to confer with, 93–94; Churchill's intentions misunderstood by, 95; compared with Samuel, 76, 171, 203; early estimate of sharifians, 96, 101–2; eliminates all opposition to Faysal, 139–49; engineers campaign by Faysal, 150–59; Faysal challenge handled by, 162–66; initiates election, 160–62; and the Kurds, 110, 168; and Philby, 156–57, 224; success of, 168–70

Crowe, Sir Eyre, 151, 213

Curzon, George Nathaniel: on Abdullah, 221–23; becomes foreign secretary, 32; critic of French Syrian policy, 46, 52, 71; and France's opposition to the sharifians, 99, 151–52, 213–14; hesitates on appointing Samuel, 63–64; implications of a sharifian in Transjordan for, 72, 207, 228; and Iraq treaty, 164; meets Faysal, 100–101; and Mesopotamia, 47, 60, 78; opinion of Churchill and Cairo policy, 125–26, 134, 207, 216, 218, 222; recognizes Zionist interest in Transjordan, 70; and responsibility for Middle East, 59, 86, 89, 93–94; Samuel reports to, 205–6; and Syria, 29–30, 50; Turkish problem for, 6, 81–83; urges approval of mandates, 80, 232

Cyprus, 1, 4

Daily Mail, 137, 239–40

Daily Telegraph, 147

Damascus, 10–13, 34–41, 45–46, 49–50, 64–65, 68, 71, 97, 101, 115–17, 153, 214, 218–22, 227, 242

Daraa, 51, 69, 71, 74

de Bunsen, Sir Maurice, 4

de Bunsen committee, 4–6

de Caix, Robert, 132, 214, 227

132, 151, 210, 214–17, 220–21, 226–27

Great Britain: aims and interests in Ottoman Empire, 2–5, 16–20; and Arab nationalism, 22–24, 35–39, 46–47, 66–67, 74, 127–28, 172, 176–77, 190–97, 202, 207–9, 227, 244, 249, 251–52; and Bolsheviks, 80–83, 240–41; Churchill takes charge of Colonial Office, 93; divorces herself from Syria, 39–42; domestic difficulties of, 28–32, 83–85, 137; and Egypt, 78–79, 126; and France, 26–28, 46–52, 125, 132–33, 151–52, 213–16; and mandates, 47, 115–16, 122–23, 164–65, 223–30; and Mesopotamia, 53–62, 84, 105–14, 140–49, 151–71, 241; and Palestine, 62–68, 114–20, 123, 171–204, 241–42, 250; reorganizes Colonial Office, 30–32, 85–93; sharifian policy of, 51, 96–103, 120, 136, 210, 245–46; summary of Cairo Conference, 237–40, 242–47; and Transjordan, 68–76, 115–20, 125, 127, 130–31, 209–35, 242; and Turkey, 24, 80–83, 143, 168–69, 241; war aims of, 4–7; wartime agreements of, 8–22

Grey, Sir Edward, 4, 12–13

Haddad, General, 47–48, 51–52, 97–99, 126, 154, 197, 207
Haifa, 12, 72, 98, 122, 177, 214
Haldane, General Aylmer, 54–57, 106, 147
Hananu, Ibrahim, 220–21
Hankey, Maurice, 188
Hardinge, Lord, 151, 166, 221
Haycraft, Sir Thomas, 174
Haycraft commission, 174–76, 180
Haydar, Sharif Ali, 141
Hijaz, the: army of, 11, 19, 23, 55, 208; delegation headed by Faysal, 34–35; differentiated from other Arab sectors, 23, 144; independence of, 78; insured against Wahhabi attack, 122, 142; involvement in Arabian feuds, 121–22; Lawrence mission to, 221–23, 227; return of Fay-

sal to, 153–54; Sa'udi conquest of, 246; and Transjordan, 74–75, 208, 210, 219, 223
Hijaz Railway, 69–70, 123, 214
Hirtzel, Sir Arthur, 22–23, 55
Hogarth, D. G., 3, 16, 28, 35
Homs-Hama-Aleppo line, 10–13, 38–39, 49–50, 101, 214. *See also* Husayn-McMahon correspondence
Hurst, Sir Cecil J. B., 167, 232
Husayn, sharif of Mecca: alienated from Great Britain, 24, 50, 74, 79, 245; approves Faysal for Iraq, 153–54; Arab opponents of, 22–24, 31, 141; British obligations to, 5, 7, 15, 20–21, 26, 30, 253; corresponds with McMahon, 8–11; French not bound by promises to, 27; Hogarth mission to, 16; refuses to ratify wartime treaties, 100–101, 223, 227; relations with sons, 19, 24, 38, 74, 212, 245; and sharifian solution, 96–101, 136, 222; subsidies to, 100, 121–22
Husayn-McMahon correspondence, 21, 42, 242; letters exchanged, 7–11; McMahon clarification of, 228–29n; sharifian claims based on, 48, 100–101
al-Husayni, Haj Amin, 185, 197, 253
al-Husayni, Musa Kazim, 66, 127, 190, 193

Ibn Sa'ud, Abd al-Aziz, 31, 253; Cairo policy toward, 120–22, 243; and Iraq, 107, 142–43, 146; and rivalry with sharifians, 23–24, 99–100, 120
Idris of Asir, 120, 122
Imam Yahya, 120, 122
India, strategic importance of for British Empire, 2–4, 122, 144
India Office: alerted to Mesopotamian unrest, 54; consulted on subsidies, 125; and interdepartmental rivalries, 6, 31, 59–60, 87, 89; interests in Mesopotamia and Persia, 30; partial to Ibn Sa'ud, 31; sensitive to India's reactions, 81; stand on reorganization, 85, 88, 91. *See also* Montagu

Interdepartmental Conference on Middle Eastern Affairs, 31

Iraq (Mesopotamia): Abdullah as possible ruler of, 23, 46–47, 96; assets for Britain, 3, 5, 78, 242; basis for sharifian policy, 102; Britain's entrenchment in, 20, 42; Britain's position weakened in, 55–57; British public opinion on involvement in, 84–85, 240; Cabinet debate over, 87–89; candidates for throne of, 139–52; Churchill's aims for, 95; Colonial Office responsibility for, 89–92; compared with Palestine, 171, 173, 189; Council of State, 60–62, 106–7, 110, 155; Cox appointed high commissioner of, 59–61; and de Bunsen report, 5–6; delegation to Cairo, 94; Faysal considered for, 97–98, 101–2; feelings toward sharifians, 23; financial status of, 112–13, 120–21; and France, 48, 99, 150–52; future decided at Cairo, 106–14, 119, 122, 125, 130–32, 135–36; Husayn defers claim to, 10; in interwar period, 238, 241–46, 249, 253; and Kurdistan, 122, 160, 167–68, 230; mandate status of, 47, 94, 122–23, 163–65, 222, 230, 232, 238, 241–43, 245, 249; military campaigns in, 7, 15; monarchy under Faysal, 151–70; preserve of India Office, 30–31, 84; refugees, 112; Turkish-Russian threat to, 25, 78–81, 168–69; under A. T. Wilson, 53–55; uprising, 55–59

Italy, 30

Jabotinsky, Vladimir, 231, 251

Jaffa riots, 173–80, 183–85, 190–91. *See also* Haycraft commission Jerusalem, 45, 63, 75, 230; phase of Cairo Conference, 120, 127–34, 173, 177, 209–11

Jewish Chronicle, 137, 183

Jidda, 24, 75, 122, 152, 224

Jordan River, 48, 67–69, 74, 115, 123, 129, 214

Kemal, Mustafa, 24–25, 80. *See also* Turkey

King-Crane commission, 36–39

Kirkbride, Sir Alec, 231

Kitchener, Lord, 7, 30

Kurdistan, 48; discussed at Cairo, 110, 123, 125; and Iraq, 122, 160, 167–68, 230

Kuwayt, 121

Landman, Samuel, 186–87, 231

Landon, Percival, 147

Lawrence, T. E.: critic of Mesopotamian policy, 84; enlisted by Churchill, 93, 248; favors sharifian solution, 96, 107–8; Faysal timetable drawn up by, 109, 158; leans toward Abdullah for Transjordan, 117, 119; meets Faysal at Port Said, 126, 152–53, 163–64, 230; present at Jerusalem talks, 129, 210; supports Young on Kurdistan, 168; in Transjordan, 211, 219, 221–27, 233

League of Nations: created by Paris Peace Conference, 2, 33, 36; defers confirmation of "A" mandates, 94, 228, 231–32; low regard of Churchill for, 167; and Mesopotamia, 53, 60, 164–65, 167–68; obligations of Britain to, 234–35, 242; Palestine Arab delegation's case before, 194–95; and protest by Arabs over assignment of mandates, 47–48; and White Paper (1922), 203

Lebanon, 19, 51

Leyguès, Georges, 51, 82

Lindsay, R. C., 100–101, 152, 207

Lloyd George, David: appealed to by Faysal, 40; and Clemenceau, 28, 34–35, 38–39, 42, 46, 49; concern over Mesopotamian uprisings, 56, 84; critic of France in Syria, 58; cultivated by Zionists, 62; decides to appoint Samuel, 63–64; describes Churchill, 82; hostile to Turks, 82–83; makes Churchill colonial secretary, 90, 247; opinion of Faysal, 99; at Paris Peace Conference, 19, 37; telegrams to Cairo, 108–9, 113–14, 119–20, 124–25, 230; Weizmann meets with, 188–89

London Conference on Turkey (1921), 138, 168
Lowther, Sir G. A., 4

Ma'an, 69, 74–75, 116, 122, 206
McMahon, Sir Henry, 7–11, 228–29n. See also Husayn-McMahon correspondence
Masterton Smith, Sir James, 91, 93
Masterton Smith committee, 92–93
Maude, Sir Stanley, 15
Maysalun, 50–51, 55, 65, 107, 228
Mecca, 10, 40, 109, 119, 122, 125–26, 216
Mediterranean Sea, 3, 5, 7, 30, 51, 91
Meinertzhagen, Colonel Richard, 93, 188, 204, 222, 227, 231, 233
Mersina, 8, 10
Mesopotamia. See Iraq
Middle East Department: formation of, 89–93, 253; outlines for Cairo policy prepared by, 102, 115, 121, 124, 162, 173, 245; and Palestine, 188, 192, 204, 232; reaction to events in Transjordan, 211, 217, 225, 230; satisfaction with results, 237
Milner, Lord Alfred, 57, 70, 78, 88–90, 247
Milner commission, 78, 126
Montagu, Edwin: on Mesopotamia, 53, 55, 59, 82, 145, 164; views on reorganization of Middle Eastern affairs, 85–86, 88
Morning Post, 137
Mosul, 35, 40, 48, 50, 112
Mudros, Armistice of, 17
Muraywad, Ahmad, 208, 220

Naqib of Baghdad: appointed first president of Council of State, 61, 106, 110; association with Sayyid Talib, 140, 143–46, 149, 154; consents to Faysal, 150, 155–56; as a potential candidate, 107; selected as prime minister, 165
Near and Middle East, 1, 2n, 22, 49, 80, 85, 102, 136
Newcombe, Colonel S. F., 221
Noel, Major E. W. C., 110

Oliphant, Lancelot, 222
Ormsby-Gore, David, 86
Ottoman Empire. See Turkey

Palestine, 73, 137, 231
Palestine: Advisory Council, 65, 172–74, 182; Arab claims to, 24, 50, 62–63, 79; Arab-Zionist accord, 34–35; Article 25 of mandate, 123, 230–34, 250; boundaries, 40, 67, 122, 221, 229; and de Bunsen report, 5–6; discussed at Cairo, 114–20, 122–23, 127–30, 135–36; Jaffa riots, 173–77; Jewish immigration into, 65, 67, 175, 180–83, 191, 198; Jewish national home in, 13–16; lack of leadership in, 66, 252; local objection to Husayn, 23; mandate, 47, 94, 122, 171, 183, 191, 194, 200, 203, 221, 223, 226, 228; 1920 violence in, 62–63; plan for a defense force in, 118, 173, 180; Samuel's policy in, 63–68; strategic importance of, 79; and Sykes-Picot agreement, 11–12, 35–36, 39; and Transjordan, 68–69, 72, 75, 79, 91, 215, 219, 221, 226, 228–29, 232–33, 241–45, 249–52
Palestine Arab Congress, 66, 127, 177, 181, 190
Palestine Arab delegation: formation of, 190; London activities of, 191–94, 201–3; meeting with Weizmann, 195–97
Palestinian Arabs, 62, 96, 115–16, 127, 133, 176, 190–95, 203, 229–30, 235, 251
Palmer, Consul, 208, 226
Paris Peace Conference, 2, 13, 19, 30, 33, 35, 42, 46, 61, 70, 79
Peake, Captain F. G., 117, 180
Persia, 30, 56, 60, 77–79, 241
Persian Gulf, 3, 5, 19, 92, 105, 122
Philby, H. St. John: career in Mesopotamian politics, 144, 147–48, 151; dismissed by Cox, 155–57; reassigned to Transjordan, 224–25, 227, 233
Picot, Georges, 11–13

Radcliffe, General, 117

Red Sea, 9, 92, 121
Royal Air Force, 111–12, 122, 212, 244, 248
Russia: British suspicions of, 58; calls Baku Conference, 80–81; and Churchill, 82–83, 181; designs on Ottoman Empire, 4, 11–12; foments unrest in Arab world, 77–78, 80–82, 127; interests in Middle East, 25–26; and Palestine, 181–82, 190; publishes Sykes-Picot text, 16; refugees, 112; treaty with Kemalists, 168–69; withdraws from Middle East involvement, 240–41
Rutenberg, Pinchas, 179

al-Sa'id, Nuri, 140, 157, 244, 249, 253
Salmond, General Sir Geoffrey, 118
Samuel, Sir Herbert: appointed high commissioner for Palestine, 63–64; compared with Cox, 76, 171, 203; conception of task, 63–65, 68, 182, 203–4; early record in Palestine, 64, 170–72; favors Arab confederation, 97; impartiality questioned by Arabs, 127–28, 177, 190; invited to Cairo, 94; joins Churchill's talks with Abdullah, 129–30; limits Jewish immigration, 180–83; memoranda on Palestine, 13–14; participant at Cairo, 105, 114, 116–18, 122; reaction to Jaffa riots, 173–77, 180; supervises Abdullah, 210–12, 214–15, 225–26; supports Arab delegation to London, 190–92; urges occupation of Transjordan, 68, 70–76, 205–6, 209, 229; voices dissatisfaction with Abdullah, 216–17, 219, 222, 227; and Weizmann, 66, 178–79, 185–87, 189–201, 251; Zionist disillusionment with, 185–88, 199
San Remo, 47, 52, 60, 63, 69, 80
al-Sanusi, Shaykh Ahmad, 143
Sassoon Effendi, 110
Sayyid Talib: candidacy of, 107, 110, 140, 143–45; deportation of, 146–49, 152, 156
Sèvres, Treaty of, 80, 83, 100, 115, 121, 160

Sharifian policy: early attitudes toward, 23–24, 30–31, 51, 74–76; genesis of, 96–103; implemented at Cairo, 107–8, 116, 119–20, 124, 129, 132, 244–46, 248; in Iraq, 140, 148–70; objections of French to, 99–100, 213–17; in Transjordan, 206–7, 209–10, 228
Shaykh of Muhammara, 107, 141–42, 146
Shuckburgh, John: assigned to Colonial Office, 93; helps draft Cairo agenda, 94; involved in coordinating government policy, 123, 134, 141; on Iraq, 148, 153, 159, 166; on Palestine, 192, 194–96, 199–200, 204; on Transjordan, 217, 222, 231, 233
Smuts, General Jan, 86
Sokolow, Nahum, 13, 70, 178–79, 187
Somaliland, 79, 120–21
Somerset, Major (Lord Raglan), 117
Spectator, 240
Stein, Leonard, 178, 187, 198
Subsidies, 100, 121, 125, 132–36, 142, 210, 222, 226, 244, 248
Suez Canal, 3, 79
al-Sulh, Riad, 198–99
Sykes, Sir Mark, 11–13
Sykes-Picot agreement, 11–13, 26, 31, 35, 42, 69, 71, 115
Syria: British troops withdrawn from, 29–30, 39–41; contested by Arabs and French, 14, 19, 35–42, 48; demanded by sharifians, 24, 101, 207; end of Faysal administration in, 50–52, 67; excluded from sharifian solution, 53, 129, 132; France given mandate for, 47; French interests in, 48–49; French suspicions of British designs on, 26–27; Gouraud arrives in, 41; idea of Greater Syria, 46, 62, 216, 249; impact on Mesopotamia and Palestine, 53, 55, 57–58, 62; McMahon on, 10; negotiations on frontiers, 67, 122, 221, 229; objections to Faysal in Iraq, 99, 125, 139–40, 151–52, 215; overland route across, 3; and raids from

sponse to Churchill White Paper, 203

Zionists, 6; as allies of Great Britain, 250–51; and Balfour Declaration, 13–16, 21; claim to Transjordan, 69–70, 72–73, 228–29; criticism of Samuel, 63–64, 175–76, 180, 183, 185–87; dealt with at Cairo, 115–16, 118, 133; described in Parliament, 136; early contacts with British government, 7; and Faysal, 35; meeting with Palestine Arab delegation, 194–98; meeting with Riad al-Sulh, 198–99; objected to by Arab spokesmen, 127–29; and Palestine Arabs, 55–56, 119, 176, 251–52; policy in Palestine, 62, 67, 184; silence at loss of Transjordan, 231, 249; submit memo to Churchill, 128–29. *See also* Palestine; Weizmann

DATE DUE			

B L A C K

G A R I A

TIRNOVA

C. Baltakra

E. R O U M E L I A

CONSTANTINOPLE

G   G

EGEAN

SEA

A C I A

M

H

ADALIA

CRETE OR CANDIA

CYPRUS
British

Tripoli

M E D I T E R R A N E A N   S E A

Beyroot

Akka or Acre
& Ba

E

D

MOUTHS OF THE NILE

Alexandria

Rosetta

A MAP OF

TURKEY IN ASIA

SCALE OF ENGLISH STATUTE MILES

CAIRO

Suez

E G Y P T

ARAB

Longitude East 28 of Greenwich

A & B - Independent Arab State, A being in the French,
         B in the British, sphere of control
    C - Italian sphere of influence
    D - International sphere